Run-Time Library Reference

Microsoft® Visual C++™

**Development System for Windows™ and Windows NT™
Version 2.0**

D1405108

Microsoft Corporation

PUBLISHED BY
Microsoft Press
A Division of Microsoft Corporation
One Microsoft Way
Redmond, Washington 98052-6399

Copyright © 1994 by Microsoft Corporation

Library of Congress Cataloging-in-Publication Data
Microsoft Visual C++ run-time library reference / Microsoft
    Corporation.
        p.   cm.
    Includes index.
    ISBN 1-55615-803-3
    1. C++ (Computer program language)   2. Microsoft Visual C++.
I. Microsoft Corporation.
QA76.73.C153M53   1994
005.265--dc20   94-30464
                                                              CIP

Printed and bound in the United States of America.

1 2 3 4 5 6 7 8 9   MLML   9 8 7 6 5 4

Distributed to the book trade in Canada by Macmillan of Canada, a division of Canada Publishing Corporation.

A CIP catalogue record for this book is available from the British Library.

Microsoft Press books are available through booksellers and distributors worldwide. For further information about international editions, contact your local Microsoft Corporation office. Or contact Microsoft Press International directly at fax (206) 936-7329.

U.S. Patent No. 4955066

For Run-Time Library Reference: Intel is a registered trademark of Intel Corporation. OS/2 is a registered trademark of International Business Machines Corporation. Microsoft, MS, MS-DOS, and XENIX are registered trademarks and Visual C++, Windows, and Windows NT are trademarks of Microsoft Corporation in the U.S. and other countries. MIPS is a registered trademark of MIPS Computer Systems, Inc. Unicode is a trademark of Unicode, Incorporated. UNIX is a registered trademark of UNIX Systems Laboratories.

Document No. DB57163-0694

For iostream Class Library Reference: Intel is a registered trademark of Intel Corporation. IBM is a registered trademark of International Business Machines Corporation. Lotus is a registered trademark of Lotus Development Corporation. CodeView, Microsoft, MS, MS-DOS, QuickC, Win32, and XENIX are registered trademarks and Visual C++, Win32s, Windows, and Windows NT are trademarks of Microsoft Corporation in the U.S. and other countries. Tandy is a registered trademark of Tandy Corporation.

Document No. DB57169-0694

Contents

Appendixes

Tables

Introduction

The Microsoft® run-time library provides routines for programming for the Microsoft Windows NT™ operating system. These routines automate many common programming tasks that are not provided by the C and C++ languages.

Compatibility

The Microsoft run-time library supports American National Standards Institute (ANSI) C and UNIX® C. (In this book, references to UNIX include XENIX®, other UNIX-like systems, and the POSIX subsystem in Windows NT.) The description of each run-time library routine in Part 2 of this book includes a compatibility section for ANSI, UNIX, and the Win32s application programming interface (API). All run-time library routines included with this product are compatible with the Win32 API.

ANSI C Compliance

The naming convention for all Microsoft-specific identifiers in the run-time system (such as functions, macros, constants, variables, and type definitions) is ANSI-compliant.

The names of Microsoft-specific functions and global variables begin with a single underscore. These names can be overridden only locally, within the scope of your code. For example, when you include Microsoft run-time header files, you can still locally override the Microsoft-specific function named **_open** by declaring a local variable of the same name. However, you cannot use this name for your own global function or global variable.

The names of Microsoft-specific macros and manifest constants begin with two underscores, or with a single leading underscore immediately followed by an uppercase letter. The scope of these identifiers is absolute. For example, you cannot use the Microsoft-specific identifier **_UPPER** for this reason.

UNIX

If you plan to transport your programs to UNIX, follow these guidelines:

- Do not remove header files from the SYS subdirectory. You can place the SYS header files elsewhere only if you do not plan to transport your programs to UNIX.

- Use the UNIX-compatible path delimiter in routines that take strings representing paths and filenames as arguments. UNIX supports only the forward slash (/) for this purpose, whereas Windows NT supports both the backslash (\) and the forward slash (/). Thus this book uses UNIX-compatible forward slashes as path delimiters in **#include** statements, for example. (However, the Windows NT command shell, CMD.EXE, does not support the forward slash in commands entered at the command prompt.)

- Use paths and filenames that work correctly in UNIX, which is case sensitive. The file allocation table (FAT) file system in Windows NT is not case sensitive; the installable NT file system (NTFS) of Windows NT preserves case for directory listings but ignores case in file searches and other system operations.

Backward Compatibility

The compiler views a structure that has both an old name and a new name as two different types. You cannot copy from an old structure type to a new structure type. Old prototypes that take **struct** pointers use the old **struct** names in the prototype.

For compatibility with Microsoft C professional development system version 6.0 and earlier Microsoft C versions, the library OLDNAMES.LIB maps old names to new names. For instance, **open** maps to **_open**. You must explicitly link with OLDNAMES.LIB only when you compile with the following combinations of command-line options:

- /Zl (omit default library name from object file) and /Ze (the default—use Microsoft extensions)

- /link (linker-control), /NOD (no default-library search), and /Ze

For more information about compiler command-line options, see the *Visual C++™ Users Guide*.

Choosing Between Functions and Macros

Most Microsoft run-time library routines are compiled or assembled functions, but some routines are implemented as macros. When a header file declares both a function and a macro version of a routine, the macro definition takes precedence, because it always appears after the function declaration. When you invoke a routine that is implemented as both a function and a macro, there are two ways to force the compiler to use the function version:

- Enclose the routine name in parentheses.

```
#include <ctype.h>
a = toupper(a);     //use macro version of toupper
a = (toupper)(a);   //force compiler to use function version
                    // of toupper
```

- "Undefine" the macro definition with the **#undef** directive:

```
#include <ctype.h>
#undef toupper
```

If you need to choose between a function and a macro implementation of a library routine, consider the following trade-offs:

- Speed versus size. The main benefit of using macros is faster execution time. During preprocessing, a macro is expanded (replaced by its definition) inline each time it is used. A function definition occurs only once regardless of how many times it is called. Macros may increase code size but do not have the overhead associated with function calls.

- Function evaluation. A function evaluates to an address; a macro does not. Thus you cannot use a macro name in contexts requiring a pointer. For instance, you can declare a pointer to a function, but not a pointer to a macro.

- Macro side effects. A macro may treat arguments incorrectly when the macro evaluates its arguments more than once. For instance, the **toupper** macro is defined as:

```
#define toupper(c) ( (islower(c)) ? _toupper(c) : (c) )
```

In the following example, the **toupper** macro produces a side effect:

```
#include <ctype.h>

int a = 'm';
a = toupper(a++);
```

The example code increments a when passing it to **toupper**. The macro evaluates the argument a++ twice, once to check case and again for the result, therefore increasing a by 2 instead of 1. As a result, the value operated on by **islower** differs from the value operated on by **toupper**.

- Type-checking. When you declare a function, the compiler can check the argument types. Because you cannot declare a macro, the compiler cannot check macro argument types, although it can check the number of arguments you pass to a macro.

Type Checking

The compiler performs limited type checking on functions that can take a variable number of arguments, as follows.

Function Call	Type-Checked Arguments
_cprintf, **_cscanf**, **printf**, **scanf**	First argument (format string)
fprintf, **fscanf**, **sprintf**, **sscanf**	First two arguments (file or buffer and format string)
_snprintf	First three arguments (file or buffer, count, and format string)
_open	First two arguments (path and **_open** flag)
_sopen	First three arguments (path, **_open** flag, and sharing mode)
_execl, **_execle**, **_execlp**, **_execlpe**	First two arguments (path and first argument pointer)
_spawnl, **_spawnle**, **_spawnlp**, **_spawnlpe**	First three arguments (mode flag, path, and first argument pointer)

The compiler performs the same limited type checking on the wide-character counterparts of these functions.

Document Conventions

This book uses the following typographic conventions.

Example	Description
STDIO.H	Uppercase letters indicate filenames, segment names, registers, and terms used at the operating-system command level.
char, **_beginthread**, **__cplusplus**	Bold type indicates C and C++ keywords, operators, language-specific characters, and library routines. Within discussions of syntax, bold type indicates that the text must be entered exactly as shown.
expression	Words in italics indicate placeholders for information that you must supply, such as a filename. Italic type is also used occasionally for emphasis in the text.
[[*option*]]	Items inside double square brackets are optional.
**#pragma pack {1	2}**	Braces and a vertical bar indicate a choice among two or more items. You must choose one of these items unless double square brackets ([[ ]]) surround the braces.
`#include <io.h>`	This font is used for examples, user input, program output, and error messages in text.

Example	Description
CL [[*option...*]] *file...*	Three dots (an ellipsis) following an item indicate that more items having the same form may appear.

`while()`
`{`
  .
  .
  .
`}`
	A column or row of three dots indicates that part of an example program has been intentionally omitted.

CTRL+ENTER	Small capital letters indicate the names of keys on the keyboard. A plus sign (+) between two key names means you hold down the first key while pressing the second.
"argument"	Quotation marks enclose a new term the first time it is defined in text.
`"C string"`	Some C constructs, such as strings, require quotation marks. Quotation marks required by the language have the form `"  "` and `'  '` rather than " " and ' '.
▶ `CEnterDlg;`	The arrow adjoining the code indicates that it has been altered from a previous example, usually because you are being instructed to edit it.

C H A P T E R   1

Run-Time Routines by Category

This chapter lists and describes Microsoft run-time library routines by category. For reference convenience, some routines are listed in more than one category. Multibyte-character routines and wide-character routines are grouped with single-byte–character counterparts, where they exist.

The main categories of Microsoft run-time library routines are:

Argument access	Floating-point support
Buffer manipulation	Input and output
Byte classification	Internationalization
Character classification	Memory allocation
Data conversion	Process and environment control
Directory control	Searching and sorting
Error handling	String manipulation
Exception handling	System calls
File handling	Time management

Argument Access

The **va_arg**, **va_end**, and **va_start** macros provide access to function arguments when the number of arguments is variable. These macros are defined in STDARG.H for ANSI C compatibility, and in VARARG.H for compatibility with UNIX System V.

Argument-Access Macros

Macro	Use
va_arg	Retrieve argument from list
va_end	Reset pointer
va_start	Set pointer to beginning of argument list

Buffer Manipulation

Use these routines to work with areas of memory on a byte-by-byte basis.

Buffer-Manipulation Routines

Routine	Use
_memccpy	Copy characters from one buffer to another until given character or given number of characters has been copied
memchr	Return pointer to first occurrence, within specified number of characters, of given character in buffer
memcmp	Compare specified number of characters from two buffers
memcpy	Copy specified number of characters from one buffer to another
_memicmp	Compare specified number of characters from two buffers without regard to case
memmove	Copy specified number of characters from one buffer to another
memset	Use given character to initialize specified number of bytes in the buffer
_swab	Swap bytes of data and store them at specified location

When the source and target areas overlap, only **memmove** is guaranteed to copy the full source properly.

Byte Classification

Each of these routines tests a specified byte of a multibyte character for satisfaction of a condition. Except where specified otherwise, the test result depends on the multibyte code page currently in use.

Note By definition, the ASCII character set is a subset of all multibyte-character sets. For example, the Japanese katakana character set includes ASCII as well as non-ASCII characters.

The manifest constants in the following table are defined in CTYPE.H.

Multibyte-Character Byte-Classification Routines

Routine	Byte Test Condition
isleadbyte	Lead byte; test result depends on **LC_CTYPE** category setting of current locale
_ismbbalnum	**isalnum || _ismbbkalnum**
_ismbbalpha	**isalpha || _ismbbkalnum**
_ismbbgraph	Same as **_ismbbprint**, but **_ismbbgraph** does not include the space character (0x20).

Multibyte-Character Byte-Classification Routines (*continued*)

Routine	Byte Test Condition
_ismbbkalnum	Non-ASCII text symbol other than punctuation. For example, in code page 932 only, **_ismbbkalnum** tests for katakana alphanumeric.
_ismbbkana	Katakana (0xA1 – 0xDF), code page 932 only.
_ismbbkprint	Non-ASCII text or non-ASCII punctuation symbol. For example, in code page 932 only, **_ismbbkprint** tests for katakana alphanumeric or katakana punctuation (range: 0xA1 – 0xDF).
_ismbbkpunct	Non-ASCII punctuation. For example, in code page 932 only, **_ismbbkpunct** tests for katakana punctuation.
_ismbblead	First byte of multibyte character. For example, in code page 932 only, valid ranges are 0x81 – 0x9F, 0xE0 – 0xFC.
_ismbbprint	**isprint || _ismbbkprint**. **ismbbprint** includes the space character (0x20).
_ismbbpunct	**ispunct || _ismbbkpunct**
_ismbbtrail	Second byte of multibyte character. For example, in code page 932 only, valid ranges are 0x40 – 0x7E, 0x80 – 0xEC.
_ismbslead	Lead byte (in string context)
_ismbstrail	Trail byte (in string context)
_mbbtype	Return byte type based on previous byte
_mbsbtype	Return type of byte within string

The **MB_LEN_MAX** macro, defined in LIMITS.H, expands to the maximum length in bytes that any multibyte character can have. **MB_CUR_MAX**, defined in STDLIB.H, expands to the maximum length in bytes of any multibyte character in the current locale.

Character Classification

Each of these routines tests a specified single-byte character, wide character, or multibyte character for satisfaction of a condition. (By definition, the ASCII character set is a subset of all multibyte-character sets. For example, Japanese katakana includes ASCII as well as non-ASCII characters.) Generally these routines execute faster than tests you might write. For example, the following code executes slower than a call to **isalpha**(*c*).

```
if ((c >= 'A') && (c <= 'Z')) || ((c >= 'a') && (c <= 'z'))
    return TRUE;
```

Character-Classification Routines

Routine	Character Test Condition
isalnum, iswalnum, **_ismbcalnum**	Alphanumeric
isalpha, iswalpha, **_ismbcalpha**	Alphabetic
__isascii, iswascii	ASCII
iscntrl, iswcntrl	Control
__iscsym	Letter, underscore, or digit
__iscsymf	Letter or underscore
isdigit, iswdigit, **_ismbcdigit**	Decimal digit
isgraph, iswgraph, **_ismbcgraph**	Printable other than space
islower, iswlower, **_ismbclower**	Lowercase
_ismbchira	Hiragana
_ismbckata	Katakana
_ismbclegal	Legal multibyte character
_ismbcl0	Japan-level 0 multibyte character
_ismbcl1	Japan-level 1 multibyte character
_ismbcl2	Japan-level 2 multibyte character
_ismbcsymbol	Non-alphanumeric multibyte character
isprint, iswprint, **_ismbcprint**	Printable
ispunct, iswpunct, **_ismbcpunct**	Punctuation
isspace, iswspace, **_ismbcspace**	White-space
isupper, iswupper, **_ismbcupper**	Uppercase
iswctype	Property specified by *desc* argument
isxdigit, iswxdigit	Hexadecimal digit
mblen	Return length of valid multibyte character; result depends on **LC_CTYPE** category setting of current locale

Data Conversion

These routines convert data from one form to another. Generally these routines execute faster than conversions you might write. Each routine that begins with a **to** prefix is implemented as a function and as a macro. See "Choosing Between Functions and Macros" on page viii for information about choosing an implementation.

Data-Conversion Routines

Routine	Use
abs	Find absolute value of integer
atof	Convert string to **float**
atoi	Convert string to **int**
atol	Convert string to **long**
_ecvt	Convert **double** to string of specified length
_fcvt	Convert **double** to string with specified number of digits following decimal point
_gcvt	Convert **double** number to string; store string in buffer
_itoa, **_itow**	Convert **int** to string
labs	Find absolute value of **long** integer
_ltoa, **_ltow**	Convert **long** to string
_mbbtombc	Convert 1-byte multibyte character to corresponding 2-byte multibyte character
_mbcjistojms	Convert Japan Industry Standard (JIS) character to Japan Microsoft (JMS) character
_mbcjmstojis	Convert JMS character to JIS character
_mbctohira	Convert multibyte character to 1-byte hiragana code
_mbctokata	Convert multibyte character to 1-byte katakana code
_mbctombb	Convert 2-byte multibyte character to corresponding 1-byte multibyte character
mbstowcs	Convert sequence of multibyte characters to corresponding sequence of wide characters
mbtowc	Convert multibyte character to corresponding wide character
strtod, wcstod	Convert string to **double**
strtol, wcstol	Convert string to **long** integer
strtoul, wcstoul	Convert string to **unsigned long** integer
strxfrm, wcsxfrm	Transform string into collated form based on locale-specific information
__toascii	Convert character to ASCII code

Data-Conversion Routines (*continued*)

Routine	Use
tolower, towlower, _mbctolower	Test character and convert to lowercase if currently uppercase
_tolower	Convert character to lowercase unconditionally
toupper, towupper, _mbctoupper	Test character and convert to uppercase if currently lowercase
_toupper	Convert character to uppercase unconditionally
_ultoa, _ultow	Convert **unsigned long** to string
wcstombs	Convert sequence of wide characters to corresponding sequence of multibyte characters
wctomb	Convert wide character to corresponding multibyte character
_wtoi	Convert wide-character string to **int**
_wtol	Convert wide-character string to **long**

Directory Control

These routines access, modify, and obtain information about the directory structure.

Directory-Control Routines

Routine	Use
_chdir, _wchdir	Change current working directory
_chdrive	Change current drive
_getcwd, _wgetcwd	Get current working directory for default drive
_getdcwd, _wgetdcwd	Get current working directory for specified drive
_getdrive	Get current (default) drive
_mkdir, _wmkdir	Make new directory
_rmdir, _wrmdir	Remove directory
_searchenv, _wsearchenv	Search for given file on specified paths

Error Handling

Use these routines to handle program errors.

Error-Handling Routines

Routine	Use
assert macro	Test for programming logic errors.
clearerr	Reset error indicator. Calling **rewind** or closing a stream also resets the error indicator.
_eof	Check for end of file in low-level I/O.
feof	Test for end of file. End of file is also indicated when **_read** returns 0.
ferror	Test for stream I/O errors.

Exception Handling

Use the C++ exception-handling functions to recover from unexpected events during program execution.

Exception-Handling Functions

Function	Use
_set_se_translator	Handle Win32 exceptions (C structured exceptions) as C++ typed exceptions.
set_terminate	Install your own termination routine to be called by **terminate**.
set_unexpected	Install your own termination function to be called by **unexpected**.
terminate	Called automatically under certain circumstances after exception is thrown. **terminate** calls **abort** or function you specify using **set_terminate**.
unexpected	Calls **terminate** or function you specify using **set_unexpected**. **unexpected** is not used in current Microsoft C++ exception-handling implementation.

File Handling

Use these routines to create, delete, and manipulate files and to set and check file-access permissions.

The following routines operate on files designated by a file handle.

File-Handling Routines (File Handle)

Routine	Use
_chsize	Change file size
_filelength	Get file length
_fstat	Get file-status information on handle
_isatty	Check for character device
_locking	Lock areas of file
_setmode	Set file-translation mode

The following routines operate on files specified by a path or filename.

File-Handling Routines (Path or Filename)

Routine	Use
_access, _waccess	Check file-permission setting
_chmod, _wchmod	Change file-permission setting
_fullpath, _wfullpath	Convert relative path to absolute path
_get_osfhandle	Return operating-system file handle associated with existing stream **FILE** pointer
_makepath, _wmakepath	Merge path components into single, full path
_mktemp, _wmktemp	Create unique filename
_open_osfhandle	Associate C run-time file handle with existing operating-system file handle
remove, _wremove	Delete file
rename, _wrename	Rename file
_splitpath, _wsplitpath	Parse path into components
_stat, _wstat	Get file-status information on named file
_umask	Set default permission mask for new files created by program
_unlink, _wunlink	Delete file

Floating-Point Support

Many Microsoft run-time library functions require floating-point support from a math coprocessor or from the floating-point libraries that accompany the compiler. Floating-point support functions are loaded only if required.

When you use a floating-point type specifier in the format string of a call to a function in the **printf** or **scanf** family, you must specify a floating-point value or a pointer to a floating-point value in the argument list to tell the compiler that floating-point support is required. The math functions in the Microsoft run-time library handle exceptions in the same way as the UNIX V math functions.

The Microsoft run-time library sets the default internal precision of the math coprocessor (or emulator) to 64 bits. This default applies only to the internal precision at which all intermediate calculations are performed; it does not apply to the size of arguments, return values, or variables. You can override this default and set the chip (or emulator) back to 80-bit precision by linking your program with LIB/FP10.OBJ. On the linker command line, FP10.OBJ must appear before LIBC.LIB, LIBCMT.LIB, or MSVCRT.LIB.

Floating-Point Functions

Function	Use
abs	Return absolute value of **int**
acos	Calculate arccosine
asin	Calculate arcsine
atan, atan2	Calculate arctangent
atof	Convert character string to double-precision floating-point value
Bessel functions	Calculate Bessel functions **_j0**, **_j1**, **_jn**, **_y0**, **_y1**, **_yn**
_cabs	Find absolute value of complex number
ceil	Find integer ceiling
_chgsign	Reverse sign of double-precision floating-point argument
_clear87, _clearfp	Get and clear floating-point status word
_control87, _controlfp	Get old floating-point control word and set new control-word value
_copysign	Return one value with sign of another
cos	Calculate cosine
cosh	Calculate hyperbolic cosine
difftime	Compute difference between two specified time values
div	Divide one integer by another, returning quotient and remainder
_ecvt	Convert **double** to character string of specified length
exp	Calculate exponential function

Floating-Point Functions (*continued*)

Function	Use
fabs	Find absolute value
_fcvt	Convert **double** to string with specified number of digits following decimal point
_finite	Determine whether given double-precision floating-point value is finite
floor	Find largest integer less than or equal to argument
fmod	Find floating-point remainder
_fpclass	Return status word containing information on floating-point class
_fpieee_flt	Invoke user-defined trap handler for IEEE floating-point exceptions
_fpreset	Reinitialize floating-point math package
frexp	Calculate exponential value
_gcvt	Convert floating-point value to character string
_hypot	Calculate hypotenuse of right triangle
_isnan	Check given double-precision floating-point value for not a number (NaN)
labs	Return absolute value of **long**
ldexp	Calculate product of argument and 2 to specified power
ldiv	Divide one **long** integer by another, returning quotient and remainder
log	Calculate natural logarithm
log10	Calculate base-10 logarithm
_logb	Extract exponential value of double-precision floating-point argument
_lrotl, _lrotr	Shift **unsigned long int** left (**_lrotl**) or right (**_lrotr**)
_matherr	Handle math errors
_ _max	Return larger of two values
_ _min	Return smaller of two values
modf	Split argument into integer and fractional parts
_nextafter	Return next representable neighbor
pow	Calculate value raised to a power
printf, wprintf	Write data to **stdout** according to specified format
rand	Get pseudorandom number
_rotl, _rotr	Shift **unsigned int** left (**_rotl**) or right (**_rotr**)

Floating-Point Functions (*continued*)

Function	Use
_scalb	Scale argument by power of 2
scanf, wscanf	Read data from **stdin** according to specified format and write data to specified location
sin	Calculate sine
sinh	Calculate hyperbolic sine
sqrt	Find square root
srand	Initialize pseudorandom series
_status87, _statusfp	Get floating-point status word
strtod	Convert character string to double-precision value
tan	Calculate tangent
tanh	Calculate hyperbolic tangent

Long Double

Previous 16-bit versions of Microsoft C/C++ and Microsoft Visual C++ supported the **long double**, 80-bit precision data type. In Win32 programming, however, the **long double** data type maps to the **double**, 64-bit precision data type. The Microsoft run-time library provides **long double** versions of the math functions only for backward compatibility. The **long double** function prototypes are identical to the prototypes for their **double** counterparts, except that the **long double** data type replaces the **double** data type. The **long double** versions of these functions should not be used in new code.

Double Functions and Their Long Double Counterparts

Function	Long Double Counterpart	Function	Long Double Counterpart
acos	acosl	frexp	frexpl
asin	asinl	_hypot	_hypotl
atan	atanl	ldexp	ldexpl
atan2	atan2l	log	logl
atof	_atold	log10	log10l
Bessel functions j0, j1, jn	Bessel functions j0l, j1l, jnl	_matherr	_matherrl
Bessel functions y0, y1, yn	Bessel functions y0l, y1l, ynl	modf	modfl

Double Functions and Their Long Double Counterparts (*continued*)

Function	Long Double Counterpart	Function	Long Double Counterpart
_cabs	_cabsl	pow	powl
ceil	ceill	sin	sinl
cos	cosl	sinh	sinhl
cosh	coshl	sqrt	sqrtl
exp	expl	strtod	_strtold
fabs	fabsl	tan	tanl
floor	floorl	tanh	tanhl
fmod	fmodl		

Input and Output

The I/O functions read and write data to and from files and devices. File I/O operations take place in text mode or binary mode. There are three types of I/O functions in the Microsoft run-time library:

- Stream I/O functions treat data as a stream of individual characters.
- Low-level I/O functions invoke the operating system directly for lower-level operation than that provided by stream I/O.
- Console and port I/O functions read or write directly to a console (keyboard and screen) or an I/O port (such as a printer port).

Warning Because stream functions are buffered and low-level functions are not, these two types of functions are generally incompatible. For processing a particular file, use either stream or low-level functions exclusively.

Text and Binary Mode File I/O

File I/O operations take place in one of two translation modes, text or binary, depending on the mode in which the file is open. Data files are usually processed in text mode. To control the file translation mode, you can:

- Retain the current default setting and specify the alternative mode only when you open selected files.

- Change the default translation mode directly by setting the global variable **_fmode** in your program. The initial default setting of **_fmode** is **_O_TEXT**, for text mode. For more information about **_fmode**, see "**_fmode**" on page 42.

When you call a file-open function such as **_open**, **fopen**, **freopen**, or **_fsopen**, you can override the current default setting of **_fmode** by specifying the appropriate argument to the function. The **stdin**, **stdout**, and **stderr** streams are always opened in text mode by default; you can also override this default when opening any of these files. Use **_setmode** to change the translation mode using the file handle after the file is open.

Unicode™ Stream I/O in Text and Binary Modes

When a Unicode stream I/O routine (such as **fwprintf**, **fwscanf**, **fgetwc**, **fputwc**, **fgetws**, or **fputws**) operates on a file that is open in text mode (the default), two kinds of character conversions take place:

- Unicode-to-MBCS or MBCS-to-Unicode conversion. When a Unicode stream-I/O function operates in text mode, the source or destination stream is assumed to be a sequence of multibyte characters. Therefore, the Unicode stream-input functions convert multibyte characters to wide characters (as if by a call to the **mbtowc** function). For the same reason, the Unicode stream-output functions convert wide characters to multibyte characters (as if by a call to the **wctomb** function).

- Carriage-return–linefeed (CR-LF) translation. This translation occurs before the MBCS–Unicode conversion (for Unicode stream input functions) and after the Unicode–MBCS conversion (for Unicode stream output functions). During input, each carriage-return–linefeed combination is translated into a single linefeed character. During output, each linefeed character is translated into a carriage-return–linefeed combination.

However, when a Unicode stream-I/O function operates in binary mode, the file is assumed to be Unicode, and no CR-LF translation or character conversion occurs during input or output.

Stream I/O

These functions process data in different sizes and formats, from single characters to large data structures. They also provide buffering, which can improve performance. The default size of a stream buffer is 4K. These routines affect only buffers created by the run-time library routines, and have no effect on buffers created by the operating system.

Stream I/O Routines

Routine	Use
clearerr	Clear error indicator for stream
fclose	Close stream
_fcloseall	Close all open streams except **stdin**, **stdout**, and **stderr**
_fdopen, wfdopen	Associate stream with handle to open file
feof	Test for end of file on stream
ferror	Test for error on stream
fflush	Flush stream to buffer or storage device
fgetc, fgetwc	Read character from stream (function versions of **getc** and **getwc**)
_fgetchar, _fgetwchar	Read character from **stdin** (function versions of **getchar** and **getwchar**)
fgetpos	Get position indicator of stream
fgets, fgetws	Read string from stream
_fileno	Get file handle associated with stream
_flushall	Flush all streams to buffer or storage device
fopen, _wfopen	Open stream
fprintf, fwprintf	Write formatted data to stream
fputc, fputwc	Write a character to a stream (function versions of **putc** and **putwc**)
_fputchar, _fputwchar	Write character to **stdout** (function versions of **putchar** and **putwchar**)
fputs, fputws	Write string to stream
fread	Read unformatted data from stream
freopen, _wfreopen	Reassign **FILE** stream pointer to new file or device
fscanf, fwscanf	Read formatted data from stream
fseek	Move file position to given location
fsetpos	Set position indicator of stream
_fsopen, _wfsopen	Open stream with file sharing
ftell	Get current file position

Stream I/O Routines (*continued*)

Routine	Use
fwrite	Write unformatted data items to stream
getc, getwc	Read character from stream (macro versions of **fgetc** and **fgetwc**)
getchar, getwchar	Read character from **stdin** (macro versions of **fgetchar** and **fgetwchar**)
gets, getws	Read line from **stdin**
_getw	Read binary **int** from stream
printf, wprintf	Write formatted data to **stdout**
putc, putwc	Write character to a stream (macro versions of **fputc** and **fputwc**)
putchar, putwchar	Write character to **stdout** (macro versions of **fputchar** and **fputwchar**)
puts, putws	Write line to stream
_putw	Write binary **int** to a stream
rewind	Move file position to beginning of stream
_rmtmp	Remove temporary files created by **tmpfile**
scanf, wscanf	Read formatted data from **stdin**
setbuf	Control stream buffering
setvbuf	Control stream buffering and buffer size
_snprintf, _snwprintf	Write formatted data of specified length to string
sprintf, swprintf	Write formatted data to string
sscanf, swscanf	Read formatted data from string
_tempnam, _wtempnam	Generate temporary filename in given directory
tmpfile	Create temporary file
tmpnam, _wtmpnam	Generate temporary filename
ungetc, ungetwc	Push character back onto stream
vfprintf, vfwprintf	Write formatted data to stream
vprintf, vwprintf	Write formatted data to **stdout**
_vsnprintf, _vsnwprintf	Write formatted data of specified length to buffer
vsprintf, vswprintf	Write formatted data to buffer

When a program begins execution, the startup code automatically opens several streams: standard input (pointed to by **stdin**), standard output (pointed to by **stdout**), and standard error (pointed to by **stderr**). These streams are directed to the console (keyboard and screen) by default. Use **freopen** to redirect **stdin**, **stdout**, or **stderr** to a disk file or a device.

Files opened using the stream routines are buffered by default. **stdout** and **stderr** are flushed whenever they are full or, if you are writing to a character device, after each library call. If a program terminates abnormally, output buffers may not be flushed, resulting in loss of data. Use **fflush** or **_flushall** to ensure that the buffer associated with a specified file or all open buffers are flushed to the operating system, which can cache data before writing it to disk. The commit-to-disk feature ensures that the flushed buffer contents are not lost in the event of a system failure.

There are two ways to commit buffer contents to disk:

- Link with the file COMMODE.OBJ to set a global commit flag. The default setting of the global flag is **n**, for "no-commit."
- Set the mode flag to **c** with **fopen** or **_fdopen**.

Any file specifically opened with either the **c** or the **n** flag behaves according to the flag, regardless of the state of the global commit/no-commit flag.

If your program does not explicitly close a stream, the stream is automatically closed when the program terminates. However, you should close a stream when your program finishes with it, as the number of streams that can be open at one time is limited.

Input can follow output directly only with an intervening call to **fflush** or to a file-positioning function (**fseek**, **fsetpos**, or **rewind**). Output can follow input without an intervening call to a file-positioning function if the input operation encounters the end of the file.

Low-level I/O

These functions invoke the operating system directly for lower-level operation than that provided by stream I/O. Low-level input and output calls do not buffer or format data.

Low-level routines can access the standard streams opened at program startup using the following predefined handles.

Stream	Handle
stdin	0
stdout	1
stderr	2

Low-level I/O routines set the **errno** global variable when an error occurs. (For more information on **errno**, see "**_doserrno, errno, _sys_errlist, and _sysnerr**" on page 39.) You must include STDIO.H when you use low-level functions only if your program requires a constant that is defined in STDIO.H, such as the end-of-file indicator (**EOF**).

Low-Level I/O Functions

Function	Use
_close	Close file
_commit	Flush file to disk
_creat, _wcreat	Create file
_dup	Return next available file handle for given file
_dup2	Create second handle for given file
_eof	Test for end of file
_lseek	Reposition file pointer to given location
_open, _wopen	Open file
_read	Read data from file
_sopen, _wsopen	Open file for file sharing
_tell	Get current file-pointer position
_umask	Set file-permission mask
_write	Write data to file

_dup and **_dup2** are typically used to associate the predefined file handles with different files.

Console and Port I/O

These routines read and write on your console or on the specified port. The console I/O routines are not compatible with stream I/O or low-level I/O library routines. The console or port does not have to be opened or closed before I/O is performed, so there are no open or close routines in this category. In Windows NT the output from these functions is always directed to the console and cannot be redirected.

Console and Port I/O Routines

Routine	Use
_cgets	Read string from console
_cprintf	Write formatted data to console
_cputs	Write string to console
_cscanf	Read formatted data from console
_getch	Read character from console
_getche	Read character from console and echo it
_inp	Read one byte from specified I/O port
_inpd	Read double word from specified I/O port
_inpw	Read 2-byte word from specified I/O port
_kbhit	Check for keystroke at console; use before attempting to read from console
_outp	Write one byte to specified I/O port
_outpd	Write double word to specified I/O port
_outpw	Write word to specified I/O port
_putch	Write character to console
_ungetch	"Unget" last character read from console so it becomes next character read

Internationalization

The Microsoft run-time library provides many routines that are useful for creating different versions of a program for international markets. This includes locale-related routines, wide-character routines, multibyte-character routines, and generic-text routines. For convenience, most locale-related routines are also categorized in this reference according to the operations they perform. In this chapter and in this book's alphabetic reference, multibyte-character routines and wide-character routines are described with single-byte–character counterparts, where they exist.

Locale

Use the **setlocale** function to change or query some or all of the current program locale information. "Locale" refers to the locality (the country and language) for which you can customize certain aspects of your program. Some locale-dependent categories include the formatting of dates and the display format for monetary values.

Locale-Dependent Routines

Routine	Use	setlocale Category Setting Dependence
atof, **atoi**, **atol**	Convert character to floating-point, integer, or long integer value, respectively	**LC_NUMERIC**
is Routines	Test given integer for particular condition.	**LC_CTYPE**
isleadbyte	Test for lead byte ( )	**LC_CTYPE**
localeconv	Read appropriate values for formatting numeric quantities	**LC_MONETARY**, **LC_NUMERIC**
MB_CUR_MAX	Maximum length in bytes of any multibyte character in current locale (macro defined in STDLIB.H)	**LC_CTYPE**
_mbccpy	Copy one multibyte character	**LC_CTYPE**
_mbclen	Return length, in bytes, of given multibyte character	**LC_CTYPE**
mblen	Validate and return number of bytes in multibyte character	**LC_CTYPE**
_mbstrlen	For multibyte-character strings: validate each character in string; return string length	**LC_CTYPE**
mbstowcs	Convert sequence of multibyte characters to corresponding sequence of wide characters	**LC_CTYPE**
mbtowc	Convert multibyte character to corresponding wide character	**LC_CTYPE**
printf family	Write formatted output	**LC_NUMERIC** (determines radix character output)
scanf family	Read formatted input	**LC_NUMERIC** (determines radix character recognition)
setlocale. **_wsetlocale**	Select locale for program	Not applicable
strcoll, **wcscoll**	Compare characters of two strings	**LC_COLLATE**
strncoll, **wcsncoll**	Compare first n characters of two strings	**LC_COLLATE**
_stricoll, **_wcsicoll**	Compare characters of two strings (case insensitive)	**LC_COLLATE**
_strnicoll, **_wcsnicoll**	Compare first n characters of two strings (case insensitive)	**LC_COLLATE**
strftime, **wcsftime**	Format date and time value according to supplied *format* argument	**LC_TIME**
_strlwr	Convert, in place, each uppercase letter in given string to lowercase	**LC_CTYPE**

Locale-Dependent Routines (*continued*)

Routine	Use	setlocale Category Setting Dependence
strtod, wcstod, strtol, wcstol, strtoul, wcstoul	Convert character string to double, long, or unsigned long value	**LC_NUMERIC** (determines radix character recognition)
_strupr	Convert, in place, each lowercase letter in string to uppercase	**LC_CTYPE**
strxfrm, wcsxfrm	Transform string into collated form according to locale	**LC_COLLATE**
tolower, towlower	Convert given character to corresponding lowercase character	**LC_CTYPE**
toupper, towupper	Convert given character to corresponding uppercase letter	**LC_CTYPE**
wcstombs	Convert sequence of wide characters to corresponding sequence of multibyte characters	**LC_CTYPE**
wctomb	Convert wide character to corresponding multibyte character	**LC_CTYPE**
_wtoi, _wtol	Convert wide-character string to **int** or **long**	**LC_NUMERIC**

Code Pages

A *code page* is a character set, which can include numbers, punctuation marks, and other glyphs. Different languages and locales may use different code pages. For example, ANSI code page 1252 is used for American English and most European languages; OEM code page 932 is used for Japanese Kanji.

A code page can be represented in a table as a mapping of characters to single-byte values or multibyte values. Many code pages share the ASCII character set for characters in the range 0x00–0x7F.

The Microsoft run-time library uses the following types of code pages.

- System-default ANSI code page. By default, at startup the run-time system automatically sets the multibyte code page to the system-default ANSI code page, which is obtained from the operating system. The call

  ```
  setlocale ( LC_ALL, "" );
  ```

  also sets the locale to the system-default ANSI code page.

- Locale code page. The behavior of a number of run-time routines is dependent on the current locale setting, which includes the locale code page. (For more information, see "Locale-Dependent Routines" on page 19–20.) By default, all locale-dependent routines in the Microsoft run-time library use the code page that corresponds to the "C" locale. At run-time you can change or query the locale code page in use with a call to **setlocale**.

- Multibyte code page. The behavior of most of the multibyte-character routines in the run-time library depends on the current multibyte code page setting. By default, these routines use the system-default ANSI code page. At run-time you can change the multibyte code page in use with a call to **_setmbcp**.

- The "C" locale is defined by ANSI to correspond to the locale in which C programs have traditionally executed.The code page for the "C" locale ("C" code page) corresponds to the ASCII character set. For example, in the "C" locale, **islower** returns true for the values 0x61–0x7A only. In another locale, **islower** may return true for these as well as other values, as defined by that locale.

Interpretation of Multibyte-Character Sequences

Most multibyte-character routines in the Microsoft run-time library recognize multibyte-character sequences according to the current multibyte code page setting. The following multibyte-character routines depend instead on the locale code page (specifically, on the **LC_CTYPE** category setting of the current locale):

Locale-Dependent Multibyte Routines

Routine	Use
mblen	Validate and return number of bytes in multibyte character
_mbstrlen	For multibyte-character strings: validate each character in string; return string length
mbstowcs	Convert sequence of multibyte characters to corresponding sequence of wide characters
mbtowc	Convert multibyte character to corresponding wide character
wcstombs	Convert sequence of wide characters to corresponding sequence of multibyte characters
wctomb	Convert wide character to corresponding multibyte character

Single-byte and Multibyte Character Sets

The ASCII character set defines characters in the range 0x00–0x7F. There are a number of other character sets, primarily European, that define the characters within the range 0x00–0x7F identically to the ASCII character set and also define an extended character set from 0x80–0xFF. Thus an 8-bit, single-byte–character set (SBCS) is sufficient to represent the ASCII character set as well as the character sets for many European languages. However, some non-European character sets, such as Japanese Kanji, include many more characters than can be represented in a single-byte coding scheme, and therefore require multibyte-character set (MBCS) encoding.

Note Many SBCS routines in the Microsoft run-time library handle multibyte bytes, characters, and strings as appropriate. Many multibyte-character sets define the ASCII character set as a subset. In many multibyte character sets, each character in the range 0x00–0x7F is identical to the character that has the same value in the ASCII character set. For example, in both ASCII and MBCS character strings, the one-byte **NULL** character ('\0') has value 0x00 and indicates the terminating null character.

A multibyte character set may consist of both one-byte and two-byte characters. Thus a multibyte-character string may contain a mixture of single-byte and double-byte characters. A 2-byte multibyte character has a lead byte and a trail byte. In a particular multibyte-character set, the lead bytes fall within a certain range, as do the trail bytes. When these ranges overlap, it may be necessary to evaluate the context to determine whether a given byte is functioning as a lead byte or a trail byte.

SBCS and MBCS Data Types

Any Microsoft MBCS run-time library routine that handles only one multibyte character or one byte of a multibyte character expects an unsigned **int** argument (where 0x00 <= character value <= 0xFFFF and 0x00 <= byte value <= 0xFF). An MBCS routine that handles multibyte bytes or characters in a string context expects a multibyte-character string to be represented as an unsigned **char** pointer.

Caution Each byte of a multibyte character can be represented in an 8-bit **char**. However, an SBCS or MBCS single-byte character of type **char** with a value greater than 0x7F is negative. When such a character is converted directly to an **int** or a **long**, the result is sign-extended by the compiler and can therefore yield unexpected results.

Therefore it is best to represent a byte of a multibyte character as an 8-bit **unsigned char**. Or, to avoid a negative result, simply convert a single-byte character of type **char** to an **unsigned char** before converting it to an **int** or a **long**.

Unicode: The Wide-Character Set

A wide character is a 2-byte multilingual character code. Any character in use in modern computing worldwide, including technical symbols and special publishing characters, can be represented according to the Unicode specification as a wide character. Developed and maintained by a large consortium that includes Microsoft, the Unicode standard is now widely accepted. Because every wide character is always represented in a fixed size of 16 bits, using wide characters simplifies programming with international character sets.

A wide character is of type **wchar_t**. A wide-character string is represented as a **wchar_t[]** array and is pointed to by a **wchar_t*** pointer. You can represent any ASCII character as a wide character by prefixing the letter L to the character. For example, L'\0' is the terminating wide (16-bit) **NULL** character. Similarly, you can represent any ASCII string literal as a wide-character string literal simply by prefixing the letter L to the ASCII literal (L"Hello").

Generally, wide characters take up more space in memory than multibyte characters but are faster to process. In addition, only one locale can be represented at a time in multibyte encoding, whereas all character sets in the world are represented simultaneously by the Unicode representation.

Using Generic-Text Mappings

Microsoft Specific →

To simplify code development for various international markets, the Microsoft run-time library provides Microsoft-specific "generic-text" mappings for many data types, routines, and other objects. These mappings are defined in TCHAR.H. You can use these name mappings to write generic code that can be compiled for any of the three kinds of character sets: ASCII (SBCS), MBCS, or Unicode, depending on a manifest constant you define using a **#define** statement. Generic-text mappings are Microsoft extensions that are not ANSI compatible.

Preprocessor Directives for Generic-Text Mappings

# define	Compiled Version	Example
_UNICODE	Unicode (wide-character)	**_tcsrev** maps to **_wcsrev**
_MBCS	Multibyte-character	**_tcsrev** maps to **_mbsrev**
None (the default: neither **_UNICODE** nor **_MBCS** defined)	SBCS (ASCII)	**_tcsrev** maps to **strrev**

For example, the generic-text function **_tcsrev**, defined in TCHAR.H, maps to **_mbsrev** if **_MBCS** has been defined in your program, or to **_wcsrev** if **_UNICODE** has been defined. Otherwise **_tcsrev** maps to **strrev**.

The generic-text data type **_TCHAR**, also defined in TCHAR.H, maps to type **char** if **_MBCS** is defined, to type **wchar_t** if **_UNICODE** is defined, and to type **char** if neither constant is defined. Other data type mappings are provided in TCHAR.H for programming convenience, but **_TCHAR** is the type that is most useful.

Generic-Text Data Type Mappings

Generic-Text Data Type Name	SBCS (_UNICODE, _MBCS Not Defined)	_MBCS Defined	_UNICODE Defined
_TCHAR	char	char	wchar_t
_TINT	int	int	wint_t
_TSCHAR	signed char	signed char	wchar_t
_TUCHAR	unsigned char	unsigned char	wchar_t
_TXCHAR	char	unsigned char	wchar_t
_T or **_TEXT**	No affect (removed by preprocessor)	No affect (removed by preprocessor)	**L** (converts following character or string to its Unicode counterpart)

For a complete list of generic-text mappings of routines, variables, and other objects, see Appendix B, "Generic-Text Mappings."

The following code fragments illustrate the use of **_TCHAR** and **_tcsrev** for mapping to the MBCS, Unicode, and SBCS models.

```
_TCHAR *RetVal, *szString;
RetVal = _tcsrev(szString);
```

If **_MBCS** has been defined, the preprocessor maps the preceding fragment to the following code:

```
char *RetVal, *szString;
RetVal = _mbsrev(szString);
```

If **_UNICODE** has been defined, the preprocessor maps the same fragment to the following code:

```
wchar_t *RetVal, *szString;
RetVal = _wcsrev(szString);
```

If neither **_MBCS** nor **_UNICODE** has been defined, the preprocessor maps the fragment to single-byte ASCII code, as follows:

```
char *RetVal, *szString;
RetVal = strrev(szString);
```

Thus you can write, maintain, and compile a single source code file to run with routines that are specific to any of the three kinds of character sets.

A Sample Generic-Text Program

The following program, GENTEXT.C, provides a more detailed illustration of the use of generic-text mappings defined in TCHAR.H.

```
#include <stdio.h>
#include <stdlib.h>
#include <string.h>
#include <direct.h>
#include <errno.h>
#include <tchar.h>

/* GENTEXT.C: Generic-Text-Mapping example program. */

int __cdecl _tmain(int argc, _TCHAR **argv, _TCHAR **envp)
{
        _TCHAR buff[_MAX_PATH];
        _TCHAR *str = _T("Astring");
        char *amsg = "Reversed";
        wchar_t *wmsg = L"Is";

#ifdef _UNICODE
        printf("Unicode version\n");
#else /* _UNICODE */
#ifdef _MBCS
        printf("MBCS version\n");
#else
        printf("SBCS version\n");
#endif
#endif /* _UNICODE */

        if (_tgetcwd(buff, _MAX_PATH) == NULL)
            printf("Can't Get Current Directory - errno=%d\n", errno);
        else
            _tprintf(_T("Current Directory is '%s'\n"), buff);
        _tprintf(_T("'%s' %hs %ls:\n"), str, amsg, wmsg);
        _tprintf(_T("'%s'\n"), _tcsrev(str));
        return 0;
}
```

If **_MBCS** has been defined, GENTEXT.C maps to the following MBCS program.

```
/*
 * MBCS version of GENTEXT.C.
 */
int __cdecl main(int argc, char **argv, char **envp)
{
        char buff[_MAX_PATH];
        char *str = "Astring";
        char *amsg = "Reversed";
        wchar_t *wmsg = L"Is";

        printf("MBCS version\n");
        if (_getcwd(buff, _MAX_PATH) == NULL)
            printf("Can't Get Current Directory - errno=%d\n", errno);
        else
            printf("Current Directory is '%s'\n", buff);
        printf("'%s' %hs %ls:\n", str, amsg, wmsg);
        printf("'%s'\n", _mbsrev(str));
        return 0;
}
```

If **_UNICODE** has been defined, GENTEXT.C maps to the following Unicode version of the program. For more information about using **wmain** in Unicode programs as a replacement for **main**, see "Using wmain," in the *C Language Reference*.

```
/*
 * Unicode version of GENTEXT.C.
 */
int __cdecl wmain(int argc, wchar_t **argv, wchar_t **envp)
{
        wchar_t buff[_MAX_PATH];
        wchar_t *str = L"Astring";
        char *amsg = "Reversed";
        wchar_t *wmsg = L"Is";

        printf("Unicode version\n");
        if (_wgetcwd(buff, _MAX_PATH) == NULL)
            printf("Can't Get Current Directory - errno=%d\n", errno);
        else
            wprintf(L"Current Directory is '%s'\n", buff);
        wprintf(L"'%s' %hs %ls:\n", str, amsg, wmsg);
        wprintf(L"'%s'\n", wcsrev(str));
        return 0;
}
```

If neither **_MBCS** nor **_UNICODE** has been defined, GENTEXT.C maps to single-byte ASCII code, as follows.

```
/*
 * SBCS (ASCII) version of GENTEXT.C.
 */
int __cdecl main(int argc, char **argv, char **envp)
{
        char buff[_MAX_PATH];
        char *str = "Astring";
        char *amsg = "Reversed";
        wchar_t *wmsg = L"Is";

        printf("SBCS version\n");
        if (_getcwd(buff, _MAX_PATH) == NULL)
            printf("Can't Get Current Directory - errno=%d\n", errno);
        else
            printf("Current Directory is '%s'\n", buff);
        printf("'%s' %hs %ls:\n", str, amsg, wmsg);
        printf("'%s'\n", strrev(str));
        return 0;
}
```

Using TCHAR.H Data Types with _MBCS

As the table of generic-text routine mappings indicates (see Appendix B, "Generic-Text Mappings"), when the manifest constant **_MBCS** is defined, a given generic-text routine maps to one of the following kinds of routines:

- An SBCS routine that handles multibyte bytes, characters, and strings appropriately. In this case, the string arguments are expected to be of type **char***. For example, **_tprintf** maps to **printf**; the string arguments to **printf** are of type **char***. If you use the **_TCHAR** generic-text data type for your string types, the formal and actual parameter types for **printf** match because **_TCHAR*** maps to **char***.

- An MBCS-specific routine. In this case, the string arguments are expected to be of type **unsigned char***. For example, **_tcsrev** maps to **_mbsrev**, which expects and returns a string of type **unsigned char***. Again, if you use the **_TCHAR** generic-text data type for your string types, there is a potential type conflict because **_TCHAR** maps to type **char**.

Following are three solutions for preventing this type conflict (and the C compiler warnings or C++ compiler errors that would result).

- Use the default behavior. TCHAR.H provides generic-text routine prototypes for routines in the run-time libraries, as in the following example.

```
char * _tcsrev(char *);
```

In the default case, the prototype for **_tcsrev** maps to **_mbsrev** through a thunk in LIBC.LIB. This changes the types of the **_mbsrev** incoming parameters and outgoing return value from **_TCHAR *** (i.e., **char ***) to **unsigned char ***. This method ensures type matching when you are using **_TCHAR**, but it is relatively slow due to the function call overhead.

- Use function inlining by incorporating the following preprocessor statement in your code.

```
#define _USE_INLINING
```

This method causes an inline function thunk, provided in TCHAR.H, to map the generic-text routine directly to the appropriate MBCS routine. The following code excerpt from TCHAR.H provides an example of how this is done.

```
__inline char *_tcsrev(char *_s1)
{return (char *)_mbsrev((unsigned char *)_s1);}
```

If you can use inlining, this is the best solution, because it guarantees type matching and has no additional time cost.

- Use "direct mapping" by incorporating the following preprocessor statement in your code.

```
#define _MB_MAP_DIRECT
```

This approach provides a fast alternative if you do not want to use the default behavior or cannot use inlining. It causes the generic-text routine to be mapped by a macro directly to the MBCS version of the routine, as in the following example from TCHAR.H.

```
#define _tcschr _mbschr
```

When you take this approach, you must be careful to ensure that appropriate data types are used for string arguments and string return values. You can use type casting to ensure proper type matching or you can use the **_TXCHAR** generic-text data type. **_TXCHAR** maps to type **char** in SBCS code but maps to type **unsigned char** in MBCS code. For more information about generic-text macros, see Appendix B, "Generic-Text Mappings."

END Microsoft Specific

Memory Allocation

Use these routines to allocate, free, and reallocate memory.

Memory-Allocation Routines

Routine	Use
_alloca	Allocate memory from stack
calloc	Allocate storage for array, initializing every byte in allocated block to 0
_expand	Expand or shrink block of memory without moving it
free	Free allocated block
_heapadd	Add memory to heap
_heapchk	Check heap for consistency
_heapmin	Release unused memory in heap
_heapset	Fill free heap entries with specified value
_heapwalk	Return information about each entry in heap
malloc	Allocate block of memory from heap
_msize	Return size of allocated block
_query_new_handler	Returns address of current new handler routine as set by **_set_new_handler**
_query_new_mode	Return integer indicating new handler mode set by **_set_new_mode** for **malloc**
realloc	Reallocate block to new size
_set_new_handler	Enable error-handling mechanism when **new** operator fails (to allocate memory)
_set_new_mode	Set new handler mode for **malloc**

Process and Environment Control

Use the process-control routines to start, stop, and manage processes from within a program. Use the environment-control routines to get and change information about the operating-system environment.

Process and Environment Control Functions

Routine	Use
abort	Abort process without flushing buffers or calling functions registered by **atexit** and **_onexit**
assert	Test for logic error
atexit	Schedule routines for execution at program termination
_beginthread, _beginthreadex	Begin thread in Windows NT process
_cexit	Perform **exit** termination procedures (such as flushing buffers), then return control to calling program without terminating process
_c_exit	Perform **_exit** termination procedures, then return control to calling program without terminating process
_cwait	Wait until another process terminates
_endthread, _endthreadex	Terminate Windows NT thread
_execl, _wexecl	Execute new process with argument list
_execle, _wexecle	Execute new process with argument list and given environment
_execlp, _wexeclp	Execute new process using **PATH** variable and argument list
_execlpe, _wexeclpe	Execute new process using **PATH** variable, given environment, and argument list
_execv, _wexecv	Execute new process with argument array
_execve, _wexecve	Execute new process with argument array and given environment
_execvp, _wexecvp	Execute new process using **PATH** variable and argument array
_execvpe, _wexecvpe	Execute new process using **PATH** variable, given environment, and argument array
exit	Call functions registered by **atexit** and **_onexit**, flush all buffers and close all open files, and terminate process
_exit	Terminate process immediately without calling **atexit** or **_onexit** or flushing buffers

Process and Environment Control Functions (*continued*)

Routine	Use
getenv, **_wgetenv**	Get value of environment variable
_getpid	Get process ID number
longjmp	Restore saved stack environment; use it to execute a nonlocal **goto**
_onexit	Schedule routines for execution at program termination; use for compatibility with Microsoft C/C++ version 7.0 and earlier
_pclose	Wait for new command processor and close stream on associated pipe
perror, **_wperror**	Print error message
_pipe	Create pipe for reading and writing
_popen, **_wpopen**	Create pipe and execute command
_putenv, **_wputenv**	Add or change value of environment variable
raise	Send signal to calling process
setjmp	Save stack environment; use to execute nonlocal **goto**
signal	Handle interrupt signal
_spawnl, **_wspawnl**	Create and execute new process with specified argument list
_spawnle, **_wspawnle**	Create and execute a new process with specified argument list and environment
_spawnlp, **_wspawnlp**	Create and execute new process using **PATH** variable and specified argument list
_spawnlpe, **_wspawnlpe**	Create and execute new process using **PATH** variable, specified environment, and argument list
_spawnv, **_wspawnv**	Create and execute new process with specified argument array
_spawnve, **_wspawnve**	Create and execute new process with specified environment and argument array
_spawnvp, **_wspawnvp**	Create and execute new process using **PATH** variable and specified argument array
_spawnvpe, **_wspawnvpe**	Create and execute new process using **PATH** variable, specified environment, and argument array
system, **_wsystem**	Execute operating-system command

In Windows NT, the spawned process is equivalent to the spawning process.
Therefore, the OS/2® **wait** function, which allows a parent process to wait for its

children to terminate, is not available. Instead, any process can use **_cwait** to wait for any other process for which the process ID is known.

The difference between the **_exec** and **_spawn** families is that a **_spawn** function can return control from the new process to the calling process. In a **_spawn** function, both the calling process and the new process are present in memory unless **_P_OVERLAY** is specified. In an **_exec** function, the new process overlays the calling process, so control cannot return to the calling process unless an error occurs in the attempt to start execution of the new process.

The differences among the functions in the **_exec** family, as well as among those in the **_spawn** family, involve the method of locating the file to be executed as the new process, the form in which arguments are passed to the new process, and the method of setting the environment, as shown in the following table. Use a function that passes an argument list when the number of arguments is constant or is known at compile time. Use a function that passes a pointer to an array containing the arguments when the number of arguments is to be determined at run time. The information in the following table also applies to the wide-character counterparts of the **_spawn** and **_exec** functions.

_spawn and _exec Function Families

Functions	Use PATH Variable to Locate File	Argument-Passing Convention	Environment Settings
_execl, _spawnl	No	List	Inherited from calling process
_execle, _spawnle	No	List	Pointer to environment table for new process passed as last argument
_execlp, _spawnlp	Yes	List	Inherited from calling process
_execlpe, _spawnlpe	Yes	List	Pointer to environment table for new process passed as last argument
_execv, _spawnv	No	Array	Inherited from calling process
_execve, _spawnve	No	Array	Pointer to environment table for new process passed as last argument
_execvp, _spawnvp	Yes	Array	Inherited from calling process
_execvpe, _spawnvpe	Yes	Array	Pointer to environment table for new process passed as last argument

Searching and Sorting

Use the following functions for searching and sorting.

Searching and Sorting Functions

Function	Search or Sort
bsearch	Binary search
_lfind	Linear search for given value
_lsearch	Linear search for given value, which is added to array if not found
qsort	Quick sort

String Manipulation

These routines operate on null-terminated single-byte character, wide-character, and multibyte-character strings. Use the buffer-manipulation routines, described in "Buffer Manipulation" on page 2, to work with character arrays that do not end with a null character.

String-Manipuoalation Routines

Routine	Use
_mbscoll, _mbsicoll, _mbsncoll, _mbsnicoll	Compare two multitype-character strings using multibyte code page information (**_mbsicoll** and **_mbsnicoll** are case-insensitive)
_mbsdec, _strdec, _wcsdec	Move string pointer back one character
_mbsinc, _strinc, _wcsinc	Advance string pointer by one character
_mbslen	Get number of multibyte characters in multibyte-character string; dependent upon OEM code page
_mbsnbcat	Append, at most, first *n* bytes of one multibyte-character string to another
_mbsnbcmp	Compare first *n* bytes of two multibyte-character strings
_mbsnbcnt	Return number of multibyte-character bytes within supplied character count
_mbsnbcpy	Copy *n* bytes of string
_mbsnbicmp	Compare *n* bytes of two multibyte-character strings, ignoring case
_mbsnbset	Set first *n* bytes of multibyte-character string to specified character
_mbsnextc, _strnextc, _wcsnextc	Find next character in string
_mbsninc. _strninc, _wcsninc	Advance string pointer by *n* characters

String-Manipulation Routines (*continued*)

Routine	Use
_mbsspnp, _strspnp, _wcsspnp	Return pointer to first character in given string not in another given string
_mbstrlen	Get number of multibyte characters in multibyte-character string; locale-dependent
strcat, wcscat, _mbscat	Append one string to another
strchr, wcschr, _mbschr	Find first occurrence of specified character in string
strcmp, wcscmp, _mbscmp	Compare two strings
strcoll, wcscoll, _stricoll, _wcsicoll, _strncoll, _wcsncoll, _strnicoll, _wcsnicoll	Compare two strings using current locale code page information (**_stricoll, _wcsicoll, _strnicoll,** and **_wcsnicoll** are case-insensitive)
strcpy, wcscpy, _mbscpy	Copy one string to another
strcspn, wcscspn, _mbscspn,	Find first occurrence of character from specified character set in string
_strdup, _wcsdup, _mbsdup	Duplicate string
strerror	Map error number to message string
_strerror	Map user-defined error message to string
strftime, wcsftime	Format date-and-time string
_stricmp, _wcsicmp, _mbsicmp	Compare two strings without regard to case
strlen, wcslen, _mbslen, _mbstrlen	Find length of string
_strlwr, _wcslwr, _mbslwr	Convert string to lowercase
strncat, wcsncat, _mbsncat	Append characters of string
strncmp, wcsncmp, _mbsncmp	Compare characters of two strings
strncpy, wcsncpy, _mbsncpy	Copy characters of one string to another
_strnicmp, _wcsnicmp, _mbsnicmp	Compare characters of two strings without regard to case
_strnset, _wcsnset, _mbsnset	Set first *n* characters of string to specified character

String-Manipulation Routines (*continued*)

Routine	Use
strpbrk, wcspbrk, _mbspbrk	Find first occurrence of character from one string in another string
strrchr, wcsrchr, _mbsrchr	Find last occurrence of given character in string
_strrev, _wcsrev, _mbsrev	Reverse string
_strset, _wcsset, _mbsset	Set all characters of string to specified character
strspn, wcsspn, _mbsspn	Find first substring from one string in another string
strstr, wcsstr, _mbsstr	Find first occurrence of specified string in another string
strtok, wcstok, _mbstok	Find next token in string
_strupr, _wcsupr, _mbsupr	Convert string to uppercase
strxfrm, wcsxfrm	Transform string into collated form based on locale-specific information

System Calls

The following functions are Windows NT operating-system calls.

Windows NT System Call Functions

Function	Use
_findclose	Release resources from previous find operations
_findfirst, _wfindfirst	Find file with specified attributes
_findnext, _wfindnext	Find next file with specified attributes

Time Management

Use these functions to get the current time and convert, adjust, and store it as necessary. The current time is the system time.

The **_ftime** and **localtime** routines use the **TZ** environment variable. If **TZ** is not set, the run-time library attempts to use the time-zone information specified by the operating system. If this information is unavailable, these functions use the default value of PST8PDT. For more information on **TZ**, see **_tzset**; also see "**_daylight, _timezone, and _tzname**" on page 38.

Time Routines

Function	Use
asctime, _wasctime	Convert time from type **struct tm** to character string
clock	Return elapsed CPU time for process
ctime, _wctime	Convert time from type **time_t** to character string
difftime	Compute difference between two times
_ftime	Store current system time in variable of type **struct _timeb**
_futime	Set modification time on open file
gmtime	Convert time from type **time_t** to **struct tm**
localtime	Convert time from type **time_t** to **struct tm** with local correction
mktime	Convert time to calendar value
_strdate, _wstrdate	Return current system date as string
strftime	Format date-and-time string for international use
_strtime, _wstrtime	Return current system time as string
time	Get current system time as type **time_t**
_tzset	Set external time variables from environment time variable **TZ**
_utime, _wutime	Set modification time for specified file using either current time or time value stored in structure

Note In all versions of Microsoft C/C++ except Microsoft C/C++ version 7.0, and in all versions of Microsoft Visual C++, the **time** function returns the current time as the number of seconds elapsed since midnight on January 1, 1970. In Microsoft C/C++ version 7.0, **time** returned the current time as the number of seconds elapsed since midnight on December 31, 1899.

CHAPTER 2

Global Variables and Standard Types

The Microsoft run-time library contains definitions for global variables and standard types used by library routines. Access these variables and types by declaring them in your program or by including the appropriate header files.

Global Variables

The Microsoft run-time library provides the following global variables.

Variable	Description
_amblksiz	Controls memory heap granularity
daylight, _timezone, _tzname	Adjust for local time; used in some date and time functions
_doserrno, errno, _sys_errlist, _sys_nerr	Store error codes and related information
_environ, _wenviron	Pointers to arrays of pointers to strings that constitute process environment
_fileinfo	Specifies whether information regarding open files of a process is passed to new processes
_fmode	Sets default file-translation mode
_osver, _winmajor, _winminor, _winver	Store build and version numbers of operating system
_pgmptr, _wpgmptr	Initialized at program startup to value such as program name, filename, relative path, or full path

_amblksiz

_amblksiz controls memory heap granularity. It is declared in MALLOC.H as

extern unsigned int _amblksiz;

The value of **_amblksiz** specifies the size of blocks allocated by the operating system for the heap. The initial requested size for a segment of heap memory is just enough to satisfy the current allocation request (for example, a call to **malloc**) plus memory required for heap manager overhead. The value of **_amblksiz** should represent a trade-off between the number of times the operating system is to be called to increase the heap to required size and the amount of memory potentially wasted (available but not used) at the end of the heap.

The default value of **_amblksiz** is 8K. You can change this value by direct assignment in your program. For example:

```
_amblksiz = 2045;
```

If you assign a value to **_amblksiz,** the actual value used internally by the heap manager is the assigned value rounded up to the nearest whole power of 2. Thus, in the previous example, the heap manager would reset the value of **_amblksize** to 2048.

_daylight, _timezone, and _tzname

_daylight, **_timezone**, and **_tzname** are used in some time and date routines to make local-time adjustments. They are declared in TIME.H as

extern int _daylight;

extern long _timezone;

extern char *_tzname[2];

On a call to **_ftime, localtime,** or **_tzset**, the values of **_daylight**, **_timezone**, and **_tzname** are determined from the value of the **TZ** environment variable. If you do not explicitly set the value of **TZ**, **_tzname[0]** and **_tzname[1]** contain empty strings, but the time-manipulation functions (**_tzset**, **_ftime**, and **localtime**) attempt to set the values of **_daylight** and **_timezone** using the time-zone information specified in the Windows NT Control Panel Date/Time application. If the time-zone information cannot be obtained from the operating system, the time-management functions use the default value PST8PDT. The time-zone global variable values are as follows.

Variable	Value
_daylight	Nonzero if daylight-saving-time zone (DST) is specified in **TZ**; otherwise, 0. Default value is 1.
_timezone	Difference in seconds between universal coordinated time and local time. Default value is 28,800.
_tzname[0]	Three-letter time-zone name derived from **TZ** environment variable.
_tzname[1]	Three-letter DST zone name derived from **TZ** environment variable. Default value is PDT (Pacific daylight time). If DST zone is omitted from **TZ**, **_tzname[1]** is empty string.

_doserrno, errno, _sys_errlist, and _sys_nerr

These global variables hold error codes used by the **perror** and **strerror** functions for printing error messages. Manifest constants for these variables are declared in STDLIB.H as follows:

extern int _doserrno;

extern int errno;

extern char *_sys_errlist[ ];

extern int _sys_nerr;

errno is set on an error in a system-level call. Because **errno** holds the value for the last call that set it, this value may be changed by succeeding calls. Always check **errno** immediately before and after a call that may set it. All **errno** values, defined as manifest constants in ERRNO.H, are UNIX-compatible. The values valid for Windows NT are a subset of these UNIX values.

On an error, **errno** is not necessarily set to the same value as the error code returned by a system call. For I/O operations only, use **_doserrno** to access the operating-system error-code equivalents of **errno** codes. For other operations the value of **_doserrno** is undefined.

Each **errno** value is associated with an error message that can be printed using **perror** or stored in a string using **strerror**. **perror** and **strerror** use the **_sys_errlist** array and **_sys_nerr**, the number of elements in _sys_errlist, to process error information.

Library math routines set **errno** by calling **_matherr**. To handle math errors differently, write your own routine according to the **_matherr** reference description and name it **_matherr**.

The following **errno** values are Windows NT–compatible. Only **ERANGE** and **EDOM** are specified in the ANSI standard.

Constant	System Error Message	Value
E2BIG	Argument list too long	7
EACCES	Permission denied	13
EBADF	Bad file number	9
EDEADLOCK	Resource deadlock would occur	36
EDOM	Math argument	33
EEXIST	File exists	17
EINVAL	Invalid argument	22
EMFILE	Too many open files	24
ENOENT	No such file or directory	2
ENOEXEC	Exec format error	8
ENOMEM	Not enough memory	12
ENOSPC	No space left on device	28
ERANGE	Result too large	34
EXDEV	Cross-device link	18

_environ, _wenviron

The **_environ** variable is a pointer to an array of pointers to the multibyte-character strings that constitute the process environment. **_environ** is declared in STDLIB.H as

extern char **_environ;

In a program that uses the **main** function, **_environ** is initialized at program startup according to settings taken from the operating-system environment. The environment consists of one or more entries of the form

ENVVARNAME=*string*

getenv and **_putenv** use the **_environ** variable to access and modify the environment table. When **_putenv** is called to add or delete environment settings, the environment table changes size. Its location in memory may also change, depending on the program's memory requirements. The value of **_environ** is automatically adjusted accordingly.

The **_wenviron** variable, declared in STDLIB.H as

extern wchar_t **_wenviron;

is a wide-character version of **_environ**. In a program that uses the **wmain** function, **_wenviron** is initialized at program startup according to settings taken from the operating-system environment.

In a program that uses **main**, **_wenviron** is initially **NULL**, because the environment is composed of multibyte-character strings. On the first call to **_wgetenv** or **_wputenv**, a corresponding wide-character string environment is created and is pointed to by **_wenviron**.

Similarly, in a program that uses **wmain**, **_environ** is initially **NULL** because the environment is composed of wide-character strings. On the first call to **_getenv** or **_putenv**, a corresponding wide-character string environment is created and is pointed to by **_environ**.

When two copies of the environment (MBCS and Unicode) exist simultaneously in a program, the run-time system must maintain both copies, resulting in slower execution time. For example, whenever you call **_putenv**, a call to **_wputenv** is also executed automatically, so that the two environment strings correspond.

Caution   In rare instances, when the run-time system is maintaining both a Unicode version and a multibyte version of the environment, these two environment versions may not correspond exactly. This is because, although any unique multibyte-character string maps to a unique Unicode string, the mapping from a unique Unicode string to a multibyte-character string is not necessarily unique. Therefore, two distinct Unicode strings may map to the same multibyte string.

The following pseudocode illustrates how this can happen.

```
int i, j;
i = _wputenv( "env_var_x=string1" );    // results in the implicit call:
                                         // putenv ("env_var_z=string1")
j = _wputenv( "env_var_y=string2" );    // also results in implicit call:
                                         // putenv("env_var_z=string2")
```

In the notation used for this example, the character strings are not C string literals; rather they are placeholders that represent Unicode environment string literals in the **_wputenv** call and multibyte environment strings in the **putenv** call. The character-placeholders '*x*' and '*y*' in the two distinct Unicode environment strings do not map uniquely to characters in the current MBCS; instead, both map to some MBCS character '*z*' that is the default result of the attempt to convert the strings.

Thus in the multibyte environment the value of "*env_var_z*" after the first implicit call to **putenv** would be "*string1*", but this value would be overwritten on the second implicit call to **putenv**, when the value of "*env_var_z*" is set to "*string2*". The Unicode environment (in **_wenviron**) and the multibyte environment (in **_environ**) would therefore differ following this series of calls.

_fileinfo

_fileinfo determines whether information about the open files of a process is passed to new processes by functions such as **_spawn**. **_fileinfo** is declared in STDLIB.H as

extern int _fileinfo;

If **_fileinfo** is 0 (the default), information about open files is not passed to new processes; otherwise the information is passed. You can modify the default value of **_fileinfo** in either of two ways:

- Set the **_fileinfo** variable to a nonzero value in your program.
- Link FILEINFO.OBJ with your program, using the /NOE LINK option to avoid multiple symbol definitions.

_fmode

_fmode sets the default file-translation mode for text or binary translation. It is declared in STDLIB.H as

extern int _fmode;

The default setting of **_fmode** is **_O_TEXT**, for text-mode translation. **_O_BINARY** is the setting for binary mode.

You can change the value of **_fmode** in either of two ways:

- Link with BINMODE.OBJ. This changes the initial setting of **_fmode** to **_O_BINARY**, causing all files except **stdin**, **stdout**, and **stderr** to be opened in binary mode.
- Change the value of **_fmode** directly by setting it in your program.

_osver, _winmajor, _winminor, _winver

These variables store build and version numbers of the operating system. Declarations for these variables in STDLIB.H are as follows:

extern unsigned int _osver;

extern unsigned int _winmajor;

extern unsigned int _winminor;

extern unsigned int _winver;

These variables are useful in programs that run in different versions of Windows NT.

Variable	Description	Value in Windows NT 3.1
_osver	Windows NT build number currently in use	Depends on Windows NT build number
_winmajor	Windows NT major version number	3
_winminor	Windows NT minor version number	10 (Windows NT minor version number is specified with a trailing 0)
_winver	Holds value of **_winmajor** in high byte and value of **_winminor** in low byte	0x30A (value represented in high-order byte is 3; value in low-order byte is 10)

_pgmptr, _wpgmptr

When a program is run from the command interpreter (CMD.EXE), **_pgmptr** is automatically initialized to the full path of the executable file. For example, if HELLO.EXE is in C:\BIN and C:\BIN is in the path, **_pgmptr** is set to C:\BIN\HELLO.EXE when you execute

```
C> hello
```

When a program is not run from the command line, **_pgmptr** may be initialized to the program name (the file's base name without the extension), or to a filename, a relative path, or a full path.

_wpgmptr is the wide-character counterpart of **_pgmptr** for use with programs that use **wmain**. **_pgmptr** and **_wpgmptr** are declared in STDLIB.H as

extern char *_pgmptr;

extern wchar_t *_pgmptr;

The following program demonstrates the use of **_pgmptr**.

```
#include <stdio.h>
#include <stdlib.h>
void main( void )
{
    printf("The full path of the executing program is : %Fs\n",
           _pgmptr);
}
```

Standard Types

The Microsoft run-time library defines the following standard types.

Type	Description	Declared In
clock_t structure	Stores time values; used by **clock**.	TIME.H
_complex structure	Stores real and imaginary parts of complex numbers; used by **_cabs**.	MATH.H
_dev_t short or unsigned integer	Represents device handles.	SYS\TYPES.H
div_t, ldiv_t structures	Store values returned by **div** and **ldiv**, respectively.	STDLIB.H
_exception structure	Stores error information for **_matherr**.	MATH.H
FILE structure	Stores information about current state of stream; used in all stream I/O operations.	STDIO.H
_finddata_t, _wfinddata_t structures	**_finddata_t** stores file-attribute information returned by **_findfirst** and **_findnext**. **_wfinddata_t** stores file-attribute information returned by **_wfindfirst** and **_wfindnext**.	**_finddata_t**: IO.H **_wfinddata_t**: IO.H, WCHAR.H
_FPIEEE_RECORD structure	Contains information pertaining to IEEE floating-point exception; passed to user-defined trap handler by **_fpieee_flt**.	FPIEEE.H
fpos_t long integer	Used by **fgetpos** and **fsetpos** to record information for uniquely specifying every position within a file.	STDIO.H
_HEAPINFO structure	Contains information about next heap entry for **_heapwalk**.	MALLOC.H
jmp_buf array	Used by **setjmp** and **longjmp** to save and restore program environment.	SETJMP.H

Type	Description	Declared In
lconv structure	Contains formatting rules for numeric values in different countries.	LOCALE.H
_off_t long integer	Represents file-offset value.	SYS\TYPES.H
_onexit_t pointer	Returned by **_onexit**.	STDLIB.H
_PNH pointer to function	Type of argument to **_set_new_handler**.	NEW.H
ptrdiff_t integer	Result of subtraction of two pointers.	STDDEF.H
sig_atomic_t integer	Type of object that can be modified as atomic entity, even in presence of asynchronous interrupts; used with **signal**.	SIGNAL.H
size_t unsigned integer	Result of **sizeof** operator.	STDDEF.H and other include files
_stat structure	Contains file-status information returned by **_stat** and **_fstat**.	SYS\STAT.H
time_t long integer	Represents time values in **mktime** and **time**.	TIME.H
_timeb structure	Used by **_ftime** to store current system time.	SYS\TIMEB.H
tm structure	Used by **asctime**, **gmtime**, **localtime**, **mktime**, and **strftime** to store and retrieve time information.	TIME.H
_utimbuf structure	Stores file access and modification times used by **_utime** to change file-modification dates.	SYS\UTIME.H
va_list structure	Used to hold information needed by **va_arg** and **va_end** macros. Called function declares variable of type **va_list** that can be passed as argument to another function.	STDARG.H
wchar_t internal type of a wide character	Useful for writing portable programs for international markets.	STDDEF.H, STDLIB.H
wctype_t integer	Can represent all characters of any national character set.	STDDEF.H, STDLIB.H
wint_t integer	Type of data object that can hold any wide character or wide end-of-file value.	WCHAR.H

abort

void abort(void);

ANSI   UNIX   WIN32S

#include <process.h>   Use either PROCESS.H or STDLIB.H.
#include <stdlib.h>

Return Value   **abort** does not return control to the caller. Instead it terminates the process and returns an exit code of 3 to the calling process by default.

Remarks   In Windows, **abort** does not call **raise(SIGABRT)**. Instead, it terminates the process with an `abnormal program termination` pop-up message. In Windows multithread libraries, **abort** does not call **raise(SIGABRT)**. Instead, it terminates the process with exit code 3. **abort** does not flush stream buffers or do **atexit/_onexit** processing.

See Also   **_exec** Functions, **exit**, **raise**, **signal**, **_spawn** Functions

Example
```
/* ABORT.C:  This program tries to open a
 * file and aborts if the attempt fails.
 */

#include  <stdio.h>
#include  <stdlib.h>

void main( void )
{
   FILE *stream;

   if( (stream = fopen( "NOSUCHF.ILE", "r" )) == NULL )
   {
      perror( "Couldn't open file" );
      abort();
   }
   else
      fclose( stream );
}
```

Output
```
Couldn't open file: No such file or directory

abnormal program termination
```

abs

int abs(int *n*);

ANSI   UNIX   WIN32S

#include <stdlib.h>   Use STDLIB.H OR MATH.H.
#include <math.h>

Return Value   The **abs** function returns the absolute value of its parameter. There is no error return.

Parameter   *n*   Integer value

See Also   **_cabs, fabs, labs**

Example
```
/* ABS.C: This program computes and displays
 * the absolute values of several numbers.
 */

#include  <stdio.h>
#include  <math.h>
#include  <stdlib.h>

void main( void )
{
    int    ix = -4, iy;
    long   lx = -41567L, ly;
    double dx = -3.141593, dy;

    iy = abs( ix );
    printf( "The absolute value of %d is %d\n", ix, iy);

    ly = labs( lx );
    printf( "The absolute value of %ld is %ld\n", lx, ly);

    dy = fabs( dx );
    printf( "The absolute value of %f is %f\n", dx, dy );
}
```

Output
```
The absolute value of -4 is 4
The absolute value of -41567 is 41567
The absolute value of -3.141593 is 3.141593
```

_access, _waccess

int _access(const char *_path_, int _mode_);

int _waccess(const wchar_t *_path_, int _mode_);

    _access: ~~ANSI~~ UNIX WIN32S
    _waccess: ~~ANSI~~ ~~UNIX~~ ~~WIN32S~~

Use **_access** for compatibility with ANSI naming conventions of non-ANSI functions. Use **access** and link with OLDNAMES.LIB for UNIX compatibility.

#include <io.h> For **_access**.
#include <wchar.h> For **_waccess** use WCHAR.H or IO.H.
#include <errno.h> For definition of **errno** constants.

Return Value   Each of these functions returns 0 if the file has the given mode. The function returns −1 if the named file does not exist or is not accessible in the given mode; in this case, **errno** is set as follows:

EACCES   Access denied: file's permission setting does not allow specified access.

ENOENT   Filename or path not found.

Parameters   *path*   File or directory path
    mode   Permission setting

Remarks   When used with files, the **_access** function determines whether the specified file exists and can be accessed as specified by the value of *mode*. When used with directories, **_access** determines only whether the specified directory exists; in Windows NT, all directories have read and write access.

mode Value	Checks File For
00	Existence only
02	Write permission
04	Read permission
06	Read and write permission

_waccess is a wide-character version of **_access**; the *path* argument to **_waccess** is a wide-character string. **_waccess** and **_access** behave identically otherwise.

See Also   **_chmod, _fstat, _open, _stat**

Example

```
/* ACCESS.C: This example uses _access to check the
 * file named "ACCESS.C" to see if it exists and if
 * writing is allowed.
 */

#include  <io.h>
#include  <stdio.h>
#include  <stdlib.h>

void main( void )
{
    /* Check for existence */
    if( (_access( "ACCESS.C", 0 )) != -1 )
    {
        printf( "File ACCESS.C exists\n" );
        /* Check for write permission */
        if( (_access( "ACCESS.C", 2 )) != -1 )
            printf( "File ACCESS.C has write permission\n" );
    }
}
```

Output

```
File ACCESS.C exists
```

acos

double acos(double *x*);

ANSI   UNIX   WIN32S

#include <math.h>

Return Value

The **acos** function returns the arccosine of x in the range 0 to π radians. If x is less than -1 or greater than 1, **acos** returns an indefinite (same as a quiet NaN). You can modify error handling with the **_matherr** routine.

Parameter

x Value between -1 and 1 whose arccosine is to be calculated

See Also

asin, atan, cos, _matherr, sin, tan

Example

```
/* ASINCOS.C: This program prompts for a value in the range
 * -1 to 1. Input values outside this range will produce
 * _DOMAIN error messages.If a valid value is entered, the
 * program prints the arcsine and the arccosine of that value.
 */

#include <math.h>
#include <stdio.h>
#include <stdlib.h>
#include <errno.h>
```

```
void main( void )
{
    double x, y;

    printf( "Enter a real number between -1 and 1: " );
    scanf( "%lf", &x );
    y = asin( x );
    printf( "Arcsine of %f = %f\n", x, y );
    y = acos( x );
    printf( "Arccosine of %f = %f\n", x, y );
}
```

Output

```
Enter a real number between -1 and 1: .32696
Arcsine of 0.326960 = 0.333085
Arccosine of 0.326960 = 1.237711
```

_alloca

void *_alloca(size_t *size*);

~~ANSI~~   UNIX   WIN32S

Use **_alloca** for compatibility with ANSI naming conventions of non-ANSI functions. Use **alloca** and compile with /Ze (enable Microsoft language extensions) for UNIX compatibility.

#include <malloc.h>

Return Value

The **_alloca** routine returns a **void** pointer to the allocated space, which is guaranteed to be suitably aligned for storage of any type of object. To get a pointer to a type other than **char**, use a type cast on the return value. A stack overflow exception is generated if the space cannot be allocated.

Parameter

size   Bytes to be allocated from stack

Remarks

_alloca allocates *size* bytes from the program stack. The allocated space is automatically freed when the calling function exits. Therefore, do not pass the pointer value returned by **_alloca** as an argument to **free**.

See Also

calloc, malloc, realloc

asctime, _wasctime

char *asctime(const struct tm *timeptr);

wchar_t *_wasctime(const struct tm *timeptr);

asctime: ANSI   UNIX   WIN32S
_wasctime: ~~ANSI~~   ~~UNIX~~   ~~WIN32S~~

#include <time.h>   For **asctime**.
#include <wchar.h>   For **_wasctime** use TIME.H or WCHAR.H.

Return Value   **asctime** returns a pointer to the character string result; **_wasctime** returns a pointer to the wide-character string result. There is no error return.

Parameter   *timeptr*   Time/date structure

Remarks   The **asctime** function converts a time stored as a structure to a character string. The *timeptr* value is usually obtained from a call to **gmtime** or **localtime**, which return a pointer to a **tm** structure, defined in TIME.H.

timeptr Field	Value
tm_hour	Hours since midnight (0 – 23)
tm_isdst	Positive if daylight saving time is in effect; 0 if daylight savings time is not in effect; negative if status of daylight saving time is unknown.
tm_mday	Day of month (1 – 31)
tm_min	Minutes after hour (0 – 59)
tm_mon	Month (0 – 11; January = 0)
tm_sec	Seconds after minute (0 – 59)
tm_wday	Day of week (0 – 6; Sunday = 0)
tm_yday	Day of year (0 – 365; January 1 = 0)
tm_year	Year (current year minus 1900)

The string result produced by **asctime** contains exactly 26 characters and has the form Wed Jan 02 02:03:55 1980\n\0. A 24-hour clock is used. All fields have a constant width. The newline character and the null character occupy the last two positions of the string. **asctime** uses a single, statically allocated buffer to hold the return string. Each call to this function destroys the result of the previous call.

_wasctime is a wide-character version of **_asctime**. **_wasctime** and **_asctime** behave identically otherwise.

See Also   **ctime, _ftime, gmtime, localtime, time, _tzset**

Example

```
/* ASCTIME.C: This program places the system time
 * in the long integer aclock, translates it into the
 * structure newtime and then converts it to string
 * form for output, using the asctime function.
 */

#include <time.h>
#include <stdio.h>

struct tm *newtime;
time_t aclock;

void main( void )
{
    time( &aclock );                     /* Get time in seconds */

    newtime = localtime( &aclock );  /* Convert time to struct */
                                     /* tm form */

    /* Print local time as a string */
    printf( "The current date and time are: %s", asctime( newtime ) );
}
```

Output

```
The current date and time are: Sun May 01 20:27:01 1994
```

asin

double asin(double *x*);

ANSI   UNIX   WIN32S

#include <math.h>

Return Value   The **asin** function returns the arcsine of x in the range $-\pi/2$ to $\pi/2$ radians. If x is less than -1 or greater than 1, **asin** returns an indefinite (same as a quiet NaN). You can modify error handling with the **_matherr** routine.

Parameter x Value whose arcsine is to be calculated

See Also   **acos, atan, cos, _matherr, sin, tan**

Example   See the example for **acos**.

assert

void assert(int *expression* **);**

ANSI   UNIX   WIN32S

#include <assert.h>
#include <stdio.h>

Return Value   None

Parameter   *expression*   C expression specifying assertion being tested

Remarks   The **assert** macro prints a diagnostic message and calls **abort** if *expression* is false
(0). The diagnostic message has the form

Assertion failed: *expression*, **file** *filename*, **line** *linenumber*

where *filename* is the name of the source file and *linenumber* is the line number of
the assertion that failed in the source file. No action is taken if *expression* is true
(nonzero).

assert is typically used during program development to identify program logic
errors. Choose the given expression so that it holds true only if the program is
operating as intended. After debugging a program, you can turn off assertion
checking without modifying the source file by defining the identifier **NDEBUG** to
any value. You can define **NDEBUG** with a /D command-line option or with a
#define directive. If you define **NDEBUG** with **#define**, the directive must appear
before ASSERT.H.

See Also   **abort, raise, signal**

Example
```
/* ASSERT.C: In this program, the analyze_string function uses
 * the assert function to test several conditions related to
 * string and length. If any of the conditions fails, the program
 * prints a message indicating what caused the failure.
 */

#include <stdio.h>
#include <assert.h>
#include <string.h>

void analyze_string( char *string );    /* Prototype */

void main( void )
{
    char  test1[] = "abc", *test2 = NULL, test3[] = "";
```

```
            printf ( "Analyzing string '%s'\n", test1 );
            analyze_string( test1 );
            printf ( "Analyzing string '%s'\n", test2 );
            analyze_string( test2 );
            printf ( "Analyzing string '%s'\n", test3 );
            analyze_string( test3 );
        }

        /* Tests a string to see if it is NULL, */
        /*    empty, or longer than 0 characters */
        void analyze_string( char * string )
        {
            assert( string != NULL );        /* Cannot be NULL */
            assert( *string != '\0' );       /* Cannot be empty */
            assert( strlen( string ) > 2 );  /* Length must exceed 2 */
        }
```

Output

```
Analyzing string 'abc'
Analyzing string '(null)'
Assertion failed: string != NULL, file assert.c, line 29

abnormal program termination
```

atan, atan2

double atan(double *x*);

double atan2(double *y*, double *x*);

ANSI   UNIX   WIN32S

#include <math.h>

Return Value   **atan** returns the arctangent of *x*. **atan2** returns the arctangent of *y/x*. If *x* is 0, **atan** returns 0. If both parameters of **atan2** are 0, the function returns 0. You can modify error handling by using the **_matherr** routine. **atan** returns a value in the range $-\pi/2$ to $\pi/2$ radians; **atan2** returns a value in the range $-\pi$ to π radians, using the signs of both parameters to determine the quadrant of the return value.

Parameters   *x, y*   Any numbers

Remarks   The **atan** function calculates the arctangent of *x*. **atan2** calculates the arctangent of *y/x*. **atan2** is well defined for every point other than the origin, even if *x* equals 0 and *y* does not equal 0.

See Also   **acos, asin, cos, _matherr, sin, tan**

Example

```
/* ATAN.C: This program calculates
 * the arctangent of 1 and -1.
 */

#include <math.h>
#include <stdio.h>
#include <errno.h>

void main( void )
{
   double x1, x2, y;

   printf( "Enter a real number: " );
   scanf( "%lf", &x1 );
   y = atan( x1 );
   printf( "Arctangent of %f: %f\n", x1, y );
   printf( "Enter a second real number: " );
   scanf( "%lf", &x2 );
   y = atan2( x1, x2 );
   printf( "Arctangent of %f / %f: %f\n", x1, x2, y );
}
```

Output

```
Enter a real number: -862.42
Arctangent of -862.420000: -1.569637
Enter a second real number: 78.5149
Arctangent of -862.420000 / 78.514900: -1.480006
```

atexit

int atexit(void (__cdecl *_func_)(void));

ANSI   ~~UNIX~~   WIN32S

For ANSI portability, use the ANSI-standard **atexit** function (rather than the similar **_onexit** function).

#include <stdlib.h>

Return Value   **atexit** returns 0 if successful, or a nonzero value if an error occurs.

Parameter   _func_   Function to be called

Remarks   The **atexit** function is passed the address of a function (_func_) to be called when the program terminates normally. Successive calls to **atexit** create a register of functions that are executed in LIFO (last-in-first-out) order. The functions passed to **atexit** cannot take parameters. **atexit** and **_onexit** use the heap to hold the register of functions. Thus, the number of functions that can be registered is limited only by heap memory.

See Also   **abort, exit, _onexit**

Example

```
/* ATEXIT.C: This program pushes four functions onto
 * the stack of functions to be executed when atexit
 * is called. When the program exits, these programs
 * are executed on a "last in, first out" basis.
 */

#include <stdlib.h>
#include <stdio.h>

void fn1( void ), fn2( void ), fn3( void ), fn4( void );

void main( void )
{
   atexit( fn1 );
   atexit( fn2 );
   atexit( fn3 );
   atexit( fn4 );
   printf( "This is executed first.\n" );
}

void fn1()
{
   printf( "next.\n" );
}

void fn2()
{
   printf( "executed " );
}

void fn3()
{
   printf( "is " );
}

void fn4()
{
   printf( "This " );
}
```

Output

```
This is executed first.
This is executed next.
```

atof, atoi, atol

double atof(const char *string* **);**

int atoi(const char *string* **);**

long atol(const char *string* **);**

ANSI   UNIX   WIN32S

#include<math.h>   For **atof**.
#include <stdlib.h>   For **atof, atoi**, and **atol**.

Return Value   Each function returns the **double**, **int**, or **long** value produced by interpreting the input characters as a number. The return value is 0 (for **atoi**), 0L (for **atol**), or 0.0 (for **atof**) if the input cannot be converted to a value of that type. The return value is undefined in case of overflow.

Parameter   *string*   String to be converted

Remarks   These functions convert a character string to a double-precision floating-point value (**atof**), an integer value (**atoi**), or a long integer value (**atol**). The input string is a sequence of characters that can be interpreted as a numerical value of the specified type. The output value is affected by the setting of the **LC_NUMERIC** category in the current locale. For more information on the **LC_NUMERIC** category, see **setlocale**.The longest string size that **atof** can handle is 100 characters. The function stops reading the input string at the first character that it cannot recognize as part of a number. This character may be the null character ('\0') terminating the string.

The *string* argument to **atof** has the following form:

[[*whitespace*]] [[*sign*]] [[*digits*]] [[.*digits*]] [[{ **d** | **D** | **e** | **E** }[[*sign*]]*digits*]]

A *whitespace* consists of space and/or tab characters, which are ignored; *sign* is either plus (+) or minus (–); and *digits* are one or more decimal digits. If no digits appear before the decimal point, at least one must appear after the decimal point. The decimal digits may be followed by an exponent, which consists of an introductory letter (**d**, **D**, **e**, or **E**) and an optionally signed decimal integer.

atoi and **atol** do not recognize decimal points or exponents. The *string* argument for these functions has the form:

[[*whitespace*]] [[*sign*]]*digits*

where *whitespace*, *sign*, and *digits* are exactly as described above for **atof**.

See Also   **_ecvt**, **_fcvt**, **_gcvt**, **setlocale**, **strtod**, **wcstol**, **strtoul**

Example
```
/* ATOF.C: This program shows how numbers stored
 * as strings can be converted to numeric values
 * using the atof, atoi, and atol functions.
 */

#include <stdlib.h>
#include <stdio.h>

void main( void )
{
    char *s; double x; int i; long l;

    s = "  -2309.12E-15";    /* Test of atof */
    x = atof( s );
    printf( "atof test: ASCII string: %s\tfloat:  %e\n", s, x );

    s = "7.8912654773d210"; /* Test of atof */
    x = atof( s );
    printf( "atof test: ASCII string: %s\tfloat:  %e\n", s, x );

    s = "  -9885 pigs";      /* Test of atoi */
    i = atoi( s );
    printf( "atoi test: ASCII string: %s\t\tinteger: %d\n", s, i );

    s = "98854 dollars";     /* Test of atol */
    l = atol( s );
    printf( "atol test: ASCII string: %s\t\tlong: %ld\n", s, l );
}
```

Output
```
atof test: ASCII string:   -2309.12E-15   float:  -2.309120e-012
atof test: ASCII string: 7.8912654773d210  float:  7.891265e+210
atoi test: ASCII string:   -9885 pigs       integer: -9885
atol test: ASCII string: 98854 dollars      long: 98854
```

_beginthread, _beginthreadex

unsigned long _beginthread(void(*start_address**)(void *), unsigned *stack_size*, void ****arglist**);**

unsigned long _beginthreadex(
    void *security,
    unsigned *stack_size*,
    unsigned (* ** *start_address* **) (void *),
    **void * ** *arglist*,
    unsigned *initflag*,
    unsigned *thrdaddr)

~~ANSI~~ ~~UNIX~~ ~~WIN32S~~

#include <process.h>

Return Value

If successful, each of these functions returns a handle to the newly created thread. **_beginthread** returns −1 on an error, in which case **errno** is set to **EAGAIN** if there are too many threads, or to **EINVAL** if the argument is invalid or the stack size is incorrect. **_beginthreadex** returns 0 on an error, in which case **errno** and **doserrno** are set.

Parameters

start_address   Start address of routine that begins execution of new thread
stack_size   Stack size for new thread
arglist   Argument list to be passed to new thread
security   Security descriptor for new thread
initflag   Initial state of new thread (running or suspended)
thrdaddr   Address of new thread

Remarks

The **_beginthread** function creates a thread that begins execution of a routine at *start_address*. The routine at *start_address* should have no return value. When the thread returns from that routine, it is terminated automatically.

_beginthreadex resembles the Win32 **CreateThread** API more closely than does **_beginthread**. **_beginthreadex** differs from **_beginthread** in the following ways:

- **_beginthreadex** has three additional parameters: *initflag, security, threadaddr*. The new thread can be created in a suspended state, with a specified security, and can be accessed using *thrdaddr*, which is the thread identifier.

- The routine at *start_address* passed to **_beginthreadex** must use the **__stdcall** calling convention and must return a thread exit code.

- **_beginthreadex** returns 0 on failure, rather than −1.

- A thread created with **_beginthreadex** is terminated by a call to **_endthreadex.**

You can call **_endthread** or **_endthreadex** explicitly to terminate a thread; however, **_endthread** or **_endthreadex** is called automatically when the thread returns from the routine passed as a parameter. Terminating a thread with a call to **endthread** or **_endthreadex** helps to ensure proper recovery of resources allocated for the thread.

_endthread automatically closes the thread handle (whereas **_endthreadex** does not). Therefore, when using **_beginthread** and **_endthread**, do not explicitly close the thread handle by calling the Win32 **CloseHandle** API. This behavior differs from the Win32 **ExitThread** API.

Note For an executable file linked with LIBCMT.LIB, do not call the Win32 **ExitThread** API; this prevents the run-time system from reclaiming allocated resources. **_endthread** and **_endthreadex** reclaim allocated thread resources and then call **ExitThread**.

Windows NT handles the allocation of the stack when either **_beginthread** or **_beginthreadex** is called; you do not need to pass the address of the thread stack to either of these functions. The *stack_size* argument can be 0, in which case Windows NT uses the same value as the stack specified for the main thread.

arglist is a parameter to be passed to the newly created thread. Typically it is the address of a data item, such as a character string. *arglist* may be NULL if it is not needed, but **_beginthread** and **_beginthreadex** must be provided with some value to pass to the new thread. All threads are terminated if any thread calls **abort**, **exit**, **_exit**, or **ExitProcess**.

To use **_beginthread** or **_beginthreadex**, link with one of the multithreaded C run-time libraries rather than with the default run-time library.

See Also **_endthread**, **abort**, **exit**

Example

```
/* BEGTHRD.C illustrates multiple threads using functions:
 *
 *      _beginthread            _endthread
 *
 *
 * This program requires the multithreaded run-time library.
 * To compile at the command line, use the command line:
 *     CL /MT /D "_X86_" BEGTHRD.C
 *
 * To compile using the Visual C++ development environment, select
 * the Multi-Threaded runtime library in the C/C++ tab of the
 * Project Settings dialog box.
 */
```

```c
#include <windows.h>
#include <process.h>      /* _beginthread, _endthread */
#include <stddef.h>
#include <stdlib.h>
#include <conio.h>

void Bounce( void *ch );
void CheckKey( void *dummy );

/* GetRandom returns a random integer between min and max. */
#define GetRandom( min, max ) ((rand() % (int)(((max) + 1) - (min))) +
(min))

BOOL repeat = TRUE;      /* Global repeat flag and video variable */
HANDLE hStdOut;               /* Handle for console window */
CONSOLE_SCREEN_BUFFER_INFO csbi;     /* Console information structure */

void main()
{
    CHAR    ch = 'A';

    hStdOut = GetStdHandle( STD_OUTPUT_HANDLE );

    /* Get display screen's text row and column information. */
    GetConsoleScreenBufferInfo( hStdOut, &csbi );

    /* Launch CheckKey thread to check for terminating keystroke. */
    _beginthread( CheckKey, 0, NULL );

    /* Loop until CheckKey terminates program. */
    while( repeat )
    {
        /* On first loops, launch character threads. */
        _beginthread( Bounce, 0, (void *) (ch++)  );

        /* Wait one second between loops. */
        Sleep( 1000L );
    }
}


/* CheckKey - Thread to wait for a keystroke, then clear repeat flag. */
void CheckKey( void *dummy )
{
    _getch();
    repeat = 0;      /* _endthread implied */

}
```

```
/* Bounce - Thread to create and and control a colored letter that moves
 * around on the screen.
 *
 * Params: ch - the letter to be moved
 */
void Bounce( void *ch )
{
    /* Generate letter and color attribute from thread argument. */
    char    blankcell = 0x20;
    char    blockcell = (char) ch;
    BOOL    first = TRUE;
    COORD   oldcoord, newcoord;
    DWORD   result;


    /* Seed random number generator and get initial location. */
    srand( _threadid );
    newcoord.X = GetRandom( 0, csbi.dwSize.X - 1 );
    newcoord.Y = GetRandom( 0, csbi.dwSize.Y - 1 );
    while( repeat )
    {
        /* Pause between loops. */
        Sleep( 100L );

        /* Blank out our old position on the screen, and draw new
letter. */
        if( first )
            first = FALSE;
        else
         WriteConsoleOutputCharacter( hStdOut, &blankcell, 1, oldcoord,
&result );
         WriteConsoleOutputCharacter( hStdOut, &blockcell, 1, newcoord,
&result );

        /* Increment the coordinate for next placement of the block. */
        oldcoord.X = newcoord.X;
        oldcoord.Y = newcoord.Y;
        newcoord.X += GetRandom( -1, 1 );
        newcoord.Y += GetRandom( -1, 1 );

        /* Correct placement (and beep) if about to go off the screen.
*/
        if( newcoord.X < 0 )
            newcoord.X = 1;
        else if( newcoord.X == csbi.dwSize.X )
            newcoord.X = csbi.dwSize.X - 2;
        else if( newcoord.Y < 0 )
            newcoord.Y = 1;
        else if( newcoord.Y == csbi.dwSize.Y )
            newcoord.Y = csbi.dwSize.Y - 2;
```

```
                              /* If not at a screen border, continue, otherwise beep. */
                              else
                                  continue;
                              Beep( ((char) ch - 'A') * 100, 175 );
                          }
                          /* _endthread given to terminate */
                          _endthread();
                      }
```

Bessel Functions

double _j0(double *x* **);**

double _j1(double *x* **);**

double _jn(int *n***, double** *x* **);**

double _y0(double *x* **);**

double _y1(double *x* **);**

double _yn(int *n***, double** *x* **);**

~~ANSI~~   UNIX   WIN32S

Use **_j0**, **_j1**, **_jn**, **_y0**, **_y1**,and **_yn** for compatibility with ANSI naming conventions of non-ANSI functions. Use **j0**, **j1**, **jn**, **y0**, **y1**, and **yn** and link with OLDNAMES.LIB for UNIX compatibility.

#include <math.h>

Return Value   Each of these routines returns a Bessel function of *x*. For **_y0**, **_y1**, or **_yn**, if *x* is negative, the routine sets **errno** to **EDOM**, prints a **_DOMAIN** error message to **stderr**, and returns **_HUGE_VAL**. You can modify error handling by using **_matherr**.

Parameters   *x*   Positive floating-point value
                  n   Integer order

Remarks   The Bessel functions are commonly used in the mathematics of electromagnetic wave theory. The **_j0**, **_j1**, and **_jn** routines return Bessel functions of the first kind, orders 0, 1, and *n*, respectively. The **_y0**, **_y1**, and **_yn** routines return Bessel functions of the second kind, orders 0, 1, and *n*, respectively.

See Also   **_matherr**

Example
```
/* BESSEL.C: This program illustrates Bessel functions,
 * including:   _j0   _j1   _jn   _y0   _y1   _yn
 */

#include <math.h>
#include <stdio.h>

void main( void )
{
   double x = 2.387;
   int n = 3, c;

   printf( "Bessel functions for x = %f:\n", x );
   printf( " Kind\t\tOrder\tFunction\tResult\n\n" );
   printf( " First\t\t0\t_j0( x )\t%f\n", _j0( x ) );
   printf( " First\t\t1\t_j1( x )\t%f\n", _j1( x ) );
   for( c = 2; c < 5; c++ )
      printf( " First\t%d\t_jn( n, x )\t%f\n", c, _jn( c, x ) );
   printf( " Second\t0\t_y0( x )\t%f\n", _y0( x ) );
   printf( " Second\t1\t_y1( x )\t%f\n", _y1( x ) );
   for( c = 2; c < 5; c++ )
      printf( " Second\t%d\t_yn( n, x )\t%f\n", c, _yn( c, x ) );
}
```

Output
```
Bessel functions for x = 2.387000:
  Kind      Order   Function    Result

  First       0     _j0( x )    0.009288
  First       1     _j1( x )    0.522941
  First       2     _jn( n, x )    0.428870
  First       3     _jn( n, x )    0.195734
  First       4     _jn( n, x )    0.063131
  Second    0     _y0( x )    0.511681
  Second    1     _y1( x )    0.094374
  Second    2     _yn( n, x )    -0.432608
  Second    3     _yn( n, x )    -0.819314
  Second    4     _yn( n, x )    -1.626833
```

bsearch

void *bsearch(const void **key***, const void ****base***, size_t** *num***, size_t** *width***,**
   int (_ _ cdecl *compare **)(const void ****elem1***, const void ****elem2* **));**

ANSI   UNIX   WIN32S

#include <stdlib.h>   Required for ANSI compatibility.
#include <search.h>

Return Value   **bsearch** returns a pointer to an occurrence of *key* in the array pointed to by *base*. If
key is not found, the function returns **NULL**. If the array is not in ascending sort
order or contains duplicate records with identical keys, the result is unpredictable.

Parameters   *key*   Object to search for
base   Pointer to base of search data
num   Number of elements
width   Width of elements
compare   Function that compares two elements: *elem1* and *elem2*
elem1   Pointer to the key for the search
elem2   Pointer to the array element to be compared with the key

Remarks   The **bsearch** function performs a binary search of a sorted array of *num* elements,
each of *width* bytes in size. The *base* value is a pointer to the base of the array to be
searched, and *key* is the value being sought. The *compare* parameter is a pointer to
a user-supplied routine that compares two array elements and returns a value
specifying their relationship. **bsearch** calls the *compare* routine one or more times
during the search, passing pointers to two array elements on each call. The *compare*
routine compares the elements, then returns one of the following values:

Value Returned by Compare Routine	Description
< 0	*elem1* less than *elem2*
0	*elem1* equal to *elem2*
> 0	*elem1* greater than *elem2*

See Also   **_lfind, _lsearch, qsort**

Example

```
/* BSEARCH.C: This program reads the command-line
 * parameters, sorting them with qsort, and then
 * uses bsearch to find the word "cat."
 */

#include <search.h>
#include <string.h>
#include <stdio.h>

int compare( char **arg1, char **arg2 ); /* Declare a function for
compare */

void main( int argc, char **argv )
{
    char **result;
    char *key = "cat";
    int i;

    /* Sort using Quicksort algorithm: */
    qsort( (void *)argv, (size_t)argc, sizeof( char * ), (int (*)(const
    void*, const void*))compare );

    for( i = 0; i < argc; ++i )      /* Output sorted list */
        printf( "%s ", argv[i] );

    /* Find the word "cat" using a binary search algorithm: */
    result = (char **)bsearch( (char *) &key, (char *)argv, argc,
                               sizeof( char * ), (int (*)(const void*,
const void*))compare );
    if( result )
        printf( "\n%s found at %Fp\n", *result, result );
    else
        printf( "\nCat not found!\n" );
}

int compare( char **arg1, char **arg2 )
{
    /* Compare all of both strings: */
    return _strcmpi( *arg1, *arg2 );
}
```

Output

```
[C:\work]bsearch dog pig horse cat human rat cow goat
bsearch cat cow dog goat horse human pig rat
cat found at 002C0008
```

_cabs

double _cabs(struct _complex *z* **);**

ANSI UNIX WIN32S

Use **_cabs** for compatibility with ANSI naming conventions of non-ANSI functions. Use **cabs** and link with OLDNAMES.LIB for UNIX compatibility.

#include <math.h>

Return Value

_cabs returns the absolute value of its argument if successful. On overflow **_cabs** returns **HUGE_VAL** and sets **errno** to **ERANGE**. You can change error handling with **_matherr**.

Parameter

z　Complex number

Remarks

The **_cabs** function calculates the absolute value of a complex number, which must be a structure of type **_complex**. The structure *z* is composed of a real component *x* and an imaginary component *y*. A call to **_cabs** produces a value equivalent to that of the expression **sqrt(** $z.x*z.x + z.y*z.y$ **).**

See Also

abs, fabs, labs

Example

```
/* CABS.C: Using _cabs, this program calculates
 * the absolute value of a complex number.
 */
#include <math.h>
#include <stdio.h>

void main( void )
{
    struct _complex number = { 3.0, 4.0 };
    double d;

    d = _cabs( number );
    printf( "The absolute value of %f + %fi is %f\n",
            number.x, number.y, d );
}
```

Output

```
The absolute value of 3.000000 + 4.000000i is 5.000000
```

calloc

void *calloc(size_t *num*, **size_t** *size* **);**

ANSI UNIX WIN32S

#include <stdlib.h>　For ANSI compatibility.
#include <malloc.h>

Return Value	**calloc** returns a pointer to the allocated space. The storage space pointed to by the return value is guaranteed to be suitably aligned for storage of any type of object. To get a pointer to a type other than **void**, use a type cast on the return value.
Parameters	*num* Number of elements *size* Length in bytes of each element
Remarks	The **calloc** function allocates storage space for an array of *num* elements, each of length *size* bytes. Each element is initialized to 0.
See Also	**free, malloc, realloc**

Example

```
/* CALLOC.C: This program uses calloc to allocate space for
 * 40 long integers. It initializes each element to zero.
 */
#include <stdio.h>
#include <malloc.h>

void main( void )
{
   long *buffer;

   buffer = (long *)calloc( 40, sizeof( long ) );
   if( buffer != NULL )
      printf( "Allocated 40 long integers\n" );
   else
      printf( "Can't allocate memory\n" );
   free( buffer );
}
```

Output

```
Allocated 40 long integers
```

ceil

double ceil(double *x*);

ANSI   UNIX   WIN32S

#include <math.h>

Return Value	The **ceil** function returns a **double** value representing the smallest integer that is greater than or equal to *x*. There is no error return.
Parameter	*x* Floating-point value
See Also	**floor, fmod**
Example	See the example for **floor**.

_cexit, _c_exit

void _cexit(void);

void _c_exit(void);

~~ANSI~~   ~~UNIX~~   WIN32S

#include <process.h>

Return Value   None

Remarks   The **_cexit** function calls, in last-in-first-out (LIFO) order, the functions registered by **atexit** and **_onexit**. Then **_cexit** flushes all I/O buffers and closes all open streams before returning. **_c_exit** is the same as **_exit** but returns to the calling process without processing **atexit** or **_onexit** or flushing stream buffers. The behavior of **exit, _exit, _cexit,** and **_c_exit** is as follows:

Function	Behavior
exit	Performs complete C library termination procedures, terminates process, and exits with supplied status code
_exit	Performs "quick" C library termination procedures, terminates process, and exits with supplied status code
_cexit	Performs complete C library termination procedures and returns to caller, but does not terminate process
_c_exit	Performs "quick" C library termination procedures and returns to caller, but does not terminate process

See Also   **abort, atexit, _exec** Functions, **exit, _onexit, _spawn** Functions, **system**

_cgets

char *_cgets(char **buffer***);**

~~ANSI~~   ~~UNIX~~   WIN32S

#include <conio.h>

Return Value   **_cgets** returns a pointer to the start of the string, at *buffer*[2]. No error return.

Parameter   *buffer*   Storage location for data

Remarks   The **_cgets** function reads a string of characters from the console and stores the string and its length in the location pointed to by *buffer*. The *buffer* parameter must be a pointer to a character array. The first element of the array, *buffer*[0], must contain the maximum length (in characters) of the string to be read. The array must contain enough elements to hold the string, a terminating null character ('\0'), and two additional bytes. The function reads characters until a carriage-return–line-feed (CR-LF) combination or the specified number of characters is read. The string is stored starting at *buffer*[2]. If the function reads a CR-LF, it stores the null character ('\0'). **_cgets** then stores the actual length of the string in the second array element, *buffer* [1]. Because all editing keys are active when **_cgets** is called, pressing F3 repeats the last entry.

See Also   **_getch**

Example

```
/* CGETS.C: This program creates a buffer and initializes
 * the first byte to the size of the buffer: 2. Next, the
 * program accepts an input string using _cgets and displays
 * the size and text of that string.
 */

#include <conio.h>
#include <stdio.h>

void main( void )
{
    char buffer[82] = { 80 };  /* Maximum characters in 1st byte */
    char *result;

    printf( "Input line of text, followed by carriage return:\n");
    result = _cgets( buffer );  /* Input a line of text */
    printf( "\nLine length = %d\nText = %s\n", buffer[1], result );
}
```

Output

```
Input line of text, followed by carriage return:
This is a line of text

Line length = 22
Text = This is a line of text.
```

_chdir, _wchdir

int _chdir(const char **dirname**);

int _wchdir(const wchar_t **dirname**);

_chdir: ~~ANSI~~   UNIX   WIN32S
_wchdir: ~~ANSI~~   ~~UNIX~~   ~~WIN32S~~

Use **_chdir** for compatibility with ANSI naming conventions of non-ANSI functions. Use **chdir** and link with OLDNAMES.LIB for UNIX compatibility.

#include <direct.h>   For **_chdir**.
#include <wchar.h>   For **_wchdir** use DIRECT.H or WCHAR.H.
#include <errno.h>   For **errno** constants

Return Value   Each of these functions returns a value of 0 if successful. A return value of −1 indicates that the specified path could not be found, in which case **errno** is set to **ENOENT**.

Parameter   *dirname*   Path of new working directory

Remarks   The **_chdir** function changes the current working directory to the directory specified by *dirname*. The *dirname* parameter must refer to an existing directory. This function can change the current working directory on any drive as well as the default working drive itself. For example, if A is the default drive and \BIN is the current working directory, the following call changes the current working directory for drive C:

```
_chdir("c:\\temp");
```

When you use the optional backslash character (\) in paths, you must place two backslashes (\\) in a C string literal to represent a single backslash (\).

If **_chdir** is called to change the directory on a drive other than the default drive, this function call may have no apparent immediate effect. However, when **_chdrive** is called to change the default drive to C, the current working directory becomes C:\TEMP. The new directory set by the program becomes the new current working directory.

_wchdir is a wide-character version of **_chdir**; the *dirname* argument to **_wchdir** is a wide-character string. **_wchdir** and **_chdir** behave identically otherwise.

See Also   **_mkdir, _rmdir, system**

Example
```
/* CHGDIR.C: This program uses the _chdir function to verify
 * that a given directory exists.
 */

#include <direct.h>
#include <stdio.h>
#include <stdlib.h>

void main( int argc, char *argv[] )
{
   if( _chdir( argv[1] )    )
      printf( "Unable to locate the directory: %s\n", argv[1] );
   else
      system( "dir *.wri");
}
```

Output	Volume in drive C is CDRIVE Volume Serial Number is 0E17-1702

```
Directory of C:\msvc20

04/29/94  01:06p                      3,200 ERRATA.WRI
04/29/94  01:06p                      2,816 README.WRI
                  2 File(s)           6,016 bytes
                               86,433,792 bytes free
```

_chdrive

int _chdrive(int *drive* **);**

~~ANSI~~ ~~UNIX~~ WIN32S

#include <direct.h>

Return Value	**_chdrive** returns a value of 0 if the working drive is successfully changed. A return value of −1 indicates an error.
Parameter	*drive* Number of new working drive
Remarks	The **_chdrive** function changes the current working drive to the drive specified by *drive*. The *drive* parameter uses an integer to specify the new working drive (1=A, 2=B, and so forth). This function changes only the working drive; **_chdir** changes the working directory.
See Also	**_chdir, _fullpath, _getcwd, _getdrive, _mkdir, _rmdir, system**
Example	See the example for **_getdrive**.

_chgsign

double _chgsign(double *x* **);**

~~ANSI~~ ~~UNIX~~ WIN32S

#include <float.h>

Return Value	**_chgsign** returns a value equal to its double-precision floating-point argument *x*, but with its sign reversed. There is no error return.
Parameter	*x* Double-precision floating-point value to be changed
See Also	**fabs, _copysign**

_chmod, _wchmod

int **_chmod**(const char *filename, int pmode);

int **_wchmod**(const wchar_t *filename, int pmode);

> **_chmod:** ~~ANSI~~ UNIX WIN32S
> **_wchmod:** ~~ANSI~~ ~~UNIX~~ ~~WIN32S~~
>
> Use **_chmod** for compatibility with ANSI naming conventions of non-ANSI
> functions. Use **chmod** and link with OLDNAMES.LIB for UNIX compatibility.
>
> #include <io.h>   For **_chmod**.
> #include <wchar.h>   For **_wchmod** use IO.H or WCHAR.H.
> #include <sys/types.h>
> #include <sys/stat.h>
> #include <errno.h>

Return Value

Each of these functions returns 0 if the permission setting is successfully changed.
A return value of –1 indicates that the specified file could not be found, in which
case **errno** is set to **ENOENT**.

Parameters

filename   Name of existing file
pmode   Permission setting for file

Remarks

The **_chmod** function changes the permission setting of the file specified by
filename. The permission setting controls read and write access to the file. The
integer expression *pmode* contains one or both of the following manifest constants,
defined in SYS\STAT.H:

_S_IWRITE   Writing permitted

_S_IREAD   Reading permitted

_S_IREAD | _S_IWRITE   Reading and writing permitted

Any other values for *pmode* are ignored. When both constants are given, they are
joined with the bitwise-OR operator (|). If write permission is not given, the file is
read-only. Note that all files are always readable; it is not possible to give write-
only permission. Thus the modes **_S_IWRITE** and **_S_IREAD | _S_IWRITE** are
equivalent.

_wchmod is a wide-character version of **_chmod**; the *filename* argument to
_wchmod is a wide-character string. **_wchmod** and **_chmod** behave identically
otherwise.

See Also   **_access, _creat, _fstat, _open, _stat**

Example

```
/* CHMOD.C: This program uses _chmod to
 * change the mode of a file to read-only.
 * It then attempts to modify the file.
 */

#include <sys/types.h>
#include <sys/stat.h>
#include <io.h>
#include <stdio.h>
#include <stdlib.h>

void main( void )
{
   /* Make file read-only: */
   if( _chmod( "CHMOD.C", _S_IREAD ) == -1 )
      perror( "File not found\n" );
   else
      printf( "Mode changed to read-only\n" );
   system( "echo /* End of file */ >> CHMOD.C" );

   /* Change back to read/write: */
   if( _chmod( "CHMOD.C", _S_IWRITE ) == -1 )
      perror( "File not found\n" );
   else
      printf( "Mode changed to read/write\n" );
   system( "echo /* End of file */ >> CHMOD.C" );
}
```

Output

```
Mode changed to read-only
Access is denied
Mode changed to read/write
```

_chsize

int _chsize(int *handle***, long** *size* **);**

~~ANSI~~   UNIX   WIN32S

Use **_chsize** for compatibility with ANSI naming conventions of non-ANSI functions. Use **chsize** and link with OLDNAMES.LIB for UNIX compatibility.

#include <io.h>
#include <errno.h>

Return Value

_chsize returns the value 0 if the file size is successfully changed. A return value of −1 indicates an error: **errno** is set to **EACCES** if the specified file is locked against access, to **EBADF** if the specified file is read-only or the handle is invalid, or to **ENOSPC** if no space is left on the device.

Parameters   *handle*   Handle referring to open file
                     size   New length of file in bytes

Remarks   The **_chsize** function extends or truncates the file associated with *handle* to the
                     length specified by *size*. The file must be open in a mode that permits writing. Null
                     characters ('\0') are appended if the file is extended. If the file is truncated, all data
                     from the end of the shortened file to the original length of the file is lost.

See Also   **_close, _creat, _open**

Example
```
/* CHSIZE.C: This program uses _filelength to report the size
 * of a file before and after modifying it with _chsize.
 */

#include <io.h>
#include <fcntl.h>
#include <sys/types.h>
#include <sys/stat.h>
#include <stdio.h>

void main( void )
{
    int fh, result;
    unsigned int nbytes = BUFSIZ;

    /* Open a file */
    if( (fh = _open( "data", _O_RDWR | _O_CREAT, _S_IREAD
                    | _S_IWRITE )) != -1 )
    {
        printf( "File length before: %ld\n", _filelength( fh ) );
        if( ( result = _chsize( fh, 329678 ) ) == 0 )
            printf( "Size successfully changed\n" );
        else
            printf( "Problem in changing the size\n" );
        printf( "File length after:  %ld\n", _filelength( fh ) );
        _close( fh );
    }
}
```

Output
```
File length before: 0
Size successfully changed
File length after:  329678
```

_clear87, _clearfp

unsigned int _clear87(void);

unsigned int _clearfp(void);

~~ANSI~~ ~~UNIX~~ WIN32S

#include <float.h>

Return Value

The bits in the value returned indicate the floating-point status. See FLOAT.H for a complete definition of the bits returned by **_clear87**. Many of the math library functions modify the 8087/80287 status word, with unpredictable results. Return values from **_clear87** and **_status87** become more reliable as fewer floating-point operations are performed between known states of the floating-point status word.

Remarks

The **_clear87** function clears the exception flags in the floating-point status word, sets the busy bit to 0, and returns the status word. The floating-point status word is a combination of the 8087/80287 status word and other conditions detected by the 8087/80287 exception handler, such as floating-point stack overflow and underflow.

_clearfp is a platform-independent, portable version of the **_clear87** routine. It is identical to **_clear87** on Intel® (x86) platforms and is also supported by the MIPS® and ALPHA platforms. To ensure that your floating-point code is portable to MIPS or ALPHA, use **_clearfp**. If you are only targeting x86 platforms, you can use either **_clear87** or **_clearfp**.

See Also

_control87, _status87

Example

```
/* CLEAR87.C: This program creates various floating-point
 * problems, then uses _clear87 to report on these problems.
 * Compile this program with Optimizations disabled (/Od).
 * Otherwise the optimizer will remove the code associated with
 * the unused floating-point values.
 */

#include <stdio.h>
#include <float.h>

void main( void )
{
    double a = 1e-40, b;
    float x, y;
```

```
                   printf( "Status: %.4x - clear\n", _clear87()  );

                   /* Store into y is inexact and underflows: */
                   y = a;
                   printf( "Status: %.4x - inexact, underflow\n", _clear87() );

                   /* y is denormal: */
                   b = y;
                   printf( "Status: %.4x - denormal\n", _clear87() );
               }
```

Output
```
               Status: 0000 - clear
               Status: 0003 - inexact, underflow
               Status: 80000 - denormal
```

clearerr

void clearerr(FILE *stream);

ANSI   UNIX   WIN32S

#include <stdio.h>

Return Value   None

Parameter   *stream*   Pointer to **FILE** structure

Remarks   The **clearerr** function resets the error indicator and end-of-file indicator for *stream*.
Error indicators are not automatically cleared; once the error indicator for a
specified stream is set, operations on that stream continue to return an error value
until **clearerr**, **fseek**, **fsetpos**, or **rewind** is called.

See Also   **_eof, feof, ferror, perror**

Example
```
/* CLEARERR.C: This program creates an error
 * on the standard input stream, then clears
 * it so that future reads won't fail. */

#include <stdio.h>

void main( void )
```

```
{
    int c;
    /* Create an error by writing to standard input. */
    putc( 'c', stdin );
    if( ferror( stdin ) )
    {
        perror( "Write error" );
        clearerr( stdin );
    }
    /* See if read causes an error. */
    printf( "Will input cause an error? " );
    c = getc( stdin );
    if( ferror( stdin ) )
    {
        perror( "Read error" );
        clearerr( stdin );
    }
}
```

Output

```
Write error: No error
Will input cause an error? n
```

clock

clock_t clock(void);

ANSI ~~UNIX~~ WIN32S

#include <time.h>

Return Value

clock returns the product of the time in seconds that has elapsed since the start of the process and the value of the **CLOCKS_PER_SEC** constant. If the processor time is unavailable, the function returns the value -1, cast as **clock_t**. Note that the elapsed time may not be equal to the actual amount of time the process has used.

Remarks

The **clock** function tells how much processor time the calling process has used. The time in seconds is approximated by dividing the clock return value by the value of the **CLOCKS_PER_SEC** constant. In other words, **clock** returns the number of processor timer ticks that have elapsed. A timer tick is approximately equal to 1/**CLOCKS_PER_SEC** second. In versions of Microsoft C before 6.0, the **CLOCKS_PER_SEC** constant was called **CLK_TCK**.

See Also   **difftime, time**

Example

```
/* CLOCK.C: This example prompts for how long
 * the program is to run and then continuously
 * displays the elapsed time for that period. */

#include <stdio.h>
#include <stdlib.h>
#include <time.h>

void sleep( clock_t wait );

void main( void )
{
   long    i = 600000L;
   clock_t start, finish;
   double  duration;

   /* Delay for a specified time. */
   printf( "Delay for three seconds\n" );
   sleep( (clock_t)3 * CLOCKS_PER_SEC );
   printf( "Done!\n" );

   /* Measure the duration of an event. */
   printf( "Time to do %ld empty loops is ", i );
   start = clock();
   while( i-- )
      ;
   finish = clock();
   duration = (double)(finish - start) / CLOCKS_PER_SEC;
   printf( "%2.1f seconds\n", duration );
}

/* Pauses for a specified number of microseconds. */
void sleep( clock_t wait )
{
   clock_t goal;
   goal = wait + clock();
   while( goal > clock() )
      ;
}
```

Output

```
Delay for three seconds
Done!
Time to do 600000 empty loops is 0.1 seconds
```

_close

int _close(int *handle* **);**

<del>ANSI</del> UNIX WIN32S

Use **_close** for compatibility with ANSI naming conventions of non-ANSI functions. Use **close** and link with OLDNAMES.LIB for UNIX compatibility.

#include <io.h>
#include <errno.h>

Return Value   **_close** returns 0 if the file was successfully closed. A return value of –1 indicates an error, in which case **errno** is set to **EBADF**, indicating an invalid file-handle parameter.

Parameter   *handle*   Handle referring to open file

Remarks   The **_close** function closes the file associated with *handle*.

See Also   **_chsize, _creat, _dup, _open, _unlink**

Example   See the example for **_open**.

_commit

int _commit(int *handle* **);**

<del>ANSI</del> <del>UNIX</del> WIN32S

#include <io.h>
#include <errno.h>

Return Value   **_commit** returns 0 if the file was successfully flushed to disk. A return value of –1 indicates an error, and **errno** is set to **EBADF**, indicating an invalid file-handle parameter.

Parameter   *handle*   Handle referring to open file

Remarks   The **_commit** function forces the operating system to write the file associated with *handle* to disk. This call ensures that the specified file is flushed immediately, not at the operating system's discretion.

See Also   **_creat, _open, _read, _write**

Example

```
/* COMMIT.C illustrates low-level file I/O functions including:
 *
 *      _close    _commit    memset    _open    _write
 *
 * This is example code; to keep the code simple and readable
 * return values are not checked.
 */

#include <io.h>
#include <stdio.h>
#include <fcntl.h>
#include <memory.h>
#include <errno.h>

#define MAXBUF 32

int log_receivable( int );

void main( void )
{
    int fhandle;
    fhandle = _open( "TRANSACT.LOG", _O_APPEND | _O_CREAT |
                                     _O_BINARY | _O_RDWR );
    log_receivable( fhandle );
    _close( fhandle );
}

int log_receivable( int fhandle )
{
/* The log_receivable function prompts for a name and a monetary
 * amount and places both values into a buffer (buf). The _write
 * function writes the values to the operating system and the
 * _commit function ensures that they are written to a disk file.
 */

    int i;
    char  buf[MAXBUF];

    memset( buf, '\0', MAXBUF );
    /* Begin Transaction. */
    printf( "Enter name: " );
    gets( buf );
    for( i = 1; buf[i] != '\0'; i++ );
    /* Write the value as a '\0' terminated string. */
    _write( fhandle, buf, i+1 );
    printf( "\n" );
```

```
            memset( buf, '\0', MAXBUF );
            printf( "Enter amount: $" );
            gets( buf );
            for( i = 1; buf[i] != '\0'; i++ );
            /* Write the value as a '\0' terminated string. */
            _write( fhandle, buf, i+1 );
            printf( "\n" );

            /* The _commit function ensures that two important pieces of
             * data are safely written to disk. The return value of the
             * _commit function is returned to the calling function.
             */
            return _commit( fhandle );
        }
```

_control87, _controlfp

unsigned int _control87(unsigned int *new*, **unsigned int** *mask* **);**

unsigned int _controlfp(unsigned int *new*, **unsigned int** *mask* **);**

~~ANSI~~ ~~UNIX~~ WIN32S

#include <float.h>

Return Value	The bits in the value returned indicate the floating-point control state. See FLOAT.H for a complete definition of the bits returned by **_control87**.
Parameters	*new* New control-word bit values
	mask Mask for new control-word bits to set
Remarks	The **_control87** function gets and sets the floating-point control word. The floating-point control word allows the program to change the precision, rounding, and infinity modes in the floating-point math package. You can also mask or unmask floating-point exceptions using **_control87**. If the value for *mask* is equal to 0, **_control87** gets the floating-point control word. If *mask* is nonzero, a new value for the control word is set: For any bit that is on (equal to 1) in *mask*, the corresponding bit in *new* is used to update the control word. In other words, *fpcntrl* = ((*fpcntrl* **& ~mask)	(new & mask)**) where *fpcntrl* is the floating-point control word.

Note The run-time libraries mask all floating-point exceptions by default.

_controlfp is a platform-independent, portable version of **_control87**. It is nearly identical to the **_control87** function on Intel (x86) platforms and is also supported by the MIPS and ALPHA platforms. To ensure that your floating-point code is portable to MIPS or ALPHA, use **_controlfp**. If you are targeting x86 platforms, use either **_control87** or **_controlfp**.

The only other difference between **_control87** and **_controlfp** is that **_controlfp** does not interfere with the DENORMAL OPERAND exception mask. The following example demonstrates the difference:

```
_control87( _EM_INVALID, _MCW_EM ); // DENORMAL is unmasked by this call
_controlfp( _EM_INVALID, _MCW_EM ); // DENORMAL exception mask remains
unchanged
```

The possible values for the mask constant (*mask*) and new control values (*new*) are shown in Table R.1. Use the portable constants listed below (**_MCW_EM**, **_EM_INVALID**, and so forth) as arguments to these functions, rather than supplying the hexadecimal values explicitly.

Table R.1   Hexadecimal Values

Mask	Hexadecimal Value	Constant	Hexadecimal Value
_MCW_EM (Interrupt exception)	0x0008001F		
		_EM_INVALID	0x00000010
		_EM_DENORMAL	0x00080000
		_EM_ZERODIVIDE	0x00000008
		_EM_OVERFLOW	0x00000004
		_EM_UNDERFLOW	0x00000002
		_EM_INEXACT	0x00000001
_MCW_IC (Infinity control)	0x00040000		
		_IC_AFFINE	0x00040000
		_IC_PROJECTIVE	0x00000000
_MCW_RC (Rounding control)	0x00000300		
		_RC_CHOP	0x00000300
		_RC_UP	0x00000200
		_RC_DOWN	0x00000100
		_RC_NEAR	0x00000000
_MCW_PC (Precision control)	0x00030000		
		_PC_24 (24 bits)	0x00020000
		_PC_53 (53 bits)	0x00010000
		_PC_64 (64 bits)	0x00000000

See Also   **_clear87**, **_status87**

Example

```
/* CNTRL87.C: This program uses _control87 to output the control
 * word, set the precision to 24 bits, and reset the status to
 * the default.
 */

#include <stdio.h>
#include <float.h>

void main( void )
{
    double a = 0.1;

    /* Show original control word and do calculation. */
    printf( "Original: 0x%.4x\n", _control87( 0, 0 ) );
    printf( "%1.1f * %1.1f = %.15e\n", a, a, a * a );

    /* Set precision to 24 bits and recalculate. */
    printf( "24-bit:   0x%.4x\n", _control87( _PC_24, MCW_PC ) );
    printf( "%1.1f * %1.1f = %.15e\n", a, a, a * a );

    /* Restore to default and recalculate. */
    printf( "Default:  0x%.4x\n",
            _control87( _CW_DEFAULT, 0xfffff ) );
    printf( "%1.1f * %1.1f = %.15e\n", a, a, a * a );
}
```

Output

```
Original: 0x9001f
0.1 * 0.1 = 1.000000000000000e-002
24-bit:   0xa001f
0.1 * 0.1 = 9.999999776482582e-003
Default:  0x001f
0.1 * 0.1 = 1.000000000000000e-002
```

_copysign

double _copysign(double *x*, double *y*);

~~ANSI~~   ~~UNIX~~   WIN32S

#include <float.h>

Return Value

_copysign returns its double-precision floating point argument *x* with the same sign as its double-precision floating-point argument *y*. There is no error return.

Parameters

x   Double-precision floating-point value to be changed
y   Double-precision floating-point value

See Also

fabs, _chgsign

cos, cosh

double cos(double *x* **);**

double cosh(double *x* **);**

ANSI   UNIX   WIN32S

#include <math.h>

Return Value   The **cos** and **cosh** functions return the cosine and hyperbolic cosine, respectively, of *x*. If *x* is greater than or equal to 2^{63}, or less than or equal to -2^{63}, a loss of significance in the result of a call to **cos** occurs, in which case the function generates a **_TLOSS** error and returns an indefinite (same as a quiet NaN).

If the result is too large in a **cosh** call, the function returns **HUGE_VAL** and sets **errno** to **ERANGE**. You can modify error handling with **_matherr**.

Parameter   *x*   Angle in radians

See Also   **acos**, **asin**, **atan**, **_matherr**, **sin**, **tan**

Example   See the example for **sin**.

_cprintf

int _cprintf(const char *format **[[,** *argument***]]** ... **);**

~~ANSI~~   ~~UNIX~~   WIN32S

#include <conio.h>

Return Value   **_cprintf** returns the number of characters printed.

Parameters   *format*   Format-control string
argument   Optional parameters

Remarks   The **_cprintf** function formats and prints a series of characters and values directly to the console, using the **_putch** function to output characters. Each *argument* (if any) is converted and output according to the corresponding format specification in *format*. The format has the same form and function as the *format* parameter for the **printf** function; for a description of the format and parameters, see **printf**. Unlike the **fprintf**, **printf**, and **sprintf** functions, **_cprintf** does not translate linefeed characters into carriage-return−linefeed (CR-LF) combinations on output.

| See Also | **_cscanf, fprintf, printf, sprintf, vfprintf** |

Example

```
/* CPRINTF.C: This program displays
 * some variables to the console.
 */

#include <conio.h>

void main( void )
{
    int      i = -16, h = 29;
    unsigned u = 62511;
    char     c = 'A';
    char     s[] = "Test";

    /* Note that console output does not translate \n as
     * standard output does. Use \r\n instead.
     */
    _cprintf( "%d  %.4x  %u  %c %s\r\n", i, h, u, c, s );
}
```

Output

```
-16  001d  62511  A Test
```

_cputs

int _cputs(const char *_string_);

~~ANSI~~ ~~UNIX~~ WIN32S

#include <conio.h>

Return Value If successful, **_cputs** returns a 0. If the function fails, it returns a nonzero value.

Parameter _string_ Output string

Remarks The **_cputs** function writes the null-terminated string pointed to by _string_ directly to the console. A carriage-return–linefeed (CR-LF) combination is not automatically appended to the string.

See Also **_putch**

Example

```
/* CPUTS.C: This program first displays
 * a string to the console.
 */

#include <conio.h>

void main( void )
{
    /* String to print at console.
     * Note the \r (return) character.
     */
    char *buffer = "Hello world (courtesy of _cputs)!\r\n";

    _cputs( buffer );
}
```

Output

```
Hello world (courtesy of _cputs)!
```

_creat, _wcreat

int _creat(const char *_filename_, int _pmode_);

int _wcreat(const wchar_t *_filename_, int _pmode_);

> **_creat:**   ~~ANSI~~   UNIX   WIN32S
> **_wcreat:**   ~~ANSI~~   ~~UNIX~~   ~~WIN32S~~

Use **_creat** for compatibility with ANSI naming conventions of non-ANSI functions. Use **creat** and link with OLDNAMES.LIB for UNIX compatibility.

#include <io.h>   For **_creat**.
#include <wchar.h>   For **_wcreat** use IO.H or WCHAR.H.
#include <sys/types.h>
#include <sys/stat.h>
#include <errno.h>

Return Value

Each of these functions, if successful, returns a handle to the created file. Otherwise the function returns –1 and sets **errno** as follows.

errno Setting	Description
EACCES	Filename specifies an existing read-only file or specifies a directory instead of a file
EMFILE	No more file handles are available
ENOENT	The specified file could not be found

Parameters

filename   Name of new file
pmode   Permission setting

Remarks

The **_creat** function creates a new file or opens and truncates an existing one. **_wcreat** is a wide-character version of **_creat**; the *filename* argument to **_wcreat** is a wide-character string. **_wcreat** and **_creat** behave identically otherwise.

If the file specified by *filename* does not exist, a new file is created with the given permission setting and is opened for writing. If the file already exists and its permission setting allows writing, **_creat** truncates the file to length 0, destroying the previous contents, and opens it for writing. The permission setting, *pmode*, applies to newly created files only. The new file receives the specified permission setting after it is closed for the first time. The integer expression *pmode* contains one or both of the manifest constants **_S_IWRITE** and **_S_IREAD**, defined in SYS\STAT.H. When both constants are given, they are joined with the bitwise-OR operator (|). The *pmode* parameter is set to one of the following values:

_S_IWRITE   Writing permitted

_S_IREAD   Reading permitted

_S_IREAD | _S_IWRITE   Reading and writing permitted

If write permission is not given, the file is read-only. All files are always readable; it is impossible to give write-only permission. Thus the modes **_S_IWRITE** and **_S_IREAD | _S_IWRITE** are equivalent. Files opened using **_creat** are always opened in compatibility mode (see **_sopen**) with **_SH_DENYNO**.

_creat applies the current file-permission mask to *pmode* before setting the permissions (see **_umask**). **_creat** is provided primarily for compatibility with previous libraries. A call to **_open** with **_O_CREAT** and **_O_TRUNC** in the *oflag* parameter is equivalent to **_creat** and is preferable for new code.

See Also

_chmod, **_chsize**, **_close**, **_dup**, **_open**, **_sopen**, **_umask**

Example

```
/* CREAT.C: This program uses _creat to create
 * the file (or truncate the existing file)
 * named data and open it for writing.
 */

#include <sys/types.h>
#include <sys/stat.h>
#include <io.h>
#include <stdio.h>
#include <stdlib.h>
```

```
void main( void )
{
    int fh;

    fh = _creat( "data", _S_IREAD | _S_IWRITE );
    if( fh == -1 )
        perror( "Couldn't create data file" );
    else
    {
        printf( "Created data file.\n" );
        _close( fh );
    }
}
```

Output   Created data file.

_cscanf

int _cscanf(const char *_format_ [[, _argument_]] ...);

~~ANSI~~ ~~UNIX~~ WIN32S

#include <conio.h>

Return Value   _**cscanf**_ returns the number of fields that were successfully converted and assigned. The return value does not include fields that were read but not assigned. The return value is **EOF** for an attempt to read at end of file. This can occur when keyboard input is redirected at the operating-system command-line level. A return value of 0 means that no fields were assigned.

Parameters   _format_   Format-control string
argument   Optional parameters

Remarks   The _**cscanf**_ function reads data directly from the console into the locations given by _argument_. The _**getche**_ function is used to read characters. Each optional parameter must be a pointer to a variable with a type that corresponds to a type specifier in _format_. The format controls the interpretation of the input fields and has the same form and function as the _format_ parameter for the **scanf** function; for a description of _format_, see **scanf**. While _**cscanf**_ normally echoes the input character, it does not do so if the last call was to _**ungetch**_.

See Also   **_cprintf, fscanf, scanf, sscanf**

Example

```
/* CSCANF.C: This program prompts for a string
 * and uses _cscanf to read in the response.
 * Then _cscanf returns the number of items
 * matched, and the program displays that number.
 */

#include <stdio.h>
#include <conio.h>

void main( void )
{
   int    result, i[3];

   _cprintf( "Enter three integers: " );
   result = _cscanf( "%i %i %i", &i[0], &i[1], &i[2] );
   _cprintf( "\r\nYou entered " );
   while( result-- )
      _cprintf( "%i ", i[result] );
   _cprintf( "\r\n" );
}
```

Output

```
Enter three integers: 1  2  3
You entered 3 2 1
```

ctime, _wctime

char *ctime(const time_t *_timer_);

wchar_t *_wctime(const time_t *_timer_);

> **ctime:**   ANSI   UNIX   WIN32S
> **_wctime:**   ~~ANSI~~   ~~UNIX~~   ~~WIN32S~~
>
> **#include <time.h>**   For _ctime.
> **#include <wchar.h>**   For **_wctime** use TIME.H or WCHAR.H.

Return Value   Each of these functions returns a pointer to the character string result. If _time_ represents a date before midnight, January 1, 1970, UCT, the function returns **NULL.**

Parameter   _timer_   Pointer to stored time

Remarks The **ctime** function converts a time stored as a **time_t** value to a character string. The *timer* value is usually obtained from a call to **time**, which returns the number of seconds elapsed since midnight (00:00:00), January 1, 1970, universal coordinated time (UCT). The string result produced by **ctime** contains exactly 26 characters and has the form

```
Wed Jan 02 02:03:55 1980\n\0
```

A 24-hour clock is used. All fields have a constant width. The newline character ('\n') and the null character ('\0') occupy the last two positions of the string.

A call to **ctime** modifies the single statically allocated buffer used by the **gmtime** and **localtime** functions. Each call to one of these routines destroys the result of the previous call. **ctime** shares a static buffer with the **asctime** function. Thus, a call to **ctime** destroys the results of any previous call to **asctime**, **localtime**, or **gmtime**.

_wctime is a wide-character version of **ctime**; _wctime returns a pointer to a wide-character string. _wctime and **ctime** behave identically otherwise.

See Also asctime, _ftime, gmtime, localtime, time

Example
```c
/* CTIME.C: This program gets the current
 * time in time_t form, then uses ctime to
 * display the time in string form.
 */

#include <time.h>
#include <stdio.h>

void main( void )
{
   time_t ltime;

   time( &ltime );
   printf( "The time is %s\n", ctime( &ltime ) );
}
```

Output
```
The time is Fri Apr 29 12:25:12 1994
```

_cwait

int _cwait(int *_termstat_, int _procid_, int _action_);

~~ANSI~~ ~~UNIX~~ ~~WIN32S~~

#include <process.h>

Return Value   If **_cwait** returns after normal termination of the new process, it returns the process ID of the new process. If **_cwait** returns after abnormal termination of the new process, it returns −1 and sets **errno** to **EINTR**. Otherwise, **_cwait** returns −1 immediately and sets **errno** to **ECHILD** if no new process exists or the process ID is invalid, or to **EINVAL** if the action code is invalid.

Parameters   _termstat_   Address for termination status code
procid   Process ID of new process
action   Action code

Remarks   The **_cwait** function suspends the calling process until the specified new process terminates. **_cwait** can be used by any process to wait for any other process for which the process ID is known.

If not **NULL**, _termstat_ points to a buffer where **_cwait** places the termination-status word and the return code of the terminated process. The termination-status word indicates whether the called process terminated normally by calling the Windows NT **ExitProcess** API. **ExitProcess** is called internally if the new process calls **exit** or **_exit**, returns from **main**, or reaches the end of **main**.

Termination-status word values are as follows.

Termination	Status Word
Normal	Result code that new process code passed to **ExitProcess.** This is the argument to **_exit** or **exit**, the return value from **main**, or if called process reached end of **main**, a random value .
Abnormal (no call to ExitProcess)	1 = Hard-error abort 2 = Trap operation 3 = SIGTERM signal not intercepted

The _procid_ argument specifies the new-process termination to wait for. This value is returned by the call to the **_spawn** function that started the new process. If the specified spawned process terminates before **_cwait** is called, **_cwait** returns immediately.

The *action* argument specifies when the calling process resumes execution. This argument is ignored in Windows NT, but it is accepted for compatibility with OS/2. In Windows NT, there is no parent-child relationship, as in OS/2. Therefore, the OS/2 **wait** function, which allows a parent process to wait for any of its immediate children to terminate, is not available in Windows NT. The *action* argument can takeone of the following values, defined in PROCESS.H:

_WAIT_CHILD

The calling process waits until the specified new process has ended.

_WAIT_GRANDCHILD

The calling process waits until the specified new process and all spawned processes of that new process have ended.

See Also   **_spawn** Functions

Example

```
/* CWAIT.C: This program launches several processes and waits
 * for a specified process to finish.
 */

#include <windows.h>
#include <process.h>
#include <stdlib.h>
#include <stdio.h>
#include <time.h>

/* Macro to get a random integer within a specified range */
#define getrandom( min, max )
                    (( rand() % (int)((( max ) + 1 ) - ( min ))) + ( min ))

struct PROCESS
{

    int     nPid;
    char    name[40];

} process[4] =
    { { 0, "Ann" }, { 0, "Beth" }, { 0, "Carl" }, { 0, "Dave" } };
```

```
void main( int argc, char *argv[] )
{

    int termstat, c;

    srand( (unsigned)time( NULL ) );    /* Seed randomizer */
    /* If no arguments, this is the calling process */
    if( argc == 1 )
    {

        /* Spawn processes in numeric order */
        for( c = 0; c < 4; c++ ){
            _flushall();
            process[c].nPid = spawnl( _P_NOWAIT, argv[0], argv[0],
                                process[c].name, NULL );
        }

        /* Wait for randomly specified process, and respond when done */
        c = getrandom( 0, 3 );
        printf( "Come here, %s\n", process[c].name );
        _cwait( &termstat, process[c].nPid, _WAIT_CHILD );
        printf( "Thank you, %s\n", process[c].name );

    }

    /* If there are arguments, this must be a spawned process */
    else
    {

        /* Delay for a period determined by process number */
        Sleep( (argv[1][0] - 'A' + 1) * 1000L );
        printf( "Hi, Dad. It's %s.\n", argv[1] );

    }

}
```

Output

```
Hi, Dad. It's Ann.
Come here, Ann.
Thank you, Ann.
Hi, Dad. It's Beth.
Hi, Dad. It's Carl.
Hi, Dad. It's Dave.
```

difftime

double difftime(time_t *timer1*, **time_t** *timer0* **);**

> ANSI   UNIX   WIN32S

> **#include <time.h>**

Return Value   **difftime** returns, in seconds, the elapsed time from *timer0* to *timer1*. The value returned is a double-precision floating-point number.

Parameters   *timer1*   Ending time
timer0   Beginning time

Remarks   The **difftime** function computes the difference between the supplied time values *timer0* and *timer1*.

See Also   **time**

Example

```
/* DIFFTIME.C: This program calculates the amount of time
 * needed to do a floating-point multiply 10 million times.
 */

#include <stdio.h>
#include <stdlib.h>
#include <time.h>

void main( void )
{
    time_t    start, finish;
    long loop;
    double    result, elapsed_time;

    printf("Multiplying 2 floating point numbers 10 million times...\n");

    time( &start );
    for( loop = 0; loop < 10000000; loop++ )
        result = 3.63 * 5.27;
    time( &finish );

    elapsed_time = difftime( finish, start );
    printf( "\nProgram takes %6.0f seconds.\n", elapsed_time );
}
```

Output

```
Multiplying 2 floats 10 million times...

Program takes      2 seconds.
```

div

div_t div(int *numer*, **int** *denom* **);**

ANSI   ~~UNIX~~   WIN32S

#include <stdlib.h>

Return Value

div returns a structure of type **div_t**, comprising the quotient and the remainder. The structure is defined in STDLIB.H.

Parameters

numer   Numerator
denom   Denominator

Remarks

The **div** function divides *numer* by *denom*, computing the quotient and the remainder. The **div_t** structure contains **int quot**, the quotient, and **int rem**, the remainder. The sign of the quotient is the same as that of the mathematical quotient. Its absolute value is the largest integer that is less than the absolute value of the mathematical quotient. If the denominator is 0, the program terminates with an error message.

See Also

ldiv

Example

```
/* DIV.C: This example takes two integers as command-line
 * arguments and displays the results of the integer
 * division. This program accepts two arguments on the
 * command line following the program name, then calls
 * div to divide the first argument by the second.
 * Finally, it prints the structure members quot and rem. */

#include <stdlib.h>
#include <stdio.h>
#include <math.h>

void main( int argc, char *argv[] )
{
    int x,y;
    div_t div_result;

    x = atoi( argv[1] );
    y = atoi( argv[2] );

    printf( "x is %d, y is %d\n", x, y );
    div_result = div( x, y );
    printf( "The quotient is %d, and the remainder is %d\n",
            div_result.quot, div_result.rem );
}
```

Output

```
x is 876, y is 13
The quotient is 67, and the remainder is 5
```

_dup, _dup2

int _dup(int *handle*);

int _dup2(int *handle1*, int *handle2*);

~~ANSI~~   UNIX   WIN32S

Use **_dup** and **_dup2** for compatibility with ANSI naming conventions of non-ANSI functions. Use **dup** and **dup2** and link with OLDNAMES.LIB for UNIX compatibility.

#include <io.h>

Return Value

_dup returns a new file handle. **_dup2** returns 0 to indicate success. If an error occurs, each function returns –1 and sets **errno** to **EBADF** if the file handle is invalid, or to **EMFILE** if no more file handles are available.

Parameters

handle, handle1   Handles referring to open file
handle2   Any handle value

Remarks

The **_dup** and **_dup2** functions associate a second file handle with a currently open file. These functions can be used to associate a predefined file handle, such as that for **stdout**, with a different file. Operations on the file can be carried out using either file handle. The type of access allowed for the file is unaffected by the creation of a new handle. **_dup** returns the next available file handle for the given file. **_dup2** forces *handle2* to refer to the same file as *handle1*. If *handle2* is associated with an open file at the time of the call, that file is closed.

Both **_dup** and **_dup2** accept file handles as parameters. To pass a stream (**FILE ***) to either of these functions, use **_fileno**. The **fileno** routine returns the file handle currently associated with the given stream. The following example shows how to associate **stderr** (defined as **FILE *** in STDIO.H) with a handle:

```
cstderr = _dup( _fileno( stderr ));
```

See Also

_close, _creat, _open

Example

```
/* DUP.C: This program uses the variable old to save
 * the original stdout. It then opens a new file named
 * new and forces stdout to refer to it. Finally, it
 * restores stdout to its original state. */

#include <io.h>
#include <stdlib.h>
#include <stdio.h>
```

```
void main( void )
{
    int old;
    FILE *new;

    old = _dup( 1 );    /* "old" now refers to "stdout" */
                        /* Note:  file handle 1 == "stdout" */
    if( old == -1 )
    {
        perror( "_dup( 1 ) failure" );
        exit( 1 );
    }
    write( old, "This goes to stdout first\r\n", 27 );
    if( ( new = fopen( "data", "w" ) ) == NULL )
    {
        puts( "Can't open file 'data'\n" );
        exit( 1 );
    }

    /* stdout now refers to file "data" */
    if( -1 == _dup2( _fileno( new ), 1 ) )
    {
        perror( "Can't _dup2 stdout" );
        exit( 1 );
    }
    puts( "This goes to file 'data'\r\n" );

    /* Flush stdout stream buffer so it goes to correct file */
    fflush( stdout );
    fclose( new );

    /* Restore original stdout */
    _dup2( old, 1 );
    puts( "This goes to stdout\n" );
    puts( "The file 'data' contains:" );
    system( "type data" );
}
```

Output

```
This goes to stdout first
This goes to file 'data'

This goes to stdout

The file 'data' contains:

This goes to file 'data'
```

_ecvt

char *_ecvt(double *value*, **int** *count*, **int** *dec, **int** *sign **);**

~~ANSI~~   UNIX   WIN32S

Use **_ecvt** for compatibility with ANSI naming conventions of non-ANSI functions.
Use **ecvt** and link with OLDNAMES.LIB for UNIX compatibility.

#include <stdlib.h>

Return Value   **_ecvt** returns a pointer to the string of digits. There is no error return.

Parameters   *value*   Number to be converted
count   Number of digits stored
dec   Stored decimal-point position
sign   Sign of converted number

Remarks   The **_ecvt** function converts a floating-point number to a character string. The
value parameter is the floating-point number to be converted. This function stores
up to *count* digits of *value* as a string and appends a null character ('\0'). If the
number of digits in *value* exceeds *count,* the low-order digit is rounded. If there are
fewer than *count* digits, the string is padded with zeros.

Only digits are stored in the string. The position of the decimal point and the sign of
value can be obtained from *dec* and *sign* after the call. The *dec* parameter points to
an integer value giving the position of the decimal point with respect to the
beginning of the string. A 0 or negative integer value indicates that the decimal
point lies to the left of the first digit. The *sign* parameter points to an integer that
indicates the sign of the converted number. If the integer value is 0, the number is
positive. Otherwise, the number is negative.

_ecvt and **_fcvt** use a single statically allocated buffer for the conversion. Each call
to one of these routines destroys the result of the previous call.

See Also   **atof, _fcvt, _gcvt**

Example
```
/* ECVT.C: This program uses _ecvt to convert a
 * floating-point number to a character string.
 */

#include <stdlib.h>
#include <stdio.h>
```

```
void main( void )
{
    int     decimal,   sign;
    char    *buffer;
    int     precision = 10;
    double  source = 3.1415926535;

    buffer = _ecvt( source, precision, &decimal, &sign );
    printf( "source: %2.10f   buffer: '%s'  decimal: %d  sign: %d\n",
            source, buffer, decimal, sign );
}
```

Output   source: 3.1415926535   buffer: '3141592654' decimal: 1   sign: 0

_endthread, _endthreadex

void _endthread(void);

void _endthreadex(unsigned *retval* **);**

~~ANSI~~ ~~UNIX~~ ~~WIN32S~~

#include <process.h>

Return Value   None

Parameter   *retval*   Thread exit code

Remarks   The **_endthread** and **_endthreadex** functions terminate a thread created by
_beginthread or **_beginthreadex**, respectively. You can call **_endthread** or
_endthreadex explicitly to terminate a thread; however, **_endthread** or
_endthreadex is called automatically when the thread returns from the routine
passed as a parameter to **_beginthread** or **_beginthreadex**. Terminating a thread
with a call to **endthread** or **_endthreadex** helps to ensure proper recovery of
resources allocated for the thread.

Note For an executable file linked with LIBCMT.LIB, do not call the Win32
ExitThread API; this prevents the run-time system from reclaiming allocated
resources. **_endthread** and **_endthreadex** reclaim allocated thread resources and
then call **ExitThread**.

_endthread automatically closes the thread handle. (This behavior differs from the Win32 **ExitThread** API.) Therefore, when you use **_beginthread** and **_endthread**, do not explicitly close the thread handle by calling the Win32 **CloseHandle** API.

Like the Win32 **ExitThread** API, _endthreadex does not close the thread handle. Therefore, when you use **_beginthreadex** and **_endthreadex**, you must close the thread handle by calling the Win32 **CloseHandle** API.

See Also   **_beginthread**

Example   See the example for **_beginthread**.

_eof

int _eof(int *handle* **);**

~~ANSI~~ ~~UNIX~~ WIN32S

#include <io.h>

Return Value   **_eof** returns 1 if the current position is end of file, or 0 if it is not. A return value of −1 indicates an error; in this case, **errno** is set to **EBADF**, which indicates an invalid file handle.

Parameter   *handle*   Handle referring to open file

Remarks   The **_eof** function determines whether the end of the file associated with *handle* has been reached.

See Also   **clearerr, feof, ferror, perror**

Example

```
/* EOF.C: This program reads data from a file
 * ten bytes at a time until the end of the
 * file is reached or an error is encountered.
 */

#include <io.h>
#include <fcntl.h>
#include <stdio.h>
#include <stdlib.h>

void main( void )
{
   int  fh, count, total = 0;
   char buf[10];
   if( (fh = _open( "eof.c", _O_RDONLY )) == - 1 )
   {
       perror( "Open failed");
       exit( 1 );
   }
   /* Cycle until end of file reached: */
   while( !_eof( fh ) )
   {
      /* Attempt to read in 10 bytes: */
      if( (count = _read( fh, buf, 10 )) == -1 )
      {
         perror( "Read error" );
         break;
      }
      /* Total actual bytes read */
      total += count;
   }
   printf( "Number of bytes read = %d\n", total );
   _close( fh );
}\
```

Output

```
Number of bytes read = 754
```

_exec, _wexec Functions

int _execl(const char *cmdname, const char *arg0, ... const char *argn, NULL);

int _wexecl(const wchar_t *cmdname, const wchar_t *arg0, ... const wchar_t *argn, NULL);

int _execle(const char *cmdname, const char *arg0, ... const char *argn, NULL, const char * const *envp);

int _wexecle(const wchar_t *cmdname, const wchar_t *arg0, ... const wchar_t *argn, NULL, const char * const *envp);

int _execlp(const char *cmdname, const char *arg0, ... const char *argn, NULL);

int _wexeclp(const wchar_t *cmdname, const wchar_t *arg0, ... const wchar_t *argn, NULL);

int _execlpe(const char *cmdname, const char *arg0, ... const char *argn, NULL, const char * const *envp);

int _wexeclpe(const wchar_t *cmdname, const wchar_t *arg0, ... const wchar_t *argn, NULL, const wchar_t * const *envp);

int _execv(const char *cmdname, const char *const *argv);

int _wexecv(const wchar_t *cmdname, const wchar_t *const *argv);

int _execve(const char *cmdname, const char *const *argv, const char * const *envp);

int _wexecve(const wchar_t *cmdname, const wchar_t *const *argv, const wchar_t * const *envp);

int _execvp(const char *cmdname, const char *const *argv);

int _wexecvp(const wchar_t *cmdname, const wchar_t *const *argv);

int _execvpe(const char *cmdname, const char *const *argv, const char * const *envp);

int _wexecvpe(const wchar_t *cmdname, const wchar_t *const *argv, const wchar_t * const *envp);

_exec functions: ~~ANSI~~ UNIX WIN32S
_wexec functions: ~~ANSI~~ ~~UNIX~~ ~~WIN32S~~

Use _exec for compatibility with ANSI naming conventions of non-ANSI functions.
Use exec and link with OLDNAMES.LIB for UNIX compatibility.

#include <process.h>   For exec functions.
#include <wchar.h>   For _wexec functions use PROCESS.H or WCHAR.H.

Return Value

If successful, these functions do not return to the calling process. A return value of −1 indicates an error, in which case the **errno** global variable is set to one of the following values.

errno Value	Description
E2BIG	The parameter list exceeds 1024 bytes, or the space required for the environment information exceeds 32K.
EACCES	The specified file has a locking or sharing violation.
EMFIL	Too many files open (the specified file must be opened to determine whether it is executable).
ENOENT	File or path not found.
ENOEXEC	The specified file is not executable or has an invalid executable-file format.
ENOMEM	Not enough memory is available to execute the new process; or the available memory has been corrupted; or an invalid block exists, indicating that the calling process was not allocated properly.

Parameters

cmdname   Path of file to be executed
arg0, ... argn   List of pointers to parameters
argv   Array of pointers to parameters
envp   Array of pointers to environment settings

Remarks

Each of the _exec functions loads and execute a new process. The **_exec** functions automatically handle multibyte-character string arguments as appropriate, recognizing multibyte-character sequences according to the multibyte code page currently in use. The **_wexec** functions are wide-character versions of the **_exec** functions. The **_wexec** functions behave identically to their **_exec** counterparts except that they do not handle multibyte-character strings.

When a call to an **_exec** function is successful, the new process is placed in the memory previously occupied by the calling process. Sufficient memory must be available for loading and executing the new process.

All **_exec** functions use the same operating-system function. The letter(s) at the end of the function name determine the variation, as follows.

_exec Function Suffix	Description
e	*envp*, array of pointers to environment settings, is passed to new process.
l	Command-line arguments are passed individually to **_exec** function.
p	**PATH** environment variable is used to find file to execute.
v	*argv*, array of pointers to command-line arguments, is passed to **_exec**.

The *cmdname* parameter specifies the file to be executed as the new process. It can specify a full path (from the root), a partial path (from the current working directory), or a filename. If *cmdname* does not have a filename extension or does not end with a period (.), the **_exec** function searches for the named file. If the search is unsuccessful, it tries the same base name with the .COM extension and then with the .EXE, .BAT, and .CMD extensions. If *cmdname* has an extension, only that extension is used in the search. If *cmdname* ends with a period, the **_exec** function searches for *cmdname* with no extension. **_execlp**, **_execlpe**, **_execvp**, and **_execvpe** search for *cmdname* (using the same procedures) in the directories specified by the **PATH** environment variable. If *cmdname* contains a drive specifier or any slashes (that is, if it is a relative path), the **_exec** call searches only for the specified file; the path is not searched.

Parameters are passed to the new process by giving one or more pointers to character strings as parameters in the **_exec** call. These character strings form the parameter list for the new process. The combined length of the strings forming the parameter list for the new process must not exceed 1024 bytes. The terminating null character ('\0') for each string is not included in the count, but space characters (inserted automatically to separate the parameters) are counted.

The argument pointers can be passed as separate parameters (in **_execl**, **_execle**, **_execlp**, and **_execlpe**) or as an array of pointers (in **_execv**, **_execve**, **_execvp**, and **_execvpe**). At least one parameter, *arg0*, must be passed to the new process; this parameter is *argv*[0] of the new process. Usually, this parameter is a copy of *cmdname*. (A different value does not produce an error.)

The **_execl**, **_execle**, **_execlp**, and **_execlpe** calls are typically used when the number of parameters is known in advance. The parameter *arg0* is usually a pointer to *cmdname*. The parameters *arg1* through *argn* point to the character strings forming the new parameter list. A null pointer must follow *argn* to mark the end of the parameter list.

The **_execv**, **_execve**, **_execvp**, and **_execvpe** calls are useful when the number of parameters to the new process is variable. Pointers to the parameters are passed as an array, *argv*. The parameter *argv*[0] is usually a pointer to *cmdname*. The parameters *argv*[1] through *argv*[*n*] point to the character strings forming the new parameter list. The parameter *argv*[*n*+1] must be a **NULL** pointer to mark the end of the parameter list.

Files that are open when an **_exec** call is made remain open in the new process. In **_execl**, **_execlp**, **_execv**, and **_execvp** calls, the new process inherits the environment of the calling process. **_execle**, **_execlpe**, **_execve**, and **_execvpe** calls alter the environment for the new process by passing a list of environment settings through the *envp* parameter. *envp* is an array of character pointers, each element of which (except for the final element) points to a null-terminated string defining an environment variable. Such a string usually has the form *NAME=value* where *NAME* is the name of an environment variable and *value* is the string value to which that variable is set. (Note that *value* is not enclosed in double quotation marks.) The final element of the *envp* array should be **NULL**. When *envp* itself is **NULL**, the new process inherits the environment settings of the calling process.

A program executed with one of the **_exec** functions is always loaded into memory as if the "maximum allocation" field in the program's .EXE file header were set to the default value of 0xFFFFH. You can use the EXEHDR utility to change the maximum allocation field of a program; however, such a program invoked with one of the **_exec** functions may behave differently from a program invoked directly from the operating-system command line or with one of the **_spawn** functions.

The **_exec** calls do not preserve the translation modes of open files. If the new process must use files inherited from the calling process, use the **_setmode** routine to set the translation mode of these files to the desired mode. You must explicitly flush (using **fflush** or **_flushall**) or close any stream before the **_exec** function call. Signal settings are not preserved in new processes that are created by calls to **_exec** routines. The signal settings are reset to the default in the new process.

See Also   **abort, atexit, exit, _onexit, _spawn** Functions, **system**

Example

```
/* EXEC.C illustrates the different versions of exec including:
 *      _execl          _execle         _execlp         _execlpe
 *      _execv          _execve         _execvp         _execvpe
 *
 * Although EXEC.C can exec any program, you can verify how
 * different versions handle arguments and environment by
 * compiling and specifying the sample program ARGS.C. See
 * SPAWN.C for examples of the similar spawn functions.
 */

#include <stdio.h>
#include <conio.h>
#include <process.h>

char *my_env[] =                    /* Environment for exec?e */
{
   "THIS=environment will be",
   "PASSED=to new process by",
   "the EXEC=functions",
   NULL
};

void main()
{
   char *args[4], prog[80];
   int ch;
```

```
printf( "Enter name of program to exec: " );
gets( prog );
printf( " 1. _execl  2. _execle  3. _execlp  4. _execlpe\n" );
printf( " 5. _execv  6. _execve  7. _execvp  8. _execvpe\n" );
printf( "Type a number from 1 to 8 (or 0 to quit): " );
ch = _getche();
if( (ch < '1') || (ch > '8') )
    exit( 1 );
printf( "\n\n" );

/* Arguments for _execv? */
args[0] = prog;
args[1] = "exec??";
args[2] = "two";
args[3] = NULL;

switch( ch )
{
case '1':
    _execl( prog, prog, "_execl", "two", NULL );
    break;
case '2':
    _execle( prog, prog, "_execle", "two", NULL, my_env );
    break;
case '3':
    _execlp( prog, prog, "_execlp", "two", NULL );
    break;
case '4':
    _execlpe( prog, prog, "_execlpe", "two", NULL, my_env );
    break;
case '5':
    _execv( prog, args );
    break;
case '6':
    _execve( prog, args, my_env );
    break;
case '7':
    _execvp( prog, args );
    break;
case '8':
    _execvpe( prog, args, my_env );
    break;
default:
    break;
}

/* This point is reached only if exec fails. */
printf( "\nProcess was not execed." );
exit( 0 );
}
```

exit, _exit

void exit(int *status* **);**

void _exit(int *status* **);**

exit: ANSI   UNIX   WIN32S
_exit: ~~ANSI~~   ~~UNIX~~   WIN32S

#include <process.h>
#include <stdlib.h>   Use either PROCESS.H or STDLIB.H.

Return Value   None

Parameter   *status*   Exit status

Remarks   The **exit** and **_exit** functions terminate the calling process. **exit** calls, in last-in-first-out (LIFO) order, the functions registered by **atexit** and **_onexit**, then flushes all file buffers before terminating the process. **_exit** terminates the process without processing **atexit** or **_onexit** or flushing stream buffers. The *status* value is typically set to 0 to indicate a normal exit and set to some other value to indicate an error.

Although the **exit** and **_exit** calls do not return a value, the low-order byte of *status* is made available to the waiting calling process, if one exists, after the calling process exits. The *status* value is available to the operating-system batch command **ERRORLEVEL** and is represented by one of two constants: **EXIT_SUCCESS**, which represents a value of 0, or **EXIT_FAILURE**, which represents a value of 1. The behavior of **exit**, **_exit**, **_cexit**, and **_c_exit** is as follows.

Function	Description
exit	Performs complete C library termination procedures, terminates the process, and exits with the supplied status code.
_exit	Performs "quick" C library termination procedures, terminates the process, and exits with the supplied status code.
_cexit	Performs complete C library termination procedures and returns to the caller, but does not terminate the process.
_c_exit	Performs "quick" C library termination procedures and returns to the caller, but does not terminate the process.

See Also   **abort**, **atexit**, **_cexit**, **_exec** Functions, **_onexit**, **_spawn** Functions, **system**

Example

```
/* EXITER.C: This program prompts the user for a yes
 * or no and returns an exit code of 1 if the
 * user answers Y or y; otherwise it returns 0. The
 * error code could be tested in a batch file.
 */

#include <conio.h>
#include <stdlib.h>

void main( void )
{
   int ch;

   _cputs( "Yes or no? " );
   ch = _getch();
   _cputs( "\r\n" );
   if( toupper( ch ) == 'Y' )
      exit( 1 );
   else
      exit( 0 );
}
```

exp

double exp(double *x*);

ANSI   UNIX   WIN32S

#include <math.h>

Return Value   The **exp** function returns the exponential value of the floating-point parameter, *x*, if successful. On overflow, the function returns INF (infinite). On underflow, or if *x* is 0, **exp** returns 0.

Parameter   *x*   Floating-point value

See Also   **log**

Example

```
/* EXP.C */

#include <math.h>
#include <stdio.h>

void main( void )
{
    double x = 2.302585093, y;

    y = exp( x );
    printf( "exp( %f ) = %f\n", x, y );
}
```

Output

```
exp( 2.302585 ) = 10.000000
```

_expand

void *_expand(void *_memblock_, size_t _size_);

ANSI   UNIX   WIN32S

#include <malloc.h>

Return Value

_expand returns a void pointer to the reallocated memory block. **_expand,** unlike **realloc**, cannot move a block to change its size. Thus, if there is sufficient memory available to expand the block without moving it, the _memblock_ parameter to _expand is the same as the return value.

_expand returns **NULL** if there is insufficient memory available to expand the block to the given size without moving it. The item pointed to by _memblock_ is expanded as much as possible in its current location.

The return value points to a storage space that is guaranteed to be suitably aligned for storage of any type of object. To check the new size of the item, use **_msize**. To get a pointer to a type other than **void**, use a type cast on the return value.

Parameters

memblock   Pointer to previously allocated memory block
size   New size in bytes

Remarks

The **_expand** function changes the size of a previously allocated memory block by trying to expand or contract the block without moving its location in the heap. The _memblock_ parameter points to the beginning of the block. The _size_ parameter gives the new size of the block, in bytes. The contents of the block are unchanged up to the shorter of the new and old sizes. _memblock_ can also point to a block that has been freed, as long as there has been no intervening call to **calloc**, **_expand**, **malloc**, or **realloc**. If *memblock* points to a freed block, the block remains free after a call to **_expand**.

See Also   **calloc, free, malloc, _msize, realloc**

Example

```
/* EXPAND.C */

#include <stdio.h>
#include <malloc.h>
#include <stdlib.h>

void main( void )
{
   char *bufchar;
   printf( "Allocate a 512 element buffer\n" );
   if( (bufchar = (char *)calloc( 512, sizeof( char ) )) == NULL )
      exit( 1 );
   printf( "Allocated %d bytes at %Fp\n",
         _msize( bufchar ), (void *)bufchar );
   if( (bufchar = (char *)_expand( bufchar, 1024 )) == NULL )
      printf( "Can't expand" );
   else
      printf( "Expanded block to %d bytes at %Fp\n",
            _msize( bufchar ), (void *)bufchar );
   /* Free memory */
   free( bufchar );
   exit( 0 );
}
```

Output

```
Allocate a 512 element buffer
Allocated 512 bytes at 002C12BC
Expanded block to 1024 bytes at 002C12BC
```

fabs

double fabs(double *x* **);**

ANSI   UNIX   WIN32S

#include <math.h>

Return Value   **fabs** returns the absolute value of its argument. There is no error return.

Parameter   *x*   Floating-point value

See Also   **abs, _cabs, labs**

Example   See the example for **abs.**

fclose, _fcloseall

int fclose(FILE *stream **);**

int _fcloseall(void);

fclose: ANSI   UNIX   WIN32S
_fcloseall: ~~ANSI~~   ~~UNIX~~   WIN32S

#include <stdio.h>

Return Value   **fclose** returns 0 if the stream is successfully closed. **_fcloseall** returns the total number of streams closed. Both functions return **EOF** to indicate an error.

Parameter   *stream*   Pointer to **FILE** structure

Remarks   The **fclose** function closes *stream*. **_fcloseall** closes all open streams except **stdin**, **stdout**, **stderr** (and, in MS-DOS®, **_stdaux** and **_stdprn**). It also closes and deletes any temporary files created by **tmpfile**. In both functions, all buffers associated with the stream are flushed prior to closing. System-allocated buffers are released when the stream is closed. Buffers assigned by the user with **setbuf** and **setvbuf** are not automatically released.

See Also   **_close, _fdopen, fflush, fopen, freopen**

Example   See the example for **fopen.**

_fcvt

char *_fcvt(double *value*, **int** *count*, **int** **dec*, **int** **sign* **);**

~~ANSI~~   UNIX   WIN32S

Use **_fcvt** for compatibility with ANSI naming conventions of non-ANSI functions. Use **fcvt** and link with OLDNAMES.LIB for UNIX compatibility.

#include <stdlib.h>

Return Value   **_fcvt** returns a pointer to the string of digits. There is no error return.

Parameters   *value*   Number to be converted
count   Number of digits after decimal point
dec   Pointer to stored decimal-point position
sign   Pointer to stored sign indicator

Remarks   The **_fcvt** function converts a floating-point number to a null-terminated character string. The *value* parameter is the floating-point number to be converted. **_fcvt** stores the digits of *value* as a string and appends a null character ('\0'). The *count* parameter specifies the number of digits to be stored after the decimal point. Excess digits are rounded off to *count* places. If there are fewer than *count* digits of precision, the string is padded with zeros.

Only digits are stored in the string. The position of the decimal point and the sign of *value* can be obtained from *dec* and *sign* after the call. The *dec* parameter points to an integer value; this integer value gives the position of the decimal point with respect to the beginning of the string. A zero or negative integer value indicates that the decimal point lies to the left of the first digit. The parameter *sign* points to an integer indicating the sign of *value*. The integer is set to 0 if *value* is positive and is set to a nonzero number if *value* is negative.

_ecvt and **_fcvt** use a single statically allocated buffer for the conversion. Each call to one of these routines destroys the results of the previous call.

See Also   **atof**, **_ecvt**, **_gcvt**

Example

```
/* FCVT.C: This program converts the constant
 * 3.1415926535 to a string and sets the pointer
 * *buffer to point to that string.
 */

#include <stdlib.h>
#include <stdio.h>

void main( void )
{
    int  decimal, sign;
    char *buffer;
    double source = 3.1415926535;

    buffer = _fcvt( source, 7, &decimal, &sign );
    printf( "source: %2.10f   buffer: '%s'   decimal: %d   sign: %d\n",
            source, buffer, decimal, sign );
}
```

Output

```
source: 3.1415926535   buffer: '31415927'   decimal: 1   sign: 0
```

_fdopen, _wfdopen

FILE *_fdopen(int *handle*, **const char ****mode* **);**

FILE *_wfdopen(int *handle*, **const wchar_t ****mode* **);**

_fdopen: ~~ANSI~~ UNIX WIN32S
_wfdopen: ~~ANSI~~ ~~UNIX~~ ~~WIN32S~~

Use **_fdopen** for compatibility with ANSI naming conventions of non-ANSI functions. Use **fdopen** and link with OLDNAMES.LIB for UNIX compatibility. The **t**, **c**, and **n** *mode* options are Microsoft extensions for **fopen** and **_fdopen** and should not be used where ANSI portability is desired.

#include <stdio.h>   For **_fdopen**.
#include <wchar.h>   For **_wfdopen** use STDIO.H or WCHAR.H.

Return Value

Each of these functions returns a pointer to the open stream. A null pointer value indicates an error.

Parameters

handle   Handle to open file
mode   Type of file access

Remarks

The **_fdopen** function associates an I/O stream with the file identified by *handle*, thus allowing a file opened for low-level I/O to be buffered and formatted. **_wfdopen** is a wide-character version of **_fdopen**; the *mode* argument to **_wfdopen** is a wide-character string. **_wfdopen** and **_fdopen** behave identically otherwise.

The *mode* character string specifies the type of file and file access.

The character string *mode* specifies the type of access requested for the file, as follows:

"r"   Opens for reading. If the file does not exist or cannot be found, the **fopen** call fails.

"w"   Opens an empty file for writing. If the given file exists, its contents are destroyed.

"a"   Opens for writing at the end of the file (appending); creates the file first if it doesn't exist.

"r+"   Opens for both reading and writing. (The file must exist.)

"w+"   Opens an empty file for both reading and writing. If the given file exists, its contents are destroyed.

"a+"   Opens for reading and appending; creates the file first if it doesn't exist.

When a file is opened with the **"a"** or **"a+"** access type, all write operations occur at the end of the file. The file pointer can be repositioned using **fseek** or **rewind**, but is always moved back to the end of the file before any write operation is carried out. Thus, existing data cannot be overwritten. When the **"r+"**, **"w+"**, or **"a+"** access type is specified, both reading and writing are allowed (the file is said to be open for "update"). However, when you switch between reading and writing, there must be an intervening **fflush**, **fsetpos**, **fseek**, or **rewind** operation. The current position can be specified for the **fsetpos** or **fseek** operation, if desired.

In addition to the above values, the following characters can be included in *mode* to specify the translation mode for newline characters:

t   Open in text (translated) mode. In this mode, carriage-return–linefeed (CR-LF) combinations are translated into single linefeeds (LF) on input, and LF characters are translated to CR-LF combinations on output. Also, CTRL+Z is interpreted as an end-of-file character on input. In files opened for reading/writing, **fopen** checks for a CTRL+Z at the end of the file and removes it, if possible. This is done because using the **fseek** and **ftell** functions to move within a file that ends with a CTRL+Z may cause **fseek** to behave improperly near the end of the file.

b   Open in binary (untranslated) mode; the above translations are suppressed.

c   Enable the commit flag for the associated *filename* so that the contents of the file buffer are written directly to disk if either **fflush** or **_flushall** is called.

n   Reset the commit flag for the associated *filename* to "no-commit." This is the default. It also overrides the global commit flag if you link your program with COMMODE.OBJ. The global commit flag default is "no-commit" unless you explicitly link your program with COMMODE.OBJ.

If **t** or **b** is not given in *mode*, the default translation mode is defined by the global variable **_fmode**. If **t** or **b** is prefixed to the argument, the function fails and returns **NULL**. For a discussion of text and binary modes, see "Text and Binary Mode File I/O" on page 12.

Valid characters for the *mode* string used in **fopen** and **_fdopen** correspond to *oflag* arguments used in **_open** and **_sopen**, as follows.

Characters in *mode* String	Equivalent *oflag* Value for _open/_sopen
a	**_O_WRONLY	_O_APPEND** (usually **_O_WRONLY | _O_CREAT | _O_APPEND**)
a+	**_O_RDWR	_O_APPEND** (usually **_O_RDWR | _O_APPEND | _O_CREAT**)
r	**_O_RDONLY**
r+	**_O_RDWR**
w	**_O_WRONLY** (usually **_O_WRONLY | _O_CREAT | _O_TRUNC**)
w+	**_O_RDWR** (usually **_O_RDWR | _O_CREAT | _O_TRUNC**)
b	**_O_BINARY**
t	**_O_TEXT**
c	None
n	None

See Also   **_dup, fclose, fopen, freopen, _open**

Example

```
/* _FDOPEN.C: This program opens a file using low-
 * level I/O, then uses _fdopen to switch to stream
 * access. It counts the lines in the file.
 */

#include <stdlib.h>
#include <stdio.h>
#include <fcntl.h>
#include <io.h>

void main( void )
{
    FILE *stream;
    int  fh, count = 0;
    char inbuf[128];

    /* Open a file handle. */
    if( (fh = _open( "_fdopen.c", _O_RDONLY )) == -1 )
        exit( 1 );
```

```
                    /* Change handle access to stream access. */
                    if( (stream = _fdopen( fh, "r" )) == NULL )
                        exit( 1 );

                    while( fgets( inbuf, 128, stream ) != NULL )
                        count++;

                    /* After _fdopen, close with fclose, not _close. */
                    fclose( stream );
                    printf( "Lines in file: %d\n", count );
                }
```

Output

```
Lines in file: 32
```

feof

int feof(FILE *stream);

ANSI   UNIX   WIN32S

#include <stdio.h>

Return Value   The **feof** function returns a nonzero value after the first read operation that attempts to read past the end of the file. It returns 0 if the current position is not end of file. There is no error return.

Parameter   *stream*   Pointer to **FILE** structure

Remarks   The **feof** routine (implemented both as a function and as a macro) determines whether the end of *stream* has been reached. When end of file is reached, read operations return an end-of-file indicator until the stream is closed or until **rewind**, **fsetpos**, **fseek**, or **clearerr** is called against it.

See Also   **clearerr, _eof, ferror, perror**

Example

```
/* FEOF.C: This program uses feof to indicate when
 * it reaches the end of the file FEOF.C. It also
 * checks for errors with ferror.
 */

#include <stdio.h>
#include <stdlib.h>
```

```
void main( void )
{
    int  count, total = 0;
    char buffer[100];
    FILE *stream;

    if( (stream = fopen( "feof.c", "r" )) == NULL )
        exit( 1 );

    /* Cycle until end of file reached: */
    while( !feof( stream ) )
    {
        /* Attempt to read in 10 bytes: */
        count = fread( buffer, sizeof( char ), 100, stream );
        if( ferror( stream ) )        {
            perror( "Read error" );
            break;
        }

        /* Total up actual bytes read */
        total += count;
    }
    printf( "Number of bytes read = %d\n", total );
    fclose( stream );
}
```

Output   Number of bytes read = 745

ferror

int ferror(FILE *stream);

ANSI   UNIX   WIN32S

#include <stdio.h>

Return Value   If no error has occurred on *stream*, **ferror** returns 0. Otherwise, it returns a nonzero value.

Parameter   *stream*   Pointer to **FILE** structure

Remarks   The **ferror** routine (implemented both as a function and as a macro) tests for a reading or writing error on the file associated with *stream*. If an error has occurred, the error indicator for the stream remains set until the stream is closed or rewound, or until **clearerr** is called against it.

See Also   **clearerr, _eof, feof, fopen, perror**

Example   See the example for **feof**.

fflush

int fflush(FILE *stream);

ANSI   UNIX   WIN32S

#include <stdio.h>

Return Value   **fflush** returns 0 if the buffer was successfully flushed. The value 0 is also returned in cases in which the specified stream has no buffer or is open for reading only. A return value of **EOF** indicates an error.

Note If **fflush** returns **EOF**, data may have been lost due to a write failure. When setting up a critical error handler, it is safest to turn buffering off with the **setvbuf** function or to use low-level I/O routines such as **_open**, **_close**, and **_write** instead of the stream I/O functions.

Parameter   *stream*   Pointer to **FILE** structure

Remarks   The **fflush** function flushes a stream. If the file associated with *stream* is open for output, **fflush** writes to that file the contents of the buffer associated with the stream. If the stream is open for input, **fflush** clears the contents of the buffer. **fflush** negates the effect of any prior call to **ungetc** against *stream*. Also, **fflush(NULL)** flushes all streams opened for output. The stream remains open after the call. **fflush** has no effect on an unbuffered stream.

Buffers are normally maintained by the operating system, which determines the optimal time to write the data automatically to disk: when a buffer is full, when a stream is closed, or when a program terminates normally without closing the stream. The commit-to-disk feature of the run-time library lets you ensure that critical data is written directly to disk rather than to the operating-system buffers. Without rewriting an existing program, you can enable this feature by linking the program's object files with COMMODE.OBJ. In the resulting executable file, calls to **_flushall** write the contents of all buffers to disk. Only **_flushall** and **fflush** are affected by COMMODE.OBJ.

For information about controlling the commit-to-disk feature, see "Stream I/O" on page 14, **fopen**, and **_fdopen**.

See Also   **fclose**, **_flushall**, **setvbuf**

Example

```
/* FFLUSH.C */

#include <stdio.h>
#include <conio.h>

void main( void )
{
   int integer;
   char string[81];

   /* Read each word as a string. */
   printf( "Enter a sentence of four words with scanf: " );
   for( integer = 0; integer < 4; integer++ )
   {
      scanf( "%s", string );
      printf( "%s\n", string );
   }

   /* You must flush the input buffer before using gets. */
   fflush( stdin );
   printf( "Enter the same sentence with gets: " );
   gets( string );
   printf( "%s\n", string );
}
```

Output

```
Enter a sentence of four words with scanf: This is a test
This
is
a
test
Enter the same sentence with gets: This is a test
This is a test
```

fgetc, fgetwc, _fgetchar, _fgetwchar

int fgetc(FILE *stream);

wint_t fgetwc(FILE *stream);

int _fgetchar(void);

wint_t _fgetwchar(void);

fgetc: ANSI   UNIX   WIN32S
fgetwc: ANSI   UNIX   ~~WIN32S~~
_fgetchar: ~~ANSI~~   ~~UNIX~~   WIN32S
_fgetwchar: ~~ANSI~~   ~~UNIX~~   ~~WIN32S~~

#include <stdio.h>   For **fgetc** and **_fgetchar**.
#include <wchar.h>   For **fgetwc** and **_fgetwchar** use STDIO.H or WCHAR.H.

Return Value   **fgetc** and **_fgetchar** return the character read as an **int** or return **EOF** to indicate an error or end of file. **fgetwc** and **_fgetwchar** return, as a **wint_t**, the wide character that corresponds to the character read or return **WEOF** to indicate an error or end of file. For all four functions, use **feof** or **ferror** to distinguish between an error and an end-of-file condition. For **fgetc** and **fgetwc**, if a read error occurs, the error indicator for the stream is set.

Parameter   *stream*   Pointer to **FILE** structure

Remarks   Each of these functions reads a single character from the current position of a file; in the case of **fgetc** and **fgetwc**, this is the file associated with *stream*. The function then increments the associated file pointer (if defined) to point to the next character. If the stream is at end of file, the end-of-file indicator for the stream is set. Routine-specific remarks follow.

Routine	Remarks
fgetc	Equivalent to **getc**, but implemented only as a function, rather than as a function and a macro.
fgetwc	Wide-character version of **fgetc.** Reads *c* as a multibyte character or a wide character according to whether *stream* is opened in text mode or binary mode.
_fgetchar	Equivalent to **fgetc(stdin)**. Also equivalent to **getchar**, but implemented only as a function, rather than as a function and a macro. Microsoft-specific; not ANSI-compatible.
_fgetwchar	Wide-character version of **_fgetchar.** Reads *c* as a multibyte character or a wide character according to whether *stream* is opened in text mode or binary mode. Microsoft-specific; not ANSI-compatible.

For more information about processing wide characters and multibyte characters in text and binary modes, see "Unicode Stream I/O in Text and Binary Modes" on page 13.

See Also   **fputc, getc**

Example

```
/* FGETC.C: This program uses getc to read the first
 * 80 input characters (or until the end of input)
 * and place them into a string named buffer.
 */

#include <stdio.h>
#include <stdlib.h>

void main( void )
{
    FILE *stream;
    char buffer[81];
    int  i, ch;

    /* Open file to read line from: */
    if( (stream = fopen( "fgetc.c", "r" )) == NULL )
        exit( 0 );

    /* Read in first 80 characters and place them in "buffer": */
    ch = fgetc( stream );
    for( i=0; (i < 80 ) && ( feof( stream ) == 0 ); i++ )
    {
        buffer[i] = (char)ch;
        ch = fgetc( stream );
    }

    /* Add null to end string */
    buffer[i] = '\0';
    printf( "%s\n", buffer );
    fclose( stream );
}
```

Output

```
/* FGETC.C: This program uses getc to read the first
 * 80 input characters (or
```

fgetpos

int fgetpos(FILE *_stream_, fpos_t *_pos_);

ANSI   ~~UNIX~~   WIN32S

#include <stdio.h>

Return Value

If successful, **fgetpos** returns 0. On failure, it returns a nonzero value and sets **errno** to one of the following manifest constants (defined in STDIO.H): **EBADF**, which means the specified stream is not a valid file handle or is not accessible, or **EINVAL**, which means the _stream_ value is invalid.

Parameters

    stream   Target stream
    pos   Position-indicator storage

Remarks

The **fgetpos** function gets the current value of the *stream* argument's file-position indicator and stores it in the object pointed to by *pos*. The **fsetpos** function can later use information stored in *pos* to reset the *stream* argument's pointer to its position at the time **fgetpos** was called. The *pos* value is stored in an internal format and is intended for use only by **fgetpos** and **fsetpos**.

See Also

fsetpos

Example

```
/* FGETPOS.C: This program opens a file and reads
 * bytes at several different locations.
 */

#include <stdio.h>

void main( void )
{
   FILE    *stream;
   fpos_t  pos;
   char    buffer[20];

   if( (stream = fopen( "fgetpos.c", "rb" )) == NULL )
      printf( "Trouble opening file\n" );
   else
   {
      /* Read some data and then check the position. */
      fread( buffer, sizeof( char ), 10, stream );
      if( fgetpos( stream, &pos ) != 0 )
         perror( "fgetpos error" );
      else
      {
         fread( buffer, sizeof( char ), 10, stream );
         printf( "10 bytes at byte %ld: %.10s\n", pos, buffer );
      }

      /* Set a new position and read more data */
      pos = 140;
      if( fsetpos( stream, &pos ) != 0 )
         perror( "fsetpos error" );

      fread( buffer, sizeof( char ), 10, stream );
      printf( "10 bytes at byte %ld: %.10s\n", pos, buffer );
      fclose( stream );
   }
}
```

Output
```
10 bytes at byte 10: .C: This p
10 bytes at byte 140:
{
    FIL
```

fgets, fgetws

char *fgets(char *_string_, **int** _n_, **FILE** *_stream_);

wchar_t *fgetws(wchar_t *_string_, **int** _n_, **FILE** *_stream_);

> **fgets:** ANSI UNIX WIN32S
> **fgetws:** ANSI UNIX ~~WIN32S~~
>
> **#include <stdio.h>**   For **fgets**.
> **#include <wchar.h>**   For **fgetws** use STDIO.H or WCHAR.H.

Return Value
Each of these functions returns _string_. **NULL** is returned to indicate an error or an end-of-file condition. Use **feof** or **ferror** to determine whether an error occurred.

Parameters
string   Storage location for data
_n_   Maximum number of characters to read
stream   Pointer to **FILE** structure

Remarks
The **fgets** function reads a string from the input _stream_ argument and stores it in _string_. **fgets** reads characters from the current stream position to and including the first newline character, to the end of the stream, or until the number of characters read is equal to _n_−1, whichever comes first. The result stored in _string_ is appended with a null character. The newline character, if read, is included in the string.

fgets is similar to the **gets** function; however, **gets** replaces the newline character with **NULL**. **fgetws** is a wide-character version of **fgets**.

fgetws reads the wide-character argument _string_ as a multibyte-character string or a wide-character string according to whether _stream_ is opened in text mode or binary mode, respectively. For more information about using text and binary modes in Unicode and multibyte stream-I/O, see "Text and Binary Mode File I/O" on page 12 and "Unicode Stream I/O in Text and Binary Modes" on page 13.

See Also
fputs, gets, puts

Example

```
/* FGETS.C: This program uses fgets to display
 * a line from a file on the screen.
 */

#include <stdio.h>

void main( void )
{
   FILE *stream;
   char line[100];

   if( (stream = fopen( "fgets.c", "r" )) != NULL )
   {
      if( fgets( line, 100, stream ) == NULL)
         printf( "fgets error\n" );
      else
         printf( "%s", line);
      fclose( stream );
   }
}
```

Output

```
/* FGETS.C: This program uses fgets to display
```

_filelength

long _filelength(int *handle* **);**

ANSI   UNIX   WIN32S

#include <io.h>

Return Value

_filelength returns the file length, in bytes, in bytes, of the target file associated with *handle*. A return value of –1L indicates an error, and an invalid handle sets **errno** to **EBADF**.

Parameter

handle   Target file handle

See Also

_chsize, _fileno, _fstat, _stat

Example

See the example for **_chsize**.

_fileno

int _fileno(FILE *_stream_);

~~ANSI~~   UNIX   WIN32S

Use **_fileno** for compatibility with ANSI naming conventions of non-ANSI functions. Use **fileno** and link with OLDNAMES.LIB for UNIX compatibility.

#include <stdio.h>

Return Value

_fileno returns the file handle. There is no error return. The result is undefined if _stream_ does not specify an open file.

Parameter

stream   Pointer to **FILE** structure

Remarks

The **_fileno** routine returns the file handle currently associated with _stream_. This routine is implemented both as a function and as a macro. For details on choosing either implementation, see "Choosing Between Functions and Macros" on page viii.

See Also

_fdopen, _filelength, fopen, freopen

Example

```
/* FILENO.C: This program uses _fileno to obtain
 * the file handle for some standard C streams.
 */

#include <stdio.h>

void main( void )
{
    printf( "The file handle for stdin is %d\n", _fileno( stdin ) );
    printf( "The file handle for stdout is %d\n", _fileno( stdout ) );
    printf( "The file handle for stderr is %d\n", _fileno( stderr ) );
}
```

Output

```
The file handle for stdin is 0
The file handle for stdout is 1
The file handle for stderr is 2
```

_find, _wfind Functions

long **_findfirst**(char *_filespec_, struct **_finddata_t** *_fileinfo_);

long **_wfindfirst**(wchar_t *_filespec_, struct **_wfinddata_t** *_fileinfo_);

int **_findnext**(long _handle_, struct **_finddata_t** *_fileinfo_);

int **_wfindnext**(long _handle_, struct **_wfinddata_t** *_fileinfo_);

int **_findclose**(long _handle_);

~~ANSI~~ ~~UNIX~~ ~~WIN32S~~

#include <io.h>   For **_find** functions.
#include <wchar.h>   For **_wfind** functions use IO.H or WCHAR.H.

Return Value

If successful, **_findfirst** and **_wfindfirst** return a unique search handle identifying the file or group of files matching the _filespec_ specification, which can be used in a subsequent call to **_findnext** or **_wfindnext**, respectively, or to **_findclose**. Otherwise, **_findfirst** and **_wfindfirst** return –1 and set **errno** to one of the following values:

ENOENT   File specification that could not be matched

EINVAL   Invalid filename specification

If successful, **_findnext, _wfindnext,** and **_findclose** return 0. Otherwise, they return –1 and set **errno** to **ENOENT**, indicating that no more matching files could be found.

Parameters

filespec   Target file specification (may include wildcards)
handle   Search handle returned by a previous call to **_findfirst**
fileinfo   File information buffer

Remarks

The **_findfirst** function provides information about the first instance of a filename that matches the file specified in the _filespec_ argument. Any wildcard combination supported by the host operating system can be used in _filespec_. File information is returned in a **_finddata_t** structure, defined in IO.H. The **_finddata_t** structure includes the following elements:

unsigned attrib   File attribute

time_t time_create   Time of file creation (–1L for FAT file systems)

time_t time_access   Time of last file access (–1L for FAT file systems)

time_t time_write   Time of last write to file

_fsize_t size   Length of file in bytes

char name[_MAX_FNAME]   Null-terminated name of matched file/directory, without the path

In file systems that do not support the creation and last access times of a file, such as the FAT system, the **time_create** and **time_access** fields are always –1L.

_MAX_FNAME is defined in STDLIB.H as 256 bytes.

You cannot specify target attributes (such as **_A_RDONLY**) by which to limit the find operation. This attribute is returned in the **attrib** field of the **_finddata_t** structure and can have the following values (defined in IO.H).

_A_ARCH   Archive. Set whenever the file is changed, and cleared by the BACKUP command. Value: 0x20

_A_HIDDEN   Hidden file. Not normally seen with the DIR command, unless the /AH option is used. Returns information about normal files as well as files with this attribute. Value: 0x02

_A_NORMAL   Normal. File can be read or written to without restriction. Value: 0x00

_A_RDONLY   Read-only. File cannot be opened for writing, and a file with the same name cannot be created. Value: 0x01

_A_SUBDIR   Subdirectory. Value: 0x10

_A_SYSTEM   System file. Not normally seen with the DIR command, unless the /A or /A:S option is used. Value: 0x04

_findnext finds the next name, if any, that matches the *filespec* argument specified in a prior call to **_findfirst**. The *fileinfo* argument should point to a structure initialized by a previous call to **_findfirst**. If a match is found, the *fileinfo* structure contents are altered as described above. **_findclose** closes the specified search handle and releases associated resources.

The **_find** functions allow nested calls. For example, if the file found by a call to **_findfirst** or **_findnext** is a subdirectory, a new search can be initiated with another call to **_findfirst** or **_findnext**.

_wfindfirst and **_wfindnext** are wide-character versions of **_findfirst** and **_findnext**. The structure argument of the wide-character versions has the **_wfinddata_t** data type, which is defined in IO.H and in WCHAR.H. The fields of this data type are the same as those of the **_finddata_t** data type, except that in **_wfinddata_t** the name field is of type **wchar_t** rather than type **char**. Otherwise **_wfindfirst** and **_wfindnext** behave identically to **_findfirst** and **_findnext**.

Example

```c
/* FFIND.C: This program uses the _find functions to print
 * a list of all files (and their attributes) with a .C extension
 * in the current directory. */

#include <stdio.h>
#include <io.h>
#include <time.h>

void main( void )
{
    struct _finddata_t c_file;
    long hFile;

    /* Find first .c file in current directory */
    if( (hFile = _findfirst( "*.c", &c_file )) == -1L )
        printf( "No *.c files in current directory!\n" );
    else
    {
            printf( "Listing of .c files\n\n" );
            printf( "\nRDO HID SYS ARC  FILE          DATE %25c SIZE\n",
                    ' ' );
            printf( "--- --- --- ---  ----          ---- %25c ----\n",
                    ' ' );
            printf( ( c_file.attrib & _A_RDONLY ) ? " Y  " : " N  " );
            printf( ( c_file.attrib & _A_SYSTEM ) ? " Y  " : " N  " );
            printf( ( c_file.attrib & _A_HIDDEN ) ? " Y  " : " N  " );
            printf( ( c_file.attrib & _A_ARCH )   ? " Y  " : " N  " );
            printf( " %-12s %.24s  %9ld\n", c_file.name,
                ctime( &( c_file.time_write ) ), c_file.size );

            /* Find the rest of the .c files */
            while( _findnext( hFile, &c_file ) == 0 )
            {
                printf( ( c_file.attrib & _A_RDONLY ) ? " Y  " :
                    " N  " );
                printf( ( c_file.attrib & _A_SYSTEM ) ? " Y  " :
                    " N  " );
                printf( ( c_file.attrib & _A_HIDDEN ) ? " Y  " :
                    " N  " );
                printf( ( c_file.attrib & _A_ARCH )   ? " Y  " :
                    " N  " );
                printf( " %-12s %.24s  %9ld\n", c_file.name,
                    ctime( &( c_file.time_write ) ), c_file.size );
            }
        _findclose( hFile );
    }
}
```

Output   Listing of .c files

```
RDO HID SYS ARC  FILE      DATE                         SIZE
--- --- --- ---  ----      ----                         ----
 N   N   N   Y   CWAIT.C   Tue Jun 01 04:07:26 1993     1611
 N   N   N   Y   SPRINTF.C Thu May 27 04:59:18 1993      617
 N   N   N   Y   CABS.C    Thu May 27 04:58:46 1993      359
 N   N   N   Y   BEGTHRD.C Tue Jun 01 04:00:48 1993     3726
```

_finite

int _finite(double *x*);

~~ANSI~~ ~~UNIX~~ ~~WIN32S~~

#include <float.h>

Return Value   **_finite** returns a nonzero value (TRUE) if its argument *x* is not infinite, that is, if $-INF < x < +INF$. It returns 0 (FALSE) if the argument is infinite or a NaN.

Parameter   *x*   Double-precision floating-point value

See Also   **_isnan, _fpclass**

floor

double floor(double *x*);

ANSI   UNIX   WIN32S

#include <math.h>

Return Value   The **floor** function returns a floating-point value representing the largest integer that is less than or equal to *x*. There is no error return.

Parameter   *x*   Floating-point value

See Also   **ceil, fmod**

Example
```
/* FLOOR.C: This example displays the largest integers
 * less than or equal to the floating-point values 2.8
 * and -2.8. It then shows the smallest integers greater
 * than or equal to 2.8 and -2.8.
 */

#include <math.h>
#include <stdio.h>
```

```
void main( void )
{
    double y;

    y = floor( 2.8 );
    printf( "The floor of 2.8 is %f\n", y );
    y = floor( -2.8 );
    printf( "The floor of -2.8 is %f\n", y );

    y = ceil( 2.8 );
    printf( "The ceil of 2.8 is %f\n", y );
    y = ceil( -2.8 );
    printf( "The ceil of -2.8 is %f\n", y );
}
```

Output

```
The floor of 2.8 is 2.000000
The floor of -2.8 is -3.000000
The ceil of 2.8 is 3.000000
The ceil of -2.8 is -2.000000
```

_flushall

int _flushall(void);

~~ANSI~~ ~~UNIX~~ WIN32S

#include <stdio.h>

Return Value

_flushall returns the number of open streams (input and output). There is no error return.

Remarks

By default, the **_flushall** function writes to appropriate files the contents of all buffers associated with open output streams. All buffers associated with open input streams are cleared of their current contents. (These buffers are normally maintained by the operating system, which determines the optimal time to write the data automatically to disk: when a buffer is full, when a stream is closed, or when a program terminates normally without closing streams.)

If a read follows a call to **_flushall**, new data is read from the input files into the buffers. All streams remain open after the call to **_flushall**.

The commit-to-disk feature of the run-time library lets you ensure that critical data is written directly to disk rather than to the operating system buffers. Without rewriting an existing program, you can enable this feature by linking the program's object files with COMMODE.OBJ. In the resulting executable file, calls to **_flushall** write the contents of all buffers to disk. Only **_flushall** and **fflush** are affected by COMMODE.OBJ.

For information about controlling the commit-to-disk feature, see "Stream I/O" on page 14, **fopen**, and **_fdopen**.

See Also   **_commit, fclose, fflush, _flushall, setvbuf**

Example

```
/* FLUSHALL.C: This program uses _flushall
 * to flush all open buffers.
 */

#include <stdio.h>

void main( void )
{
    int numflushed;

    numflushed = _flushall();
    printf( "There were %d streams flushed\n", numflushed );
}
```

Output

```
There were 3 streams flushed
```

fmod

double fmod(double x, double y);

ANSI   UNIX   WIN32S

#include <math.h>

Return Value   **fmod** returns the floating-point remainder of x / y. If the value of y is 0.0, **fmod** returns a quiet NaN. For information about representation of a quiet NaN by the **printf** family, see **printf**.

Parameters x, y Floating-point values

Remarks	The **fmod** function calculates the floating-point remainder f of x / y such that $x = i * y + f$, where i is an integer, f has the same sign as x, and the absolute value of f is less than the absolute value of y.
See Also	**ceil, fabs, floor**

Example

```
/* FMOD.C: This program displays a
 * floating-point remainder.
 */

#include <math.h>
#include <stdio.h>

void main( void )
{
    double w = -10.0, x = 3.0, y = 0.0, z;

    z = fmod( x, y );
    printf( "The remainder of %.2f / %.2f is %f\n", w, x, z );
    printf( "The remainder of %.2f / %.2f is %f\n", x, y, z );
}
```

Output

```
The remainder of -10.00 / 3.00 is -1.000000
The remainder of 3.00 / 0.00 is -1.#IND00
```

fopen, _wfopen

FILE *fopen(const char **filename***, const char ****mode***);**

FILE *_wfopen(const wchar_t **filename***, const wchar_t ****mode***);**

fopen: ANSI UNIX WIN32S
_wfopen: ~~ANSI~~ ~~UNIX~~ ~~WIN32S~~

The **c**, **n**, and **t** *mode* options are Microsoft extensions for **fopen** and **_fdopen** and should not be used where ANSI portability is desired.

#include <stdio.h>   For **fopen**.
#include <wchar.h>   For **_wfopen** use STDIO.H or WCHAR.H..

Return Value	Each of these functions returns a pointer to the open file. A null pointer value indicates an error.
Parameters	*filename* Filename
	mode Type of access permitted

Remarks   The **fopen** function opens the file specified by *filename*. **_wfopen** is a wide-character version of **fopen**; the arguments to **_wfopen** are wide-character strings. **_wfopen** and **fopen** behave identically otherwise.

The character string *mode* specifies the type of access requested for the file, as follows:

"r"   Opens for reading. If the file does not exist or cannot be found, the **fopen** call fails.

"w"   Opens an empty file for writing. If the given file exists, its contents are destroyed.

"a"   Opens for writing at the end of the file (appending); creates the file first if it doesn't exist.

"r+"   Opens for both reading and writing. (The file must exist.)

"w+"   Opens an empty file for both reading and writing. If the given file exists, its contents are destroyed.

"a+"   Opens for reading and appending; creates the file first if it doesn't exist.

When a file is opened with the **"a"** or **"a+"** access type, all write operations occur at the end of the file. The file pointer can be repositioned using **fseek** or **rewind**, but is always moved back to the end of the file before any write operation is carried out. Thus, existing data cannot be overwritten. When the **"r+"**, **"w+"**, or **"a+"** access type is specified, both reading and writing are allowed (the file is said to be open for "update"). However, when you switch between reading and writing, there must be an intervening **fflush**, **fsetpos**, **fseek**, or **rewind** operation. The current position can be specified for the **fsetpos** or **fseek** operation, if desired.

In addition to the above values, the following characters can be included in *mode* to specify the translation mode for newline characters:

t   Open in text (translated) mode. In this mode, CTRL+Z is interpreted as an end-of-file character on input. In files opened for reading/writing, **fopen** checks for a CTRL+Z at the end of the file and removes it, if possible. This is done because using **fseek** and **ftell** to move within a file that ends with a CTRL+Z may cause **fseek** to behave improperly near the end of the file.

Also, in text mode, carriage-return–linefeed combinations are translated into single linefeeds on input, and linefeed characters are translated to carriage-return–linefeed combinations on output. When a Unicode stream-I/O function operates in text mode (the default), the source or destination stream is assumed to be a sequence of multibyte characters. Therefore, the Unicode stream-input functions convert multibyte characters to wide characters (as if by a call to the **mbtowc** function). For the same reason, the Unicode stream-output functions convert wide characters to multibyte characters (as if by a call to the **wctomb** function).

b   Open in binary (untranslated) mode; translations involving carriage-return and linefeed characters are suppressed.

If **t** or **b** is not given in *mode*, the default translation mode is defined by the global variable **_fmode**. If **t** or **b** is prefixed to the argument, the function fails and returns **NULL**.

For more information about using text and binary modes in Unicode and multibyte stream-I/O, see "Text and Binary Mode File I/O" on page 12 and "Unicode Stream I/O in Text and Binary Modes" on page 13.

c   Enable the commit flag for the associated *filename* so that the contents of the file buffer are written directly to disk if either **fflush** or **_flushall** is called.

n   Reset the commit flag for the associated *filename* to "no-commit." This is the default. It also overrides the global commit flag if you link your program with COMMODE.OBJ. The global commit flag default is "no-commit" unless you explicitly link your program with COMMODE.OBJ.

Valid characters for the *mode* string used in **fopen** and **_fdopen** correspond to *oflag* arguments used in **_open** and **_sopen**, as follows.

Characters in *mode* String	Equivalent *oflag* Value for _open/_sopen
a	**_O_WRONLY	_O_APPEND** (usually **_O_WRONLY | _O_CREAT | _O_APPEND**)
a+	**_O_RDWR	_O_APPEND** (usually **_O_RDWR | _O_APPEND | _O_CREAT**)
r	**_O_RDONLY**
r+	**_O_RDWR**
w	**_O_WRONLY** (usually **_O_WRONLY | _O_CREAT | _O_TRUNC**)
w+	**_O_RDWR** (usually **_O_RDWR | _O_CREAT | _O_TRUNC**)
b	**_O_BINARY**
t	**_O_TEXT**
c	None
n	None

See Also   fclose, _fdopen, ferror, _fileno, freopen, _open, _setmode

Example

```
/* FOPEN.C: This program opens files named "data"
 * and "data2".It  uses fclose to close "data" and
 * _fcloseall to close all remaining files.
 */

#include <stdio.h>

FILE *stream, *stream2;

void main( void )
{
   int numclosed;

   /* Open for read (will fail if file "data" does not exist) */
   if( (stream  = fopen( "data", "r" )) == NULL )
      printf( "The file 'data' was not opened\n" );
   else
      printf( "The file 'data' was opened\n" );

   /* Open for write.*/
   if( (stream2 = fopen( "data2", "w+" )) == NULL )
      printf( "The file 'data2' was not opened\n" );
   else
      printf( "The file 'data2' was opened\n" );

   /* Close stream */
   if( fclose( stream ) )
      printf( "The file 'data' was not closed\n" );

   /* All other files are closed: */
   numclosed = _fcloseall( );
   printf( "Number of files closed by _fcloseall: %u\n", numclosed );
}
```

Output

```
The file 'data' was opened
The file 'data2' was opened
Number of files closed by _fcloseall: 1
```

_fpclass

int   _fpclass(double *x*);

ANSI   UNIX   WIN32S

#include <float.h>

Return Value   _fpclass returns an integer value that indicates the floating-point class of its argument *x*. The status word may have one of the following values, defined in FLOAT.H.

Value	Meaning
_FPCLASS_SNAN	Signaling NaN
_FPCLASS_QNAN	Quiet NaN
_FPCLASS_NINF	Negative infinity (– INF)
_FPCLASS_NN	Negative normalized non-zero
_FPCLASS_ND	Negative denormalized
_FPCLASS_NZ	Negative zero (– 0)
_FPCLASS_PZ	Positive 0 (+ 0)
_FPCLASS_PD	Positive denormalized
_FPCLASS_PN	Positive normalized non-zero
_FPCLASS_PINF	Positive infinity (+ INF)

Parameter   *x*   Double-precision floating-point value

See Also   _isnan

_fpieee_flt

int _fpieee_flt(unsigned long *exc_code*, struct _EXCEPTION_POINTERS **exc_info*, int *handler*(_FPIEEE_RECORD **));

ANSI   UNIX   WIN32S

include <fpieee.h>

Return Value   The return value of **_fpieee_flt** is the value returned by *handler*. As such, the IEEE filter routine may be used in the except clause of a structured exception-handling (SEH) mechanism.

Parameters   *exc_code*   Exception code
exc_info   Pointer to the Windows NT exception information structure
handler   Pointer to user's IEEE trap-handler routine

Remarks   The **_fpieee_flt** function invokes a user-defined trap handler for IEEE floating-point exceptions and provides it with all relevant information. This routine serves as an exception filter in the SEH mechanism, which invokes your own IEEE exception handler when necessary.

The **_FPIEEE_RECORD** structure, defined in FPIEEE.H, contains information pertaining to an IEEE floating-point exception. This structure is passed to the user-defined trap handler by **_fpieee_flt**.

_FPIEEE_RECORD Field	Description
unsigned int RoundingMode, unsigned int Precision	These fields contain information on the floating-point environment at the time the exception occurred.
unsigned int Operation	Indicates the type of operation that caused the trap. If the type is a comparison (**_FpCodeCompare**), you can supply one of the special **_FPIEEE_COMPARE_RESULT** values (as defined in FPIEEE.H) in the **Result.Value** field. The conversion type (**_FpCodeConvert**) indicates that the trap occurred during a floating-point conversion operation. You can look at the **Operand1** and **Result** types to determine the type of conversion being attempted.
_FPIEEE_VALUE Operand1, _FPIEEE_VALUE Operand2, _FPIEEE_VALUE Result	These structures indicate the types and values of the proposed result and operands: **OperandValid** Flag indicating whether the responding value is valid. **Format** Data type of the corresponding value. The format type may be returned even if the corresponding value is not valid. **Value** Result or operand data value.

See Also   **_control87**

Example
```
/* FPIEEE.C: This program demonstrates the implementation of
 * a user-defined floating-point exception handler using the
 * _fpieee_flt function.
 */

#include <fpieee.h>
#include <excpt.h>
#include <float.h>
```

```c
int fpieee_handler( _FPIEEE_RECORD * );

int fpieee_handler( _FPIEEE_RECORD *pieee )
{
   // user-defined ieee trap handler routine:
   // there is one handler for all
   // IEEE exceptions

   // Assume the user wants all invalid
   // operations to return 0.

   if ((pieee->Cause.InvalidOperation) &&
       (pieee->Result.Format == _FpFormatFp32))
   {
       pieee->Result.Value.Fp32Value = 0.0F;
       return EXCEPTION_CONTINUE_EXECUTION;
   }
   else
      return EXCEPTION_EXECUTE_HANDLER;
}

#define _EXC_MASK    \
   _EM_UNDERFLOW  + \
   _EM_OVERFLOW   + \
   _EM_ZERODIVIDE + \
   _EM_INEXACT

void main( void )
{
   // ...

   __try {
      // unmask invalid operation exception
      _controlfp(_EXC_MASK, _MCW_EM);

      // code that may generate
      // fp exceptions goes here
   }
   __except ( _fpieee_flt( GetExceptionCode(),
              GetExceptionInformation(),
              fpieee_handler ) ){

      // code that gets control
      // if fpieee_handler returns
      // EXCEPTION_EXECUTE_HANDLER goes here

   }

   // ...
}
```

_fpreset

void _fpreset(void);

~~ANSI~~   ~~UNIX~~   WIN32S

#include <float.h>

Return Value   None

Remarks   The **_fpreset** function reinitializes the floating-point math package. **_fpreset** is usually used with **signal**, **system**, or the **_exec** or **_spawn** functions. If a program traps floating-point error signals (**SIGFPE**) with **signal**, it can safely recover from floating-point errors by invoking **_fpreset** and using **longjmp**.

See Also   **_exec** Functions, **signal**, **_spawn** Functions, **system**

Example

```
/* FPRESET.C: This program uses signal to set up a
 * routine for handling floating-point errors.
 */

#include <stdio.h>
#include <signal.h>
#include <setjmp.h>
#include <stdlib.h>
#include <float.h>
#include <math.h>
#include <string.h>

jmp_buf mark;                  /* Address for long jump to jump to */
int     fperr;                 /* Global error number */

void __cdecl fphandler( int sig, int num );   /* Prototypes */
void fpcheck( void );

void main( void )
{
    double n1, n2, r;
    int jmpret;
    /* Unmask all floating-point exceptions. */
    _control87( 0, _MCW_EM );
    /* Set up floating-point error handler. The compiler
     * will generate a warning because it expects
     * signal-handling functions to take only one argument.
     */
    if( signal( SIGFPE, fphandler ) == SIG_ERR )
    {
        fprintf( stderr, "Couldn't set SIGFPE\n" );
        abort();    }
```

```
      /* Save stack environment for return in case of error. First
       * time through, jmpret is 0, so true conditional is executed.
       * If an error occurs, jmpret will be set to -1 and false
       * conditional will be executed.
       */
      jmpret = setjmp( mark );
      if( jmpret == 0 )
      {
         printf( "Test for invalid operation - " );
         printf( "enter two numbers: " );
         scanf( "%lf %lf", &n1, &n2 );
         r = n1 / n2;
         /* This won't be reached if error occurs. */
         printf( "\n\n%4.3g / %4.3g = %4.3g\n", n1, n2, r );
         r = n1 * n2;
         /* This won't be reached if error occurs. */
         printf( "\n\n%4.3g * %4.3g = %4.3g\n", n1, n2, r );
      }
      else
         fpcheck();
   }
/* fphandler handles SIGFPE (floating-point error) interrupt. Note
 * that this prototype accepts two arguments and that the
 * prototype for signal in the run-time library expects a signal
 * handler to have only one argument.
 *
 * The second argument in this signal handler allows processing of
 * _FPE_INVALID, _FPE_OVERFLOW, _FPE_UNDERFLOW, and
 * _FPE_ZERODIVIDE, all of which are Microsoft-specific symbols
 * that augment the information provided by SIGFPE. The compiler
 * will generate a warning, which is harmless and expected.
 */
void fphandler( int sig, int num )
{
   /* Set global for outside check since we don't want
    * to do I/O in the handler.
    */
   fperr = num;
   /* Initialize floating-point package. */
   _fpreset();
   /* Restore calling environment and jump back to setjmp. Return
    * -1 so that setjmp will return false for conditional test.
    */
   longjmp( mark, -1 );
}
```

```
void fpcheck( void )
{
    char fpstr[30];
    switch( fperr )
    {
    case _FPE_INVALID:
        strcpy( fpstr, "Invalid number" );
        break;
    case _FPE_OVERFLOW:
        strcpy( fpstr, "Overflow" );
        break;
    case _FPE_UNDERFLOW:
        strcpy( fpstr, "Underflow" );
        break;
    case _FPE_ZERODIVIDE:
        strcpy( fpstr, "Divide by zero" );
        break;
    default:
        strcpy( fpstr, "Other floating point error" );
        break;
    }
    printf( "Error %d: %s\n", fperr, fpstr );
}
```

Output

```
Test for invalid operation - enter two numbers: 5 0
Error 131: Divide by zero
```

fprintf, fwprintf

int fprintf(FILE **stream*, **const char** **format* [[, *argument*]]...**);**

int fwprintf(FILE **stream*, **const wchar_t** **format* [[, *argument*]]...**);**

> **fprintf:**　ANSI　UNIX　WIN32S
> **fwprintf:**　ANSI　UNIX　~~WIN32S~~
>
> **#include <stdio.h>**　For **fprintf**.
> **#include <wchar.h>**　For **fwprintf** use STDIO.H or WCHAR.H.

Return Value

fprintf returns the number of bytes written. **fwprintf** returns the number of wide characters written. Each of these functions returns a negative value instead when an output error occurs.

Parameters

stream　Pointer to **FILE** structure
format　Format-control string
argument　Optional arguments

Remarks   **fprintf** formats and prints a series of characters and values to the output *stream*. Each function *argument* (if any) is converted and output according to the corresponding format specification in *format.* For **fprintf**, the *format* argument has the same syntax and use that it has in **printf**.

fwprintf is a wide-character version of **fprintf**; in **fwprintf**, *format* is a wide-character string. These functions behave identically otherwise.

For more information on *format* and *argument,* see **printf**.

See Also   **_cprintf, fscanf, sprintf**

Example
```
/* FPRINTF.C: This program uses fprintf to format various
 * data and print it to the file named FPRINTF.OUT. It
 * then displays FPRINTF.OUT on the screen using the system
 * function to invoke the operating-system TYPE command.
 */

#include <stdio.h>
#include <process.h>

FILE *stream;

void main( void )
{
    int    i = 10;
    double fp = 1.5;
    char   s[] = "this is a string";
    char   c = '\n';

    stream = fopen( "fprintf.out", "w" );
    fprintf( stream, "%s%c", s, c );
    fprintf( stream, "%d\n", i );
    fprintf( stream, "%f\n", fp );
    fclose( stream );
    system( "type fprintf.out" );
}
```

Output
```
this is a string
10
1.500000
```

fputc, fputwc, _fputchar, _fputwchar

int fputc(int *c*, **FILE ****stream* **);**

wint_t fputwc(wint_t *c*, **FILE ****stream* **);**

int _fputchar(int *c* **);**

wint_t _fputwchar(wint_t *c* **);**

fputc: ANSI   UNIX   WIN32S
fputwc: ANSI   UNIX   ~~WIN32S~~
_fputchar: ~~ANSI~~   ~~UNIX~~   WIN32S
_fputwchar: ~~ANSI~~   ~~UNIX~~   ~~WIN32S~~

#include <stdio.h>   For **fputc** and **_fputchar**.
#include <wchar.h>   For **fputwc** and **_fputwchar** use STDIO.H or WCHAR.H.

Return Value   Each of these functions returns the character written. For **fputc** and **_fputchar**, a return value of **EOF** indicates an error. For **fputwc** and **_fputwchar**, a return value of **WEOF** indicates an error.

Parameters   *c*   Character to be written
stream   Pointer to **FILE** structure

Remarks   Each of these functions writes the single character *c* to a file at the position indicated by the associated file position indicator (if defined) and advances the indicator as appropriate. In the case of **fputc** and **fputwc**, the file is associated with *stream*. If the file cannot support positioning requests or was opened in append mode, the character is appended to the end of the stream. Routine-specific remarks follow.

Routine	Remarks
fputc	Equivalent to **putc**, but implemented only as a function, rather than as a function and a macro.
fputwc	Wide-character version of **fputc**. Writes *c* as a multibyte character or a wide character according to whether *stream* is opened in text mode or binary mode.
_fputchar	Equivalent to **fputc(stdout)**. Also equivalent to **putchar**, but implemented only as a function, rather than as a function and a macro. Microsoft-specific; not ANSI-compatible.
_fputwchar	Wide-character version of **_fputchar**. Writes *c* as a multibyte character or a wide character according to whether *stream* is opened in text mode or binary mode. Microsoft-specific; not ANSI-compatible.

See Also   **fgetc, putc**

Example

```
/* FPUTC.C: This program uses fputc and _fputchar
 * to send a character array to stdout.
 */

#include <stdio.h>

void main( void )
{
    char strptr1[] = "This is a test of fputc!!\n";
    char strptr2[] = "This is a test of _fputchar!!\n";
    char *p;

    /* Print line to stream using fputc. */
    p = strptr1;
    while( (*p != '\0') && fputc( *(p++), stdout ) != EOF ) ;

    /* Print line to stream using _fputchar. */
    p = strptr2;
    while( (*p != '\0') && _fputchar( *(p++) ) != EOF )
        ;
}
```

Output

```
This is a test of fputc!!
This is a test of _fputchar!!
```

fputs, fputws

int fputs(const char **string***, FILE ****stream** **);**

int fputws(const wchar_t **string***, FILE ****stream** **);**

> **fputs:** ANSI UNIX WIN32S
> **fputws:** ANSI UNIX ~~WIN32S~~
>
> **#include <stdio.h>**   For **fputs**.
> **#include <wchar.h>**   For **fputws** use STDIO.H or WCHAR.H.

Return Value   Each of these functions returns a nonnegative value if it is successful. On an error, **fputs** returns **EOF**, and **fputws** returns **WEOF**.

Parameters   *string*   Output string
stream   Pointer to **FILE** structure

Remarks   Each of these functions copies *string* to the output *stream* at the current position. **fputws** copies the wide-character argument *string* to *stream* as a multibyte-character string or a wide-character string according to whether *stream* is opened in text mode or binary mode, respectively. Neither function copies the terminating null character.

See Also   **fgets, gets, puts**

Example

```
/* FPUTS.C: This program uses fputs to write
 * a single line to the stdout stream.
 */

#include <stdio.h>

void main( void )
{
    fputs( "Hello world from fputs.\n", stdout );
}
```

Output

```
Hello world from fputs.
```

fread

size_t fread(void **buffer*, **size_t** *size*, **size_t** *count*, **FILE** **stream* **);**

ANSI   UNIX   WIN32S

#include <stdio.h>

Return Value

fread returns the number of full items actually read, which may be less than *count* if an error occurs or if the end of the file is encountered before reaching *count*. Use the **feof** or **ferror** function to distinguish a read error from an end-of-file condition. If *size* or *count* is 0, **fread** returns 0 and the buffer contents are unchanged.

Parameters

buffer   Storage location for data
size   Item size in bytes
count   Maximum number of items to be read
stream   Pointer to **FILE** structure

Remarks

The **fread** function reads up to *count* items of *size* bytes from the input *stream* and stores them in *buffer*. The file pointer associated with *stream* (if there is one) is increased by the number of bytes actually read. If the given stream is opened in text mode, carriage-return–linefeed pairs are replaced with single linefeed characters. The replacement has no effect on the file pointer or the return value. The file-pointer position is indeterminate if an error occurs. The value of a partially read item cannot be determined.

See Also

fwrite, _read

Example

```
/* FREAD.C: This program opens a file named FREAD.OUT and
 * writes 25 characters to the file. It then tries to open
 * FREAD.OUT and read in 25 characters. If the attempt succeeds,
 * the program displays the number of actual items read.
 */

#include <stdio.h>

void main( void )
{
   FILE *stream;
   char list[30];
   int  i, numread, numwritten;

   /* Open file in text mode: */
   if( (stream = fopen( "fread.out", "w+t" )) != NULL )
   {
      for ( i = 0; i < 25; i++ )
         list[i] = (char)('z' - i);
      /* Write 25 characters to stream */
      numwritten = fwrite( list, sizeof( char ), 25, stream );
      printf( "Wrote %d items\n", numwritten );
      fclose( stream );
   }
   else
      printf( "Problem opening the file\n" );

   if( (stream = fopen( "fread.out", "r+t" )) != NULL )
   {
      /* Attempt to read in 25 characters */
      numread = fread( list, sizeof( char ), 25, stream );
      printf( "Number of items read = %d\n", numread );
      printf( "Contents of buffer = %.25s\n", list );
      fclose( stream );
   }
   else
      printf( "File could not be opened\n" );
}
```

Output

```
Wrote 25 items
Number of items read = 25
Contents of buffer = zyxwvutsrqponmlkjihgfedcb
```

free

void free(void *memblock);

ANSI   UNIX   WIN32S

#include <stdlib.h>
#include <malloc.h>

Return Value   None

Parameter   *memblock*   Allocated memory block

Remarks   The **free** function deallocates a memory block. The argument *memblock* points to a
                      memory block previously allocated through a call to **calloc**, **malloc**, or **realloc**. A
                      NULL pointer argument is ignored. The number of bytes freed is the number of
                      bytes specified when the block was allocated (or reallocated, in the case of
                      realloc). After the call, the freed block is available for allocation. Attempting to
                      free an invalid pointer may affect subsequent allocation and cause errors. An
                      invalid pointer is one not allocated with the appropriate call.

                      Blocks allocated with **calloc**, **malloc**, and **realloc** should be freed with **free**.

See Also   **_alloca**, **calloc**, **malloc**, **realloc**

Example   See the example for **malloc**.

freopen, _wfreopen

FILE *freopen(const char *path, const char *mode, FILE *stream);

FILE *_wfreopen(const wchar_t *path, const wchar_t *mode, FILE *stream);

freopen: ANSI   UNIX   WIN32S
_wfreopen: ANSI   ~~UNIX~~   ~~WIN32S~~

#include <stdio.h>   For **freopen**.
#include <wchar.h>   For **_wfreopen** use STDIO.H or WCHAR.H.

Return Value   Each of these functions returns a pointer to the newly opened file. If an error occurs,
                      the original file is closed and the function returns a **NULL** pointer value.

Parameters   *path*   Path of new file
                      mode   Type of access permitted
                      stream   Pointer to **FILE** structure

Remarks   The **freopen** function closes the file currently associated with *stream* and reassigns *stream* to the file specified by *path*. _**wfreopen** is a wide-character version of _**freopen**; the *path* and *mode* arguments to _**wfreopen** are wide-character strings. _**wfreopen** and _**freopen** behave identically otherwise.

freopen is typically used to redirect the pre-opened files **stdin**, **stdout**, and **stderr** to files specified by the user. The new file associated with *stream* is opened with *mode,* which is a character string specifying the type of access requested for the file, as follows:

"r"   Opens for reading. If the file does not exist or cannot be found, the **freopen** call fails.

"w"   Opens an empty file for writing. If the given file exists, its contents are destroyed.

"a"   Opens for writing at the end of the file (appending); creates the file first if it does not exist.

"r+"   Opens for both reading and writing. (The file must exist.)

"w+"   Opens an empty file for both reading and writing. If the given file exists, its contents are destroyed.

"a+"   Opens for reading and appending; creates the file first if it does not exist.

Use the **"w"** and **"w+"** types with care, as they can destroy existing files.

When a file is opened with the **"a"** or **"a+"** access type, all write operations take place at the end of the file. Although the file pointer can be repositioned using **fseek** or **rewind**, the file pointer is always moved back to the end of the file before any write operation is carried out. Thus, existing data cannot be overwritten. When the **"r+"**, **"w+"**, or **"a+"** access type is specified, both reading and writing are allowed (the file is said to be open for "update"). However, when you switch between reading and writing, there must be an intervening **fsetpos**, **fseek**, or **rewind** operation. The current position can be specified for the **fsetpos** or **fseek** operation, if desired. In addition to the above values, one of the following characters may be included in the *mode* string to specify the translation mode for new lines.

t   Open in text (translated) mode; carriage-return–linefeed (CR-LF) combinations are translated into single linefeed (LF) characters on input; LF characters are translated to CR-LF combinations on output. Also, CTRL+Z is interpreted as an end-of-file character on input. In files opened for reading or for writing and reading, the run-time library checks for a CTRL+Z at the end of the file and removes it, if possible. This is done because using **fseek** and **ftell** to move within a file may cause **fseek** to behave improperly near the end of the file. The **t** option is a Microsoft extension that should not be used where ANSI portability is desired.

b   Open in binary (untranslated) mode; the above translations are suppressed.

If **t** or **b** is not given in the *mode* string, the translation mode is defined by the default mode variable **_fmode**.

For a discussion of text and binary modes, see "Text and Binary Mode File I/O" on page 12.

See Also   **fclose, _fdopen, _fileno, fopen, _open, _setmode**

Example

```
/* FREOPEN.C: This program reassigns stderr to the file
 * named FREOPEN.OUT and writes a line to that file.
 */

#include <stdio.h>
#include <stdlib.h>

FILE *stream;

void main( void )
{
    /* Reassign "stderr" to "freopen.out": */
    stream = freopen( "freopen.out", "w", stderr );

    if( stream == NULL )
        fprintf( stdout, "error on freopen\n" );
    else
    {
        fprintf( stream, "This will go to the file 'freopen.out'\n" );
        fprintf( stdout, "successfully reassigned\n" );
        fclose( stream );
    }
    system( "type freopen.out" );
}
```

Output

```
successfully reassigned
This will go to the file 'freopen.out
```

frexp

double frexp(double *x*, int **expptr*);

ANSI   UNIX   WIN32S

#include <math.h>

Return Value   **frexp** returns the mantissa. If *x* is 0, the function returns 0 for both the mantissa and the exponent. There is no error return.

Parameters   *x*   Floating-point value
expptr   Pointer to stored integer exponent

Remarks   The **frexp** function breaks down the floating-point value (x) into a mantissa (m) and an exponent (n), such that the absolute value of m is greater than or equal to 0.5 and less than 1.0, and $x = m*2^n$. The integer exponent n is stored at the location pointed to by *expptr*.

See Also   **ldexp, modf**

Example
```
/* FREXP.C: This program calculates frexp( 16.4, &n )
 * then displays y and n.
 */

#include <math.h>
#include <stdio.h>

void main( void )
{
    double x, y;
    int n;

    x = 16.4;
    y = frexp( x, &n );
    printf( "frexp( %f, &n ) = %f, n = %d\n", x, y, n );
}
```

Output
```
frexp( 16.400000, &n ) = 0.512500, n = 5
```

fscanf, fwscanf

int fscanf(FILE **stream,* **const char** **format* [[, *argument*]]... **);**

int fwscanf(FILE **stream,* **const wchar_t** **format* [[, *argument*]]... **);**

fscanf: ANSI   UNIX   WIN32S
fwscanf: ANSI   UNIX   ~~WIN32S~~

#include <stdio.h>   For **fscanf.**
#include <wchar.h>   For **fwscanf** use STDIO.H or WCHAR.H.

Return Value   Each of these functions returns the number of fields successfully converted and assigned; the return value does not include fields that were read but not assigned. A return value of 0 indicates that no fields were assigned. If an error occurs, or if the end of the file stream is reached before the first conversion, the return value is **EOF** for fscanf or **WEOF** for **fwscanf.**

Parameters   *stream*   Pointer to **FILE** structure
format   Format-control string
argument   Optional arguments

Remarks   The **fscanf** function reads data from the current position of *stream* into the locations given by *argument* (if any). Each *argument* must be a pointer to a variable of a type that corresponds to a type specifier in *format*. *format* controls the interpretation of the input fields and has the same form and function as the *format* argument for **scanf**; see **scanf** for a description of *format*. If copying takes place between strings that overlap, the behavior is undefined.

fwscanf is a wide-character version of **fscanf**; the format argument to **fwscanf** is a wide-character string. These functions behave identically otherwise.

See Also   **_cscanf, fprintf, scanf, sscanf**

Example

```
/* FSCANF.C: This program writes formatted
 * data to a file. It then uses fscanf to
 * read the various data back from the file.
 */

#include <stdio.h>

FILE *stream;

void main( void )
{
   long l;
   float fp;
   char s[81];
   char c;

   stream = fopen( "fscanf.out", "w+" );
   if( stream == NULL )
      printf( "The file fscanf.out was not opened\n" );
   else
   {
      fprintf( stream, "%s %ld %f%c", "a-string",
               65000, 3.14159, 'x' );

      /* Set pointer to beginning of file: */
      fseek( stream, 0L, SEEK_SET );

      /* Read data back from file: */
      fscanf( stream, "%s", s );
      fscanf( stream, "%ld", &l );
      fscanf( stream, "%f", &fp );
      fscanf( stream, "%c", &c );
```

```
                        /* Output data read: */
                        printf( "%s\n", s );
                        printf( "%ld\n", l );
                        printf( "%f\n", fp );
                        printf( "%c\n", c );

                        fclose( stream );
                    }
                }
```

Output

```
a-string
65000
3.141590
x
```

fseek

int fseek(FILE **stream*, **long** *offset*, **int** *origin* **);**

ANSI   UNIX   WIN32S

include <stdio.h>

Return Value

If successful, **fseek** returns 0. Otherwise, it returns a nonzero value. On devices incapable of seeking, the return value is undefined.

Parameters

stream   Pointer to **FILE** structure
offset   Number of bytes from *origin*
origin   Initial position

Remarks

The **fseek** function moves the file pointer (if any) associated with *stream* to a new location that is *offset* bytes from *origin*. The next operation on the stream takes place at the new location. On a stream open for update, the next operation can be either a read or a write. The argument origin must be one of the following constants, defined in STDIO.H:

SEEK_CUR   Current position of file pointer

SEEK_END   End of file

SEEK_SET   Beginning of file

You can use **fseek** to reposition the pointer anywhere in a file. The pointer can also be positioned beyond the end of the file. Attempting to position the pointer before the beginning of the file causes an error only if you explicitly link with LSEEKCHK.OBJ (16-bit). **fseek** clears the end-of-file indicator and negates the effect of any prior **ungetc** calls against *stream*.

When a file is opened for appending data, the current file position is determined by the last I/O operation, not by where the next write would occur. If no I/O operation has yet occurred on a file opened for appending, the file position is the start of the file.

For streams opened in text mode, **fseek** has limited use, because carriage-return–linefeed translations can cause **fseek** to produce unexpected results. The only **fseek** operations guaranteed to work on streams opened in text mode are:

- Seeking with an offset of 0 relative to any of the origin values.
- Seeking from the beginning of the file with an offset value returned from a call to **ftell**.

See Also   **ftell**, **_lseek**, **rewind**

Example

```
/* FSEEK.C: This program opens the file FSEEK.OUT and
 * moves the pointer to the file's beginning.
 */

#include <stdio.h>

void main( void )
{
   FILE *stream;
   char line[81];
   int  result;

   stream = fopen( "fseek.out", "w+" );
   if( stream == NULL )
      printf( "The file fseek.out was not opened\n" );
   else
   {
      fprintf( stream, "The fseek begins here: "
                       "This is the file 'fseek.out'.\n" );
      result = fseek( stream, 23L, SEEK_SET);
      if( result )
         perror( "Fseek failed" );
      else
      {
         printf( "File pointer is set to middle of first line.\n" );
         fgets( line, 80, stream );
         printf( "%s", line );
      }
      fclose( stream );
   }
}
```

Output

```
File pointer is set to middle of first line.
This is the file 'fseek.out'.
```

fsetpos

int fsetpos(FILE *_stream_, const fpos_t *_pos_);

ANSI ~~UNIX~~ WIN32S

#include <stdio.h>

Return Value   If successful, **fsetpos** returns 0. On failure, the function returns a nonzero value and sets **errno** to one of the following manifest constants (defined in ERRNO.H): **EBADF**, which means the file is not accessible or the object that _stream_ points to is not a valid file handle; or **EINVAL**, which means an invalid stream value was passed.

Parameters   _stream_   Pointer to **FILE** structure
pos   Position-indicator storage

Remarks   The **fsetpos** function sets the file-position indicator for _stream_ to the value of _pos,_ which is obtained in a prior call to **fgetpos** against _stream._ The function clears the end-of-file indicator and undoes any effects of **ungetc**on _stream._ After calling **fsetpos**, the next operation on _stream_ may be either input or output.

See Also   **fgetpos**

Example   See the example for **fgetpos**.

_fsopen, _wfsopen

FILE *_fsopen(const char *_filename_, const char *_mode_, int _shflag_);

FILE *_wfsopen(const wchar_t *_filename_, const wchar_t *_mode_,
   int _shflag_);

_fsopen: ~~ANSI~~ ~~UNIX~~ WIN32S
_wfsopen: ~~ANSI~~ ~~UNIX~~ ~~WIN32S~~

#include <stdio.h>   For **_fsopen.**
#include <wchar.h>   For **_wfsopen** use STDIO.H or WCHAR.H.
#include <share.h>   _shflag_ constants

Return Value   Each of these functions returns a pointer to the stream. A **NULL** pointer value indicates an error.

Parameters   _filename_   Name of file to open
mode   Type of access permitted
shflag   Type of sharing allowed

Remarks   The **_fsopen** function opens the file specified by *filename* as a stream and prepares the file for subsequent shared reading or writing, as defined by the mode and *shflag* arguments. **_wfsopen** is a wide-character version of **_fsopen**; the *filename* and *mode* arguments to **_wfsopen** are wide-character strings. **_wfsopen** and **_fsopen** behave identically otherwise.

The character string *mode* specifies the type of access requested for the file, as follows:

"r"   Opens for reading. If the file does not exist or cannot be found, the **_fsopen** call fails.

"w"   Opens an empty file for writing. If the given file exists, its contents are destroyed.

"a"   Opens for writing at the end of the file (appending); creates the file first if it does not exist.

"r+"   Opens for both reading and writing. (The file must exist.)

"w+"   Opens an empty file for both reading and writing. If the given file exists, its contents are destroyed.

"a+"   Opens for reading and appending; creates the file first if it does not exist.

Use the **"w"** and **"w+"** types with care, as they can destroy existing files.

When a file is opened with the **"a"** or **"a+"** access type, all write operations occur at the end of the file. The file pointer can be repositioned using **fseek** or **rewind**, but is always moved back to the end of the file before any write operation is carried out. Thus existing data cannot be overwritten. When the **"r+"**, **"w+"**, or **"a+"** access type is specified, both reading and writing are allowed (the file is said to be open for "update"). However, when switching between reading and writing, there must be an intervening **fsetpos**, **fseek**, or **rewind**operation. The current position can be specified for the **fsetpos** or **fseek** operation, if desired. In addition to the above values, one of the following characters can be included in *mode* to specify the translation mode for new lines:

t   Opens a file in text (translated) mode. In this mode, carriage-return–linefeed (CR-LF) combinations are translated into single linefeeds (LF) on input and LF characters are translated to CR-LF combinations on output. Also, CTRL+Z is interpreted as an end-of-file character on input. In files opened for reading or reading/writing, **_fsopen** checks for a CTRL+Z at the end of the file and removes it, if possible. This is done because using **fseek** and **ftell** to move within a file that ends with a CTRL+Z may cause **fseek** to behave improperly near the end of the file.

b   Opens a file in binary (untranslated) mode; the above translations are suppressed.

If **t** or **b** is not given in *mode,* the translation mode is defined by the default-mode variable **_fmode**. If **t** or **b** is prefixed to the argument, the function fails and returns **NULL**. For a discussion of text and binary modes, see "Text and Binary Mode File I/O" on page 12.

The argument *shflag* is a constant expression consisting of one of the following manifest constants, defined in SHARE.H:

_SH_DENYNO   Permits read and write access

_SH_DENYRD   Denies read access to file

_SH_DENYRW   Denies read and write access to file

_SH_DENYWR   Denies write access to file

See Also

fclose, _fdopen, ferror, _fileno, fopen, freopen, _open, _setmode, _sopen

Example

```
/* FSOPEN.C:
 */

#include <stdio.h>
#include <stdlib.h>
#include <share.h>

void main( void )
{
    FILE *stream;

    /* Open output file for writing. Using _fsopen allows us to
     * ensure that no one else writes to the file while we are
     * writing to it.
     */
    if( (stream = _fsopen( "outfile", "wt", _SH_DENYWR )) != NULL )
    {
        fprintf( stream, "No one else in the network can write "
                         "to this file until we are done.\n" );
        fclose( stream );
    }
    /* Now others can write to the file while we read it. */
    system( "type outfile" );
}
```

Output

```
No one else in the network can write to this file until we are done.
```

_fstat

int _fstat(int *handle,* **struct _stat** **buffer* **);**

~~ANSI~~   UNIX   ~~WIN32S~~

Use **_fstat** for compatibility with ANSI naming conventions of non-ANSI functions. Use **fstat** and link with OLDNAMES.LIB for UNIX compatibility.

#include <sys/types.h>
#include <sys/stat.h>

Return Value

_fstat returns 0 if the file-status information is obtained. A return value of −1 indicates an error, in which case **errno** is set to **EBADF**, indicating an invalid file handle.

Parameters

handle   Handle of open file
buffer   Pointer to structure to store results

Remarks

The **_fstat** function obtains information about the open file associated with *handle* and stores it in the structure pointed to by *buffer.* The **_stat** structure, defined in SYS\STAT.H, contains the following fields:

st_atime   Time of last file access.

st_ctime   Time of creation of file.

st_dev   If a device, *handle*; otherwise 0.

st_mode   Bit mask for file-mode information. The **_S_IFCHR** bit is set if *handle* refers to a device. The **_S_IFREG** bit is set if *handle* refers to an ordinary file. The read/write bits are set according to the file's permission mode. **_S_IFCHR** and other constants are defined in SYS\STAT.H.

st_mtime   Time of last modification of file.

st_nlink   Always 1 on non-NTFS file systems.

st_rdev   If a device, *handle*; otherwise 0.

st_size   Size of the file in bytes.

If *handle* refers to a device, the **st_atime, st_ctime,** and **st_mtime** and **st_size** fields are not meaningful.

Because STAT.H uses the **_dev_t** type, which is defined in TYPES.H, you must include TYPES.H before STAT.H in your code.

See Also

_access, _chmod, _filelength, _stat

Example

```
/* FSTAT.C: This program uses _fstat to report
 * the size of a file named F_STAT.OUT.
 */

#include <io.h>
#include <fcntl.h>
#include <time.h>
#include <sys/types.h>
#include <sys/stat.h>
#include <stdio.h>
#include <stdlib.h>
#include <string.h>

void main( void )
{
   struct _stat buf;
   int fh, result;
   char buffer[] = "A line to output";

   if( (fh = _open( "f_stat.out", _O_CREAT | _O_WRONLY |
                                  _O_TRUNC )) == -1 )
   _write( fh, buffer, strlen( buffer ) );

   /* Get data associated with "fh": */
   result = _fstat( fh, &buf );

   /* Check if statistics are valid: */
   if( result != 0 )
      printf( "Bad file handle\n" );
   else
   {
      printf( "File size     : %ld\n", buf.st_size );
      printf( "Time modified : %s", ctime( &buf.st_ctime ) );
   }
   _close( fh );
}
```

Output

```
File size     : 0
Time modified : Tues May 03 07:49:16 1994
```

ftell

long ftell(FILE **stream* **);**

ANSI   UNIX   WIN32S

#include <stdio.h>

Return Value

ftell returns the current file position. The value returned by **ftell** may not reflect the physical byte offset for streams opened in text mode, because text mode causes carriage-return–linefeed translation. Use **ftell** with **fseek** to return to file locations correctly. On error, **ftell** returns −1L and **errno** is set to one of two constants, defined in ERRNO.H. The **EBADF** constant means the *stream* argument is not a valid file-handle value or does not refer to an open file. **EINVAL** means an invalid *stream* argument was passed to the function. On devices incapable of seeking (such as terminals and printers), or when *stream* does not refer to an open file, the return value is undefined.

Parameter

stream   Target **FILE** structure

Remarks

The **ftell** function gets the current position of the file pointer (if any) associated with *stream*. The position is expressed as an offset relative to the beginning of the stream.

Note that when a file is opened for appending data, the current file position is determined by the last I/O operation, not by where the next write would occur. For example, if a file is opened for an append and the last operation was a read, the file position is the point where the next read operation would start, not where the next write would start. (When a file is opened for appending, the file position is moved to end of file before any write operation.) If no I/O operation has yet occurred on a file opened for appending, the file position is the beginning of the file.

See Also

fgetpos, fseek, _lseek, _tell

Example

```
/* FTELL.C: This program opens a file named FTELL.C
 * for reading and tries to read 100 characters. It
 * then uses ftell to determine the position of the
 * file pointer and displays this position.
 */

#include <stdio.h>

FILE *stream;
```

```
void main( void )
{
    long position;
    char list[100];
    if( (stream = fopen( "ftell.c", "rb" )) != NULL )
    {
        /* Move the pointer by reading data: */
        fread( list, sizeof( char ), 100, stream );
        /* Get position after read: */
        position = ftell( stream );
        printf( "Position after trying to read 100 bytes: %ld\n",
                position );
        fclose( stream );
    }
}
```

Output   `Position after trying to read 100 bytes: 100`

_ftime

void _ftime(struct _timeb *_timeptr_);

~~ANSI~~ ~~UNIX~~ WIN32S

#include <sys/types.h>
#include <sys/timeb.h>

Return Value   _ftime gives values to the fields in the structure pointed to by _timeptr_. It does not return a value.

Parameter   _timeptr_   Pointer to structure defined in SYS\TIMEB.H

Remarks   The **_ftime** function gets the current time and stores it in the structure pointed to by _timeptr_. The **_timeb** structure is defined in SYS\TIMEB.H. It contains four fields:

dstflag   Nonzero if daylight saving time is currently in effect for the local time zone. (See **_tzset** for an explanation of how daylight saving time is determined.)

millitm   Fraction of a second in milliseconds.

time   Time in seconds since midnight (00:00:00), January 1, 1970, universal coordinated time (UCT).

timezone   Difference in minutes, moving westward, between UCT and local time. The value of _timezone_ is set from the value of the global variable **_timezone** (see **_tzset**).

See Also   **asctime, ctime, gmtime, localtime, time**

Example

```
/* FTIME.C: This program uses _ftime to obtain the current
 * time and then stores this time in timebuffer.
 */

#include <stdio.h>
#include <sys/timeb.h>
#include <time.h>

void main( void )
{
    struct _timeb timebuffer;
    char *timeline;

    _ftime( &timebuffer );
    timeline = ctime( & ( timebuffer.time ) );

    printf( "The time is %.19s.%hu %s", timeline, timebuffer.millitm,
            &timeline[20] );
}
```

Output

```
The time is Tues May 03 08:01:41.946 1994
```

_fullpath, _wfullpath

char *_fullpath(char *_buffer_, const char *_path_, size_t _maxlen_);

**wchar_t *_wfullpath(wchar_t *_buffer_, const wchar_t *_path_,
    size_t _maxlen_);**

> **_fullpath:** ~~ANSI~~ ~~UNIX~~ WIN32S
> **_wfullpath:** ~~ANSI~~ ~~UNIX~~ ~~WIN32S~~
>
> **#include <stdlib.h>**   For **_fullpath**.
> **#include <wchar.h>**   For **_wfullpath** use STDLIB.H or WCHAR.H.

Return Value

Each of these functions returns a pointer to the buffer containing the absolute path (_buffer_). If there is an error (for example, if the _path_ argument specifies a drive that is not valid, or if the length of the fully qualified path is greater than the value of _maxlen_) the function returns **NULL**.

Parameters

buffer   Full path buffer
path   Relative path
maxlen   Length of the buffer pointed to by _buffer_

Remarks   The **_fullpath** function converts the partial path stored in *path* to a fully qualified path that is stored in *buffer*. **_fullpath** automatically handles multibyte-character string arguments as appropriate, recognizing multibyte-character sequences according to the multibyte code page currently in use. **_wfullpath** is a wide-character version of **_fullpath**; the string arguments to **_wfullpath** are wide-character strings. **_wfullpath** and **_fullpath** behave identically except that **_wfullpath** does not handle multibyte-character strings.

Unlike **_makepath**, **_fullpath** can be used with ./ and ../ in the path. If buffer is **NULL**, **_fullpath** calls **malloc** to allocate a buffer of size **_MAX_PATH** and ignores the *maxlen* argument. It is the caller's responsibility to deallocate this buffer (using **free**) as appropriate. If the *path* argument specifies a disk drive, the current directory of this drive is combined with the path.

See Also   **_getcwd, _getdcwd, _makepath, _splitpath**

Example
```
/* FULLPATH.C: This program demonstrates how _fullpath
 * creates a full path from a partial path.
 */

#include <stdio.h>
#include <conio.h>
#include <stdlib.h>
#include <direct.h>

char full[_MAX_PATH], part[_MAX_PATH];

void main( void )
{
   while( 1 )
   {
      printf( "Enter partial path or ENTER to quit: " );
      gets( part );
      if( part[0] == 0 )
         break;

      if( _fullpath( full, part, _MAX_PATH ) != NULL )
         printf( "Full path is: %s\n", full );
      else
         printf( "Invalid path\n" );
   }
}
```

_futime

int _futime(int *handle*, struct _utimbuf **filetime*);

~~ANSI~~ ~~UNIX~~ ~~WIN32S~~

#include <sys/utime.h>

Return Value

_futime returns 0 if successful. A return value of −1 indicates an error; in this case, **errno** is set to **EBADF**, indicating an invalid file handle.

Parameters

handle   Handle to open file
filetime   Pointer to structure containing new modification date

Remarks

The **_futime** routine sets the modification date and the access time on the open file associated with *handle*. **_futime** is identical to **_utime**, except that its argument is the handle to an open file, rather than the name of a file or a path to a file. The **_utimbuf** structure contains fields for the new modification date and access time. Both fields must contain valid values.

Example

```
/* FUTIME.C: This program uses _futime to set the
 * file-modification time to the current time.
 */

#include <stdio.h>
#include <stdlib.h>
#include <fcntl.h>
#include <io.h>
#include <sys/types.h>
#include <sys/stat.h>
#include <sys/utime.h>

void main( void )
{

    int hFile;

    /* Show file time before and after. */
    system( "dir futime.c" );

    hFile = _open("futime.c", _O_RDWR);

    if( _futime( hFile, NULL ) == -1 )
       perror( "_futime failed\n" );
    else
       printf( "File time modified\n" );
    system( "dir futime.c" );
}
```

Output

```
Volume in drive C is CDRIVE
Volume Serial Number is 0E17-1702

Directory of C:\code

05/03/94  08:06p                   578 FUTIME.C
              1 File(s)            578 bytes
                          80,396,288 bytes free
Volume in drive C is CDRIVE
Volume Serial Number is 0E17-1702

Directory of C:\code

05/03/94  08:07p                   578 FUTIME.C
              1 File(s)            578 bytes
                          80,396,288 bytes free
File time modified
```

fwrite

size_t fwrite(const void *buffer**, size_t** size**, size_t** count**, FILE ***stream **);**

ANSI   UNIX   WIN32S

#include <stdio.h>

Return Value   **fwrite** returns the number of full items actually written, which may be less than *count* if an error occurs. Also, if an error occurs, the file-position indicator cannot be determined.

Parameters   *buffer*   Pointer to data to be written
size   Item size in bytes
count   Maximum number of items to be written
stream   Pointer to **FILE** structure

Remarks   The **fwrite** function writes up to *count* items, of *size* length each, from *buffer* to the output *stream*. The file pointer associated with *stream* (if there is one) is incremented by the number of bytes actually written. If *stream* is opened in text mode, each carriage return is replaced with a carriage-return–linefeed pair. The replacement has no effect on the return value.

See Also   **fread**, **_write**

Example   See the example for **fread**.

_gcvt

char *_gcvt(double *value***, int** *digits***, char** **buffer* **);**

~~ANSI~~   UNIX   WIN32S

Use **_gcvt** for compatibility with ANSI naming conventions of non-ANSI functions. Use **gcvt** and link with OLDNAMES.LIB for UNIX compatibility.

#include <stdlib.h>

Return Value   **_gcvt** returns a pointer to the string of digits. There is no error return.

Parameters   *value*   Value to be converted
digits   Number of significant digits stored
buffer   Storage location for result

Remarks   The **_gcvt** function converts a floating-point *value* to a character string (which includes a decimal point and a possible sign byte) and stores the string in *buffer*. The *buffer* should be large enough to accommodate the converted value plus a terminating null character, which is appended automatically. If a buffer size of *digits* + 1 is used, the function overwrites the end of the buffer. This is because the converted string includes a decimal point and can contain sign and exponent information. There is no provision for overflow. **_gcvt** attempts to produce *digits* digits in decimal format. If it cannot, it produces *digits* digits in exponential format. Trailing zeros may be suppressed in the conversion.

See Also   **atof, _ecvt, _fcvt**

Example
```
/* _GCVT.C: This program converts -3.1415e5
 * to its string representation.
 */

#include <stdlib.h>
#include <stdio.h>

void main( void )
{
   char buffer[50];
   double source = -3.1415e5;
   _gcvt( source, 7, buffer );
   printf( "source: %f  buffer: '%s'\n", source, buffer );
   _gcvt( source, 7, buffer );
   printf( "source: %e  buffer: '%s'\n", source, buffer );
}
```

Output
```
source: -314150.000000  buffer: '-314150.'
source: -3.141500e+005  buffer: '-314150.'
```

getc, getwc, getchar, getwchar

int getc(FILE **stream* **);**

wint_t getwc(FILE **stream* **);**

int getchar(void);

wint_t getwchar(void);

> **getc, getchar:**   ANSI   UNIX   WIN32S
> **getwc, getwchar:**   ANSI   UNIX   ~~WIN32S~~
>
> **#include <stdio.h>**   For **getc** and **getchar**.
> **#include <wchar.h>**   For **getwc** and **getwchar** use STDIO.H or WCHAR.H.

Return Value   Each of these functions returns the character read. To indicate an read error or end-of-file condition, **getc** and **getchar** return **EOF**, and **getwc** and **getwchar** return **WEOF**. For **getc** and **getchar**, use **ferror** or **feof** to check for an error or for end of file.

Parameter   *stream*   Input stream

Remarks   Each of these routines reads a single character from a file at the current position and increments the associated file pointer (if defined) to point to the next character. In the case of **getc** and **getwc**, the file is associated with *stream* (see "Choosing Between Functions and Macros" on page viii). Routine-specific remarks follow.

Routine	Remarks
getc	Same as **fgetc**, but implemented as a function and as a macro.
getwc	Wide-character version of **getc**. Reads a multibyte character or a wide character according to whether *stream* is opened in text mode or binary mode.
getchar	Same as **_fgetchar**, but implemented as a function and as a macro.
getwchar	Wide-character version of **getchar**. Reads a multibyte character or a wide character according to whether *stream* is opened in text mode or binary mode.

See Also   **fgetc, _getch, putc, ungetc**

Example
```
/* GETC.C: This program uses getchar to read a single line
 * of input from stdin, places this input in buffer, then
 * terminates the string before printing it to the screen.
 */

#include <stdio.h>
```

```
void main( void )
{
    char buffer[81];
    int i, ch;

    printf( "Enter a line: " );

    /* Read in single line from "stdin": */
    for( i = 0; (i < 80) && ((ch = getchar()) != EOF)
                    && (ch != '\n'); i++ )
        buffer[i] = (char)ch;

    /* Terminate string with null character: */
    buffer[i] = '\0';
    printf( "%s\n", buffer );
}
```

Output

```
Enter a line: This is a test
This is a test
```

_getch, _getche

int _getch(void);

int _getche(void);

~~ANSI~~ ~~UNIX~~ WIN32S

#include <conio.h>

Return Value Both **_getch** and **_getche** return the character read. There is no error return.

Remarks The **_getch** function reads a single character from the console without echoing. **_getche** reads a single character from the console and echoes the character read. Neither function can be used to read CTRL+C. When reading a function key or an arrow key, **_getch** and **_getche** must be called twice; the first call returns 0 or 0xE0, and the second call returns the actual key code.

See Also **_cgets, getc, _ungetch**

Example

```
/* GETCH.C: This program reads characters from
 * the keyboard until it receives a 'Y' or 'y'.
 */

#include <conio.h>
#include <ctype.h>

void main( void )
{
   int ch;

   _cputs( "Type 'Y' when finished typing keys: " );
   do
   {
      ch = _getch();
      ch = toupper( ch );
   } while( ch != 'Y' );

   _putch( ch );
   _putch( '\r' );     /* Carriage return */
   _putch( '\n' );     /* Line feed       */
}
```

Output

```
Type 'Y' when finished typing keys: Y
```

_getcwd, _wgetcwd

char *_getcwd(char **buffer***, int** *maxlen* **);**

wchar_t *_wgetcwd(wchar_t **buffer***, int** *maxlen* **);**

_getcwd: ~~ANSI~~   UNIX   WIN32S
_wgetcwd: ~~ANSI~~   ~~UNIX~~   ~~WIN32S~~

Use **_getcwd** for compatibility with ANSI naming conventions of non-ANSI functions. Use **getcwd** and link with OLDNAMES.LIB for UNIX compatibility.

#include <direct.h>   For **_getcwd**.
#include <wchar.h>   For **_wgetcwd** use DIRECT.H or WCHAR.H.

Return Value

Each of these functions returns a pointer to *buffer*. A **NULL** return value indicates an error, and **errno** is set either to **ENOMEM**, indicating that there is insufficient memory to allocate *maxlen* bytes (when a **NULL** argument is given as *buffer*), or to **ERANGE**, indicating that the path is longer than *maxlen* characters.

Parameters

buffer   Storage location for path
maxlen   Maximum length of path

Remarks

The **_getcwd** function gets the full path of the current working directory for the default drive and stores it at *buffer*. The integer argument *maxlen* specifies the maximum length for the path. An error occurs if the length of the path (including the terminating null character) exceeds *maxlen*. The *buffer* argument can be **NULL**; a buffer of at least size *maxlen* (more only if necessary) will automatically be allocated, using **malloc**, to store the path. This buffer can later be freed by calling **free** and passing it the **_getcwd** return value (a pointer to the allocated buffer).

_getcwd returns a string that represents the path of the current working directory. If the current working directory is the root, the string ends with a backslash (\ ). If the current working directory is a directory other than the root, the string ends with the directory name and not with a backslash.

_wgetcwd is a wide-character version of **_getcwd**; the *buffer* argument and return value of **_wgetcwd** are wide-character strings. **_wgetcwd** and **_getcwd** behave identically otherwise.

See Also   **_chdir, _mkdir, _rmdir**

Example
```
// GETCWD.C
/* This program places the name of the current directory in the
 * buffer array, then displays the name of the current directory
 * on the screen. Specifying a length of _MAX_PATH leaves room
 * for the longest legal path name.
 */

#include <direct.h>
#include <stdlib.h>
#include <stdio.h>

void main( void )
{
    char buffer[_MAX_PATH];

    /* Get the current working directory: */
    if( _getcwd( buffer, _MAX_PATH ) == NULL )
        perror( "_getcwd error" );
    else
        printf( "%s\n", buffer );
}
```

Output   C:\msvc20

_getdcwd, _wgetdcwd

char *_getdcwd(int *drive***, char ****buffer***, int** *maxlen* **);**

wchar_t *_wgetdcwd(int *drive***, wchar_t ****buffer***, int** *maxlen* **);**

_getdcwd: ~~ANSI~~ ~~UNIX~~ WIN32S
_wgetdcwd: ~~ANSI~~ ~~UNIX~~ ~~WIN32S~~

#include <direct.h> For **_getdcwd**.
#include <wchar.h> For **_wgetdcwd** use DIRECT.H or WCHAR.H.

Return Value

Each of these functions returns *buffer*. A **NULL** return value indicates an error, and **errno** is set either to **ENOMEM**, indicating that there is insufficient memory to allocate *maxlen* bytes (when a **NULL** argument is given as *buffer*), or to **ERANGE**, indicating that the path is longer than *maxlen* characters.

Parameters

drive   Disk drive
buffer   Storage location for path
maxlen   Maximum length of path

Remarks

The **_getdcwd** function gets the full path of the current working directory on the specified drive and stores it at *buffer*. An error occurs if the length of the path (including the terminating null character) exceeds *maxlen*. The *drive* argument specifies the drive (0 = default drive, 1 = A, 2 = B, and so on). The *buffer* argument can be **NULL**; a buffer of at least size *maxlen* (more only if necessary) will automatically be allocated, using **malloc**, to store the path. This buffer can later be freed by calling **free** and passing it the **_getdcwd** return value (a pointer to the allocated buffer).

_getdcwd returns a string that represents the path of the current working directory. If the current working directory is set to the root, the string ends with a backslash (\). If the current working directory is set to a directory other than the root, the string ends with the name of the directory and not with a backslash.

_wgetdcwd is a wide-character version of **_getdcwd**; the *buffer* argument and return value of **_wgetdcwd** are wide-character strings. **_wgetdcwd** and **_getdcwd** behave identically otherwise.

See Also

_chdir, _getcwd, _getdrive, _mkdir, _rmdir

Example

See the example for **_getdrive**.

_getdrive

int _getdrive(void);

~~ANSI~~ ~~UNIX~~ WIN32S

#include <direct.h>

Return Value

_getdrive returns the current (default) drive (1=A, 2=B, and so on). There is no error return.

See Also

_chdrive, _getcwd, _getdcwd

Example

```
/* GETDRIVE.C illustrates drive functions including:
 *      _getdrive       _chdrive        _getdcwd
 */

#include <stdio.h>
#include <conio.h>
#include <direct.h>
#include <stdlib.h>
#include <ctype.h>

void main( void )
{
    int ch, drive, curdrive;
    static char path[_MAX_PATH];

    /* Save current drive. */
    curdrive = _getdrive();

    printf( "Available drives are: \n" );

    /* If we can switch to the drive, it exists. */
    for( drive = 1; drive <= 26; drive++ )
      if( !_chdrive( drive ) )
         printf( "%c: ", drive + 'A' - 1 );
```

```
while( 1 )
{
    printf( "\nType drive letter to check or ESC to quit: " );
    ch = _getch();
    if( ch == 27 )
        break;
    if( isalpha( ch ) )
        _putch( ch );
    if( _getdcwd( toupper( ch ) - 'A' + 1, path, _MAX_PATH ) != NULL )
        printf( "\nCurrent directory on that drive is %s\n", path );
}

/* Restore original drive.*/
_chdrive( curdrive );
printf( "\n" );
}
```

Output

```
Available drives are:
A: B: C: L: M: O: U: V:
Type drive letter to check or ESC to quit: c
Current directory on that drive is C:\CODE

Type drive letter to check or ESC to quit: m
Current directory on that drive is M:\

Type drive letter to check or ESC to quit:
```

getenv, _wgetenv

char *getenv(const char *varname **);**

wchar_t *_wgetenv(const wchar_t *varname **);**

getenv: ANSI   UNIX   WIN32S
_wgetenv: ~~ANSI~~   ~~UNIX~~   ~~WIN32S~~

#include <stdlib.h>   For **getenv**.
#include <wchar.h>   For **_wgetenv** use STDLIB.H or WCHAR.H.

Return Value   Each of these functions returns a pointer to the environment table entry containing *varname*. It is not safe to modify the value of the environment variable using the returned pointer. Use the **_putenv** function to modify the value of an environment variable. The return value is **NULL** if *varname* is not found in the environment table.

Parameter   *varname*   Environment variable name

Remarks

The **getenv** function searches the list of environment variables for *varname*. **getenv** is not case sensitive in Windows NT. **getenv** and **_putenv** use the copy of the environment pointed to by the global variable **_environ** to access the environment. **getenv** operates only on the data structures accessible to the run-time library and not on the environment "segment" created for the process by the operating system. Therefore, programs that use the *envp* argument to **main** or **wmain** may retrieve invalid information. For more information on **wmain**, see "Using **wmain**" in the *C Language Reference*.

_wgetenv is a wide-character version of **getenv**; the argument and return value of **_wgetenv** are wide-character strings. The **_wenviron** global variable is a wide-character version of **_environ**.

In an MBCS program (for example, in an SBCS ASCII program), **_wenviron** is initially **NULL** because the environment is composed of multibyte-character strings. Then, on the first call to **_wputenv**, or on the first call to **_wgetenv** if an (MBCS) environment already exists, a corresponding wide-character string environment is created and is then pointed to by **_wenviron**.

Similarly in a Unicode (**_wmain**) program, **_environ** is initially **NULL** because the environment is composed of wide-character strings. Then, on the first call to **_putenv**, or on the first call to **getenv** if a (Unicode) environment already exists, a corresponding MBCS environment is created and is then pointed to by **_environ**.

When two copies of the environment (MBCS and Unicode) exist simultaneously in a program, the run-time system must maintain both copies, resulting in slower execution time. For example, whenever you call **_putenv**, a call to **_wputenv** is also executed automatically, so that the two environment strings correspond.

Caution In rare instances, when the run-time system is maintaining both a Unicode version and a multibyte version of the environment, these two environment versions may not correspond exactly. This is because, although any unique multibyte-character string maps to a unique Unicode string, the mapping from a unique Unicode string to a multibyte-character string is not necessarily unique. For more information, see "**_environ** and **_wenviron**" on page 40.

To check or change the value of the **TZ** environment variable, use **getenv**, **_putenv** and **_tzset** as necessary. For more information about **TZ**, see **_tzset** and "**_daylight, timezone,** and **_tzname**" on page 38.

See Also

_putenv

Example

```
/* GETENV.C: This program uses getenv to retrieve
 * the LIB environment variable and then uses
 * _putenv to change it to a new value.
 */

#include <stdlib.h>
#include <stdio.h>

void main( void )
{
   char *libvar;

   /* Get the value of the LIB environment variable. */
   libvar = getenv( "LIB" );

   if( libvar != NULL )
      printf( "Original LIB variable is: %s\n", libvar );

   /* Attempt to change path. Note that this only affects the
environment
      * variable of the current process. The command processor's
environment
      * is not changed.
      */
   _putenv( "LIB=c:\\mylib;c:\\yourlib" );

   /* Get new value. */
   libvar = getenv( "LIB" );

   if( libvar != NULL )
      printf( "New LIB variable is: %s\n", libvar );
}
```

Output

```
Original LIB variable is: C:\MSVC20
New LIB variable is: c:\mylib;c:\yourlib
```

_getmbcp

int _getmbcp (void);

~~ANSI~~ ~~UNIX~~ ~~WIN32S~~

#include <mbstring.h>

Return Value

_getmbcp returns the current multibyte code page. A return value of 0 indicates that a single byte code page is in use.

See Also   **_setmbcp**

_get_osfhandle

long _get_osfhandle (int *filehandle***);**

~~ANSI~~   ~~UNIX~~   ~~WIN32S~~

#include <io.h>

Return Value   If successful, **_get_osfhandle** returns an operating-system file handle corresponding to *filehandle*. Otherwise, it returns −1 and sets **errno** to **EBADF**, indicating an invalid file handle.

Parameter   *filehandle*   User file handle

Remarks   The **_get_osfhandle** function returns *filehandle* if it is in range and if it is internally marked as free.

See Also   **_close, _creat, _dup, _open**

_getpid

int _getpid(void);

~~ANSI~~   UNIX   WIN32S

Use **_getpid** for compatibility with ANSI naming conventions of non-ANSI functions. Use **getpid** and link with OLDNAMES.LIB for UNIX compatibility.

#include <process.h>

Return Value   **_getpid** returns the process ID obtained from the system. There is no error return.

Remarks   The **_getpid** function obtains the process ID from the system. The process ID uniquely identifies the calling process.

See Also   **_mktemp**

Example
```
/* GETPID.C: This program uses _getpid to obtain
 * the process ID and then prints the ID.
 */

#include <stdio.h>
#include <process.h>

void main( void )
{
    /* If run from command line, shows different ID for
     * command line than for operating system shell.
     */
    printf( "\nProcess id: %d\n", _getpid() );
}
```

Output   `Process id: 193`

gets, getws

char *gets(char **buffer***);**

wchar_t *getws(wchar_t **buffer***);**

> **gets:**   ANSI   UNIX   WIN32S
> **getws:**   ANSI   UNIX   ~~WIN32S~~
>
> **#include <stdio.h>**   For **gets**.
> **#include <wchar.h>**   For **getws** use STDIO.H or WCHAR.H.

Return Value   Each of these functions returns its argument if successful. A **NULL** pointer indicates an error or end-of-file condition. Use **ferror** or **feof** to determine which one has occurred.

Parameter   *buffer*   Storage location for input string

Remarks   The **gets** function reads a line from the standard input stream **stdin** and stores it in *buffer*. The line consists of all characters up to and including the first newline character ('\n'). **gets** then replaces the newline character with a null character ('\0') before returning the line. In contrast, the **fgets** function retains the newline character. **getws** is a wide-character version of **gets**; its argument and return value are wide-character strings.

See Also   **fgets, fputs, puts**

Example
```
/* GETS.C */

#include <stdio.h>

void main( void )
{
    char line[81];

    printf( "Input a string: " );
    gets( line );
    printf( "The line entered was: %s\n", line );
}
```

Output
```
Input a string: Hello!
The line entered was: Hello!
```

_getw

int _getw(FILE *stream);

~~ANSI~~   UNIX   WIN32S

Use **_getw** for compatibility with ANSI naming conventions of non-ANSI functions. Use **getw** and link with OLDNAMES.LIB for UNIX compatibility. **getw** is provided only for backward compatibility. Problems with porting may occur with **_getw** because the size of the **int** type and the ordering of bytes within the **int** type differ across systems.

#include <stdio.h>

Return Value

_getw returns the integer value read. A return value of **EOF** indicates either an error or end of file. However, because the **EOF** value is also a legitimate integer value, use **feof** or **ferror** to verify an end-of-file or error condition.

Parameter

stream   Pointer to **FILE** structure

Remarks

The **_getw** function reads the next binary value of type **int** from the file associated with *stream* and increments the associated file pointer (if there is one) to point to the next unread character. **_getw** does not assume any special alignment of items in the stream.

See Also

_putw

Example

```
/* GETW.C: This program uses _getw to read a word
 * from a stream, then performs an error check.
 */

#include <stdio.h>
#include <stdlib.h>

void main( void )
{
   FILE *stream;
   int i;

   if( (stream = fopen( "getw.c", "rb" )) == NULL )
     printf( "Couldn't open file\n" );
   else
   {
      /* Read a word from the stream: */
      i = _getw( stream );
```

```
                      /* If there is an error... */
                      if( ferror( stream ) )
                      {
                          printf( "_getw failed\n" );
                          clearerr( stream );
                      }
                      else
                          printf( "First data word in file: 0x%.4x\n", i );
                      fclose( stream );
                  }
              }
```

Output   First data word in file: 0x47202a2f

gmtime

struct tm *gmtime(const time_t **timer***);**

ANSI   UNIX   WIN32S

#include <time.h>

Return Value   **gmtime** returns a pointer to a structure of type **tm**. The fields of the returned structure hold the evaluated value of the *timer* argument in UCT rather than in local time. Each of the structure fields is of type **int,** as follows:

tm_sec   Seconds after minute (0–59)

tm_min   Minutes after hour (0–59)

tm_hour   Hours since midnight (0–23)

tm_mday   Day of month (1–31)

tm_mon   Month (0–11; January = 0)

tm_year   Year (current year minus 1900)

tm_wday   Day of week (0–6; Sunday = 0)

tm_yday   Day of year (0–365; January 1 = 0)

tm_isdst Always 0 for **gmtime**

The **gmtime, mktime,** and **localtime** functions use the same single, statically allocated structure to hold their results. Each call to one of these functions destroys the result of any previous call. If *timer* represents a date before midnight, January 1, 1970, **gmtime** returns **NULL**. There is no error return.

Parameter

timer   Pointer to stored time. The time is represented as seconds elapsed since midnight (00:00:00), January 1, 1970, universal coordinated time (UCT).

Remarks

The **gmtime** function breaks down the *timer* value and stores it in a statically allocated structure of type **tm**, defined in TIME.H. The value of *timer* is usually obtained from a call to the **time** function.

Note   The target environment should try to determine whether daylight saving time is in effect.

See Also

asctime, ctime, _ftime, localtime, mktime, time

Example

```
/* GMTIME.C: This program uses gmtime to convert a long-
 * integer representation of universal coordinated time
 * to a structure named newtime, then uses asctime to
 * convert this structure to an output string.
 */

#include <time.h>
#include <stdio.h>

void main( void )
{
    struct tm *newtime;
    long ltime;

    time( &ltime );

    /* Obtain universal coordinated time: */
    newtime = gmtime( &ltime );
    printf( "Universal coordinated time is %s\n",
                                asctime( newtime ) );
}
```

Output

```
Universal coordinated time is Wed May 04 01:01:25 1994
```

_heapadd

int _heapadd(void *memblock***, size_t** *size* **);**

ANSI UNIX WIN32S

#include <malloc.h>

Return Value	**_heapadd** returns 0 if successful or −1 if an error occurred.
Parameters	*memblock* Pointer to heap memory
	size Size in bytes of memory to add
Remarks	The **_heapadd** function adds an unused piece of memory to the heap.
See Also	**free, _heapchk, _heapmin, _heapset, _heapwalk, malloc, realloc**

_heapchk

int _heapchk(void);

ANSI UNIX WIN32S

#include <malloc.h>

Return Value   **_heapchk** returns one of the following integer manifest constants defined in MALLOC.H:

_HEAPBADBEGIN   Initial header information is bad or cannot be found

_HEAPBADNODE   Bad node has been found or heap is damaged

_HEAPBADPTR   Pointer into heap is not valid

_HEAPEMPTY   Heap has not been initialized

_HEAPOK   Heap appears to be consistent

Remarks   The **_heapchk** function helps debug heap-related problems by checking for minimal consistency of the heap.

See Also   _heapadd, _heapmin, _heapset, _heapwalk

Example

```c
/* HEAPCHK.C: This program checks the heap for
 * consistency and prints an appropriate message.
 */

#include <malloc.h>
#include <stdio.h>

void main( void )
{
   int  heapstatus;
   char *buffer;

   /* Allocate and deallocate some memory */
   if( (buffer = (char *)malloc( 100 )) != NULL )
      free( buffer );

   /* Check heap status */
   heapstatus = _heapchk();
   switch( heapstatus )
   {
   case _HEAPOK:
      printf(" OK - heap is fine\n" );
      break;
   case _HEAPEMPTY:
      printf(" OK - heap is empty\n" );
      break;
   case _HEAPBADBEGIN:
      printf( "ERROR - bad start of heap\n" );
      break;
   case _HEAPBADNODE:
      printf( "ERROR - bad node in heap\n" );
      break;
   }
}
```

Output

```
OK - heap is fine
```

_heapmin

int _heapmin(void);

ANSI   UNIX   WIN32S

#include <malloc.h>

Return Value   _heapmin returns 0 if the function completed successfully or −1 in the case of an error.

Remarks   The **_heapmin** function minimizes the heap by releasing unused heap memory to the operating system.

See Also   **free, _heapadd, _heapchk, _heapset, _heapwalk, malloc**

_heapset

int _heapset(unsigned int *fill* **);**

ANSI   UNIX   WIN32S

#include <malloc.h>

Return Value   **_heapset** returns one of the following integer manifest constants defined in MALLOC.H:

_HEAPBADBEGIN   Initial header information invalid or not found

_HEAPBADNODE   Heap damaged or bad node found

_HEAPEMPTY   Heap not initialized

_HEAPOK   Heap appears to be consistent

Parameter   *fill*   Fill character

Remarks   The **_heapset** function shows free memory locations or nodes that have been unintentionally overwritten.

_heapset checks for minimal consistency on the heap, then sets each byte of the heap's free entries to the *fill* value. This known value shows which memory locations of the heap contain free nodes and which contain data that were unintentionally written to freed memory.

See Also   **_heapadd, _heapchk , _heapmin, _heapwalk**

Example

```
/* HEAPSET.C: This program checks the heap and
 * fills in free entries with the character 'Z'.
 */

#include <malloc.h>
#include <stdio.h>
#include <stdlib.h>

void main( void )
{
   int heapstatus;
   char *buffer;

   if( (buffer = malloc( 1 )) == NULL ) /* Make sure heap is */
      exit( 0 );                        /*    initialized    */
   heapstatus = _heapset( 'Z' );        /* Fill in free entries */
   switch( heapstatus )
   {
   case _HEAPOK:
      printf( "OK - heap is fine\n" );
      break;
   case _HEAPEMPTY:
      printf( "OK - heap is empty\n" );
      break;
   case _HEAPBADBEGIN:
      printf( "ERROR - bad start of heap\n" );
      break;
   case _HEAPBADNODE:
      printf( "ERROR - bad node in heap\n" );
      break;
   }
   free( buffer );
}
```

Output

```
OK - heap is fine
```

_heapwalk

int _heapwalk(_HEAPINFO *entryinfo);

~~ANSI~~   ~~UNIX~~   WIN32S

#include <malloc.h>

Return Value   _heapwalk returns one of the following integer manifest constants defined in MALLOC.H:

_HEAPBADBEGIN   Initial header information invalid or not found

_HEAPBADNODE   Heap damaged or bad node found

_HEAPBADPTR   **_pentry** field of **_HEAPINFO** structure does not contain valid pointer into heap

_HEAPEND   End of heap reached successfully

_HEAPEMPTY   Heap not initialized

_HEAPOK   No errors so far; **_HEAPINFO** structure contains information about next entry.

Parameter   *entryinfo*   Buffer to contain heap information

Remarks   The **_heapwalk** function helps debug heap-related problems in programs. The function walks through the heap, traversing one entry per call, and returns a pointer to a structure of type **_HEAPINFO** that contains information about the next heap entry. The **_HEAPINFO** type, defined in MALLOC.H, contains the following elements:

int *_pentry   Heap entry pointer

size_t _size   Size of heap entry

int _useflag   Flag that indicates whether heap entry is in use

A call to **_heapwalk** that returns **_HEAPOK** stores the size of the entry in the **_size** field and sets the **_useflag** field to either **_FREEENTRY** or **_USEDENTRY** (both are constants defined in MALLOC.H). To obtain this information about the first entry in the heap, pass **_heapwalk** a pointer to a **_HEAPINFO** structure whose **_pentry** member is **NULL**.

See Also   **_heapadd, _heapchk, _heapmin, _heapset**

Example
```
/* HEAPWALK.C: This program "walks" the heap, starting
 * at the beginning (_pentry = NULL). It prints out each
 * heap entry's use, location, and size. It also prints
 * out information about the overall state of the heap as
 * soon as _heapwalk returns a value other than _HEAPOK.
 * The output is abridged to save space.
 */

#include <stdio.h>
#include <malloc.h>
```

```
void heapdump( void );

void main( void )
{
   char *buffer;

   heapdump();
   if( (buffer = malloc( 59 )) != NULL )
   {
      heapdump();
      free( buffer );
   }
   heapdump();
}

void heapdump( void )
{
   _HEAPINFO hinfo;
   int heapstatus;
   hinfo._pentry = NULL;
   while( ( heapstatus = _heapwalk( &hinfo ) ) == _HEAPOK )
   { printf( "%6s block at %Fp of size %4.4X\n",
         ( hinfo._useflag == _USEDENTRY ? "USED" : "FREE" ),
            hinfo._pentry, hinfo._size );
   }

   switch( heapstatus )
   {
   case _HEAPEMPTY:
      printf( "OK - empty heap\n" );
      break;
   case _HEAPEND:
      printf( "OK - end of heap\n" );
      break;
   case _HEAPBADPTR:
      printf( "ERROR - bad pointer to heap\n" );
      break;
   case _HEAPBADBEGIN:
      printf( "ERROR - bad start of heap\n" );
      break;
   case _HEAPBADNODE:
      printf( "ERROR - bad node in heap\n" );
      break;
   }
}
```

Output
```
        USED block at 002C0004 of size 0014
        USED block at 002C001C of size 0054
        USED block at 002C0074 of size 0024
        USED block at 002C009C of size 0010
        USED block at 002C00B0 of size 0018
        USED block at 002C00CC of size 000C
        USED block at 002C00DC of size 001C
        USED block at 002C00FC of size 0010
        USED block at 002C0110 of size 0014
        USED block at 002C0128 of size 0010
        USED block at 002C013C of size 0028
        USED block at 002C0168 of size 0088
        USED block at 002C01F4 of size 001C
        USED block at 002C0214 of size 0014
        USED block at 002C022C of size 0010
        USED block at 002C0240 of size 0014
        USED block at 002C0258 of size 0010
        USED block at 002C026C of size 000C
        USED block at 002C027C of size 0010
        USED block at 002C0290 of size 0014
        USED block at 002C02A8 of size 0010
        USED block at 002C02BC of size 0010
        USED block at 002C02D0 of size 1000
        FREE block at 002C12D4 of size ED2C
OK - end of heap
        .
        .
        .
```

_hypot

double _hypot(double *x*, double *y*);

~~ANSI~~   UNIX   WIN32S

Use **_hypot** for compatibility with ANSI naming conventions of non-ANSI functions. Use **hypot** and link with OLDNAMES.LIB for UNIX compatibility.

#include <math.h>

Return Value

_hypot returns the length of the hypotenuse if successful or INF (infinity) on overflow. The **errno** variable is set to **ERANGE** on overflow. You can modify error handling with **_matherr**.

Parameters

x, *y*   Floating-point values

Remarks

The **_hypot** function calculates the length of the hypotenuse of a right triangle, given the length of the two sides *x* and *y*. A call to **_hypot** is equivalent to the square root of $x^2 + y^2$.

See Also   _cabs, _matherr

Example
```
/* HYPOT.C: This program prints the
 * hypotenuse of a right  triangle.
 */

#include <math.h>
#include <stdio.h>

void main( void )
{
    double x = 3.0, y = 4.0;

    printf( "If a right triangle has sides %2.1f and %2.1f, "
            "its hypotenuse is %2.1f\n", x, y, _hypot( x, y ) );
}
```

Output   If a right triangle has sides 3.0 and 4.0, its hypotenuse is 5.0

_inp, _inpw, _inpd

int _inp(unsigned short *port* **);**

unsigned short _inpw(unsigned short *port* **);**

unsigned long _inpd(unsigned short *port* **);**

~~ANSI~~ ~~UNIX~~ WIN32S

#include <conio.h>

Return Value   The functions return the byte, word, or double word read from *port*. There is no error return.

Parameter   *port*   Port number

Remarks   The **_inp**, **_inpw**, and **_inpd** functions read a byte, a word, and a double word, respectively, from the specified input port. The input value can be any unsigned short integer in the range 0–65,535.

See Also   **_outp**

is, isw Routines

int isalnum(int *c*);

int isalpha(int *c*);

int __isascii(int *c*);

int iscntrl(int *c*);

int __iscsym(int *c*);

int __iscsymf(int *c*);

int isdigit(int *c*);

int isgraph(int *c*);

int islower(int *c*);

int isprint(int *c*);

int ispunct(int *c*);

int isspace(int *c*);

int isupper(int *c*);

int isxdigit(int *c*);

int iswalnum(wint_t *c*);

int iswalpha(wint_t *c*);

int iswascii(wint_t *c*);

int iswcntrl(wint_t *c*);

int iswctype(wint_t *c*, wctype_t *desc*);

int iswdigit(wint_t *c*);

int iswgraph(wint_t *c*);

int iswlower(wint_t *c*);

int iswprint(wint_t *c*);

int iswpunct(wint_t *c*);

int iswspace(wint_t *c*);

int iswupper(wint_t *c*);

int iswxdigit(wint_t *c*);

isalnum, isalpha, iscntrl, isdigit, isgraph, islower, isprint, ispunct, isspace, isupper, isxdigit, iswxdigit: ANSI UNIX WIN32S
__isascii: ~~ANSI~~ UNIX WIN32S
__iscsym, __iscsymf: ~~ANSI~~ ~~UNIX~~ WIN32S
iswalnum, iswalpha, iswascii, iswcntrl, iswctype, iswdigit, iswgraph, iswlower, iswprint, iswpunct, iswspace, iswupper: ANSI UNIX ~~WIN32S~~

Use **__isascii** for compatibility with ANSI naming conventions of non-ANSI functions. Use **isascii** and link with OLDNAMES.LIB for UNIX compatibility.

#include <ctype.h>   For **is** routines.
#include <wchar.h>   For **isw** routines use CTYPE.H or WCHAR.H.

Return Value

Each of the **is** and **isw** routines returns a nonzero value if the integer satisfies the test condition or 0 if it does not.

Parameters

c   Integer to test
desc   Property to test for

Remarks

The **is** routines produce meaningful results for any integer argument from −1 (**EOF**) to **UCHAR_MAX** (0xFF), inclusive. The expected argument type is **int**.

Warning For the **is** routines, passing an argument of type **char** may yield unpredictable results. An SBCS or MBCS single-byte character of type **char** with a value greater than 0x7F is negative. If a **char** is passed, the compiler may convert the value to a signed **int** or a signed **long**. This value may be sign-extended by the compiler, with unexpected results.

The **isw** routines produce meaningful results for any integer value from 0 (**WEOF**) to 0xFFFF, inclusive. The **wint_t** data type is defined in WCHAR.H as an **unsigned short**; it can hold any wide character or the wide-character end-of-file (**WEOF**) value.

For each of the **is** routines, the result of the test for the specified condition depends on the **LC_CTYPE** category setting of the current locale; see **setlocale** for more information. In the "C" locale, the test conditions for the **is** routines are as follows:

isalnum   Alphanumeric (A–Z, a–z, or 0–9)

isalpha   Alphabetic (A–Z or a–z)

__isascii   ASCII character (0x00–0x7F)

iscntrl   Control character (0x00–0x1F or 0x7F)

__iscsym   Letter, underscore, or digit

__iscsymf   Letter or underscore

isdigit   Decimal digit (0–9)

isgraph   Printable character except space ( )

islower   Lowercase letter (a–z)

isprint   Printable character (0x20–0x7E)

ispunct   Punctuation character

isspace   White-space character (0x09–0x0D or 0x20)

isupper   Uppercase letter (A–Z)

isxdigit   Hexadecimal digit (A–F, a–f, or 0–9)

The test result of all **isw** routines is independent of the locale. The test conditions for the **isw** functions are as follows:

iswalnum   iswalpha or iswdigit

iswalpha   Any wide character that is one of an implementation-defined set for which none of iswcntrl, iswdigit, iswpunct, or iswspace is true. iswalpha returns true only for wide characters for which iswupper or iswlower is true.

iswascii   Wide-character representation of ASCII character.

iswcntrl   Control wide character.

iswctype   Character has property specified by the *desc* argument. For each valid value of the *desc* argument of **iswctype**, there is an equivalent wide-character classification routine, as shown in the following table:

R.2   Equivalence of iswctype(*c*, *desc*) to Other isw Testing Routines

Value of *desc* Argument	iswctype(*c*, *desc*) Equivalent
_ALPHA	iswalpha(*c*)
_ALPHA I _DIGIT	iswalnum(*c*)
_CONTROL	iswcntrl(*c*)
_DIGIT	iswdigit(*c*)
_ALPHA I _DIGIT I _PUNCT	iswgraph(*c*)
_LOWER	iswlower(*c*)
_ALPHA I _BLANK I _DIGIT I _PUNCT	iswprint(*c*)
_PUNCT	iswpunct(*c*)
_SPACE	iswspace(*c*)
_UPPER	iswupper(*c*)
_HEX	iswxdigit(*c*)

iswdigit   Wide character corresponding to a decimal-digit character.

iswgraph   Printable wide character except space wide character (L' ').

iswlower   Lowercase letter, or one of implementation-defined set of wide characters for which none of **iswcntrl**, **iswdigit**, **iswpunct**, or **iswspace** is true. **iswlower** returns true only for wide characters that correspond to lowercase letters.

iswprint   Printable wide character, including space wide character (L' ').

iswpunct   Printable wide character that is neither space wide character (L' ') nor wide character for which **iswalnum** is true.

iswspace   Wide character that corresponds to standard white-space character or is one of implementation-defined set of wide characters for which **iswalnum** is false. Standard white-space characters are: space (L' '), formfeed (L'\f'), newline (L'\n'), carriage return (L'\r'), horizontal tab (L'\t'), and vertical tab (L'\v').

iswupper   Wide character that is uppercase or is one of an implementation-defined set of wide characters for which none of **iswcntrl**, **iswdigit**, **iswpunct**, or **iswspace** is true. **iswupper** returns true only for wide characters that correspond to uppercase characters.

iswxdigit   Wide character that corresponds to a hexadecimal-digit character.

See Also   **setlocale, to** Functions

Example

```
/* ISFAM.C: This program tests all characters between 0x0
 * and 0x7F, then displays each character with abbreviations
 * for the character-type codes that apply. The output has
 * been abridged to save space.
 */

#include <stdio.h>
#include <ctype.h>

void main( void )
{
   int ch;
   for( ch = 0; ch <= 0x7F; ch++ )
   {
      printf( "%.2x  ", ch );
      printf( " %c", isprint( ch )  ? ch   : '\0' );
      printf( "%4s", isalnum( ch )  ? "AN" : "" );
      printf( "%3s", isalpha( ch )  ? "A"  : "" );
      printf( "%3s", __isascii( ch )  ? "AS" : "" );
      printf( "%3s", iscntrl( ch )  ? "C"  : "" );
      printf( "%3s", __iscsym( ch )  ? "CS " : "" );
      printf( "%3s", __iscsymf( ch )  ? "CSF" : "" );
      printf( "%3s", isdigit( ch )  ? "D"  : "" );
      printf( "%3s", isgraph( ch )  ? "G"  : "" );
      printf( "%3s", islower( ch )  ? "L"  : "" );
      printf( "%3s", ispunct( ch )  ? "PU" : "" );
      printf( "%3s", isspace( ch )  ? "S"  : "" );
      printf( "%3s", isprint( ch )  ? "PR" : "" );
      printf( "%3s", isupper( ch )  ? "U"  : "" );
      printf( "%3s", isxdigit( ch ) ? "X"  : "" );
      printf( "\n" );
   }
}
```

Output													
00													
01													
02													
.													
.													
.													
20	′		AS							S	PR		
21	!		AS				G	PU			PR		
22	"		AS				G	PU			PR		
.													
.													
.													
39	9	AN	AS	CS		D	G				PR		X
3a	:		AS				G	PU			PR		
3b	;		AS				G	PU			PR		
.													
.													
.													
3f	?		AS				G	PU			PR		
40	@		AS				G	PU			PR		
41	A	AN	A AS	CS CSF			G				PR	U	X
.													
.													
.													
61	a	AN	A AS	CS CSF			G	L			PR		X
62	b	AN	A AS	CS CSF			G	L			PR		X
63	c	AN	A AS	CS CSF			G	L			PR		X
.													
.													
.													

_isatty

int _isatty(int *handle* **);**

~~ANSI~~   UNIX   WIN32S

Use **_isatty** for compatibility with ANSI naming conventions of non-ANSI functions. Use **isatty** and link with OLDNAMES.LIB for UNIX compatibility.

#include <io.h>

Return Value   **_isatty** returns a nonzero value handle is associated with a character device. Otherwise, **_isatty** returns 0.

Parameter   *handle*   Handle referring to device to be tested

Remarks   The **_isatty** function determines whether *handle* is associated with a character
                     device (a terminal, console, printer, or serial port).

Example
```
/* ISATTY.C: This program checks to see whether
 * stdout has been redirected to a file. */

#include <stdio.h>
#include <io.h>

void main( void )
{
   if( _isatty( _fileno( stdout ) ) )
      printf( "stdout has not been redirected to a file\n" );
   else
      printf( "stdout has been redirected to a file\n");
}
```

Output
```
stdout has been redirected to a file
```

isleadbyte

int isleadbyte(int *c*);

ANSI UNIX WIN32S

#include <ctype.h>

Return Value   **isleadbyte** returns a nonzero value if the argument satisfies the test condition or 0 if
                     it does not. In the "C" locale and in single-byte–character set (SBCS) locales,
                     isleadbyte always returns 0.

Parameter   *c*   Integer to test

Remarks   The **isleadbyte** macro returns a nonzero value if its argument is the first byte of a
                     multibyte character. **isleadbyte** produces a meaningful result for any integer
                     argument from −1 (**EOF**) to **UCHAR_MAX** (0xFF), inclusive. The result of the
                     test depends upon the **LC_CTYPE** category setting of the current locale; see
                     setlocale for more information.

The expected argument type of **isleadbyte** is **int**; if a signed character is passed, the compiler may convert it to an integer by sign extension, yielding unpredictable results.

See Also   **_ismbb** Routines

_ismbb Routines

int **_ismbbalnum**(unsigned int *c*);

int **_ismbbalpha**(unsigned int *c*);

int **_ismbbgraph**(unsigned int *c*);

int **_ismbbkalnum**(unsigned int *c*);

int **_ismbbkana**(unsigned int *c*);

int **_ismbbkprint**(unsigned int *c*);

int **_ismbbkpunct**(unsigned int *c*);

int **_ismbblead**(unsigned int *c*);

int **_ismbbprint**(unsigned int *c*);

int **_ismbbpunct**(unsigned int *c*);

int **_ismbbtrail**(unsigned int *c*);

~~ANSI~~   ~~UNIX~~   ~~WIN32S~~

#include <mbctype.h>

Return Value   Each of the **_ismbb** routines returns a nonzero value if the integer satisfies the test condition or 0 if it does not.

Parameter   *c*   Integer to be tested

Remarks   Each routine in the **_ismbb** family tests the given integer value *c* for a particular condition. The test result depends on the multibyte code page in effect. By default, the multibyte code page is set to the system-default ANSI code page obtained from the operating system at program startup. You can query or change the multibyte code page in use with **_getmbcp** or **_setmbcp**, respectively.

Routine	Byte Test Condition
_ismbbalnum	**isalnum ‖ _ismbbkalnum**
_ismbbalpha	**isalpha ‖ _ismbbkalnum**
_ismbbgraph	Same as **_ismbbprint**, but **_ismbbgraph** does not include space character (0x20).
_ismbbkalnum	Non-ASCII text symbol other than punctuation. For example, in code page 932 only, **_ismbbkalnum** tests for katakana alphanumeric.
_ismbbkana	Katakana (0xA1 – 0xDF). Specific to code page 932.
_ismbbkprint	Non-ASCII text or non-ASCII punctuation symbol. For example, in code page 932 only, **_ismbbkprint** tests for katakana alphanumeric or katakana punctuation (range: 0xA1–0xDF).
_ismbbkpunct	Non-ASCII punctuation. For example, in code page 932 only, **_ismbbkpunct** tests for katakana punctuation.
_ismbblead	First byte of multibyte character. For example, in code page 932 only, valid ranges are 0x81–0x9F, 0xE0–0xFC.
_ismbbprint	**isprint ‖ _ismbbkprint. ismbbprint** includes the space character (0x20).
_ismbbpunct	**ispunct ‖ _ismbbkpunct**
_ismbbtrail	Second byte of multibyte character. For example, in code page 932 only, valid ranges are 0x40–0x7E, 0x80–0xEC.

The following table shows the ORed values that compose the test conditions for these routines. The manifest constants **_BLANK**, **_DIGIT**, **_LOWER**, **_PUNCT**, and **_UPPER** are defined in CTYPE.H.

Routine	_BLANK	_DIGIT	_LOWER	_PUNCT	_UPPER	Non-ASCII Text	Non-ASCII Punct
_ismbbalnum	—	x	x	—	x	x	—
_ismbbalpha	—	—	x	—	x	x	—
_ismbbgraph	—	x	x	x	x	x	x
_ismbbkalnum	—	—	—	—	—	x	—
_ismbbkprint	—	—	—	—	—	x	x
_ismbbkpunct	—	—	—	—	—	—	x
_ismbbprint	x	x	x	x	x	x	x
_ismbbpunct	—	—	—	x	—	—	x

The **_ismbb** routines are implemented both as functions and as macros. For details on choosing either implementation, see "Choosing Between Functions and Macros" on page viii.

See Also   is Routines, **_mbbtombc**, **_mbctombb**

ismbc Routines

int _ismbcalnum(unsigned int c);

int _ismbcalpha(unsigned int c);

int _ismbcdigit(unsigned int c);

int _ismbcgraph(unsigned int c);

int _ismbchira(unsigned int c);

int _ismbckata(unsigned int c);

int _ismbcl0(unsigned int c);

int _ismbcl1(unsigned int c);

int _ismbcl2(unsigned int c);

int _ismbclegal(unsigned int c);

int _ismbclower(unsigned int c);

int _ismbcprint(unsigned int c);

int _ismbcpunct(unsigned int c);

int _ismbcspace(unsigned int c);

int _ismbcsymbol(unsigned int c);

int _ismbcupper(unsigned int c);

~~ANSI~~ ~~UNIX~~ ~~WIN32S~~

#include <mbstring.h>

Return Value   Each of these routines returns a nonzero value if the character satisfies the test condition or 0 if it does not. If $c <= 255$ and there is a corresponding **_ismbb** routine (for example, **_ismbcalnum** corresponds to **_ismbbalnum**), the result is the return value of the corresponding **_ismbb** routine.

Parameter c Character to be tested

Remarks

The test result of each of the **_ismbc** routines depends on the multibyte code page in effect. By default, the multibyte code page is set to the system-default ANSI code page obtained from the operating system at program startup. You can query or change the multibyte code page in use with **_getmbcp** or **_setmbcp**, respectively.

Each of these routines tests a given multibyte character for a particular condition.

Routine	Character Test Condition
_ismbcalnum	Alphanumeric
_ismbcalpha	Alphabetic. For example, in code page 932, **_ismbcalpha** returns true if and only if $0x41 <= c <= 0x51$ or $0x61 <= c <= 0x7A$.
_ismbcdigit	Digit. For example, in code page 932, **_ismbcdigit** returns true if and only if $0x30 <= c <= 0x39$.
_ismbcgraph	Graphic
_ismbclegal	Valid multibyte character. For example, in code page 932, first byte must be within ranges $0x81 - 0x9F$ or $0xE0 - 0xFC$, while second byte must be within ranges $0x40 - 0x7E$ or $0x80 - FC$.
_ismbclower	Lowercase alphabetic. For example, in code page 932, **_ismbclower** returns true if and only if $0x61 <= c <= 0x7A$..
_ismbcprint	Printable
_ismbcpunct	Punctuation
_ismbcspace	Whitespace. For example, in code page 932, **_ismbcspace** returns true if and only if $c = 0x20$ or $0x09 <= c <= 0x0D$.
_ismbcsymbol	Multibyte symbol. For example, in code page 932, **_ismbcsymbol** returns true if and only if $0x8141 <= c <= 0x81AC$.
_ismbcupper	Uppercase alphabetic. For example, in code page 932, **_ismbcupper** returns true if and only if $0x41 <= c <= 0x5A$.

Code Page 932 Specific →
The following routines are specific to code page 932.

Routine (Code Page 932 Only)	Character Test Condition
_ismbchira	Double-byte hiragana ($0x829F <= c <= 0x82F1$)
_ismbckata	Double-byte katakana ($0x8340 <= c <= 0x8396$)
_ismbcl0	JIS non-Kanji ($0x8140 <= c <= 0x889E$)
_ismbcl1	JIS level-1 ($0x889F <= c <= 0x9872$)
_ismbcl2	JIS level-2 ($0x989F <= c <= 0xEA9E$)

_ismbcl0, **_ismbcl1**, and **_ismbcl2** check that the specified value c matches the test conditions described in the preceding table, but do not check that c is a valid multibyte character. If the lower byte is in the ranges 0x00–0x3F, 0x7F, or 0xFD–0xFF, each of these routines returns a nonzero value, indicating that the character

satisfies the test condition. Use **_ismbbtrail** to test whether the multibyte character is defined.

END Code Page 932 Specific

See Also   **is** Routines, **_ismbb** Routines

_ismbslead, _ismbstrail

int **_ismbslead**(**const unsigned char** **string*, **const unsigned char** **current*);

int **_ismbstrail**(**const unsigned char** **string*, **const unsigned char** **current*);

    ~~ANSI~~   ~~UNIX~~   ~~WIN32S~~

    #include <mbctype.h>

Return Value   **_ismbslead** and **_ismbstrail** return –1 if the character is a lead or trail byte, respectively. Otherwise they return zero.

Parameters   *string*   Pointer to start of string or previous known lead byte
              current   Pointer to position in string to be tested

Remarks   The **_ismbslead** and **_ismbstrail** routines perform context-sensitive tests for multibyte-character string lead and trail bytes; they determine whether a given substring pointer points to a lead byte or a trail byte. **_ismbslead** and **_ismbstrail** are slower than their **_ismbblead** and **_ismbbtrail** counterparts because they take the string context into account.

See Also   **is** Routines, **_ismbb** Routines

_isnan

int   **_isnan**(**double** *x*);

    ~~ANSI~~   ~~UNIX~~   WIN32S

    #include <float.h>

Return Value   **_isnan** returns a nonzero value (TRUE) if the argument *x* is a NaN; otherwise it returns 0 (FALSE).

Parameter   *x*   Double-precision floating-point value

Remarks   The **_isnan** function tests a given double-precision floating-point value *x*, returning a nonzero value if *x* is a NaN. A NaN is generated when the result of a floating-point operation cannot be represented in Institute of Electrical and Electronics Engineers (IEEE) format. For information about how a NaN is represented for output, see **printf**.

See Also   **_finite, _fpclass**

_itoa, _itow

char *_itoa(int *value***, char ****string***, int** *radix* **);**

wchar_t * _itow (int *value***, wchar_t ****string***, int** *radix* **);**

_itoa: ~~ANSI~~ ~~UNIX~~ WIN32S
_itow: ~~ANSI~~ ~~UNIX~~ ~~WIN32S~~

#include <stdlib.h>   For **_itoa.**
#include <wchar.h>   For **_itow** use STDIO.H or WCHAR.H.

Return Value   Each of these functions returns a pointer to *string*. There is no error return.

Parameters   *value*   Number to be converted
                  string String result
                  radix   Base of *value*; must be in the range 2–36

Remarks   The **_itoa** function converts the digits of the given *value* argument to a null-terminated character string and stores the result (up to 17 bytes) in *string*. If *radix* equals 10 and *value* is negative, the first character of the stored string is the minus sign (–). **_itow** is a wide-character version of **_itoa**.

See Also   **_ltoa, _ultoa**

Example

```
/* ITOA.C: This program converts integers of various
 * sizes to strings in various radixes.
 */

#include <stdlib.h>
#include <stdio.h>

void main( void )
{
   char buffer[20];
   int  i = 3445;
   long l = -344115L;
   unsigned long ul = 1234567890UL;

   _itoa( i, buffer, 10 );
   printf( "String of integer %d (radix 10): %s\n", i, buffer );
   _itoa( i, buffer, 16 );
   printf( "String of integer %d (radix 16): 0x%s\n", i, buffer );
   _itoa( i, buffer, 2  );
   printf( "String of integer %d (radix 2): %s\n", i, buffer );

   _ltoa( l, buffer, 16 );
   printf( "String of long int %ld (radix 16): 0x%s\n", l,
                                               buffer );
```

```
                      _ultoa( ul, buffer, 16 );
                      printf( "String of unsigned long %lu (radix 16): 0x%s\n", ul,
                                                                        buffer );
                  }
```

Output

```
String of integer 3445 (radix 10): 3445
String of integer 3445 (radix 16): 0xd75
String of integer 3445 (radix 2): 110101110101
String of long int -344115 (radix 16): 0xfffabfcd
String of unsigned long 1234567890 (radix 16): 0x499602d2
```

_kbhit

int _kbhit(void);

~~ANSI~~ ~~UNIX~~ WIN32S

#include <conio.h>

Return Value **_kbhit** returns a nonzero value if a key has been pressed. Otherwise, it returns 0.

Remarks The **_kbhit** function checks the console for a recent keystroke. If the function returns a nonzero value, a keystroke is waiting in the buffer. The program can then call **_getch** or **_getche** to get the keystroke.

Example
```
/* KBHIT.C: This program loops until the user
 * presses a key. If _kbhit returns nonzero, a
 * keystroke is waiting in the buffer. The program
 * can call _getch or _getche to get the keystroke.
 */

#include <conio.h>
#include <stdio.h>

void main( void )
{
   /* Display message until key is pressed. */
   while( !_kbhit() )
      _cputs( "Hit me!! " );

   /* Use _getch to throw key away. */
   printf( "\nKey struck was '%c'\n", _getch() );
   _getch();
}
```

Output

```
Hit me!! Hit me!! Hit me!! Hit me!! Hit me!! Hit me!! Hit me!!
Key struck was 'q'
```

labs

long labs(long *n*);

ANSI   ~~UNIX~~   WIN32S

#include <stdlib.h>
#include <math.h>

Return Value   The **labs** function returns the absolute value of its argument. There is no error return.

Parameter   *n*   Long-integer value

See Also   **abs, _cabs, fabs**

Example   See the example for **abs**.

ldexp

double ldexp(double *x*, int *exp*);

ANSI   UNIX   WIN32S

#include <math.h>

Return Value   The **ldexp** function returns the value of $x * 2^{exp}$ if successful. On overflow (depending on the sign of x), **ldexp** returns +/–**HUGE_VAL**; the **errno** variable is set to **ERANGE**.

Parameters   *x*   Floating-point value
exp   Integer exponent

See Also   **frexp, modf**

Example

```
/* LDEXP.C */

#include <math.h>
#include <stdio.h>

void main( void )
{
    double x = 4.0, y;
    int p = 3;

    y = ldexp( x, p );
    printf( "%2.1f times two to the power of %d is %2.1f\n", x, p, y );
}
```

Output

```
4.0 times two to the power of 3 is 32.0
```

ldiv

ldiv_t ldiv (long int *numer*, **long int** *denom* **);**

ANSI ~~UNIX~~ WIN32S

#include <stdlib.h>

Return Value

ldiv returns a structure of type **ldiv_t** that comprises both the quotient and the remainder.

Parameters

numer   Numerator
denom   Denominator

Remarks

The **ldiv** function divides *numer* by *denom*, computing the quotient and remainder. The sign of the quotient is the same as that of the mathematical quotient. The absolute value of the quotient is the largest integer that is less than the absolute value of the mathematical quotient. If the denominator is 0, the program terminates with an error message. **ldiv** is the same as **div**, except that the arguments of **ldiv** and the members of the returned structure are all of type **long int**.

The **ldiv_t** structure, defined in STDLIB.H, contains **long int quot**, the quotient, and **long int rem**, the remainder.

See Also

div

Example

```
/* LDIV.C: This program takes two long integers
 * as command-line arguments and displays the
 * results of the integer division.
 */

#include <stdlib.h>
#include <math.h>
#include <stdio.h>

void main( void )
{
    long x = 5149627, y = 234879;
    ldiv_t div_result;

    div_result = ldiv( x, y );
    printf( "For %ld / %ld, the quotient is ", x, y );
    printf( "%ld, and the remainder is %ld\n",
            div_result.quot, div_result.rem );
}
```

Output

```
For 5149627 / 234879, the quotient is 21, and the remainder is 217168
```

_lfind

void *_lfind(const void *_key_**, const void ***_base_**, unsigned int ***_num_**, unsigned int** _width_**,
    int (_ _ cdecl ***_compare_**)(const void ***_elem1_**, const void ***_elem2_**));**

~~ANSI~~ UNIX   WIN32S

Use **_lfind** for compatibility with ANSI naming conventions of non-ANSI
functions. Use **lfind** and link with OLDNAMES.LIB for UNIX compatibility.

#include <search.h>

Return Value

If the key is found, **_lfind** returns a pointer to the element of the array at _base_ that
matches _key_. If the key is not found, **_lfind** returns **NULL**.

Parameters	*key* Object to search for
	base Pointer to base of search data
	num Number of array elements
	width Width of array elements
	compare Pointer to comparison routine
	elem1 Pointer to key for search
	elem2 Pointer to array element to be compared with key

Remarks

The **_lfind** function performs a linear search for the value *key* in an array of *num* elements, each of *width* bytes in size. Unlike **bsearch**, **_lfind** does not require the array to be sorted. The *base* argument is a pointer to the base of the array to be searched. The *compare* argument is a pointer to a user-supplied routine that compares two array elements and then returns a value specifying their relationship. **_lfind** calls the *compare* routine one or more times during the search, passing pointers to two array elements on each call. The *compare* routine must compare the elements then return nonzero, meaning the elements are different, or 0, meaning the elements are identical.

See Also

bsearch, **_lsearch**, **qsort**

Example

```
/* LFIND.C: This program uses _lfind to search for
 * the word "hello" in the command-line arguments.
 */

#include <search.h>
#include <string.h>
#include <stdio.h>

int compare( const void *arg1, const void *arg2 );

void main( unsigned int argc, char **argv )
{
    char **result;
    char *key = "hello";

    result = (char **)_lfind( &key, argv,
                        &argc, sizeof(char *), compare );
    if( result )
        printf( "%s found\n", *result );
    else
        printf( "hello not found!\n" );
}

int compare(const void *arg1, const void *arg2 )
{
    return( _stricmp( * (char**)arg1, * (char**)arg2 ) );
}
```

Output   [C:\code]lfind Hello
                           Hello found

localeconv

struct lconv *localeconv(void);

                           ANSI   ~~UNIX~~   WIN32S

                           #include <locale.h>

Return Value   **localeconv** returns a pointer to a filled-in object of type **struct lconv**. The values
                           contained in the object can be overwritten by subsequent calls to **localeconv** and do
                           not directly modify the object. Calls to **setlocale** with *category* values of **LC_ALL**,
                           LC_MONETARY, or **LC_NUMERIC** overwrite the contents of the structure.

Remarks   The **localeconv** function gets detailed information about numeric formatting for the
                           current locale. This information is stored in a structure of type **lconv**. The **lconv**
                           structure, defined in LOCALE.H, contains the following members:

                           char *decimal_point   Decimal-point character for nonmonetary quantities.

                           char *thousands_sep   Character that separates groups of digits to left of decimal
                           point for nonmonetary quantities.

                           char *grouping   Size of each group of digits in nonmonetary quantities.

                           char *int_curr_symbol   International currency symbol for current locale. First
                           three characters specify alphabetic international currency symbol as defined in the
                           ISO 4217 Codes for the Representation of Currency and Funds standard. Fourth
                           character (immediately preceding null character) separates international currency
                           symbol from monetary quantity.

                           char *currency_symbol   Local currency symbol for current locale.

                           char *mon_decimal_point   Decimal-point character for monetary quantities.

                           char *mon_thousands_sep   Separator for groups of digits to left of decimal place
                           in monetary quantities.

                           char *mon_grouping   Size of each group of digits in monetary quantities.

                           char *positive_sign   String denoting sign for nonnegative monetary quantities.

                           char *negative_sign   String denoting sign for negative monetary quantities.

char int_frac_digits   Number of digits to right of decimal point in internationally formatted monetary quantities.

char frac_digits   Number of digits to right of decimal point in formatted monetary quantities.

char p_cs_precedes   Set to 1 if currency symbol precedes value for nonnegative formatted monetary quantity. Set to 0 if symbol follows value.

char p_sep_by_space   Set to 1 if currency symbol is separated by space from value for nonnegative formatted monetary quantity. Set to 0 if there is no space separation.

char n_cs_precedes   Set to 1 if currency symbol precedes value for negative formatted monetary quantity. Set to 0 if symbol succeeds value.

char n_sep_by_space   Set to 1 if currency symbol is separated by space from value for negative formatted monetary quantity. Set to 0 if there is no space separation.

char p_sign_posn   Position of positive sign in nonnegative formatted monetary quantities.

char n_sign_posn   Position of positive sign in negative formatted monetary quantities.

The **char *** members of the structure are pointers to strings. Any of these (other than **char *decimal_point**) that equals "" is either of zero length or is not supported in the current locale. The **char** members of the structure are nonnegative numbers. Any of these that equals **CHAR_MAX** is not supported in the current locale.

The elements of **grouping** and **mon_grouping** are interpreted according to the following rules.

CHAR_MAX   Do not perform any further grouping:

0   Use previous element for each of remaining digits.

n   Number of digits that make up current group. Next element is examined to determine size of next group of digits before current group.

The values for **int_curr_symbol** are interpreted according to the following rules:

The first three characters specify the alphabetic international currency symbol as defined in the *ISO 4217 Codes for the Representation of Currency and Funds* standard.

The fourth character (immediately preceding the null character) separates the international currency symbol from the monetary quantity.

The values for **p_cs_precedes** and **n_cs_precedes** are interpreted according to the following rules (the **n_cs_precedes** rule is in parentheses):

0   Currency symbol follows value for nonnegative (negative) formatted monetary value.

1   Currency symbol precedes value for nonnegative (negative) formatted monetary value.

The values for **p_sep_by_space** and **n_sep_by_space** are interpreted according to the following rules (the **n_sep_by_space** rule is in parentheses):

0   Currency symbol is separated from value by space for nonnegative (negative) formatted monetary value.

1   There is no space separation between currency symbol and value for nonnegative (negative) formatted monetary value.

The values for **p_sign_posn** and **n_sign_posn** are interpreted according to the following rules:

0   Parentheses surround quantity and currency symbol

1   Sign string precedes quantity and currency symbol

2   Sign string follows quantity and currency symbol

3   Sign string immediately precedes currency symbol

4   Sign string immediately follows currency symbol

See Also   **setlocale**, **strcoll** Functions, **strftime**, **strxfrm**

localtime

struct tm *localtime(const time_t *timer**);**

ANSI   UNIX   WIN32S

#include <time.h>

Return Value   **localtime** returns a pointer to the structure result. If the value in *timer* represents a date before midnight, January 1, 1970, **localtime** returns **NULL**. The fields of the structure type **tm** store the following values, each of which is an **int**:

tm_sec   Seconds after minute (0–59)

tm_min   Minutes after hour (0–59)

tm_hour   Hours after midnight (0–23)

tm_mday   Day of month (1–31)

tm_mon   Month (0–11; January = 0)

tm_year   Year (current year minus 1900)

tm_wday   Day of week (0–6; Sunday = 0)

tm_yday   Day of year (0–365; January 1 = 0)

tm_isdst   Positive value if daylight saving time is in effect; 0 if daylight saving time is not in effect; negative value if status of daylight saving time is unknown

Parameter   *timer*   Pointer to stored time

Remarks   The **localtime** function converts a time stored as a **time_t** value and stores the result in a structure of type **tm**. The **long** value *timer* represents the seconds elapsed since midnight (00:00:00), January 1, 1970, universal coordinated time. This value is usually obtained from the **time** function.

gmtime, **mktime**, and **localtime** all use a single statically allocated **tm** structure for the conversion. Each call to one of these routines destroys the result of the previous call.

localtime corrects for the local time zone if the user first sets the global environment variable **TZ**. When **TZ** is set, three other environment variables (**_timezone**, **_daylight**, and **_tzname**) are automatically set as well. See **_tzset** for a description of these variables. **TZ** is a Microsoft extension and not part of the ANSI standard definition of **localtime**.

Note   The target environment should try to determine whether daylight saving time is in effect.

See Also   **asctime**, **ctime**, **_ftime**, **gmtime**, **time**, **_tzset**

Example

```
/* LOCALTIM.C: This program uses time to get the current time
 * and then uses localtime to convert this time to a structure
 * representing the local time. The program converts the result
 * from a 24-hour clock to a 12-hour clock and determines the
 * proper extension (AM or PM).
 */

#include <stdio.h>
#include <string.h>
#include <time.h>

void main( void )
{
        struct tm *newtime;
        char am_pm[] = "AM";
        time_t long_time;

        time( &long_time );                    /* Get time as long integer.
*/
        newtime = localtime( &long_time ); /* Convert to local time. */

        if( newtime->tm_hour > 12 )          /* Set up extension. */
                strcpy( am_pm, "PM" );
        if( newtime->tm_hour > 12 )          /* Convert from 24-hour */
                newtime->tm_hour -= 12;      /*   to 12-hour clock.  */
        if( newtime->tm_hour == 0 )          /*Set hour to 12 if midnight.
*/
                newtime->tm_hour = 12;

        printf( "%.19s %s\n", asctime( newtime ), am_pm );
}
```

Output

```
Tue Mar 23 11:28:17 AM
```

_locking

int _locking(int *handle***, int** *mode***, long** *nbytes* **);**

~~ANSI~~   UNIX   WIN32S

Use **_locking** for compatibility with ANSI naming conventions of non-ANSI functions. Use **locking** and link with OLDNAMES.LIB for UNIX compatibility.

#include <sys/locking.h>
#include <io.h>

Return Value   **_locking** returns 0 if successful. A return value of –1 indicates failure, in which case **errno** is set to one of the following values:

EACCES   Locking violation (file already locked or unlocked).

EBADF   Invalid file handle.

EDEADLOCK   Locking violation. Returned when the **_LK_LOCK** or **_LK_RLCK** flag is specified and the file cannot be locked after 10 attempts.

EINVAL   An invalid argument was given to **_locking**.

Parameters

handle   File handle
mode   Locking action to perform
nbytes   Number of bytes to lock

Remarks

The **_locking** function locks or unlocks *nbytes* bytes of the file specified by *handle*. Locking bytes in a file prevents access to those bytes by other processes. All locking or unlocking begins at the current position of the file pointer and proceeds for the next *nbytes* bytes. It is possible to lock bytes past end of file.

mode must be one of the following manifest constants, which are defined in LOCKING.H:

_LK_LOCK   Locks the specified bytes. If the bytes cannot be locked, the program immediately tries again after 1 second. If, after 10 attempts, the bytes cannot be locked, the constant returns an error.

_LK_NBLCK   Locks the specified bytes. If the bytes cannot be locked, the constant returns an error.

_LK_NBRLCK   Same as **_LK_NBLCK**.

_LK_RLCK   Same as **_LK_LOCK**.

_LK_UNLCK   Unlocks the specified bytes, which must have been previously locked.

Multiple regions of a file that do not overlap can be locked. A region being unlocked must have been previously locked. **_locking** does not merge adjacent regions; if two locked regions are adjacent, each region must be unlocked separately. Regions should be locked only briefly and should be unlocked before closing a file or exiting the program.

See Also

_creat, **_open**

Example

```
/* LOCKING.C: This program opens a file with sharing. It locks
 * some bytes before reading them, then unlocks them. Note that the
 * program works correctly only if the file exists.
 */

#include <io.h>
#include <sys/types.h>
#include <sys/stat.h>
#include <sys/locking.h>
#include <share.h>
#include <fcntl.h>
#include <stdio.h>
#include <stdlib.h>

void main( void )
{
    int  fh, numread;
    char buffer[40];

    /* Quit if can't open file or system doesn't
     * support sharing.
     */
    fh = _sopen( "locking.c", _O_RDWR, _SH_DENYNO,
                 _S_IREAD | _S_IWRITE );
    if( fh == -1 )
      exit( 1 );

    /* Lock some bytes and read them. Then unlock. */
    if( _locking( fh, LK_NBLCK, 30L ) != -1 )
    {
        printf( "No one can change these bytes while I'm reading ",
                "them\n" );
        numread = _read( fh, buffer, 30 );
        printf( "%d bytes read: %.30s\n", numread, buffer );
        lseek( fh, 0L, SEEK_SET );
        _locking( fh, LK_UNLCK, 30L );
        printf( "Now I'm done. Do what you will with them.\n" );
    }
    else
        perror( "Locking failed\n" );

    _close( fh );
}
```

Output

```
No one can change these bytes while I'm reading them
30 bytes read: /* LOCKING.C: This program ope
Now I'm done. Do what you will with them.
```

log, log10

double log(double *x* **);**

double log10(double *x* **);**

ANSI   UNIX   WIN32S

#include <math.h>

Return Value   The **log** functions return the logarithm of *x* if successful. If *x* is negative, these functions return an indefinite (same as a quiet NaN). If *x* is 0, they return INF (infinite). You can modify error handling by using the **_matherr** routine.

Parameter   *x*   Value whose logarithm is to be found

See Also   **exp, _matherr, pow**

Example

```
/* LOG.C: This program uses log and log10
 * to calculate the natural logarithm and
 * the base-10 logarithm of 9,000.
 */

#include <math.h>
#include <stdio.h>

void main( void )
{
    double x = 9000.0;
    double y;

    y = log( x );
    printf( "log( %.2f ) = %f\n", x, y );
    y = log10( x );
    printf( "log10( %.2f ) = %f\n", x, y );
}
```

Output

```
log( 9000.00 ) = 9.104980
log10( 9000.00 ) = 3.954243
```

_logb

double _logb(double *x* **);**

~~ANSI~~   ~~UNIX~~   WIN32S

#include <float.h>

Return Value   **_logb** returns the unbiased exponential value of *x*.

Parameter   *x*   Double-precision floating-point value

Remarks   The **_logb** function extracts the exponential value of its double-precision floating-point argument *x*, as though *x* were represented with infinite range. If the argument *x* is denormalized, it is treated as if it were normalized.

See Also   **frexp**

longjmp

void longjmp(jmp_buf *env*, **int** *value* **);**

ANSI   UNIX   WIN32S

#include <setjmp.h>

Return Value   None

Parameters   *env*   Variable in which environment is stored
                   value   Value to be returned to **setjmp** call

Remarks   The **longjmp** function restores a stack environment and execution locale previously saved in *env* by **setjmp**. **setjmp** and **longjmp** provide a way to execute a nonlocal **goto**; they are typically used to pass execution control to error-handling or recovery code in a previously called routine without using the normal call and return conventions.

A call to **setjmp** causes the current stack environment to be saved in *env*. A subsequent call to **longjmp** restores the saved environment and returns control to the point immediately following the corresponding **setjmp** call. Execution resumes as if *value* had just been returned by the **setjmp** call. The values of all variables (except register variables) that are accessible to the routine receiving control contain the values they had when **longjmp** was called. The values of register variables are unpredictable. The value returned by **setjmp** must be nonzero. If *value* is passed as 0, the value 1 is substituted in the actual return.

Call **longjmp** before the function that called **setjmp** returns; otherwise the results are unpredictable.

Observe the following restrictions when using **longjmp**:

- Do not assume that the values of the register variables will remain the same. The values of register variables in the routine calling **setjmp** may not be restored to the proper values after **longjmp** is executed.

- Do not use **longjmp** to transfer control out of an interrupt-handling routine unless the interrupt is caused by a floating-point exception. In this case, a program may return from an interrupt handler via **longjmp** if it first reinitializes the floating-point math package by calling **_fpreset**.

- Be careful when using **setjmp** and **longjmp** in C++ programs. Because these functions do not support C++ object semantics, it is safer to use the C++ exception-handling mechanism.

See Also   **setjmp**

Example   See the example for **_fpreset**.

_lrotl, _lrotr

unsigned long _lrotl(unsigned long *value*, **int** *shift* **);**

unsigned long _lrotr(unsigned long *value*, **int** *shift* **);**

~~ANSI~~ ~~UNIX~~ WIN32S

#include <stdlib.h>

Return Value   Both functions return the rotated value. There is no error return.

Parameters   *value*   Value to be rotated
shift   Number of bits to shift *value*

Remarks   The **_lrotl** and **_lrotr** functions rotate *value* by *shift* bits. **_lrotl** rotates the value left. **_lrotr** rotates the value right. Both functions "wrap" bits rotated off one end of *value* to the other end.

See Also   **_rotl**

Example

```
/* LROT.C */

#include <stdlib.h>
#include <stdio.h>

void main( void )
{
    unsigned long val = 0x0fac35791;

    printf( "0x%8.8lx rotated left eight times is 0x%8.8lx\n",
            val, _lrotl( val, 8 ) );
    printf( "0x%8.8lx rotated right four times is 0x%8.8lx\n",
            val, _lrotr( val, 4 ) );
}
```

Output

```
0xfac35791 rotated left eight times is 0xc35791fa
0xfac35791 rotated right four times is 0x1fac3579
```

_lsearch

void *_lsearch(const void **key***, void ****base***, unsigned int ****num***, unsigned int** *width***,
    int (_ _ cdecl ****compare* **)(const void ****elem1***, const void ****elem2* **));**

~~ANSI~~   UNIX   WIN32S

Use **_lsearch** for compatibility with ANSI naming conventions of non-ANSI
functions. Use **lsearch** and link with OLDNAMES.LIB for UNIX compatibility.

#include <search.h>

Return Value

If the key is found, **_lsearch** returns a pointer to the element of the array at *base*
that matches *key*. If the key is not found, **_lsearch** returns a pointer to the newly
added item at the end of the array.

Parameters

key   Object to search for
base   Pointer to base of array to be searched
num   Number of elements
width   Width of each array element
compare   Pointer to comparison routine
elem1   Pointer to key for search
elem2   Pointer to array element to be compared with key

Remarks   The **_lsearch** function performs a linear search for the value *key* in an array of *num* elements, each of *width* bytes in size. Unlike **bsearch**, **_lsearch** does not require the array to be sorted. If *key* is not found, **_lsearch** adds it to the end of the array and increments *num*.

The *compare* argument is a pointer to a user-supplied routine that compares two array elements and returns a value specifying their relationship. **_lsearch** calls the *compare* routine one or more times during the search, passing pointers to two array elements on each call. *compare* must compare the elements, then return either nonzero, meaning the elements are different, or 0, meaning the elements are identical.

See Also   **bsearch, _lfind**

Example   See the example for **_lfind**.

_lseek

long _lseek(int *handle***, long** *offset***, int** *origin* **);**

~~ANSI~~ UNIX WIN32S

Use **_lseek** for compatibility with ANSI naming conventions of non-ANSI functions. Use **lseek** and link with OLDNAMES.LIB for UNIX compatibility.

#include <io.h>
#include <stdio.h>

Return Value   **_lseek** returns the offset, in bytes, of the new position from the beginning of the file. The function returns −1L to indicate an error and sets **errno** either to **EBADF**, meaning the file handle is invalid, or to **EINVAL**, meaning the value for *origin* is invalid or the position specified by *offset* is before the beginning of the file. On devices incapable of seeking (such as terminals and printers), the return value is undefined.

Parameters   *handle*   Handle referring to open file
offset   Number of bytes from *origin*
origin   Initial position

Remarks   The **_lseek** function moves the file pointer associated with *handle* to a new location that is *offset* bytes from *origin*. The next operation on the file occurs at the new location. The *origin* argument must be one of the following constants, which are defined in STDIO.H:

SEEK_SET   Beginning of file

SEEK_CUR   Current position of file pointer

SEEK_END   End of file

You can use **_lseek** to reposition the pointer anywhere in a file or beyond the end of the file.

See Also   **fseek, _tell**

Example

```
/* LSEEK.C: This program first opens a file named LSEEK.C.
 * It then uses _lseek to find the beginning of the file,
 * to find the current position in the file, and to find
 * the end of the file.
 */

#include <io.h>
#include <fcntl.h>
#include <stdlib.h>
#include <stdio.h>

void main( void )
{
    int fh;
    long pos;                   /* Position of file pointer */
    char buffer[10];

    fh = _open( "lseek.c", _O_RDONLY );

    /* Seek the beginning of the file: */
    pos = _lseek( fh, 0L, SEEK_SET );
    if( pos == -1L )
        perror( "_lseek to beginning failed" );
    else
        printf( "Position for beginning of file seek = %ld\n", pos );

    /* Move file pointer a little */
     _read( fh, buffer, 10 );

    /* Find current position: */
    pos = _lseek( fh, 0L, SEEK_CUR );
    if( pos == -1L )
        perror( "_lseek to current position failed" );
    else
        printf( "Position for current position seek = %ld\n", pos );
```

```
                    /* Set the end of the file: */
                    pos = _lseek( fh, 0L, SEEK_END );
                    if( pos == -1L )
                        perror( "_lseek to end failed" );
                    else
                        printf( "Position for end of file seek = %ld\n", pos );

                    _close( fh );
                }
```

Output

```
Position for beginning of file seek = 0
Position for current position seek = 10
Position for end of file seek = 1201
```

_ltoa, _ltow

char *_ltoa(long *value***, char ****string***, int** *radix* **);**

wchar_t *_ltow (long *value***, wchar_t ****string***, int** *radix* **);**

_ltoa:	~~ANSI~~ ~~UNIX~~	WIN32S
_ltow:	~~ANSI~~ UNIX	~~WIN32S~~

#include <stdlib.h>   For **_ltoa**.
#include <wchar.h>   For **_ltow** use STDIO.H or WCHAR.H.

Return Value Each of these functions returns a pointer to *string*. There is no error return.

Parameters
value   Number to be converted
string   String result
radix   Base of *value*

Remarks The **_ltoa** function converts the digits of *value* to a null-terminated character string and stores the result (up to 33 bytes) in *string*. The *radix* argument specifies the base of *value*, which must be in the range 2–36. If *radix* equals 10 and *value* is negative, the first character of the stored string is the minus sign (–). **_ltow** is a wide-character version of **_ltoa**; the second argument and return value of **_ltow** are wide-character strings. Each of these functions is Microsoft-specific.

See Also **_itoa, _ultoa**

Example See the example for **_itoa**.

_makepath, _wmakepath

void _makepath(char *path, const char *drive, const char *dir, const char *fname,
const char *ext);

void _wmakepath(wchar_t *path, const wchar_t *drive, const wchar_t *dir, const wchar_t
*fname, const wchar_t *ext);

> _makepath: ~~ANSI~~ ~~UNIX~~ WIN32S
> _wmakepath: ~~ANSI~~ ~~UNIX~~ ~~WIN32S~~
>
> #include <stdlib.h>   For _makepath.
> #include <wchar.h>   For _wmakepath use STDLIB.H or WCHAR.H.

Return Value   None

Parameters

> path   Full path buffer
> drive   Drive letter
> dir   Directory path
> fname   Filename
> ext   File extension

Remarks

The **_makepath** function creates a single path and stores it in *path*. The path may include a drive letter, directory path, filename, and filename extension. **_wmakepath** is a wide-character version of **_makepath**; the arguments to **_wmakepath** are wide-character strings. **_wmakepath** and **_makepath** behave identically otherwise.

The following arguments point to buffers containing the path elements:

drive   Contains a letter (A, B, and so on) corresponding to the desired drive and an optional trailing colon. **_makepath** inserts the colon automatically in the composite path if it is missing. If *drive* is a null character or an empty string, no drive letter and colon appear in the composite *path* string.

dir   Contains the path of directories, not including the drive designator or the actual filename. The trailing slash is optional, and either a forward slash (/) or a backslash (\) or both may be used in a single *dir* argument. If a trailing slash (/ or \) is not specified, it is inserted automatically. If *dir* is a null character or an empty string, no slash is inserted in the composite *path* string.

fname   Contains the base filename without any extensions. If *fname* is **NULL** or points to an empty string, no filename is inserted in the composite *path* string.

ext   Contains the actual filename extension, with or without a leading period (.). **_makepath** inserts the period automatically if it does not appear in *ext*. If *ext* is a null character or an empty string, no period is inserted in the composite *path* string.

The *path* argument must point to an empty buffer large enough to hold the complete path. Although there are no size limits on any of the fields that constitute *path*, the composite *path* must be no larger than the **_MAX_PATH** constant, defined in STDLIB.H. **_MAX_PATH** may be larger than the current operating-system version will handle.

See Also   **_fullpath, _splitpath**

Example
```
/* MAKEPATH.C */

#include <stdlib.h>
#include <stdio.h>

void main( void )
{
    char path_buffer[_MAX_PATH];
    char drive[_MAX_DRIVE];
    char dir[_MAX_DIR];
    char fname[_MAX_FNAME];
    char ext[_MAX_EXT];

    _makepath( path_buffer, "c", "\\sample\\crt\\", "makepath", "c" );
    printf( "Path created with _makepath: %s\n\n", path_buffer );
    _splitpath( path_buffer, drive, dir, fname, ext );
    printf( "Path extracted with _splitpath:\n" );
    printf( "  Drive: %s\n", drive );
    printf( "  Dir: %s\n", dir );
    printf( "  Filename: %s\n", fname );
    printf( "  Ext: %s\n", ext );
}
```

Output
```
Path created with _makepath: c:\sample\crt\makepath.c

Path extracted with _splitpath:
  Drive: c:
  Dir: \sample\crt\
  Filename: makepath
  Ext: .c
```

malloc

void *malloc(size_t *size* **);**

ANSI   UNIX   WIN32S

#include <stdlib.h>
#include <malloc.h>

Return Value

malloc returns a void pointer to the allocated space, or **NULL** if there is insufficient memory available. To return a pointer to a type other than **void**, use a type cast on the return value. The storage space pointed to by the return value is guaranteed to be suitably aligned for storage of any type of object. If size is 0, **malloc** allocates a zero-length item in the heap and returns a valid pointer to that item. Always check the return from **malloc**, even if the amount of memory requested is small.

Parameter

size   Bytes to allocate

Remarks

The **malloc** function allocates a memory block of at least *size* bytes. The block may be larger than *size* bytes because of space required for alignment and maintenance information.

The startup code uses **malloc** to allocate storage for the **_environ**, **envp**, and **argv** variables. The following functions and their wide-character counterparts also call **malloc**:

calloc	**fscanf**	**_getw**	**setvbuf**
_exec functions	**fseek**	**_popen**	**_spawn functions**
fgetc	**fsetpos**	**printf**	**_strdup**
_fgetchar	**_fullpath**	**putc**	**system**
fgets	**fwrite**	**putchar**	**_tempnam**
fprintf	**getc**	**_putenv**	**ungetc**
fputc	**getchar**	**puts**	**vfprintf**
_fputchar	**_getcwd**	**_putw**	**vprintf**
fputs	**_getdcwd**	**scanf**	
fread	**gets**	**_searchenv**	

The C++ **_set_new_mode** function sets the new handler mode for **malloc**. The new handler mode indicates whether, on failure, **malloc** is to call the new handler routine as set by **_set_new_handler**. By default, **malloc** does not call the new handler routine on failure to allocate memory. You can override this default behavior so that, when **malloc** fails to allocate memory, **malloc** calls the new handler routine in the same way that the **new** operator does when it fails for the same reason. To override the default, call

```
_set_new_mode(1)
```

early in your program, or link with NEWMODE.OBJ.

See Also   **calloc, free, realloc**

Example
```
/* MALLOC.C: This program allocates memory with
 * malloc, then frees the memory with free.
 */

#include <stdlib.h>            /* For _MAX_PATH definition */
#include <stdio.h>
#include <malloc.h>

void main( void )
{
   char *string;

   /* Allocate space for a path name */
   string = malloc( _MAX_PATH );
   if( string == NULL )
      printf( "Insufficient memory available\n" );
   else
      printf( "Memory space allocated for path name\n" );
      free( string );
      printf( "Memory freed\n" );
}
```

Output
```
Memory space allocated for path name
Memory freed
```

_matherr

int _matherr(struct _exception *except);

~~ANSI~~ UNIX WIN32S

Use **_matherr** for compatibility with ANSI naming conventions of non-ANSI functions. Use **matherr** and link with OLDNAMES.LIB for UNIX compatibility.

#include <math.h>

Return Value   _matherr returns 0 to indicate an error or a non-zero value to indicate success. If _matherr returns 0, an error message can be displayed, and **errno** is set to an appropriate error value. If _matherr returns a nonzero value, no error message is displayed, and **errno** remains unchanged.

Parameter   *except*   Pointer to structure containing error information

Remarks   The _matherr function processes errors generated by the floating-point functions of the math library. These functions call _matherr when an error is detected.

For special error handling, you can provide a different definition of _matherr. However, if you use the dynamically linked version of the C run-time library (CRTDLL.DLL), you cannot replace the default _matherr routine with a user-defined version. You can only install a custom _matherr routine if you use one of the statically-linked C run-time libraries.

When an error occurs in a math routine, _matherr is called with a pointer to an _exception type structure (defined in MATH.H) as an argument. The _exception structure contains the following elements:

int type   Exception type

char *name   Name of function where error occurred

double arg1, arg2   First and second (if any) arguments to function

double retval   Value to be returned by function

The **type** specifies the type of math error. It is one of the following values, defined in MATH.H:

_DOMAIN   Argument domain error.

_SING   Argument singularity.

_OVERFLOW   Overflow range error.

_PLOSS   Partial loss of significance.

_TLOSS   Total loss of significance.

_UNDERFLOW   The result is too small to be represented. (This condition is not currently supported.)

The structure member **name** is a pointer to a null-terminated string containing the name of the function that caused the error. The structure members **arg1** and **arg2** specify the values that caused the error. (If only one argument is given, it is stored in **arg1**.)

The default return value for the given error is **retval**. If you change the return value, it must specify whether an error actually occurred.

Example

```
/* MATHERR.C illustrates writing an error routine for math
 * functions. The error function must be:
 *      _matherr
 *
 * To use _matherr, you must turn on the No Extended Dictionary
 * option within the development environment or use the /NOE
 * linker option outside the environment. For example:
 *      CL matherr.c /link /NOE
 */

#include <math.h>
#include <string.h>
#include <stdio.h>

void main()
{
    /* Do several math operations that cause errors. The _matherr
     * routine handles _DOMAIN errors, but lets the system handle
     * other errors normally.
     */
    printf( "log( -2.0 ) = %e\n", log( -2.0 ) );
    printf( "log10( -5.0 ) = %e\n", log10( -5.0 ) );
    printf( "log( 0.0 ) = %e\n", log( 0.0 ) );
}

/* Handle several math errors caused by passing a negative argument
 * to log or log10 (_DOMAIN errors). When this happens, _matherr
 * returns the natural or base-10 logarithm of the absolute value
 * of the argument and suppresses the usual error message.
 */
int _matherr( struct _exception *except )
{
    /* Handle _DOMAIN errors for log or log10. */
    if( except->type == _DOMAIN )
    {
        if( strcmp( except->name, "log" ) == 0 )
        {
            except->retval = log( -(except->arg1) );
            printf( "Special: using absolute value: %s: _DOMAIN "
                    "error\n", except->name );
            return 1;
        }
```

```
                else if( strcmp( except->name, "log10" ) == 0 )
                {
                    except->retval = log10( -(except->arg1) );
                    printf( "Special: using absolute value: %s: _DOMAIN ",
                            "error\n", except->name );
                    return 1;
                }
            }
            else
            {
                printf( "Normal: " );
                return 0;    /* Else use the default actions */
            }
        }
```

Output

```
Special: using absolute value: log: _DOMAIN error
log( -2.0 ) = 6.931472e-001
Special: using absolute value: log10: _DOMAIN error
log10( -5.0 ) = 6.989700e-001
Normal: log( 0.0 ) = -1.#INF00e+000
```

__max

type **__max**(*type a,* *type b*);

ANSI UNIX WIN32S

#include <stdlib.h>

Return Value

__max returns the larger of its arguments.

Parameters

type   Any numeric data type
a, b   Values of any numeric type to be compared

Remarks

The **__max** macro compares two values and returns the value of the larger one. The arguments can be of any numeric data type, signed or unsigned. Both arguments and the return value must be of the same data type.

See Also	__min
Example	See the example for __min.

_mbbtombc

unsigned short _mbbtombc(unsigned short *c*);

~~ANSI~~ ~~UNIX~~ ~~WIN32S~~

#include <mbstring.h>

Return Value	If **_mbbtombc** successfully converts *c*, it returns a multibyte character; otherwise it returns *c*.
Parameter	*c* Single-byte character to convert.
Remarks	The **_mbbtombc** function converts a given single-byte multibyte character to a corresponding double-byte multibyte character. Characters must be within the range 0x20–0x7E or 0xA1–0xDF to be converted.
	In earlier versions, **_mbbtombc** was called **hantozen**. For new code, use **_mbbtombc** instead.
See Also	**_mbctombb**

_mbbtype

int _mbbtype(unsigned char *c*, int *type*);

~~ANSI~~ ~~UNIX~~ ~~WIN32S~~

#include <mbstring.h>   For **_mbbtype**.
#include <mbctype.h>   For definitions of manifest constants used as return values.

Return Value	**_mbbtype** returns the type of byte within a string. This decision is context-sensitive as specified by the value of *type*, which provides the control test

condition. *type* is the type of the previous byte in the string. The manifest constants in the following table are defined in MBCTYPE.H.

Value of *type*	_mbbtype Tests For	Return Value	*c*
Any value except 1	Valid single byte or lead byte	**_MBC_SINGLE** (0)	Single byte (0x20–0x7E, 0xA1–0xDF)
Any value except 1	Valid single byte or lead byte	**_MBC_LEAD** (1)	Lead byte of multibyte character (0x81–0x9F, 0xE0–0xFC)
Any value except 1	Valid single-byte or lead byte	**_MBC_ILLEGAL** (−1)	Invalid character (any value except 0x20–0x7E, 0xA1–0xDF, 0x81–0x9F, 0xE0–0xFC
1	Valid trail byte	**_MBC_TRAIL** (2)	Trailing byte of multibyte character (0x40–0x7E, 0x80–0xFC)
1	Valid trail byte	**_MBC_ILLEGAL** (−1)	Invalid character (any value except 0x20–0x7E, 0xA1–0xDF, 0x81–0x9F, 0xE0–0xFC

Parameters

c   Character to test

type   Type of byte to test for

Remarks

The **_mbbtype** function determines the type of a byte in a multibyte character. If the value of *type* is any value except 1, **_mbbtype** tests for a valid single-byte or lead byte of a multibyte character. If the value of *type* is 1, **_mbbtype** tests for a valid trail byte of a multibyte character.

In earlier versions, **_mbbtype** was called **chkctype**. For new code, **_mbbtype** use instead.

_mbccpy

void _mbccpy(unsigned char *dest, const unsigned char *src);

~~ANSI~~ ~~UNX~~ ~~WIN32S~~

#include <mbtype.h>

Return Value

None

Parameters

dest   Copy destination

src   Multibyte character to copy

Remarks   The **_mbccpy** function copies one multibyte character from *src* to *dest*. If *src* does not point to the lead byte of a multibyte character as determined by an implicit call to **_ismbblead**, no copy is performed.

See Also   **_mbclen**

_mbcjistojms, _mbcjmstojis

unsigned int **_mbcjistojms**(unsigned int *c*);

unsigned int **_mbcjmstojis**(unsigned int *c*);

~~ANSI~~ ~~UNIX~~ ~~WIN32S~~

#include <mbstring.h>

Return Value   **_mbcjistojms** and **_mbcjmstojis** return a converted character. Otherwise they return 0.

Parameter   *c*   Character to convert

Remarks   The **_mbcjistojms** function converts a Japan Industry Standard (JIS) character to a Microsoft Kanji (Shift JIS) character. The character is converted only if the lead and trail bytes are in the range 0x21–0x7E.

The **_mbcjmstojis** function converts a Shift JIS character to a JIS character. The character is converted only if the lead byte is in the range 0x81–0x9F or 0xE0–0xFC, and the trail byte is in the range 0x40–0x7E or 0x80–0xFC.

The value *c* should be a 16-bit value whose upper eight bits represent the lead byte of the character to convert and whose lower eight bits represent the trail byte.

In earlier versions, **_mbcjistojms** and **_mbcjmstojis** were called **jistojms** and **jmstojis**, repectively. **_mbcjistojms** and **_mbcjmstojis** should be used instead.

See Also   **_ismbb** Routines

_mbclen, mblen

size_t **_mbclen**(const unsigned char **c*);

int **mblen**(const char **mbstr*, size_t *count*);

_mbclen: ~~ANSI~~ ~~UNIX~~ WIN32S
mblen: ANSI ~~UNIX~~ ~~WIN32S~~

#include <mbstring.h>   For **_mbclen**.
#include <stdlib.h>   For **mblen**.

Return Value

_mbclen returns 1 or 2, according to whether the multibyte character *c* is one or two bytes long. There is no error return for **_mbclen**. If *mbstr* is not **NULL**, **mblen** returns the length, in bytes, of the multibyte character. If *mbstr* is **NULL**, or if it points to the wide-character null character, **mblen** returns 0. If the object that *mbstr* points to does not form a valid multibyte character within the first *count* characters, **mblen** returns −1.

Parameters

c   Multibyte character
mbstr   Address of multibyte-character byte sequence
count   Number of bytes to check

Remarks

The **_mbclen** function returns the length, in bytes, of the multibyte character *c*. If *c* does not point to the lead byte of a multibyte character as determined by an implicit call to **_ismbblead**, the result of **_mbclen** is unpredictable.

mblen returns the length in bytes of *mbstr* if it is a valid multibyte character. It examines *count* or fewer bytes contained in *mbstr*, but not more than **MB_CUR_MAX** bytes. **mblen** determines multibyte-character validity according to the **LC_CTYPE** category setting of the current locale. For more information on the **LC_CTYPE** category, see **setlocale**.

See Also

_mbccpy, _mbslen

Example

```
/* MBLEN.C illustrates the behavior of the mblen function
 */

#include <stdlib.h>
#include <stdio.h>

void main( void )
{
    int     i;
    char    *pmbc = (char *)malloc( sizeof( char ) );
    wchar_t wc   = L'a';

    printf( "Convert wide character to multibyte character:\n" );
    i = wctomb( pmbc, wc );
    printf( "\tCharacters converted: %u\n", i );
    printf( "\tMultibyte character: %x\n\n", pmbc );

    i = mblen( pmbc, MB_CUR_MAX );
    printf( "Length in bytes of multibyte character %x: %u\n", pmbc,
            i );

    pmbc = NULL;
    i = mblen( pmbc, MB_CUR_MAX );
    printf( "Length in bytes of NULL multibyte character %x: %u\n",
            pmbc, i );
}
```

Output

```
Convert wide character to multibyte character:
    Characters converted: 1
    Multibyte character: 2c02cc

Length in bytes of multibyte character 2c02cc: 1
Length in bytes of NULL multibyte character 0: 0
```

_mbctohira, _mbctokata

unsigned int _mbctohira(unsigned int *c* **);**

unsigned int _mbctokata(unsigned int *c* **);**

ANSI ~~UNIX~~ ~~WIN32S~~

#include <mbstring.h>

Return Value   Each of these functions returns the converted character *c*, if possible. Otherwise it returns the character *c* unchanged.

Parameter   *c*   Multibyte character to convert

Remarks   The **_mbctohira** and **_mbctohira** functions test a character *c* and, if possible, apply one of the following conversions.

Function	Converts
_mbctohira	Multibyte katakana to multibyte hiragana
_mbctokata	Multibyte hiragana to multibyte katakana

In previous versions, **_mbctohira** was called **jtohira** and **_mbctokata** was called **jtokata**. For new code, use the new names instead.

See Also   **_mbcjistojms, _mbctolower, _mbctombb**

_mbctolower, _mbctoupper

unsigned int _mbctolower(unsigned int *c* **);**

unsigned int _mbctoupper(unsigned int *c* **);**

ANSI ~~UNIX~~ ~~WIN32S~~

#include <mbstring.h>

Return Value   Each of these functions returns the converted character *c*, if possible. Otherwise it returns the character *c* unchanged.

Parameter   *c*   Multibyte character to convert

Remarks   The **_mbctolower** and **_mbctoupper** functions test a character *c* and, if possible, apply one of the following conversions.

Function	Converts
_mbctolower	Uppercase character to lowercase character
_mbctoupper	Lowercase character to uppercase character

In previous versions, **_mbctolower** was called **jtolower**, and **_mbctoupper** was called **jtoupper**. For new code, use the new names instead.

See Also   **_mbbtombc, _mbcjistojms, _mbctohira, _mbctombb**

_mbctombb

unsigned int _mbctombb(unsigned int *c*);

~~ANSI~~ ~~UNIX~~ ~~WIN32S~~

#include <mbstring.h>

Return Value   If successful, **_mbctombb** returns the single-byte character that corresponds to *c*; otherwise it returns *c*.

Parameter   *c*   Multibyte character to convert.

Remarks   The **_mbctombb** function converts a given multibyte character to a corresponding single-byte multibyte character. Characters must correspond to single-byte characters within the range 0x20–0x7E or 0xA1–0xDF to be converted.

In previous versions, **_mbctombb** was called **zentohan**. Use **_mbctombb** instead.

See Also   **_mbbtombc, _mbcjistojms, _mbctohira, _mbctolower**

_mbsbtype

int _mbsbtype(const unsigned char **mbstr*, size_t *count*);

~~ANSI~~ ~~UNIX~~ ~~WIN32S~~

#include <mbstring.h>   For **_mbsbtype**.
#include <mbctype.h>   For manifest constants used as return values.

Return Value   **_mbsbtype** returns an integer value indicating the result of the test on the specified byte. The manifest constants in the following table are defined in MBCTYPE.H.

Return Value	Byte Type
_MBC_SINGLE (0)	Single-byte character. For example, in code page 932, _mbsbtype returns 0 if the specified byte is within the range 0x20 – 0x7E or 0xA1 – 0xDF.
_MBC_LEAD (1)	Lead byte of multibyte character. For example, in code page 932, _mbsbtype returns 1 if the specified byte is within the range 0x81 – 0x9F or 0xE0 – 0xFC.
_MBC_TRAIL (2)	Trailing byte of multibyte character. For example, in code page 932, _mbsbtype returns 2 if the specified byte is within the range 0x40–0x7E or 0x80 – 0xFC.
_MBC_ILLEGAL (–1)	Invalid character, or **NULL** byte found before the byte at offset *count* in *mbstr*.

Parameters   *mbstr*   Address of a sequence of multibyte characters
count   Byte offset from head of string

Remarks   The **_mbsbtype** function determines the type of a byte in a multibyte character string. The function examines only the byte at offset *count* in *mbstr*, ignoring invalid characters before the specified byte.

_mbsdec, _strdec, _wcsdec

unsigned char *_mbsdec(const unsigned char **start***, const unsigned char ****current***);**

For the definitions of **_strdec** and **_wcsdec**, see TCHAR.H.

~~ANSI~~ ~~UNIX~~ ~~WIN32S~~

#include <tchar.h>   For **_strdec** and **_wcsdec**.
#include <string.h>
#include <mbstring.h>   For **_mbsdec** use STRING.H or MBSTRING.H.

Return Value   Each of these routines returns a pointer to the character that immediately precedes *current*, or **NULL** if the value of *start* is greater than or equal to that of *current*. The return value from **_tcsdec** is undefined; thus, when using **_tcsdec**, you must ensure that you do not decrement the string pointer beyond *start*.

Parameters   *start*   Pointer to first byte of any multibyte character in the source string; *start* must precede *current* in the source string
current   Pointer to first byte of any multibyte character in the source string; *current* must follow *start* in the source string

Remarks   The **_mbsdec** function returns a pointer to the first byte of the multibyte-character that immediately precedes *current* in the string that contains *start*. **_mbsdec** recognizes multibyte-character sequences according to the multibyte code page currently in use.

The generic-text function **_tcsdec**, defined in TCHAR.H, maps to **_mbsdec** if **_MBCS** has been defined, or to **_wcsdec** if **_UNICODE** has been defined. Otherwise **_tcsdec** maps to **_strdec**. **_strdec** and **_wcsdec** are single-byte character and wide-character versions of **_mbsdec**. **_strdec** and **_wcsdec** are provided only for this mapping and should not be used otherwise. For more information, see "Using Generic-Text Mappings" on page 23 and Appendix B, "Generic-Text Mappings."

See Also   **_mbsinc, _mbsnextc, _mbsninc**

_mbsinc, _strinc, _wcsinc

unsigned char *_mbsinc(const unsigned char **current***);**

For the definitions of **_strinc** and **_wcsinc**, see TCHAR.H.

~~ANSI~~ ~~UNIX~~ ~~WIN32S~~

#include <tchar.h>   For **_strinc**.
#include <string.h>
#include <mbstring.h>   For **_mbsinc** use STRING.H or MBSTRING.H.

Return Value   Each of these routines returns a pointer to the character that immediately follows *current*.

Parameter   *current*   Character pointer

Remarks   The **_mbsinc** function returns a pointer to the first byte of the multibyte character that immediately follows *current*. **_mbsinc** recognizes multibyte-character sequences according to the multibyte code page currently in use.

The generic-text function **_tcsinc**, defined in TCHAR.H, maps to **_mbsinc** if **_MBCS** has been defined, or to **_wcsinc** if **_UNICODE** has been defined. Otherwise **_tcsinc** maps to **_strinc**. **_strinc** and **_wcsinc** are single-byte character and wide-character versions of **_mbsinc**. **_strinc** and **_wcsinc** are provided only for this mapping and should not be used otherwise. For more information, see "Using Generic-Text Mappings" on page 23 and Appendix B, "Generic-Text Mappings."

See Also   **_mbsdec, _mbsnextc, _mbsninc**

_mbsnbcat

unsigned char *_mbsnbcat(unsigned char **dest***, const unsigned char ****src***, size_t** *count* **);**

~~ANSI~~ ~~UNIX~~ ~~WIN32S~~

#include <mbstring.h>

Return Value	**_mbsnbcat** returns a pointer to the destination string. No return value is reserved to indicate an error.
Parameters	*dest* Null-terminated multibyte-character destination string *src* Null-terminated multibyte-character source string *count* Number of bytes from *src* to append to *dest*
Remarks	The **_mbsnbcat** function appends, at most, the first *count* bytes of *src* to *dest*. If the byte immediately preceding the null character in *dest* is a lead byte, the initial byte of *src* overwrites this lead byte. Otherwise the initial byte of *src* overwrites the terminating null character of *dest*. If a null byte appears in *src* before *count* bytes are appended, **_mbsnbcat** appends all bytes from *src*, up to the null character. If *count* is greater than the length of *src*, the length of *src* is used in place of *count*. The resulting string is terminated with a null character. If copying takes place between strings that overlap, the behavior is undefined.
See Also	**_mbsnbcmp, _mbsnbcnt, _mbsnbcpy, _mbsnbicmp, _mbsnbset, _mbsnccnt, strncat**

_mbsnbcmp

int _mbsnbcmp(const unsigned char **string1***, const unsigned char ****string2***, size_t** *count* **);**

~~ANSI~~ ~~UNIX~~ ~~WIN32S~~

#include <mbstring.h>

Return Value	The return value indicates the relation of the substrings of *string1* and *string*.

Return Value	Description
< 0	*string1* substring less than *string2* substring
0	*string1* substring identical to *string2* substring
> 0	*string1* substring greater than *string2* substring

On an error, **_mbsnbcmp** returns **_NLSCMPERROR**, which is defined in STRING.H and MBSTRING.H.

Parameters	*string1, string2* Strings to compare *count* Number of bytes to compare

Remarks   The **_mbsnbcmp** function lexicographically compares, at most, the first *count* bytes in *string1* and *string2* and returns a value indicating the relationship between the substrings. **_mbsnbcmp** is a case-sensitive version of **_mbsnbicmp**. Unlike **strcoll**, **_mbsnbcmp** is not affected by locale. **_mbsnbcmp** recognizes multibyte-character sequences according to the current multibyte code page. For more information, see "Code Pages" on page 20.

_mbsnbcmp is similar to **_mbsncmp**, except that **_mbsnbcmp** compares strings by characters rather than by bytes.

See Also   **_mbsnbcat, _mbsnbicmp, strncmp, _strnicmp**

Example
```
/* STRNBCMP.C */
#include <mbstring.h>
#include <stdio.h>

char string1[] = "The quick brown dog jumps over the lazy fox";
char string2[] = "The QUICK brown fox jumps over the lazy dog";

void main( void )
{
   char tmp[20];
   int result;
   printf( "Compare strings:\n\t\t%s\n\t\t%s\n\n", string1, string2 );
   printf( "Function:\t_mbsnbcmp (first 10 characters only)\n" );
   result = _mbsncmp( string1, string2 , 10 );
   if( result > 0 )
      _mbscpy( tmp, "greater than" );
   else if( result < 0 )
      _mbscpy( tmp, "less than" );
   else
      _mbscpy( tmp, "equal to" );
   printf( "Result:\t\tString 1 is %s string 2\n\n", tmp );
   printf( "Function:\t_mbsnicmp (first 10 characters only)\n" );
   result = _mbsnicmp( string1, string2, 10 );
   if( result > 0 )
      _mbscpy( tmp, "greater than" );
   else if( result < 0 )
      _mbscpy( tmp, "less than" );
   else
      _mbscpy( tmp, "equal to" );
   printf( "Result:\t\tString 1 is %s string 2\n\n", tmp );
}
```

Output
```
Compare strings:
        The quick brown dog jumps over the lazy fox
        The QUICK brown fox jumps over the lazy dog

Function:    _mbsnbcmp (first 10 characters only)
Result:      String 1 is greater than string 2

Function:    _mbsnicmp (first 10 characters only)
Result:      String 1 is equal to string 2
```

_mbsnbcnt, _strncnt, _wcsncnt

size_t _mbsnbcnt(const unsigned char *string, size_t n);

For the definitions of _strncnt and _wcsncnt, see TCHAR.H.

> _mbsnbcnt, _wcsncnt: ~~ANSI~~ ~~UNIX~~ ~~WIN32S~~
> _strncnt: ~~ANSI~~ ~~UNIX~~ WIN32S

#include <mbstring.h>

Return Value

_mbsnbcnt returns the number of bytes in the first *n* multibyte characters of *string*. If _mbsnbcnt finds a null character within the first *n* characters, it returns the number of bytes preceding the null character. If it finds a null character at the second byte of a multibyte character, it treats the corresponding lead byte as a null character and does not include it in the count. If *n* is less than zero, the function returns 0. In previous versions, the return value of _mbsnbcnt was of type **int** rather than of type **size_t**.

_strncnt returns the number of characters (that is, *n*) in the first *n* bytes of the single-byte string *string*; _wcsncnt returns the number of bytes (that is, 2 * *n*) in the first *n* wide characters of the wide-character string *string*.

Parameters

string   String to examine

n   Number of characters to examine in *string*.

Remarks

The _mbsnbcnt function returns the number of bytes in the first *n* multibyte characters of *string*. _mbsnbcnt replaces **mtob**, and should be used in place of **mtob**.

The generic-text routine _tcsnbcnt, defined in TCHAR.H, maps to _mbsnbcnt if _MBCS has been defined, or to _wcsncnt if _UNICODE has been defined. Otherwise _tcsnbcnt maps to _strncnt. _strncnt and _wcsncnt are single-byte–character string and wide-character–string versions of _tcsnbcnt. _strncnt and _wcsncnt are provided only for this mapping and should not be used otherwise. For more information, see "Using Generic-Text Mappings" on page 23 and Appendix B, "Generic-Text Mappings."

See Also   **_mbsnbcat, _mbsnccnt**

Example
```
#include  <mbstring.h>
#include  <stdio.h>

void main( void )
{
    unsigned char str[] = "This is a multibyte-character string.";
    unsigned int char_count, byte_count;
    char_count = _mbsnccnt( str, 10 );
    byte_count = _mbsnbcnt( str, 10 );
    if ( byte_count - char_count )
        printf( "The first 10 characters contain %s multibyte characters",
                char_count );
    else
        printf( "The first 10 characters are single-byte.");
}
```

Output   `The first 10 characters are single-byte.`

_mbsnbcpy

unsigned char * _mbsnbcpy(unsigned char **dest***, const unsigned char ****src***, size_t**
  count **);**

~~ANSI   UNIX   WIN32S~~

#include <mbstring.h>

Return Value   **_mbsnbcpy** returns a pointer to the character string that is to be copied.

Parameters   *dest*   Destination for character string to be copied
src   Character string to be copied
count   Number of bytes to be copied

Remarks   The **_mbsnbcpy** function copies count bytes from *src* to *dest*. If *src* is shorter
than *dest*, the string is padded with null characters. If *dest* is less than or equal to
count it is not terminated with a null character.

See Also   **_mbsnbcat, _mbsnbcmp, _mbsnbcnt, _mbsnbicmp, _mbsnbset, _mbsncpy**

_mbsnbicmp

int _mbsnbicmp(const unsigned char **string1***, const unsigned char ****string2***, size_t** *count* **);**

~~ANSI   UNIX   WIN32S~~

#include <mbstring.h>

Return Value   The return value indicates the relationship between the substrings.

Value	Description
< 0	*string1* substring less than *string2* substring
0	*string1* substring identical to *string2* substring
> 0	*string1* substring greater than *string2* substring

On an error, **_mbsnbcmp** returns **_NLSCMPERROR**, which is defined in STRING.H and MBSTRING.H.

Parameters   *string1, string2*   Null-terminated strings to compare
count   Number of bytes to compare

Remarks   The **_mbsnbicmp** function lexicographically compares, at most, the first *count* bytes of *string1* and *string2*. The comparison is performed without regard to case; **_mbsnbcmp** is a case-sensitive version of **_mbsnbicmp**. The comparison ends if a terminating null character is reached in either string before *count* characters are compared. If the strings are equal when a terminating null character is reached in either string before *count* characters are compared, the shorter string is lesser.

_mbsnbicmp is similar to **_mbsnicmp**, except that it compares strings by bytes instead of by characters.

Two strings containing characters located between 'Z' and 'a' in the ASCII table ('[', '\', ']', '^', '_', and '`') compare differently, depending on their case. For example, the two strings "ABCDE" and "ABCD^" compare one way if the comparison is lowercase ("abcde" > "abcd^") and the other way ("ABCDE" < "ABCD^") if it is uppercase.

_mbsnbicmp recognizes multibyte-character sequences according to the multibyte code page currently in use. It is not affected by the current locale setting.

See Also   **_mbsnbcat, _mbsnbcmp, _stricmp, _strnicmp**

Example   See the example for **_mbsnbcmp**.

_mbsnbset

unsigned char *_mbsnbset(unsigned char **string***, unsigned int** *c***, size_t** *count* **);**

~~ANSI~~   ~~UNIX~~   ~~WIN32S~~

#include <mbstring.h>

Return Value   **_mbsnbset** returns a pointer to the altered string.

Parameters   *string*   String to be altered
c   Single-byte or multibyte character setting
count   Number of bytes to be set

Remarks   The **_mbsnbset** function sets, at most, the first *count* bytes of *string* to *c*. If *count* is greater than the length of *string*, the length of *string* is used instead of *count*. If *c* is a multibyte character and cannot be set entirely into the last byte specified by *count*, then the last byte will be padded with a blank character. **_mbsnbset** does not place a terminating null at the end of *string*.

_mbsnbset is similar to **_mbsnset**, except that it sets *count* bytes rather than *count* characters of *c*.

See Also   **_mbsnbcat, _mbsnset, _mbsset**

Example
```
/* MBSNBSET.C */

#include <mbstring.h>
#include <stdio.h>

void main( void )
{
    char string[15] = "This is a test";
    /* Set not more than 4 bytes of string to be *'s */
    printf( "Before: %s\n", string );
    _mbsnbset( string, '*', 4 );
    printf( "After:  %s\n", string );
}
```

Output
```
Before: This is a test
After:  **** is a test
```

_mbsnccnt, _strncnt, _wcsncnt

size_t _mbsnccnt(const unsigned char *string, size_t n);

For the definitions of **_strncnt** and **_wcsncnt,** see TCHAR.H.

_mbsnccnt, _wcsncnt :   ~~ANSI~~   ~~UNIX~~   ~~WIN32S~~
_strncnt: ~~ANSI~~   ~~UNIX~~   WIN32S

#include <tchar.h>   For **_strncnt** and **_wcsncnt.**
#include <mbstring.h>   For **_mbsnccnt.**

Return Value   **_mbsnccnt** returns the number of multibyte characters from the beginning of the string to byte *n*. If the function finds a null character before byte *n*, it returns the number of characters before the null character. If the string consists of fewer than *n* characters, the function returns the number of characters in the string. If *n* is less than zero, the function returns 0. In previous versions the return value of **_mbsnccnt** was of type **int** rather than type **size_t**.

The generic-text routine **_tcsnccnt**, defined in TCHAR.H, maps to **_mbsnbcnt** if **_MBCS** has been defined, or to the **_wcsncnt** macro if **_UNICODE** has been defined. Otherwise **_tcsnccnt** maps to the **_strncnt** macro. **_strncnt** and **_wcsncnt** are single-byte–character string and wide-character string versions of **_tcsnccnt**. The **_strncnt** and **_wcsncnt** macros are provided only for this mapping and should not be used otherwise. For more information, see Appendix B, "Generic-Text Mappings."

Parameters

string   String to be counted

n   Number of characters to be counted in string

Remarks

The **_mbsnccnt** function counts the number of characters in the first *n* bytes of *string*. If **_mbsnccnt** finds a null as the second byte of a double-byte character, the first byte is also considered a null character and is not included in the count.

In previous versions, **_mbsnccnt** was called **btom**. For new code, use **_mbsnccnt** instead.

See Also

_mbsnbcat, _mbsnbcnt

Example

See the example for **_mbsnbcnt**.

_mbsnbcoll, _mbsnbicoll

int _mbsnbcoll(const unsigned char **string1***, const unsigned char** *string2***, size_t** *count* **);**

int _mbsnbicoll(const unsigned char **string1***, const unsigned char** *string2***, size_t** *count* **);**

~~ANSI~~ ~~UNIX~~ ~~WIN32S~~

#include <mbstring.h>

Return Value

The return value indicates the relation of the substrings of *string1* and *string2*.

Return Value	Description
< 0	*string1* substring less than *string2* substring
0	*string1* substring identical to *string2* substring
> 0	*string1* substring greater than *string2* substring

Each of these functions returns **_NLSCMPERROR** on an error. To use **_NLSCMPERROR**, include either STRING.H or MBSTRING.H.

Parameters

string1, string2   Strings to compare

count   Number of bytes to compare

Remarks

Each of these functions collates, at most, the first *count* bytes in *string1* and *string2* and returns a value indicating the relationship between the resulting substrings of *string1* and *string2*. If the final byte in the substring of *string1* or *string2* is a lead byte, it is not included in the comparison; these functions compare only complete characters in the substrings. **_mbsnbicoll** is a case-insensitive version of **_mbsnbcoll**. Like **_mbsnbcmp** and **_mbsnbicmp**, **_mbsnbcoll** and **_mbsnbicoll** collate the two multibyte-character strings according to the lexicographic order specified by the multibyte code page currently in use. For more information, see "Code Pages" on page 20.

For some code pages and corresponding character sets, the order of characters in the character set may differ from the lexicographic character order. In the "C" locale, this is not the case: the order of characters in the ASCII character set is the same as the lexicographic order of the characters. However, in certain European code pages, for example, the character 'a' (value 0x61) precedes the character 'ä' (value 0xE4) in the character set, but the character 'ä' precedes the character 'a' lexicographically. To perform a lexicographic comparison of strings by bytes in such an instance, use **_mbsnbcoll** rather than **_mbsnbcmp**; to check only for string equality, use **_mbsnbcmp**.

Because the **coll** functions collate strings lexicographically for comparison, whereas the **cmp** functions simply test for string equality, the **coll** functions are much slower than the corresponding **cmp** versions. Therefore, the **coll** functions should be used only when there is a difference between the character set order and the lexicographic character order in the current code page and this difference is of interest for the comparison.

See Also   **_mbsnbcat**, **_mbsnbcmp**, **_mbsnbicmp**, **strcoll** Functions, **strncmp**, **_strnicmp**

_mbsnextc, _strnextc, _wcsnextc

unsigned int _mbsnextc(const unsigned char *_string_);

For the definitions of **_strnextc** and **_wcsnextc**, see TCHAR.H.

> **_mbsnextc, _wcsnextc:** ~~ANSI~~ ~~UNIX~~ ~~WIN32S~~
> **_strnextc:** ~~ANSI~~ ~~UNIX~~ WIN32S

> **#include <tchar.h>**   For **_strnextc** and **_wcsnextc**.
> **#include <mbstring.h>**   For **_mbsnextc**.

Return Value   Each of these functions returns the integer value of the next character in _string_.

Parameter   _string_   Source string

Remarks   The **_mbsnextc** function returns the integer value of the next multibyte-character in _string_, without advancing the string pointer. **_mbsnextc** recognizes multibyte-character sequences according to the multibyte code page currently in use.

The generic-text function **_tcsnextc**, defined in TCHAR.H, maps to **_mbsnextc** if **_MBCS** has been defined, or to **_wcsnextc** if **_UNICODE** has been defined. Otherwise **_tcsnextc** maps to **_strnextc**. **_strnextc** and **_wcsnextc** are single-byte–character string and wide-character string versions of **_mbsnextc**. **_wcsnextc** returns the integer value of the next wide character in _string_;

_strnextc returns the integer value of the next single-byte character in *string*. _strnextc and _wcsnextc are provided only for this mapping and should not be used otherwise. For more information, see "Using Generic-Text Mappings" on page 23 and Appendix B, "Generic-Text Mappings."

See Also　　_mbsdec, _mbsinc, _mbsninc

_mbsninc, _strninc, _wcsninc

unsigned char *_mbsninc(const unsigned char **string***, size_t *****count** **);**

For the definitions of **_strninc** and **_wcsninc**, see TCHAR.H.

_mbsninc, _wcsninc: ~~ANSI~~ ~~UNIX~~ ~~WIN32S~~
_strninc: ~~ANSI~~ ~~UNIX~~ WIN32S

#include <tchar.h>　For **_strninc** and **_wcsninc**.
#include <mbstring.h>　For **_mbsninc**.

Return Value　　Each of these routines returns a pointer to *string* after *string* has been incremented by *count* characters, or **NULL** if the supplied pointer is **NULL**. If *count* is greater than or equal to the number of characters in *string,* the result is undefined.

Parameters　　*string*　　Source string
　　　　　　　　count　　Number of characters to increment string pointer

Remarks　　The **_mbsninc** function increments *string* by *count* multibyte characters. **_mbsninc** recognizes multibyte-character sequences according to the multibyte code page currently in use.

The generic-text function **_tcsninc**, defined in TCHAR.H, maps to **_mbsninc** if **_MBCS** has been defined, or to **_wcsninc** if **_UNICODE** has been defined. Otherwise **_tcsninc** maps to **_strninc**. **_strninc** and **_wcsninc** are single-byte–character string and wide-character string versions of **_mbsninc**. **_wcsninc** and **_strninc** are provided only for this mapping and should not be used otherwise. For more information, see "Using Generic-Text Mappings" on page 23 and Appendix B, "Generic-Text Mappings."

See Also　　_mbsdec, _mbsinc, _mbsnextc

mbstowcs

size_t mbstowcs(wchar_t **wcstr***, const char ****mbstr***, size_t *****count** **);**

ANSI ~~UNIX~~ WIN32S

#include <stdlib.h>

Return Value　　If **mbstowcs** successfully converts the source string, it returns the number of converted multibyte characters. If the *wcstr* argument is **NULL**, the function returns the required size of the destination string. If **mbstowcs** encounters an invalid multibyte character, it returns −1. If the return value is *count*, the wide-character string is not null-terminated.

Parameters   *wcstr*   The address of a sequence of wide characters

mbstr   The address of a sequence of multibyte characters

count   The number of multibyte characters to convert

Remarks   The **mbstowcs** function converts *count* or fewer multibyte characters pointed to by *mbstr* to a string of corresponding wide characters that are determined by the current locale. It stores the resulting wide-character string at the address represented by *wcstr*. The result is similiar to a series of calls to **mbtowc**. If **mbstowcs** encounters the single-byte null character ('\0') either before or when *count* occurs, it converts the null character to a wide-character null character (L'\0') and stops. Thus the wide-character string at *wcstr* is null-terminated only if a null character is encountered during conversion. If the sequences pointed to by *wcstr* and *mbstr* overlap, the behavior is undefined.

If the *wcstr* argument is **NULL**, **mbstowcs** returns the required size of the destination string.

See Also   **mblen, mbtowc, wcstombs, wctomb**

Example

```
/* MBSTOWCS.C illustrates the behavior of the mbstowcs function
 */

#include <stdlib.h>
#include <stdio.h>

void main( void )
{
    int i;
    char    *pmbnull  = NULL;
    char    *pmbhello = (char *)malloc( MB_CUR_MAX );
    wchar_t *pwchello = L"Hi";
    wchar_t *pwc      = (wchar_t *)malloc( sizeof( wchar_t ));

    printf( "Convert to multibyte string:\n" );
    i = wcstombs( pmbhello, pwchello, MB_CUR_MAX );
    printf( "\tCharacters converted: %u\n", i );
    printf( "\tHex value of first" );
    printf( " multibyte character: %#.4x\n\n", pmbhello );

    printf( "Convert back to wide-character string:\n" );
    i = mbstowcs( pwc, pmbhello, MB_CUR_MAX );
    printf( "\tCharacters converted: %u\n", i );
    printf( "\tHex value of first" );
    printf( " wide character: %#.4x\n\n", pwc );
}
```

Output

```
Convert to multibyte string:
    Characters converted: 1
    Hex value of first multibyte character: 0x0e1a

Convert back to wide-character string:
    Characters converted: 1
    Hex value of first wide character: 0x0e1e
```

mbtowc

int mbtowc(wchar_t *****wchar*, **const char *****mbchar*, **size_t *count* **);**

ANSI ~~UNIX~~ WIN32S

#include <stdlib.h>

Return Value   If **mbchar** is not **NULL** and if the object that *mbchar* points to forms a valid
multibyte character, **mbtowc** returns the length in bytes of the multibyte
character. If *mbchar* is **NULL** or the object that it points to is a wide-character
null character (L'\0'), the function returns 0. If the object that *mbchar* points to
does not form a valid multibyte character within the first *count* characters, it
returns −1.

Parameters   *wchar*   Address of a wide character (type **wchar_t**)
mbchar   Address of a sequence of bytes (a multibyte character)
count   Number of bytes to check

Remarks   The **mbtowc** function converts *count* or fewer bytes pointed to by *mbchar*, if
mbchar is not **NULL**, to a corresponding wide character. **mbtowc** stores the
resulting wide character at *wchar,* if *wchar* is not **NULL**. **mbtowc** does not
examine more than **MB_CUR_MAX** bytes.

See Also   **mblen, mbtowc, wcstombs, wctomb**

Example
```
/* MBTOWC.C illustrates the behavior of the mbtowc function */
#include <stdlib.h>
#include <stdio.h>

void main( void )
{
    int     i;
    char    *pmbc    = (char *)malloc( sizeof( char ) );
    wchar_t wc       = L'a';
    wchar_t *pwcnull = NULL;
    wchar_t *pwc     = (wchar_t *)malloc( sizeof( wchar_t ) );
    printf( "Convert a wide character to multibyte character:\n" );
    i = wctomb( pmbc, wc );
    printf( "\tCharacters converted: %u\n", i );
    printf( "\tMultibyte character: %x\n\n", pmbc );
```

```
                         printf( "Convert multibyte character back to a wide "
                                 "character:\n" );
                         i = mbtowc( pwc, pmbc, MB_CUR_MAX );
                         printf( "\tBytes converted: %u\n", i );
                         printf( "\tWide character: %x\n\n", pwc );
                         printf( "Attempt to convert when target is NULL\n" );
                         i = mbtowc( pwcnull, pmbc, MB_CUR_MAX );
                         printf( "\tLength of multibyte character: %u\n\n", i );

                         printf( "Attempt to convert a NULL pointer to a" );
                         printf( " wide character:\n" );
                         pmbc = NULL;
                         i = mbtowc( pwc, pmbc, MB_CUR_MAX );
                         printf( "\tBytes converted: %u\n", i );
                     }
```

Output
```
                 Convert a wide character to multibyte character:
                     Characters converted: 1
                     Multibyte character: 2d02d4

                 Convert multibyte character back to a wide character:
                     Bytes converted: 1
                     Wide character: 2d02dc

                 Attempt to convert when target is NULL
                     Length of multibyte character: 1

                 Attempt to convert a NULL pointer to a wide character:
                     Bytes converted: 0
```

_memccpy

void *_memccpy(void *_dest_, const void *_src_, int _c_, unsigned int _count_);

~~ANSI~~   UNIX   WIN32S

Use **_memccpy** for compatibility with ANSI naming conventions of non-ANSI
functions. Use **memccpy** and link with OLDNAMES.LIB for UNIX
compatibility.

#include <memory.h>
#include <string.h>   For **_memccpy** use MEMORY.H or STRING.H.

Return Value   If the character _c_ is copied, **_memccpy** returns a pointer to the byte in _dest_ that
immediately follows the character. If _c_ is not copied, it returns **NULL**.

Parameters   _dest_ Pointer to destination
src   Pointer to source
_c_   Last character to copy
count   Number of characters

Remarks	The **_memccpy** function copies 0 or more bytes of *src* to *dest*, halting when the character *c* has been copied or when *count* bytes have been copied, whichever comes first.
See Also	**memchr, memcmp, memcpy, memset**
Example	

```
/* MEMCCOPY.C */

#include <memory.h>
#include <stdio.h>
#include <string.h>

char string1[60] = "The quick brown dog jumps over the lazy fox";

void main( void )
{
   char buffer[61];
   char *pdest;

   printf( "Copy 60 characters or up to character 's'\n" );
   printf( "Source:\t\t%s\n", string1 );
   pdest = _memccpy( buffer, string1, 's', 60 );
   *pdest = '\0';
   printf( "Result:\t\t%s\n", buffer );
   printf( "Length:\t\t%d characters\n\n", strlen( buffer ) );
}
```

Output	

```
Copy 60 characters or up to character 's'
Source:     The quick brown dog jumps over the lazy fox
Result:     The quick brown dog jumps
Length:     25 characters
```

memchr

void *memchr(const void **buf***, int** *c***, size_t** *count* **);**

ANSI   UNIX   WIN32S

#include <memory.h>
#include <string.h>   For **memchr** use MEMORY.H or STRING.H.

Return Value	If successful, **memchr** returns a pointer to the first location of *c* in *buf*. Otherwise it returns **NULL**.
Parameters	*buf* Pointer to buffer *c* Character to look for *count* Number of characters to check
Remarks	The **memchr** function looks for the first occurrence of *c* in the first *count* bytes of *buf*. It stops when it finds *c* or when it has checked the first *count* bytes.

See Also	**_memccpy, memcmp, memcpy, memset, strchr**
Example	

```
/* MEMCHR.C */

#include <memory.h>
#include <stdio.h>

int  ch = 'r';
char str[] =    "lazy";
char string[] = "The quick brown dog jumps over the lazy fox";
char fmt1[] =    "         1         2         3         4         5";
char fmt2[] =    "12345678901234567890123456789012345678901234567890";

void main( void )
{
   char *pdest;
   int result;
   printf( "String to be searched:\n\t\t%s\n", string );
   printf( "\t\t%s\n\t\t%s\n\n", fmt1, fmt2 );

   printf( "Search char:\t%c\n", ch );
   pdest = memchr( string, ch, sizeof( string ) );
   result = pdest - string + 1;
   if( pdest != NULL )
      printf( "Result:\t\t%c found at position %d\n\n", ch, result );
   else
      printf( "Result:\t\t%c not found\n" );
}
```

Output

```
String to be searched:
        The quick brown dog jumps over the lazy fox
                 1         2         3         4         5
        12345678901234567890123456789012345678901234567890

Search char:    r
Result:         r found at position 12
```

memcmp

int memcmp(const void *_buf1_, const void *_buf2_, size_t _count_);

ANSI   UNIX   WIN32S

#include <memory.h>
#include <string.h>   For **memcmp** use MEMORY.H or STRING.H.

Return Value   The return value indicates the relationship between the buffers.

Value	Relationship of First *count* Bytes of *buf1* and *buf2*
< 0	*buf1* less than *buf2*
0	*buf1* identical to *buf2*
> 0	*buf1* greater than *buf2*

Parameters

buf1   First buffer
buf2   Second buffer
count   Number of characters

Remarks

The **memcmp** function compares the first *count* bytes of *buf1* and *buf2* and returns a value indicating their relationship.

See Also

_memccpy, memchr, memcpy, memset, strcmp, strncmp

Example

```
/* MEMCMP.C: This program uses memcmp to compare
 * the strings named first and second. If the first
 * 19 bytes of the strings are equal, the program
 * considers the strings to be equal. */

#include <string.h>
#include <stdio.h>
void main( void )
{
    char first[]  = "12345678901234567890";
    char second[] = "12345678901234567891";
    int result;

    printf( "Compare '%.19s' to '%.19s':\n", first, second );
    result = memcmp( first, second, 19 );
    if( result < 0 )
       printf( "First is less than second.\n" );
    else if( result == 0 )
       printf( "First is equal to second.\n" );
    else if( result > 0 )
       printf( "First is greater than second.\n" );
    printf( "Compare '%.20s' to '%.20s':\n", first, second );
    result = memcmp( first, second, 20 );
    if( result < 0 )
       printf( "First is less than second.\n" );
    else if( result == 0 )
       printf( "First is equal to second.\n" );
    else if( result > 0 )
       printf( "First is greater than second.\n" );
}
```

Output

```
Compare '1234567890123456789' to '1234567890123456789':
First is equal to second.
Compare '12345678901234567890' to '12345678901234567891':
First is less than second.
```

memcpy

void *memcpy(void **dest***, const void ****src***, size_t** *count* **);**

ANSI   UNIX   WIN32S

#include <memory.h>
#include <string.h>   For **memcpy** use MEMORY.H or STRING.H.

Return Value   **memcpy** returns the value of *dest*.

Parameters   *dest*   New buffer
src   Buffer to copy from
count   Number of characters to copy

Remarks   The **memcpy** function copies *count* bytes of *src* to *dest*. If the source and destination overlap, this function does not ensure that the original source bytes in the overlapping region are copied before being overwritten. Use **memmove** to handle overlapping regions.

See Also   **_memccpy, memchr, memcmp, memmove, memset, strcpy, strncpy**

Example

```
/* MEMCPY.C: Illustrate overlapping copy: memmove
 * handles it correctly; memcpy does not. */

#include <memory.h>
#include <string.h>
#include <stdio.h>

char string1[60] = "The quick brown dog jumps over the lazy fox";
char string2[60] = "The quick brown fox jumps over the lazy dog";
/*                         1         2         3         4         5
 *               12345678901234567890123456789012345678901234567890
 */

void main( void )
{
    printf( "Function:\tmemcpy without overlap\n" );
    printf( "Source:\t\t%s\n", string1 + 40 );
    printf( "Destination:\t%s\n", string1 + 16 );
    memcpy( string1 + 16, string1 + 40, 3 );
    printf( "Result:\t\t%s\n", string1 );
    printf( "Length:\t\t%d characters\n\n", strlen( string1 ) );

    /* Restore string1 to original contents */
    memcpy( string1 + 16, string2 + 40, 3 );
    printf( "Function:\tmemmove with overlap\n" );
    printf( "Source:\t\t%s\n", string2 + 4 );
    printf( "Destination:\t%s\n", string2 + 10 );
    memmove( string2 + 10, string2 + 4, 40 );
    printf( "Result:\t\t%s\n", string2 );
```

```
            printf( "Length:\t\t%d characters\n\n", strlen( string2 ) );
            printf( "Function:\tmemcpy with overlap\n" );
            printf( "Source:\t\t%s\n", string1 + 4 );
            printf( "Destination:\t%s\n", string1 + 10 );
            memcpy( string1 + 10, string1 + 4, 40 );
            printf( "Result:\t\t%s\n", string1 );
            printf( "Length:\t\t%d characters\n\n", strlen( string1 ) );
        }
```

Output

```
Function:    memcpy without overlap
Source:      fox
Destination: dog jumps over the lazy fox
Result:      The quick brown fox jumps over the lazy fox
Length:      43 characters

Function:    memmove with overlap
Source:      quick brown fox jumps over the lazy dog
Destination: brown fox jumps over the lazy dog
Result:      The quick quick brown fox jumps over the lazy dog
Length:      49 characters

Function:    memcpy with overlap
Source:      quick brown dog jumps over the lazy fox
Destination: brown dog jumps over the lazy fox
Result:      The quick quick brown dog jumps over the lazy fox
Length:      49 characters
```

_memicmp

int _memicmp(const void *_buf1_, const void *_buf2_, unsigned int _count_);

~~ANSI~~ UNIX WIN32S

Use **_memicmp** for compatibility with ANSI naming conventions of non-ANSI functions. Use **memicmp** and link with OLDNAMES.LIB for UNIX compatibility.

#include <memory.h>
#include <string.h>   For **_memicmp** use MEMORY.H or STRING.H.

Return Value

The return value indicates the relationship between the buffers.

Value	Relationship of First _count_ Bytes of _buf1_ and _buf2_
< 0	_buf1_ less than _buf2_
0	_buf1_ identical to _buf2_
> 0	_buf1_ greater than _buf2_

Parameters	*buf1* First buffer
	buf2 Second buffer
	count Number of characters

Remarks

The **_memicmp** function compares the first *count* characters of the two buffers *buf1* and *buf2* byte by byte. The comparison is not case sensitive.

See Also

_memccpy, memchr, memcmp, memcpy, memset, _stricmp, _strnicmp

Example

```
/* MEMICMP.C: This program uses _memicmp to compare
 * the first 29 letters of the strings named first and
 * second without regard to the case of the letters.
 */

#include <memory.h>
#include <stdio.h>
#include <string.h>

void main( void )
{
   int result;
   char first[] = "Those Who Will Not Learn from History";
   char second[] = "THOSE WHO WILL NOT LEARN FROM their mistakes";
   /* Note that the 29th character is right here ^ */

   printf( "Compare '%.29s' to '%.29s'\n", first, second );
   result = _memicmp( first, second, 29 );
   if( result < 0 )
      printf( "First is less than second.\n" );
   else if( result == 0 )
      printf( "First is equal to second.\n" );
   else if( result > 0 )
      printf( "First is greater than second.\n" );
}
```

Output

```
Compare 'Those Who Will Not Learn from' to 'THOSE WHO WILL NOT LEARN
FROM'
First is equal to second.
```

memmove

void *memmove(void **dest***, const void ****src***, size_t** *count* **);**

ANSI ~~UNIX~~ WIN32S

#include <string.h>
#include <memory.h>   For **memmove** use MEMORY.H or STRING.H.

Return Value

memmove returns the value of *dest*.

Parameters	*dest* Destination object
	src Source object
	count Number of characters to copy

Remarks The **memmove** function copies *count* characters from *src* to *dest*. If some regions of the source area and the destination overlap, **memmove** ensures that the original source bytes in the overlapping region are copied before being overwritten.

See Also **_memccpy**, **memcpy**, **strcpy**, **strncpy**

Example See the example for **memcpy**.

memset

void *memset(void **dest***, int** *c***, size_t** *count* **);**

ANSI   UNIX   WIN32S

#include <memory.h>
#include <string.h>   For **memset** use MEMORY.H or STRING.H.

Return Value **memset** returns the value of *dest*.

Parameters *dest* Pointer to destination
c Character to set
count Number of characters

Remarks The **memset** function sets the first *count* bytes of *dest* to the character *c*.

See Also **_memccpy**, **memchr**, **memcmp**, **memcpy**, **_strnset**

Example

```
/* MEMSET.C: This program uses memset to
 * set the first four bytes of buffer to "*".
 */

#include <memory.h>
#include <stdio.h>

void main( void )
{
    char buffer[] = "This is a test of the memset function";

    printf( "Before: %s\n", buffer );
    memset( buffer, '*', 4 );
    printf( "After:  %s\n", buffer );
}
```

Output

```
Before: This is a test of the memset function
After:  **** is a test of the memset function
```

__min

type __**min**(*type a*, *type b*);

ANSI   UNIX   WIN32S

#include <stdlib.h>

Return Value   The smaller of the two arguments

Parameters   *type*   Any numeric data type
                     a, b   Values of any numeric type to be compared

Remarks   The __**min** macro compares two values and returns the value of the smaller one.
                     The arguments can be of any numeric data type, signed or unsigned. Both
                     arguments and the return value must be of the same data type.

See Also   __**max**

Example
```
/* MINMAX.C */

#include <stdlib.h>
#include <stdio.h>

void main( void )
{
    int a = 10;
    int b = 21;

    printf( "The larger of %d and %d is %d\n", a, b, __max( a, b ) );
    printf( "The smaller of %d and %d is %d\n", a, b, __min( a, b ) );
}
```

Output
```
The larger of 10 and 21 is 21
The smaller of 10 and 21 is 10
```

_mkdir, _wmkdir

int _mkdir(const char *``*dirname*``);

int _wmkdir(const wchar_t *``*dirname*``);

_mkdir: ANSI   UNIX   WIN32S
_wmkdir: ANSI   UNIX   WIN32S

#include <direct.h>   For **_mkdir**.
#include <wchar.h>   For **_wmkdir** use DIRECT.H or WCHAR.H.

Return Value   Each of these functions returns the value 0 if the new directory was created. On
                     an error the function returns −1 and sets **errno** as follows:

                     EACCES   Directory was not created because *dirname* is the name of an
                     existing file, directory, or device

ENOENT   Path was not found

Parameter   *dirname*   Path for new directory

Remarks   The **_mkdir** function creates a new directory with the specified *dirname*. **_mkdir** can create only one new directory per call, so only the last component of *dirname* can name a new directory. **_mkdir** does not translate path delimiters. In Windows NT, both the backslash (\) and the forward slash (/) are valid path delimiters in character strings in run-time routines.

_wmkdir is a wide-character version of **_mkdir**; the *dirname* argument to **_wmkdir** is a wide-character string. **_wmkdir** and **_mkdir** behave identically otherwise.

See Also   **_chdir, _rmdir**

Example
```
/* MAKEDIR.C */

#include <direct.h>
#include <stdlib.h>
#include <stdio.h>

void main( void )
{
   if( _mkdir( "\\testtmp" ) == 0 )
   {
      printf( "Directory '\\testtmp' was successfully created\n" );
      system( "dir \\testtmp" );
      if( _rmdir( "\\testtmp" ) == 0 )
        printf( "Directory '\\testtmp' was successfully removed\n"  );
      else
         printf( "Problem removing directory '\\testtmp'\n" );
   }

   else
      printf( "Problem creating directory '\\testtmp'\n" );
}
```

Output
```
Directory '\testtmp' was successfully created
 Volume in drive C is CDRIVE
 Volume Serial Number is 0E17-1702

 Directory of C:\testtmp

05/03/94  12:30p         <DIR>         .
05/03/94  12:30p         <DIR>         ..
             2 File(s)          0 bytes
                          17,358,848 bytes free
Directory '\testtmp' was successfully removed
```

_mktemp, _wmktemp

char *_mktemp(char *_template_);

wchar_t *_wmktemp(wchar_t *_template_);

> _mktemp: ~~ANSI~~   UNIX   WIN32S
> _wmktemp: ~~ANSI~~   UNIX   ~~WIN32S~~

Use **_mktemp** for compatibility with ANSI naming conventions of non-ANSI functions. Use **mktemp** and link with OLDNAMES.LIB for UNIX compatibility.

#include <io.h>   For **_mktemp**.
#include <wchar.h>   For **_wmktemp** use IO.H or WCHAR.H.

Return Value   Each of these functions returns a pointer to the modified template. The function returns **NULL** if _template_ is badly formed or no more unique names can be created from the given template.

Parameter   _template_   Filename pattern

Remarks   The **_mktemp** function creates a unique filename by modifying the _template_ argument. **_mktemp** automatically handles multibyte-character string arguments as appropriate, recognizing multibyte-character sequences according to the multibyte code page currently in use by the run-time system. **_wmktemp** is a wide-character version of **_mktemp**; the argument and return value of **_wmktemp** are wide-character strings. **_wmktemp** and **_mktemp** behave identically otherwise, except that **_wmktemp** does not handle multibyte-character strings.

template has the form _base_XXXXXX where _base_ is the part of the new filename that you supply and each X is a placeholder for a character supplied by **_mktemp**. Each placeholder character in _template_ must be an uppercase X. **_mktemp** preserves _base_ and replaces the first trailing X with an alphabetic character. **_mktemp** replaces the following trailing X's with a five-digit value; this value is a unique number identifying the calling process, or in multi-threaded programs, the calling thread.

Each successful call to **_mktemp** modifies _template_. In each subsequent call from the same process or thread with the same _template_ argument, **_mktemp** checks for filenames that match names returned by **_mktemp** in previous calls. If no file exists for a given name, **_mktemp** returns that name. If files exist for all previously returned names, **_mktemp** creates a new name by replacing the alphabetic character it used in the previously returned name with the next available lowercase letter, in order, from 'a' through 'z'. For example, if _base_ is

```
fn
```

and the five-digit value supplied by **_mktemp** is 12345, the first name returned is

```
fna12345
```

If this name is used to create file FNA12345 and this file still exists, the next name returned on a call from the same process or thread with the same *base* for *template* will be

fnb12345

If FNA12345 does not exist, the next name returned will again be

fna12345

See Also   **fopen, _getmbcp, _getpid, _open, _setmbcp, _tempnam, tmpfile**

Example

```c
/* MKTEMP.C: The program uses _mktemp to create
 * five unique filenames. It opens each filename
 * to ensure that the next name is unique.
 */

#include <io.h>
#include <string.h>
#include <stdio.h>

char *template = "fnXXXXXX";
char *result;
char names[5][9];

void main( void )
{
   int i;
   FILE *fp;

   for( i = 0; i < 5; i++ )
   {
      strcpy( names[i], template );
      /* Attempt to find a unique filename: */
      result = _mktemp( names[i] );
      if( result == NULL )
         printf( "Problem creating the template" );
      else
      {
         if( (fp = fopen( result, "w" )) != NULL )
            printf( "Unique filename is %s\n", result );
         else
            printf( "Cannot open %s\n", result );
         fclose( fp );
      }
   }
}
```

Output

```
Unique filename is fna00141
Unique filename is fnb00141
Unique filename is fnc00141
Unique filename is fnd00141
Unique filename is fne00141
```

mktime

time_t mktime(struct tm *timeptr* **);**

ANSI ~~UNIX~~ WIN32S

#include <time.h>

Return Value

mktime returns the specified calendar time encoded as a value of type **time_t**. If *timeptr* references a date before midnight, January 1, 1970, or if the calendar time cannot be represented, the function returns –1 cast to type **time_t**.

Parameter

timeptr   Pointer to time structure

Remarks

The **mktime** function converts the supplied time structure (possibly incomplete) pointed to by *timeptr* into a fully defined structure with normalized values and then converts it to a **time_t** calendar time value. For description of **tm** structure fields, see **asctime**. The converted time has the same encoding as the values returned by the **time** function. The original values of the **tm_wday** and **tm_yday** components of the *timeptr* structure are ignored, and the original values of the other components are not restricted to their normal ranges.

mktime handles dates in any time zone from midnight, January 1, 1970, to midnight, February 5, 2036. If successful, **mktime** sets the values of **tm_wday** and **tm_yday** as appropriate and sets the other components to represent the specified calendar time, but with their values forced to the normal ranges; the final value of **tm_mday** is not set until **tm_mon** and **tm_year** are determined. When specifying a **tm** structure time, set the **tm_isdst** field to 0 to indicate that standard time is in effect, or to a value greater than 0 to indicate that daylight savings time is in effect, or to a value less than zero to have the C run-time library code compute whether standard time or daylight savings time is in effect. **tm_isdst** is a required field. If not set, its value is undefined and the return value from **mktime** is unpredictable. If *timeptr* points to a **tm** structure returned by a previous call to **asctime**, **gmtime**, or **localtime**, the **tm_isdst** field contains the correct value.

Note that **gmtime** and **localtime** use a single statically allocated buffer for the conversion. If you supply this buffer to **mktime**, the previous contents are destroyed.

See Also   **asctime, gmtime, localtime, time**

Example

```
/* MKTIME.C: The example takes a number of days
 * as input and returns the time, the current
 * date, and the specified number of days.
 */

#include <time.h>
#include <stdio.h>

void main( void )
{
    struct tm when;
    time_t now, result;
    int    days;

    time( &now );
    when = *localtime( &now );
    printf( "Current time is %s\n", asctime( &when ) );
    printf( "How many days to look ahead: " );
    scanf( "%d", &days );

    when.tm_mday = when.tm_mday + days;
    if( (result = mktime( &when )) != (time_t)-1 )
        printf( "In %d days the time will be %s\n",
                days, asctime( &when ) );
    else
        perror( "mktime failed" );
}
```

Output

```
Current time is Tue May 03 12:45:47 1994

How many days to look ahead: 29
In 29 days the time will be Wed Jun 01 12:45:47 1994
```

modf

double modf(double *x*, double *intptr);

ANSI   UNIX   WIN32S

#include <math.h>

Return Value   This function returns the signed fractional portion of *x*. There is no error return.

Parameters   *x*   Floating-point value
intptr   Pointer to stored integer portion

Remarks   The **modf** function breaks down the floating-point value *x* into fractional and integer parts, each of which has the same sign as *x*. The signed fractional portion of *x* is returned. The integer portion is stored as a floating-point value at *intptr*.

See Also   **frexp, ldexp**

Example
```
/* MODF.C */

#include <math.h>
#include <stdio.h>

void main( void )
{
    double x, y, n;

    x = -14.87654321;      /* Divide x into its fractional */
    y = modf( x, &n );      /* and integer parts           */

    printf( "For %f, the fraction is %f and the integer is %.f\n",
            x, y, n );
}
```

Output   `For -14.876543, the fraction is -0.876543 and the integer is -14`

_msize

size_t _msize(void *memblock **);**

ANSI   UNIX   WIN32S

#include <malloc.h>

Return Value   **_msize** returns the size (in bytes) as an unsigned integer.

Parameter   *memblock*   Pointer to memory block

Remarks   The **_msize** function returns the size, in bytes, of the memory block allocated by a call to **calloc**, **malloc**, or **realloc**.

See Also   **calloc, _expand, malloc, realloc**

Example   See the example for **realloc**.

_nextafter

double _nextafter(double *x*, **double** *y* **);**

~~ANSI~~   ~~UNIX~~   WIN32S

#include <float.h>

Return Value   If *x*=*y*, **_nextafter** returns *x*, with no exception triggered. If either *x* or *y* is a quiet NaN, then the return value is one or the other of the input NaNs.

Parameters   *x*, *y*   Double-precision floating-point values

Remarks   The **_nextafter** function returns the closest representable neighbor of *x* in the direction toward *y*.

See Also   **_isnan**

offsetof

size_t offsetof(*struct-name*, *member-name* **);**

ANSI   UNIX   WIN32S

#include <stddef.h>

Return Value   This macro returns the offset in bytes of *member-name* from the beginning of the structure. It is undefined for bit fields.

Parameters   *struct-name*
  member-name

Remarks   The **offsetof** macro returns the offset in bytes of *member-name* from the beginning of the structure specified by *struct-name*. You can specify types with the **struct** keyword.

Note   **offsetof** is not a function and cannot be described using a C prototype.

_onexit

_onexit_t _onexit(**_onexit_t** *func* **);**

~~ANSI~~   UNIX   WIN32S

Use **_onexit** for compatibility with ANSI naming conventions of non-ANSI functions. Use **onexit** and link with OLDNAMES.LIB for UNIX compatibility.

#include <stdlib.h>

Return Value   _onexit returns a pointer to the function if successful, or **NULL** if there is no space to store the function pointer.

Parameter   *func*   Pointer to function to be called at exit

Remarks   The **_onexit** function is passed the address of a function (*func*) to be called when the program terminates normally. Successive calls to **_onexit** create a register of functions that are executed in LIFO (last-in-first-out) order. The functions passed to **_onexit** cannot take parameters.

_onexit is a Microsoft extension. For ANSI portability use **atexit**.

See Also   **atexit, exit**

Example
```c
/* ONEXIT.C */

#include <stdlib.h>
#include <stdio.h>

/* Prototypes */
int fn1(void), fn2(void), fn3(void), fn4 (void);

void main( void )
{
    _onexit( fn1 );
    _onexit( fn2 );
    _onexit( fn3 );
    _onexit( fn4 );
    printf( "This is executed first.\n" );
}
int fn1()
{
    printf( "next.\n" );
    return 0;
}

int fn2()
{
    printf( "executed " );
    return 0;
}
```

```
int fn3()
{
   printf( "is " );
   return 0;
}

int fn4()
{
   printf( "This " );
   return 0;
}
```

Output

```
This is executed first.
This is executed next.
```

_open, _wopen

int _open(const char **filename***, int** *oflag* **[[, int** *pmode*]] **);**

int _wopen(const wchar_t **filename***, int** *oflag* **[[, int** *pmode*]] **);**

> **_open:** ~~ANSI~~ UNIX WIN32S
> **_wopen:** ~~ANSI~~ UNIX ~~WIN32S~~

Use **_open** for compatibility with ANSI naming conventions of non-ANSI functions. Use **open** and link with OLDNAMES.LIB for UNIX compatibility.

#include <io.h>   For **_open**.
#include <wchar.h>   For **_wopen** use IO.H or WCHAR.H.
#include <fcntl.h>
#include <sys/types.h>
#include <sys/stat.h>

Return Value

Each of these functions returns a file handle for the opened file. A return value of –1 indicates an error, in which case **errno** is set to one of the following values:

EACCES   Tried to open read-only file for writing, or file's sharing mode does not allow specified operations, or given path is directory

EEXIST   **_O_CREAT** and **_O_EXCL** flags specified, but *filename* already exists

EINVAL   Invalid *oflag* or *pmode* argument

EMFILE   No more file handles available (too many open files)

ENOENT   File or path not found

Parameters

filename   Filename
oflag   Type of operations allowed
pmode   Permission mode

Remarks

The **_open** function opens the file specified by *filename* and prepares the file for reading or writing, as specified by *oflag*. **_wopen** is a wide-character version of **_open**; the *filename* argument to **_wopen** is a wide-character string. **_wopen** and **_open** behave identically otherwise.

oflag is an integer expression formed from one or more of the following manifest constants or constant combinations defined in FCNTL.H:

_O_APPEND   Moves file pointer to end of file before every write operation.

_O_BINARY   Opens file in binary (untranslated) mode. (See **fopen** for a description of binary mode.)

_O_CREAT   Creates and opens new file for writing. Has no effect if file specified by *filename* exists. *pmode* argument is required when **_O_CREAT** is specified.

_O_CREAT | _O_SHORT_LIVED   Create file as temporary and if possible do not flush to disk. *pmode* argument is required when **_O_CREAT** is specified.

_O_CREAT | _O_TEMPORARY   Create file as temporary; file is deleted when last file handle is closed. *pmode* argument is required when **_O_CREAT** is specified.

_O_CREAT | _O_EXCL   Returns error value if file specified by *filename* exists. Applies only when used with **_O_CREAT**.

_O_RANDOM   Specifies primarily random access from disk

_O_RDONLY   Opens file for reading only; cannot be specified with **_O_RDWR** or **_O_WRONLY**.

_O_RDWR   Opens file for both reading and writing; you cannot specify this flag with **_O_RDONLY** or **_O_WRONLY**.

_O_SEQUENTIAL   Specifies primarily sequential access from disk

_O_TEXT   Opens file in text (translated) mode. (For more information, see "Text and Binary Mode File I/O" on page 12 and **fopen**.)

_O_TRUNC   Opens file and truncates it to zero length; file must have write permission. You cannot specify this flag with **_O_RDONLY**. **_O_TRUNC** used with **_O_CREAT** opens an existing file or creates a new file.

Warning The **_O_TRUNC** flag destroys the contents of the specified file.

_O_WRONLY   Opens file for writing only; cannot be specified with **_O_RDONLY** or **_O_RDWR**.

To specify the file access mode, you must specify either **_O_RDONLY**, **_O_RDWR**, or **_O_WRONLY**. There is no default value for the access mode.

When two or more manifest constants are used to form the *oflag* argument, the constants are combined with the bitwise-OR operator (|). See "Text and Binary Mode File I/O" on page 12 for a discussion of binary and text modes.

The *pmode* argument is required only when **_O_CREAT** is specified. If the file already exists, *pmode* is ignored. Otherwise, *pmode* specifies the file permission settings, which are set when the new file is closed the first time. **_open** applies the current file-permission mask to *pmode* before setting the permissions (for more information, see **_umask**). *pmode* is an integer expression containing one or both of the following manifest constants, defined in SYS\STAT.H:

_S_IREAD   Reading only permitted

_S_IWRITE   Writing permitted (effectively permits reading and writing)

_S_IREAD | _S_IWRITE   Reading and writing permitted

When both constants are given, they are joined with the bitwise-OR operator (|). In Windows NT, all files are readable, so write-only permission is not available; thus the modes **_S_IWRITE** and **_S_IREAD | _S_IWRITE** are equivalent.

See Also   **_chmod**, **_close**, **_creat**, **_dup**, **fopen**, **_sopen**

Example

```
/* OPEN.C: This program uses _open to open a file
 * named OPEN.C for input and a file named OPEN.OUT
 * for output. The files are then closed.
 */

#include <fcntl.h>
#include <sys/types.h>
#include <sys/stat.h>
#include <io.h>
#include <stdio.h>

void main( void )
{
   int fh1, fh2;

   fh1 = _open( "OPEN.C", _O_RDONLY );
   if( fh1 == -1 )
     perror( "Open failed on input file" );
   else
   {
     printf( "Open succeeded on input file\n" );
     _close( fh1 );
   }

   fh2 = _open( "OPEN.OUT", _O_WRONLY | _O_CREAT, _S_IREAD |
                               _S_IWRITE );
   if( fh2 == -1 )
     perror( "Open failed on output file" );
   else
   {
     printf( "Open succeeded on output file\n" );
     _close( fh2 );
   }
}
```

Output

```
Open succeeded on input file
Open succeeded on output file
```

_open_osfhandle

int _open_osfhandle (long *osfhandle*, **int** *flags* **);**

~~ANSI~~ ~~UNIX~~ ~~WIN32S~~

#include <io.h>

Return Value   If successful, **_open_osfhandle** returns a C run-time file handle. Otherwise, it returns –1.

Parameters   *osfhandle*   Operating-system file handle
flags   Types of operations allowed

Remarks   The **_open_osfhandle** function allocates a C run-time file handle and sets it to point to the operating-system file handle specified by *osfhandle*. The *flags* argument is an integer expression formed from one or more of the manifest constants defined in FCNTL.H. When two or more manifest constants are used to form the *flags* argument, the constants are combined with the bitwise-OR operator (|).

The FCNTL.H file defines the following manifest constants:

_O_APPEND   Positions file pointer to end of file before every write operation.

_O_RDONLY   Opens file for reading only

_O_TEXT   Opens file in text (translated) mode

_outp, _outpw, _outpd

int _outp(unsigned short *port***, int** *databyte* **);**

unsigned short _outpw(unsigned short *port***, unsigned short** *dataword* **);**

unsigned long _outpd(unsigned short *port***, unsigned long** *dataword* **);**

~~ANSI~~   ~~UNIX~~   WIN32S

#include <conio.h>

Return Value   The functions return the data output. There is no error return.

Parameters   *port*   Port number
databyte, dataword   Output values

Remarks   The **_outp**, **_outpw**, and **_outpd** functions write a byte, a word, and a double word, respectively, to the specified output port. The *port* argument can be any unsigned integer in the range 0–65,535; *databyte* can be any integer in the range 0–255; and *dataword* can be any value in the range of an integer, an unsigned short integer, and an unsigned long integer, respectively.

See Also   **_inp**

_pclose

int _pclose(FILE *stream);

~~ANSI~~ ~~UNIX~~ ~~WIN32S~~

#include <stdio.h>

Return Value	_pclose returns the exit status of the terminating command processor, or –1 if an error occurs. The format of the return value is the same as that for _cwait, except the low-order and high-order bytes are swapped.
Parameter	*stream* Return value from previous call to _popen
Remarks	The _pclose function looks up the process ID of the command processor (CMD.EXE) started by the associated _popen call, executes a _cwait call on the new command processor, and closes the stream on the associated pipe.
See Also	_pipe, _popen

perror, _wperror

void perror(const char *string);

void _wperror(const wchar_t *string);

perror: ANSI   UNIX   WIN32S
_wperror: ~~ANSI~~   UNIX   ~~WIN32S~~

#include <stdio.h>   For **perror**.
#include <wchar.h>   For **_wperror** use STDIO.H or WCHAR.H.

Return Value	None
Parameter	*string* String message to print
Remarks	The **perror** function prints an error message to **stderr**. **_wperror** is a wide-character version of **_perror**; the *string* argument to **_wperror** is a wide-character string. **_wperror** and **_perror** behave identically otherwise.

string is printed first, followed by a colon, then by the system error message for the last library call that produced the error, and finally by a newline character. If *string* is a null pointer or a pointer to a null string, **perror** prints only the system error message.

The error number is stored in the variable **errno** (defined in ERRNO.H). The system error messages are accessed through the variable **_sys_errlist**, which is an array of messages ordered by error number. **perror** prints the appropriate error message using the **errno** value as an index to **_sys_errlist**. The value of the variable **_sys_nerr** is defined as the maximum number of elements in the **_sys_errlist** array.

For accurate results, call **perror** immediately after a library routine returns with an error. Otherwise, subsequent calls can overwrite the **errno** value.

In Windows NT, some **errno** values listed in ERRNO.H are unused. These values are reserved for use by the UNIX operating system. See "**_doserrno, errno, _sys_errlist, and _sys_nerr**" on page 39 for meanings of **errno** values used in Windows NT. **perror** prints an empty string for any **errno** value not used in Windows NT.

See Also   **clearerr, ferror, strerror**

Example

```
/* PERROR.C: This program attempts to open a file named
 * NOSUCHF.ILE. Because this file probably doesn't exist,
 * an error message is displayed. The same message is
 * created using perror, strerror, and _strerror.
 */

#include <fcntl.h>
#include <sys/types.h>
#include <sys/stat.h>
#include <io.h>
#include <stdlib.h>
#include <stdio.h>
#include <string.h>

void main( void )
{
   int  fh;

   if( (fh = _open( "NOSUCHF.ILE", _O_RDONLY )) == -1 )
   {
      /* Three ways to create error message: */
      perror( "perror says open failed" );
      printf( "strerror says open failed: %s\n", strerror( errno ) );
      printf( _strerror( "_strerror says open failed" ) );
   }
   else
   {
      printf( "open succeeded on input file\n" );
      _close( fh );
   }
}
```

Output

```
perror says open failed: No such file or directory
strerror says open failed: No such file or directory
_strerror says open failed: No such file or directory
```

_pipe

int _pipe(int * *phandles*, **unsigned int** *psize*, **int** *textmode* **);**

~~ANSI~~ ~~UNIX~~ ~~WIN32S~~

#include <fcntl.h>   For **_O_BINARY** and **_O_TEXT** definitions.
#include <errno.h>   **errno** definitions.
#include <io.h>   **Prototype** declaration.

Return Value

_pipe returns 0 if successful. It returns −1 to indicate an error, in which case **errno** is set to one of two values: **EMFILE**, which indicates no more file handles available, or **ENFILE**, which indicates a system file table overflow.

Parameters

phandles[2]   Array to hold read and write handles
psize   Amount of memory to reserve
textmode   File mode

Remarks

The **_pipe** function creates a pipe. A *pipe* is an artificial I/O channel that a program uses to pass information to other programs. A pipe is similar to a file in that it has a file pointer, a file descriptor, or both, and can be read from or written to using the standard library's input and output functions. However, a pipe does not represent a specific file or device. Instead, it represents temporary storage in memory that is independent of the program's own memory and is controlled entirely by the operating system.

_pipe is similar to **_open** but opens the pipe for reading and writing, returning two file handles instead of one. The program can use both sides of the pipe or close the one it does not need. For example, the command processor in Windows NT creates a pipe when executing a command such as

```
PROGRAM1 | PROGRAM2
```

The standard output handle of PROGRAM1 is attached to the pipe's write handle. The standard input handle of PROGRAM2 is attached to the pipe's read handle. This eliminates the need for creating temporary files to pass information to other programs.

The **_pipe** function returns two handles to the pipe in the *phandles* argument. The element *phandles*[0] contains the read handle, and the element *phandles*[1] contains the write handle. Pipe file handles are used in the same way as other file handles. (The low-level input and output functions **_read** and **_write** can read from and write to a pipe.) To detect the end-of-pipe condition, check for a **_read** request that returns 0 as the number of bytes read.

The *psize* argument specifies the amount of memory, in bytes, to reserve for the pipe. The *textmode* argument specifies the translation mode for the pipe. The manifest constant **_O_TEXT** specifies a text translation, and the constant **_O_BINARY** specifies binary translation. (See **fopen** for a description of text and binary modes.) If the *textmode* argument is 0, **_pipe** uses the default translation mode specified by the default-mode variable **_fmode**.

In multithreaded programs, no locking is performed. The handles returned are newly opened and should not be referenced by any thread until after the **_pipe** call is complete.

In Windows NT, a pipe is destroyed when all its handles have been closed. (If all read handles on the pipe have been closed, writing to the pipe causes an error.) All read and write operations on the pipe wait until there is enough data or enough buffer space to complete the I/O request.

See Also   **_open**

Example

```
/* PIPE.C: This program uses the _pipe function to pass streams of
 * text to spawned processes.
 */

#include <stdlib.h>
#include <stdio.h>
#include <io.h>
#include <fcntl.h>
#include <process.h>
#include <math.h>

enum PIPES { READ, WRITE }; /* Constants 0 and 1 for READ and WRITE */
#define NUMPROBLEM 8

void main( int argc, char *argv[] )
{

    int hpipe[2];
    char hstr[20];
    int pid, problem, c;
    int termstat;

    /* If no arguments, this is the spawning process */
    if( argc == 1 )
    {

        setvbuf( stdout, NULL, _IONBF, 0 );

        /* Open a set of pipes */
        if( _pipe( hpipe, 256, O_BINARY ) == -1 )
            exit( 1 );
```

```
    /* Convert pipe read handle to string and pass as argument
     * to spawned program. Program spawns itself (argv[0]).
     */
    itoa( hpipe[READ], hstr, 10 );
    if( ( pid = spawnl( P_NOWAIT, argv[0], argv[0],
          hstr, NULL ) ) == -1 )
        printf( "Spawn failed" );

    /* Put problem in write pipe. Since spawned program is
     * running simultaneously, first solutions may be done
     * before last problem is given.
     */
    for( problem = 1000; problem <= NUMPROBLEM * 1000;
         problem += 1000)
    {
        printf( "Son, what is the square root of %d?\n", problem );
        write( hpipe[WRITE], (char *)&problem, sizeof( int ) );
    }

    /* Wait until spawned program is done processing. */
    _cwait( &termstat, pid, WAIT_CHILD );
    if( termstat & 0x0 )
        printf( "Child failed\n" );

    close( hpipe[READ] );
    close( hpipe[WRITE] );

}

/* If there is an argument, this must be the spawned process. */
else
{

    /* Convert passed string handle to integer handle. */
    hpipe[READ] = atoi( argv[1] );

    /* Read problem from pipe and calculate solution. */
    for( c = 0; c < NUMPROBLEM; c++ )
    {

        read( hpipe[READ], (char *)&problem, sizeof( int ) );
        printf( "Dad, the square root of %d is %3.2f.\n",
                problem, sqrt( ( double )problem ) );

    }
}
}
```

Output

```
Son, what is the square root of 1000?
Son, what is the square root of 2000?
Son, what is the square root of 3000?
Son, what is the square root of 4000?
Son, what is the square root of 5000?
Son, what is the square root of 6000?
Son, what is the square root of 7000?
Son, what is the square root of 8000?
Dad, the square root of 1000 is 31.62.
Dad, the square root of 2000 is 44.72.
Dad, the square root of 3000 is 54.77.
Dad, the square root of 4000 is 63.25.
Dad, the square root of 5000 is 70.71.
Dad, the square root of 6000 is 77.46.
Dad, the square root of 7000 is 83.67.
Dad, the square root of 8000 is 89.44.
```

_popen, _wpopen

FILE *_popen(const char **command***, const char ****mode***);**

FILE *_wpopen(const wchar_t **command***, const wchar_t ****mode***);**

~~ANSI~~ ~~UNIX~~ ~~WIN32S~~

#include <stdio.h>   For **_popen**.
#include <wchar.h>   For **_wpopen** use STRING.H or WCHAR.H.

Return Value

Each of these functions returns a stream associated with one end of the created pipe. The other end of the pipe is associated with the spawned command's standard input or standard output. The functions return **NULL** on an error.

Parameters

command   Command to be executed
mode   Mode of returned stream

Remarks

The **_popen** function creates a pipe and asynchronously executes a spawned copy of the command processor with the specified string *command*. The character string *mode* specifies the type of access requested, as follows:

"r"   The calling process can read the spawned command's standard output via the returned stream.

"w"   The calling process can write to the spawned command's standard input via the returned stream.

"b"   Open in binary mode.

"t"   Open in text mode.

_wpopen is a wide-character version of **_popen**; the *path* argument to **_wpopen** is a wide-character string. **_wpopen** and **_popen** behave identically otherwise.

See Also   **_pclose, _pipe**

Example
```
/* POPEN.C: This program uses _popen and _pclose to receive a
 * stream of text from a system process. */

#include <stdio.h>
#include <stdlib.h>

void main( void )
{
   char   psBuffer[128];
   FILE   *chkdsk;

       /* Run DIR so that it writes its output to a pipe. Open this
    * pipe with read text attribute so that we can read it
       * like a text file.    */
   if( (chkdsk = _popen( "dir *.c /on /p", "rt" )) == NULL )
     exit( 1 );

   /* Read pipe until end of file. End of file indicates that
    * CHKDSK closed its standard out (probably meaning it
        * terminated).
    */
   while( !feof( chkdsk ) )
   {
      if( fgets( psBuffer, 128, chkdsk ) != NULL )
        printf( psBuffer );
   }

   /* Close pipe and print return value of CHKDSK. */
   printf( "\nProcess returned %d\n", _pclose( chkdsk ) );
}
```

Output
```
Volume in drive C is CDRIVE
Volume Serial Number is 0E17-1702

Directory of C:\dolphin\crt\code\pcode

05/02/94  01:05a                   805 perror.c
05/02/94  01:05a                 2,149 pipe.c
05/02/94  01:05a                   882 popen.c
05/02/94  01:05a                   206 pow.c
05/02/94  01:05a                 1,514 printf.c
05/02/94  01:05a                   454 putc.c
05/02/94  01:05a                   162 puts.c
05/02/94  01:05a                   654 putw.c
               8 File(s)          6,826 bytes
                         86,597,632 bytes free

Process returned 0
```

pow

double pow(double *x*, double *y*);

ANSI   UNIX   WIN32S

#include <math.h>

Return Value

pow returns the value of *x^y*. No error message is printed on overflow or underflow.

Values of *x* and *y*	Return Values of pow
x <> 0 and *y* = 0.0	1
x = 0.0 and *y* < 0	INF

Parameters

x   Base
y   Exponent

Remarks

The **pow** function computes *x* raised to the power of *y*.

pow does not recognize integral floating-point values greater than 2^{64}, such as
`1.0E100`.

See Also

exp, **log**, **sqrt**

Example

```
/* POW.C
 *
 */

#include <math.h>
#include <stdio.h>

void main( void )
{
    double x = 2.0, y = 3.0, z;

    z = pow( x, y );
    printf( "%.1f to the power of %.1f is %.1f\n", x, y, z );
}
```

Output

```
2.0 to the power of 3.0 is 8.0
```

printf, wprintf

int printf(const char **format* [[, *argument*]]... **);**

int wprintf(const wchar_t **format* [[, *argument*]]... **);**

> **printf:** ANSI UNIX WIN32S
> **wprintf:** ANSI UNIX ~~WIN32S~~
>
> **#include <stdio.h>**   For **printf**.
> **#include <wchar.h>**   For **wprintf** use STDIO.H or WCHAR.H.

Return Value   Each of these functions returns the number of characters printed, or a negative value if an error occurs.

Parameters   *format*   Format control
argument   Optional arguments

Remarks   The **printf** function formats and prints a series of characters and values to the standard output stream, **stdout**. If arguments follow the *format* string, the *format* string must contain specifications that determine the output format for the arguments. **printf** and **fprintf** behave identically except that **printf** writes output to **stdout** rather than to a destination of type **FILE**.

wprintf is a wide-character version of **printf**; *format* is a wide-character string. **wprintf** and **printf** behave identically otherwise.

The *format* argument consists of ordinary characters, escape sequences, and (if arguments follow *format*) format specifications. The ordinary characters and escape sequences are copied to **stdout** in order of their appearance. For example, the line

```
printf("Line one\n\t\tLine two\n");
```

produces the output

```
Line one
        Line two
```

Format specifications always begin with a percent sign (%) and are read left to right. When **printf** encounters the first format specification (if any), it converts the value of the first argument after *format* and outputs it accordingly. The second format specification causes the second argument to be converted and output, and so on. If there are more arguments than there are format specifications, the extra arguments are ignored. The results are undefined if there are not enough arguments for all the format specifications.

Format Specification Fields

A format specification, which consists of optional and required fields, has the following form:

%[[*flags*]] [[*width*]] [[.*precision*]] [[{**h** | **l** | **L**}]]*type*

Each field of the format specification is a single character or a number signifying a particular format option. The simplest format specification contains only the percent sign and a *type* character (for example, %s). If a percent sign is followed by a character that has no meaning as a format field, the character is copied to **stdout**. For example, to print a percent-sign character, use %%.

The optional fields, which appear before the *type* character, control other aspects of the formatting, as follows:

type   Required character that determines whether the associated *argument* is interpreted as a character, a string, or a number (see Table R.3).

flags   Optional character or characters that control justification of output and printing of signs, blanks, decimal points, and octal and hexadecimal prefixes (see Table R.4). More than one flag can appear in a format specification.

width   Optional number that specifies the minimum number of characters output.

precision   Optional number that specifies the maximum number of characters printed for all or part of the output field, or the minimum number of digits printed for integer values (see Table R.5).

h | **l** | **L**   Optional prefixes to *type*-that specify the size of *argument* (seeTable R.6).

Type Field Characters

The *type* character is the only required format field for **printf**; it appears after any optional format fields. The *type* character determines whether the associated argument is interpreted as a character, string, or number The types **c**, **C**, **s**, and **S** are Microsoft extensions and are not ANSI-compatible.

Table R.3   Type Characters for printf

Character	Type	Output Format
c	**int** or **wint_t**	When used with **printf**, specifies a single-byte character; when used with **wprintf**, specifies a wide character.
C	**int** or **wint_t**	When used with **printf**, specifies a wide character; when used with **wprintf**, specifies a single-byte character.
d	**int**	Signed decimal integer.
i	**int**	Signed decimal integer.
o	**int**	Unsigned octal integer.
u	**int**	Unsigned decimal integer.
x	**int**	Unsigned hexadecimal integer, using "abcdef."
X	**int**	Unsigned hexadecimal integer, using "ABCDEF."
e	**double**	Signed value having the form $[-]d.dddd$ **e** $[sign]ddd$ where d is a single decimal digit, $dddd$ is one or more decimal digits, ddd is exactly three decimal digits, and $sign$ is + or −.
E	**double**	Identical to the **e** format except that **E** rather than **e** introduces the exponent.
f	**double**	Signed value having the form $[-]dddd.dddd$, where $dddd$ is one or more decimal digits. The number of digits before the decimal point depends on the magnitude of the number, and the number of digits after the decimal point depends on the requested precision.
g	**double**	Signed value printed in **f** or **e** format, whichever is more compact for the given value and precision. The **e** format is used only when the exponent of the value is less than −4 or greater than or equal to the *precision* argument. Trailing zeros are truncated, and the decimal point appears only if one or more digits follow it.
G	**double**	Identical to the **g** format, except that **E**, rather than **e**, introduces the exponent (where appropriate).
n	Pointer to integer	Number of characters successfully written so far to the stream or buffer; this value is stored in the integer whose address is given as the argument.
p	Pointer to **void**	Prints the address pointed to by the argument in the form $xxxx:yyyy$ where $xxxx$ is the segment and $yyyy$ is the offset, and the digits x and y are uppercase hexadecimal digits.

Table R.3 Type Characters for printf (*continued*)

Character	Type	Output Format
s	String	When used with **printf**, specifies a single-byte–character string; when used with **wprintf**, specifies a wide-character string. Characters are printed up to the first null character or until the *precision* value is reached.
S	String	When used with **printf**, specifies a wide-character string; when used with **wprintf**, specifies a single-byte–character string. Characters are printed up to the first null character or until the *precision* value is reached.

Flag Directives

The first optional field of the format specification is *flags*. A flag directive is a character that justifies output and prints signs, blanks, decimal points, and octal and hexadecimal prefixes. More than one flag directive may appear in a format specification.

Table R.4 Flag Characters for printf

Flag	Meaning	Default
–	Left align the result within the given field width.	Right align.
+	Prefix the output value with a sign (+ or –) if the output value is of a signed type.	Sign appears only for negative signed values (–).
0	If *width* is prefixed with **0**, zeros are added until the minimum width is reached. If 0 and – appear, the **0** is ignored. If **0** is specified with an integer format (**i**, **u**, **x**, **X**, **o**, **d**) the **0** is ignored.	No padding.
blank (' ')	Prefix the output value with a blank if the output value is signed and positive; the blank is ignored if both the blank and + flags appear.	No blank appears.
#	When used with the **o**, **x**, or **X** format, the **#** flag prefixes any nonzero output value with 0, 0x, or 0X, respectively.	No blank appears.
	When used with the **e**, **E**, or **f** format, the **#** flag forces the output value to contain a decimal point in all cases.	Decimal point appears only if digits follow it.
	When used with the **g** or **G** format, the **#** flag forces the output value to contain a decimal point in all cases and prevents the truncation of trailing zeros.	Decimal point appears only if digits follow it. Trailing zeros are truncated.
	Ignored when used with **c**, **d**, **i**, **u**, or **s**.	

Width Specification

The second optional field of the format specification is the width specification. The *width* argument is a nonnegative decimal integer controlling the minimum number of characters printed. If the number of characters in the output value is less than the specified width, blanks are added to the left or the right of the values—depending on whether the – flag (for left alignment) is specified—until the minimum width is reached. If *width* is prefixed with 0, zeros are added until the minimum width is reached (not useful for left-aligned numbers).

The width specification never causes a value to be truncated. If the number of characters in the output value is greater than the specified width, or if *width* is not given, all characters of the value are printed (subject to the precision specification).

If the width specification is an asterisk (*), an **int** argument from the argument list supplies the value. The *width* argument must precede the value being formatted in the argument list. A nonexistent or small field width does not cause the truncation of a field; if the result of a conversion is wider than the field width, the field expands to contain the conversion result.

Precision Specification

The third optional field of the format specification is the precision specification. It specifies a nonnegative decimal integer, preceded by a period (.), which specifies the number of characters to be printed, the number of decimal places, or the number of significant digits (see Table R.5). Unlike the width specification, the precision specification can cause either truncation of the output value or rounding of a floating-point value. If *precision* is specified as 0 and the value to be converted is 0, the result is no characters output, as shown below:

```
printf( "%.0d", 0 );      /* No characters output */
```

If the precision specification is an asterisk (*), an **int** argument from the argument list supplies the value. The *precision* argument must precede the value being formatted in the argument list.

The type determines the interpretation of *precision* and the default when *precision* is omitted, as shown in Table R.5.

Table R.5   How printf Precision Values Affect Type

	Meaning	Default
	The precision has no effect.	Character is printed.
d, i, u, o, x, X	The precision specifies the minimum number of digits to be printed. If the number of digits in the argument is less than *precision*, the output value is padded on the left with zeros. The value is not truncated when the number of digits exceeds *precision*.	Default precision is 1.
e, E	The precision specifies the number of digits to be printed after the decimal point. The last printed digit is rounded.	Default precision is 6; if *precision* is 0 or the period (.) appears without a number following it, no decimal point is printed.
f	The precision value specifies the number of digits after the decimal point. If a decimal point appears, at least one digit appears before it. The value is rounded to the appropriate number of digits.	Default precision is 6; if *precision* is 0, or if the period (.) appears without a number following it, no decimal point is printed.
g, G	The precision specifies the maximum number of significant digits printed.	Six significant digits are printed, with any trailing zeros truncated.
s, S	The precision specifies the maximum number of characters to be printed. Characters in excess of *precision* are not printed.	Characters are printed until a null character is encountered.

If the argument corresponding to a floating-point specifier is infinite, indefinite, or NaN, **printf** gives the following output.

Value	Output
+ infinity	**1.#INF***random-digits*
– infinity	**–1.#INF***random-digits*
Indefinite (same as quiet NaN)	*digit.***#IND***random-digits*
NaN	*digit.***#NAN***random-digits*

Size and Distance Specification

The optional prefixes to *type*, **h**, **l**, and **L**, specify the "size" of *argument* (long or short, single-byte character or wide character, depending upon the type specifier that they modify). These type-specifier prefixes are used with type characters in **printf** or **wprintf** to specify interpretation of arguments, as shown in the following table. These prefixes are Microsoft extensions and are not ANSI-compatible.

Table R.6   Size Prefixes for printf and wprintf Format-Type Specifiers

To Specify	Use Prefix	With Type Specifier
long int	l	**d, i, o, x,** or **X**
long unsigned int	l	**u**
short int	h	**d, i, o, x,** or **X**
short unsigned int	h	**u**
Single-byte character with **printf**	h	**c** or **C**
Single-byte character with **wprintf**	h	**c** or **C**
Wide character with **printf**	l	**c** or **C**
Wide character with **wprintf**	l	**c** or **C**
Single-byte–character string with **printf**	h	**s** or **S**
Single-byte–character string with **wprintf**	h	**s** or **S**
Wide-character string with **printf**	l	**s** or **S**
Wide-character string with **wprintf**	l	**s** or **S**

Thus to print single-byte or wide-characters with **printf** and **wprintf**, use format specifiers as follows.

To Print Character As	Use Function	With Format Specifier
single byte	printf	**c, hc,** or **hC**
single byte	wprintf	**C, hc,** or **hC**
wide	wprintf	**c, lc,** or **lC**
wide	printf	**C, lc,** or **lC**

To print strings with **printf** and **wprintf**, use the prefixes **h** and **l** analogously with format type-specifiers **s** and **S**.

See Also   **fopen**, **fprintf**, **scanf**, **sprintf**, **vprintf** Functions

Example

```
/* PRINTF.C: This program uses the printf and wprintf functions
 * to produce formatted output.
 */

#include <stdio.h>

void main( void )
{
    char    ch = 'h', *string = "computer";
    int     count = -9234;
    double fp = 251.7366;
    wchar_t wch = L'w', *wstring = L"Unicode";

    /* Display integers. */
    printf( "Integer formats:\n"
            "\tDecimal: %d  Justified: %.6d  Unsigned: %u\n",
            count, count, count, count );

    printf( "Decimal %d as:\n\tHex: %Xh  C hex: 0x%x  Octal: %o\n",
             count, count, count, count );

    /* Display in different radixes. */
    printf( "Digits 10 equal:\n\tHex: %i  Octal: %i  Decimal: %i\n",
            0x10, 010, 10 );

    /* Display characters. */

    printf( "Characters in field (1):\n%10c%5hc%5C%5lc\n", ch, ch, wch,
             wch );
    wprintf( L"Characters in field (2):\n%10C%5hc%5c%5lc\n", ch, ch, wch,
             wch );

    /* Display strings. */

    printf("Strings in field (1):\n%25s\n%25.4hs\n\t%S%25.3ls\n",
    string, string, wstring, wstring);
    wprintf(L"Strings in field (2):\n%25S\n%25.4hs\n\t%s%25.3ls\n",
        string, string, wstring, wstring);

    /* Display real numbers. */
    printf( "Real numbers:\n\t%f %.2f %e %E\n", fp, fp, fp, fp );

    /* Display pointer. */
    printf( "\nAddress as:\t%p\n", &count);

    /* Count characters printed. */
    printf( "\nDisplay to here:\n" );
    printf( "1234567890123456%n78901234567890\n", &count );
    printf( "\tNumber displayed: %d\n\n", count );
}
```

Output

```
Integer formats:
   Decimal: -9234   Justified: -009234   Unsigned: 4294958062
Decimal -9234 as:
   Hex: FFFFDBEEh   C hex: 0xffffdbee   Octal: 37777755756
Digits 10 equal:
   Hex: 16   Octal: 8   Decimal: 10
Characters in field (1):
    h    h    w    w
Characters in field (2):
    h    h    w    w
Strings in field (1):
       computer
           comp
   Unicode                    Uni
Strings in field (2):
       computer
           comp
   Unicode                    Uni
Real numbers:
   251.736600 251.74 2.517366e+002 2.517366E+002

Address as:     0012FFAC

Display to here:
123456789012345678901234567890
   Number displayed: 16
```

putc, putwc, putchar, putwchar

int putc(int *c*, **FILE** **stream* **);**

wint_t putwc(wint_t *c*, **FILE** **stream* **);**

int putchar(int *c* **);**

wint_t putwchar(wint_t *c* **);**

putc, putchar: ANSI   UNIX   WIN32S
putwc, putwchar: ANSI   UNIX   ~~WIN32S~~

#include <stdio.h>   For **putc** and **putchar**.
#include <wchar.h>   For **putwc** and **putwchar** use STDIO.H or WCHAR.H.

Return Value

Each of these functions returns the character written. To indicate an error or end-of-file condition, **putc** and **putchar** return **EOF**; **putwc** and **putwchar** return **WEOF**. For all four routines, use **ferror** or **feof** to check for an error or end of file.

Parameters

c   Character to be written
stream   Pointer to **FILE** structure

Remarks   The **putc** routine writes the single character *c* to the output *stream* at the current position. Any integer can be passed to **putc**, but only the lower 8 bits are written. The **putchar** routine is identical to **putc(*c*, stdout)**. For each routine, if a read error occurs, the error indicator for the stream is set. **putc** and **putchar** are similar to **fputc** and **_fputchar**, respectively, but are implemented both as functions and as macros (see "Choosing Between Functions and Macros" on page viii). **putwc** and **putwchar** are wide-character versions of **putc** and **putchar**, respectively.

See Also   **fputc, getc**

Example
```
/* PUTC.C: This program uses putc to write buffer
 * to a stream. If an error occurs, the program
 * stops before writing the entire buffer.
 */

#include <stdio.h>

void main( void )
{
    FILE *stream;
    char *p, buffer[] = "This is the line of output\n";
    int   ch;

    /* Make standard out the stream and write to it. */
    stream = stdout;
    for( p = buffer; (ch != EOF) && (*p != '\0'); p++ )
        ch = putc( *p, stream );
}
```

Output
```
This is the line of output
```

_putch

int _putch(int *c*);

~~ANSI~~ ~~UNIX~~ WIN32S

#include <conio.h>

Return Value   The function returns *c* if successful, and **EOF** if not.

Parameter   *c*   Character to be output

Remarks   The **_putch** function writes the character *c* directly (without buffering) to the console.

See Also   **_cprintf, _getch**

Example   See the example for **_getch**.

_putenv, _wputenv

int _putenv(const char **envstring* **);**

int _wputenv(const wchar_t **envstring* **);**

        _putenv: ~~ANSI~~ UNIX WIN32S
        _wputenv: ~~ANSI~~ UNIX ~~WIN32S~~

Use **_putenv** for compatibility with ANSI naming conventions of non-ANSI functions. Use **putenv** and link with OLDNAMES.LIB for UNIX compatibility.

#include <stdlib.h>   For **_putenv**.
#include <wchar.h>   For **_wputenv** STDLIB.H or WCHAR.H.

Return Value   **_putenv** and **_wputenv** return 0 if successful, or –1 in the case of an error.

Parameter   *envstring*   Environment-string definition

Remarks   The **_putenv** function adds new environment variables or modifies the values of existing environment variables. Environment variables define the environment in which a process executes (for example, the default search path for libraries to be linked with a program). **_wputenv** is a wide-character version of **_putenv**; the *envstring* argument to **_wputenv** is a wide-character string.

The *envstring* argument must be a pointer to a string of the form *varname=string*, where *varname* is the name of the environment variable to be added or modified and *string* is the variable's value. If *varname* is already part of the environment, its value is replaced by *string*; otherwise, the new *varname* variable and its *string* value are added to the environment. You can remove a variable from the environment by specifying an empty *string*—in other words, by specifying only *varname=*.

_putenv and **_wputenv** affect only the environment that is local to the current process; you cannot use them to modify the command-level environment. That is, these functions operate only on data structures accessible to the run-time library and not on the environment "segment" created for a process by the operating system. When the current process terminates, the environment reverts to the level of the calling process (in most cases, the operating-system level). However, the modified environment can be passed to any new processes created by **_spawn**, **_exec**, or **system**, and these new processes get any new items added by **_putenv** and **_wputenv**.

With regard to environment entries, observe the following cautions:

- Do not change an environment entry directly; instead, use **_putenv** or **_wputenv** to change it. To modify the return value of **_putenv** or **_wputenv** without affecting the environment table, use **_strdup** or **strcpy** to make a copy of the string.

- Never free a pointer to an environment entry, because the environment variable will then point to freed space. A similar problem can occur if you pass **_putenv** or **_wputenv** a pointer to a local variable, then exit the function in which the variable is declared.

getenv and **_putenv** use the global variable **_environ** to access the environment table; **_wgetenv** and **_wputenv** use **_wenviron**. **_putenv** and **_wputenv** may change the value of **_environ** and **_wenviron**, thus invalidating the *envp* argument to **main** and the *wenvp* argument to **wmain**. Therefore, it is safer to use **_environ** or **_wenviron** to access the environment information. For more information about the relation of **_putenv** and **_wputenv** to global variables, see "**_environ**, **_wenviron**," on page 40.

See Also   **getenv, _searchenv**

Example   See the example for **getenv**.

puts, putws

int puts(const char *string **);**

int putws(const wchar_t *string **);**

      puts: ANSI UNIX WIN32S
      putws: ANSI UNIX ~~WIN32S~~

      #include <stdio.h>

Return Value   Each of these returns a nonnegative value if successful. If **puts** fails it returns **EOF**; if **putws** fails it returns **WEOF**.

Parameter   *string*   Output string

Remarks   The **puts** function writes *string* to the standard output stream **stdout**, replacing the string's terminating null character ('\0') with a newline character ('\n') in the output stream.

See Also   **fputs, gets**

Example

```
/* PUTS.C: This program uses puts
 * to write a string to stdout.
 */

#include <stdio.h>

void main( void )
{
   puts( "Hello world from puts!" );
}
```

Output

```
Hello world from puts!
```

_putw

int _putw(int *binint,* **FILE ****stream* **);**

~~ANSI~~   UNIX   WIN32S

Use **_putw** for compatibility with ANSI naming conventions of non-ANSI functions. Use **putw** and link with OLDNAMES.LIB for UNIX compatibility.

#include <stdio.h>

Return Value

_putw returns the value written. A return value of **EOF** may indicate an error. Because **EOF** is also a legitimate integer value, use **ferror** to verify an error.

Parameters

binint   Binary integer to be output
stream   Pointer to **FILE** structure

Remarks

The **_putw** function writes a binary value of type **int** to the current position of *stream*. **_putw** does not affect the alignment of items in the stream, nor does it assume any special alignment. **_putw** is primarily for compatibility with previous libraries. Portability problems may occur with **_putw** because the size of an **int** and the ordering of bytes within an **int** differ across systems.

See Also

_getw

Example

```
/* PUTW.C: This program uses _putw to write a
 * word to a stream, then performs an error check.
 */

#include <stdio.h>
#include <stdlib.h>

void main( void )
{
   FILE *stream;
   unsigned u;
   if( (stream = fopen( "data.out", "wb" )) == NULL )
      exit( 1 );
   for( u = 0; u << 10; u++ )
   {
      _putw( u + 0x2132, stdout );
      _putw( u + 0x2132, stream );     /* Write word to stream. */
      if( ferror( stream ) )           /* Make error check. */
      {
         printf( "_putw failed" );
         clearerr( stream );
         exit( 1 );
      }
   }
   printf( "\nWrote ten words\n" );
   fclose( stream );
}
```

Output

```
Wrote ten words
```

_query_new_handler

_PNH _query_new_handler(void);

~~ANSI~~   ~~UNIX~~   WIN32S

#include <stdio.h>

Return Value

_query_new_handler returns the address of the current new handler routine.

Remarks

The C++ **_query_new_handler** function returns the address of the current new handler routine as set by **_set_new_handler**. The C++ **_set_new_handler** function gains control if the **new** operator fails to allocate memory. The run-time system automatically calls **_set_new_handler** when **new** fails. For more information, see **_set_new_handler**.

_query_new_mode

int _query_new_mode(void);

~~ANSI~~ ~~UNIX~~ WIN32S

#include <stdio.h>

Return Value   **_query_new_mode** returns the current new handler mode, namely 0 or 1, for
malloc. A return value of 1 indicates that, on failure to allocate memory, **malloc**
calls the new handler routine; a return value of 0 indicates that it does not.

Remarks   The C++ **_query_new_mode** function returns an integer that indicates the new
handler mode that is set by the C++ **_set_new_mode** function for **malloc**. The new
handler mode indicates whether, on failure to allocate memory, **malloc** is to call the
new handler routine as set by **_set_new_handler**. By default, **malloc** does not call
the new handler routine on failure. You can use **_set_new_mode** to override this
behavior so that on failure **malloc** calls the new handler routine in the same way
that the **new** operator does when it fails to allocate memory.

See Also   **calloc**, **free**, **malloc**, **realloc**, **_query_new_handler**, **_set_new_handler**,
_set_new_mode

qsort

**void qsort(void *_base_, size_t _num_, size_t _width_, int(_ _ cdecl *_compare_) (const void *_elem1_,
const void *_elem2_));**

ANSI UNIX WIN32S

#include <stdlib.h>
#include <search.h>

Return Value   None

Parameters   _base_   Start of target array
num   Array size in elements
width   Element size in bytes
compare   Comparison function
elem1   Pointer to the key for the search
elem2   Pointer to the array element to be compared with the key

Remarks   The **qsort** function implements a quick-sort algorithm to sort an array of _num_
elements, each of _width_ bytes. The argument _base_ is a pointer to the base of the
array to be sorted. **qsort** overwrites this array with the sorted elements. The
argument _compare_ is a pointer to a user-supplied routine that compares two array
elements and returns a value specifying their relationship. **qsort** calls the _compare_
routine one or more times during the sort, passing pointers to two array elements on
each call:

compare(**(void *)** *elem1*, **(void *)** *elem2* **);**

The routine must compare the elements, then return one of the following values:

Value	Description
< 0	*elem1* less than *elem2*
0	*elem1* equivalent to *elem2*
> 0	*elem1* greater than *elem2*

The array is sorted in increasing order, as defined by the comparison function. To sort an array in decreasing order, reverse the sense of "greater than" and "less than" in the comparison function.

See Also   **bsearch, _lsearch**

Example
```
/* QSORT.C: This program reads the command-line
 * parameters and uses qsort to sort them. It
 * then displays the sorted arguments. */

#include <stdlib.h>
#include <string.h>
#include <stdio.h>

int compare( const void *arg1, const void *arg2 );

void main( int argc, char **argv )
{
   int i;
   /* Eliminate argv[0] from sort: */
   argv++;
   argc--;

   /* Sort remaining args using Quicksort algorithm: */
   qsort( (void *)argv, (size_t)argc, sizeof( char * ), compare );

   /* Output sorted list: */
   for( i = 0; i < argc; ++i )
      printf( "%s ", argv[i] );
   printf( "\n" );
}

int compare( const void *arg1, const void *arg2 )
{
   /* Compare all of both strings: */
   return _stricmp( * ( char** ) arg1, * ( char** ) arg2 );
}
```

Output
```
[c:\code] qsort every good boy deserves favor
boy deserves every favor good
```

raise

int raise(int *sig* **);**

ANSI ~~UNIX~~ WIN32S

#include <signal.h>

Return Value   If successful, **raise** returns 0. Otherwise, it returns a nonzero value.

Parameters   *sig*   Signal to be raised

Remarks   The **raise** function sends *sig* to the executing program. If a previous call to **signal** has installed a signal-handling function for *sig*, **raise** executes that function. If no handler function has been installed, the default action associated with the signal value *sig* is taken, as follows.

Signal	Meaning	Default
SIGABRT	Abnormal termination	Terminates the calling program with exit code 3
SIGFPE	Floating-point error	Terminates the calling program
SIGILL	Illegal instruction	Terminates the calling program
SIGINT	CTRL+C interrupt	Terminates the calling program
SIGSEGV	Illegal storage access	Terminates the calling program
SIGTERM	Termination request sent to the program	Ignores the signal

See Also   **abort**, **signal**

rand

int rand(void);

ANSI UNIX WIN32S

#include <stdlib.h>

Return Value   **rand** returns a pseudorandom number, as described above. There is no error return.

Remarks   The **rand** function returns a pseudorandom integer in the range 0 to **RAND_MAX**. Use the **srand** function to seed the pseudorandom-number generator before calling **rand**.

See Also   **srand**

Example

```
/* RAND.C: This program seeds the random-number generator
 * with the time, then displays 10 random integers.
 */

#include <stdlib.h>
#include <stdio.h>
#include <time.h>

void main( void )
{
   int i;

   /* Seed the random-number generator with current time so that
    * the numbers will be different every time we run.
    */
   srand( (unsigned)time( NULL ) );

   /* Display 10 numbers. */
   for( i = 0;   i < 10;i++ )
      printf( "  %6d\n", rand() );
}
```

Output

```
 6929
 8026
21987
30734
20587
 6699
22034
25051
 7988
10104
```

_read

int _read(int *handle***, void** **buffer***, unsigned int** *count* **);**

~~ANSI~~   UNIX   WIN32S

Use **_read** for compatibility with ANSI naming conventions of non-ANSI functions. Use **read** and link with OLDNAMES.LIB for UNIX compatibility.

#include <io.h>

Return Value

_read returns the number of bytes read, which may be less than *count* if there are fewer than *count* bytes left in the file or if the file was opened in text mode, in which case each carriage-return–linefeed (CR-LF) pair is replaced with a single linefeed character. Only the single linefeed character is counted in the return value. The replacement does not affect the file pointer.

If the function tries to read at end of file, it returns 0. If the *handle* is invalid, or the file is not open for reading, or the file is locked, the function returns −1 and sets **errno** to **EBADF**.

Parameters

handle   Handle referring to open file
buffer   Storage location for data
count   Maximum number of bytes

Remarks

The **_read** function reads a maximum of *count* bytes into *buffer* from the file associated with *handle*. The read operation begins at the current position of the file pointer associated with the given file. After the read operation, the file pointer points to the next unread character.

If the file was opened in text mode, the read terminates when **_read** encounters a CTRL+Z character, which is treated as an end-of-file indicator. . Use **_lseek** to clear the end-of-file indicator.

See Also

_creat, fread, _open, _write

Example

```
/* READ.C: This program opens a file named
 * READ.C and tries to read 60,000 bytes from
 * that file using _read. It then displays the
 * actual number of bytes read from READ.C.
 */

#include <fcntl.h>       /* Needed only for _O_RDWR definition */
#include <io.h>
#include <stdlib.h>
#include <stdio.h>

char buffer[60000];

void main( void )
{
   int fh;
   unsigned int nbytes = 60000, bytesread;

   /* Open file for input: */
   if( (fh = _open( "read.c", _O_RDONLY )) == -1 )
   {
      perror( "open failed on input file" );
      exit( 1 );
   }
```

```
                    /* Read in input: */
                    if( ( bytesread = _read( fh, buffer, nbytes ) ) <= 0 )
                      perror( "Problem reading file" );
                    else
                      printf( "Read %u bytes from file\n", bytesread );

                    _close( fh );
                 }
```

Output   `Read 775 bytes from file`

realloc

void *realloc(void *__memblock__, size_t _size_);

ANSI   UNIX   WIN32S

#include <stdlib.h>   For ANSI compatibility
#include <malloc.h>

Return Value   **realloc** returns a **void** pointer to the reallocated (and possibly moved) memory block. The return value is **NULL** if the size is zero and the buffer argument is not **NULL**, or if there is not enough available memory to expand the block to the given size. In the first case, the original block is freed. In the second, the original block is unchanged. The return value points to a storage space that is guaranteed to be suitably aligned for storage of any type of object. To get a pointer to a type other than **void**, use a type cast on the return value.

Parameters   _memblock_   Pointer to previously allocated memory block
size   New size in bytes

Remarks   The **realloc** function changes the size of an allocated memory block. The _memblock_ argument points to the beginning of the memory block. If _memblock_ is **NULL**, **realloc** behaves the same way as **malloc** and allocates a new block of _size_ bytes. If _memblock_ is not **NULL**, it should be a pointer returned by a previous call to **calloc**, **malloc**, or **realloc**.

The _size_ argument gives the new size of the block, in bytes. The contents of the block are unchanged up to the shorter of the new and old sizes, although the new block can be in a different location. Because the new block can be in a new memory location, the pointer returned by **realloc** is not guaranteed to be the pointer passed through the _memblock_ argument.

See Also   **calloc, free, malloc**

Example

```
/* REALLOC.C: This program allocates a block of memory for
 * buffer and then uses _msize to display the size of that
 * block. Next, it uses realloc to expand the amount of
 * memory used by buffer and then calls _msize again to
 * display the new amount of memory allocated to buffer.
 */

#include <stdio.h>
#include <malloc.h>
#include <stdlib.h>

void main( void )
{
   long *buffer;
   size_t size;

   if( (buffer = (long *)malloc( 1000 * sizeof( long ) )) == NULL )
      exit( 1 );

   size = _msize( buffer );
   printf( "Size of block after malloc of 1000 longs: %u\n", size );

   /* Reallocate and show new size: */
   if( (buffer = realloc( buffer, size + (1000 * sizeof( long )) ))
         == NULL )
      exit( 1 );
   size = _msize( buffer );
   printf( "Size of block after realloc of 1000 more longs: %u\n",
            size );

   free( buffer );
   exit( 0 );
}
```

Output

```
Size of block after malloc of 1000 longs: 4000
Size of block after realloc of 1000 more longs: 8000
```

remove, _wremove

int remove(const char *****path **);**

int _wremove(const wchar_t *****path **);**

remove: ANSI   ~~UNIX~~   WIN32S
_wremove: ~~ANSI~~   ~~UNIX~~   ~~WIN32S~~

#include <stdio.h>   Required for ANSI compatibility
#include <io.h>   Use either IO.H or STDIO.H.
#include <wchar.h>   For **_wremove**

Return Value

Each of these functions returns 0 if the file is successfully deleted. Otherwise, it returns –1 and sets **errno** either to **EACCES** to indicate that the path specifies a read-only file, or to **ENOENT** to indicate that the filename or path was not found or that the path specifies a directory.

Parameters

path   Path of file to be removed

Remarks

The **remove** function deletes the file specified by *path*. **_wremove** is a wide-character version of **_remove**; the *path* argument to **_wremove** is a wide-character string. **_wremove** and **_remove** behave identically otherwise.

See Also

_unlink

Example

```
/* REMOVE.C: This program uses remove to delete REMOVE.OBJ. */

#include <stdio.h>

void main( void )
{
   if( remove( "remove.obj" ) == -1 )
      perror( "Could not delete 'REMOVE.OBJ'" );
   else
      printf( "Deleted 'REMOVE.OBJ'\n" );
}
```

Output

```
Deleted 'REMOVE.OBJ'
```

rename, _wrename

int rename(const char **oldname***, const char ****newname***);**

int _wrename(const wchar_t **oldname***, const wchar_t ****newname***);**

rename: ANSI ~~UNIX~~ WIN32S
_wrename: ~~ANSI~~ ~~UNIX~~ ~~WIN32S~~

#include <stdio.h>   Required for ANSI compatibility
#include <io.h>   Use either IO.H or STDIO.H.
#include <wchar.h>   For **_wrename**

Return Value

Each of these functions returns 0 if it is successful. On an error, the function returns a nonzero value and sets **errno** to one of the following values:

EACCES   File or directory specified by *newname* already exists or could not be created (invalid path); or *oldname* is a directory and *newname* specifies a different path.

ENOENT   File or path specified by *oldname* not found.

Parameters	*oldname* Pointer to old name
	newname Pointer to new name

Remarks

The **rename** function renames the file or directory specified by *oldname* to the name given by *newname*. The old name must be the path of an existing file or directory. The new name must not be the name of an existing file or directory. You can use **rename** to move a file from one directory or device to another by giving a different path in the *newname* argument. However, you cannot use **rename** to move a directory. Directories can be renamed, but not moved.

_wrename is a wide-character version of **_rename**; the arguments to **_wrename** are wide-character strings. **_wrename** and **_rename** behave identically otherwise.

Example

```
/* RENAMER.C: This program attempts to rename a file
 * named RENAMER.OBJ to RENAMER.JBO. For this operation
 * to succeed, a file named RENAMER.OBJ must exist and
 * a file named RENAMER.JBO must not exist.
 */

#include <stdio.h>

void main( void )
{
    int  result;
    char old[] = "RENAMER.OBJ", new[] = "RENAMER.JBO";

    /* Attempt to rename file: */
    result = rename( old, new );
    if( result != 0 )
        printf( "Could not rename '%s'\n", old );
    else
        printf( "File '%s' renamed to '%s'\n", old, new );
}
```

Output

```
File 'RENAMER.OBJ' renamed to 'RENAMER.JBO'
```

rewind

void rewind(FILE *stream);

ANSI UNIX WIN32S

#include <stdio.h>

Return Value

None

Parameter

stream Pointer to **FILE** structure

Remarks

The **rewind** function repositions the file pointer associated with *stream* to the beginning of the file. A call to **rewind** is similar to

(void) fseek(*stream*, **0L, SEEK_SET);**

However, unlike **fseek**, **rewind** clears the error indicators for the stream as well as the end-of-file indicator. Also, unlike **fseek**, **rewind** does not return a value to indicate whether the pointer was successfully moved.

To clear the keyboard buffer, use **rewind** with the stream **stdin**, which is associated with the keyboard by default.

Example

```
/* REWIND.C: This program first opens a file named
 * REWIND.OUT for input and output and writes two
 * integers to the file. Next, it uses rewind to
 * reposition the file pointer to the beginning of
 * the file and reads the data back in.
 */

#include <stdio.h>

void main( void )
{
    FILE *stream;
    int data1, data2;

    data1 = 1;
    data2 = -37;

    if( (stream = fopen( "rewind.out", "w+" )) != NULL )
    {
        fprintf( stream, "%d %d", data1, data2 );
        printf( "The values written are: %d and %d\n", data1, data2 );
        rewind( stream );
        fscanf( stream, "%d %d", &data1, &data2 );
        printf( "The values read are: %d and %d\n", data1, data2 );
        fclose( stream );
    }
}
```

Output

```
The values written are: 1 and -37
The values read are: 1 and -37
```

_rmdir, _wrmdir

int _rmdir(const char **dirname**);

int _rmdir(const wchar_t **dirname**);

> **_rmdir:** ~~ANSI~~ ~~UNIX~~ WIN32S
> **_wrmdir:** ~~ANSI~~ ~~UNIX~~ ~~WIN32S~~
>
> **#include <direct.h>**
> **#include <wchar.h>**   For **_wrmdir**

Return Value   Each of these functions returns 0 if the directory is successfully deleted. A return value of −1 indicates an error, and **errno** is set to one of the following values. **ENOTEMPTY** indicates that the given path is not a directory, the directory is not empty, or the directory is the current working directory or the root directory. **ENOENT** indicates that the path is invalid.

Parameters   *dirname*   Path name of directory to be removed

Remarks   The **_rmdir** function deletes the directory specified by *dirname*. The directory must be empty, and it must not be the current working directory or the root directory.

_wrmdir is a wide-character version of **_rmdir**; the *dirname* argument to **_wrmdir** is a wide-character string. **_wrmdir** and **_rmdir** behave identically otherwise.

See Also   **_chdir, _mkdir**

Example   See the example for **_mkdir**.

_rmtmp

int _rmtmp(void);

> ~~ANSI~~ ~~UNIX~~ WIN32S
>
> **#include <stdio.h>**

Return Value   **_rmtmp** returns the number of temporary files closed and deleted.

Remarks   The **_rmtmp** function cleans up all temporary files in the current directory. The function removes only those files created by **tmpfile**; use it only in the same directory in which the temporary files were created.

See Also	_flushall, tmpfile, tmpnam
Example	See the example for tmpfile.

_rotl, _rotr

unsigned int _rotl(unsigned int *value*, **int** *shift* **);**

unsigned int _rotr(unsigned int *value*, **int** *shift* **);**

~~ANSI~~   ~~UNIX~~   WIN32S

#include <stdlib.h>

Return Value	Both functions return the rotated value. There is no error return.
Parameters	*value* Value to be rotated *shift* Number of bits to shift
Remarks	The **_rotl** and **_rotr** functions rotate the unsigned *value* by *shift* bits. **_rotl** rotates the value left. **_rotr** rotates the value right. Both functions "wrap" bits rotated off one end of *value* to the other end.
See Also	_lrotl, _lrotr
Example	

```
/* ROT.C: This program uses _rotr and _rotl with
 * different shift values to rotate an integer.
 */

#include <stdlib.h>
#include <stdio.h>

void main( void )
{
   unsigned val = 0x0fd93;
   printf( "0x%4.4x rotated left three times is 0x%4.4x\n",
           val, _rotl( val, 3 ) );
   printf( "0x%4.4x rotated right four times is 0x%4.4x\n",
           val, _rotr( val, 4 ) );
}
```

Output	0xfd93 rotated left three times is 0x7ec98 0xfd93 rotated right four times is 0x30000fd9

_scalb

double _scalb(double *x*, **long** *exp* **);**

~~ANSI~~   ~~UNIX~~   WIN32S

#include <float.h>

Return Value   **_scalb** returns an exponential value if successful. On overflow (depending on the sign of *x*), **_scalb** returns +/–**HUGE_VAL**; the **errno** variable is set to **ERANGE**.

Parameters   *x*   Double-precision floating-point value
exp   Long integer exponent

Remarks   The **_scalb** function calculates the value of $x * 2^{exp}$.

See Also   **ldexp**

scanf, wscanf

int scanf(const char **format* [[,*argument*]]... **);**

int wscanf(const wchar_t **format* [[,*argument*]]... **);**

scanf: ANSI   UNIX   WIN32S
wscanf: ANSI   UNIX   ~~WIN32S~~

#include <stdio.h>   For **scanf**.
#include <wchar.h>   For **wscanf** use STDIO.H or WCHAR.H.

Return Value   Both **scanf** and **wscanf** return the number of fields successfully converted and assigned; the return value does not include fields that were read but not assigned. A return value of 0 indicates that no fields were assigned. The return value is **EOF** for an error or if the end-of-file character or the end-of-string character is encountered in the first attempt to read a character.

Parameters   *format*   Format control string
argument   Optional arguments

Remarks   The **scanf** function reads data from the standard input stream **stdin** and writes the data into the location given by *argument*. Each *argument* must be a pointer to a variable of a type that corresponds to a type specifier in *format*. If copying takes place between strings that overlap, the behavior is undefined.

wscanf is a wide-character version of **scanf**; the *format* argument to **wscanf** is a wide-character string. **wscanf** and **scanf** behave identically otherwise.

The *format* argument specifies the interpretation of the input and can contain one or more of the following:

- White-space characters: blank (' '); tab ('\t'); or newline ('\n'). A white-space character causes **scanf** to read, but not store, all consecutive white-space characters in the input up to the next non–white-space character. One white-space character in the format matches any number (including 0) and combination of white-space characters in the input.

- Non–white-space characters, except for the percent sign (%). A non–white-space character causes **scanf** to read, but not store, a matching non–white-space character. If the next character in **stdin** does not match, **scanf** terminates.

- Format specifications, introduced by the percent sign (%). A format specification causes **scanf** to read and convert characters in the input into values of a specified type. The value is assigned to an argument in the argument list.

The format is read from left to right. Characters outside format specifications are expected to match the sequence of characters in **stdin**; the matching characters in **stdin** are scanned but not stored. If a character in **stdin** conflicts with the format specification, **scanf** terminates, and the character is left in **stdin** as if it had not been read.

When the first format specification is encountered, the value of the first input field is converted according to this specification and stored in the location that is specified by the first *argument*. The second format specification causes the second input field to be converted and stored in the second *argument*, and so on through the end of the format string.

An input field is defined as all characters up to the first white-space character (space, tab, or newline), or up to the first character that cannot be converted according to the format specification, or until the field width (if specified) is reached. If there are too many arguments for the given specifications, the extra arguments are evaluated but ignored. The results are unpredictable if there are not enough arguments for the format specification.

A format specification has the form

%[[*]] [[*width*]] [[{**h** | **l** | **L**}]]*type*

Each field of the format specification is a single character or a number signifying a particular format option. The *type* character, which appears after the last optional format field, determines whether the input field is interpreted as a character, a string, or a number.

The simplest format specification contains only the percent sign and a *type* character (for example, %s). If a percent sign (%) is followed by a character that has no meaning as a format-control character, that character and the following characters (up to the next percent sign) are treated as an ordinary sequence of characters, that is, a sequence of characters that must match the input. For example, to specify that a percent-sign character is to be input, use %%.

An asterisk (*) following the percent sign suppresses assignment of the next input field, which is interpreted as a field of the specified type. The field is scanned but not stored.

width is a positive decimal integer controlling the maximum number of characters to be read from **stdin**. No more than *width* characters are converted and stored at the corresponding *argument*. Fewer than *width* characters may be read if a white-space character (space, tab, or newline) or a character that cannot be converted according to the given format occurs before *width* is reached.

The optional prefixes **h**, **l**, and **L** indicate the "size" of the *argument* (long or short, single-byte character or wide character, depending upon the type character that they modify). These format-specification characters are used with type characters in **scanf** or **wscanf** to specify interpretation of arguments as shown in the following table. The type prefixes **h**, **l**, and **L** are Microsoft extensions and are not ANSI-compatible. The type characters and their meanings are described in Table R.8.

Table R.7   Size Prefixes for scanf and wscanf Format-Type Specifiers

To Specify	Use Prefix	With Type Specifier
double	l	**e, E, f, g, or G**
long int	l	**d, i, o, x, or X**
long unsigned int	l	**u**
short int	h	**d, i, o, x, or X**
short unsigned int	h	**u**
Single-byte character with **scanf**	h	**c or C**
Single-byte character with **wscanf**	h	**c or C**
Wide character with **scanf**	l	**c or C**
Wide character with **wscanf**	l	**c, or C**
Single-byte–character string with **scanf**	h	**s or S**
Single-byte–character string with **wscanf**	h	**s or S**
Wide-character string with **scanf**	l	**s or S**
Wide-character string with **wscanf**	l	**s or S**

Following are examples of the use of **h** and **l** with **scanf** and **wscanf**:

```
scanf( "%ls", &x );      // Read a wide-character string
wscanf( "%lC", &x );     // Read a single-byte character
```

To read strings not delimited by space characters, a set of characters in brackets ([ ]) can be substituted for the **s** (string) type character. The corresponding input field is read up to the first character that does not appear in the bracketed character set. If the first character in the set is a caret (^), the effect is reversed: The input field is read up to the first character that does appear in the rest of the character set.

Note that %[a-z] and %[z-a] are interpreted as equivalent to %[abcde...z]. This is a common **scanf** extension, but note that the ANSI standard does not require it.

To store a string without storing a terminating null character ('\0'), use the specification %nc where *n* is a decimal integer. In this case, the **c** type character indicates that the argument is a pointer to a character array. The next *n* characters are read from the input stream into the specified location, and no null character ('\0') is appended. If *n* is not specified, its default value is 1.

scanf scans each input field, character by character. It may stop reading a particular input field before it reaches a space character for a variety of reasons:

- The specified width has been reached.
- The next character cannot be converted as specified.
- The next character conflicts with a character in the control string that it is supposed to match.
- The next character fails to appear in a given character set.

For whatever reason, when **scanf** stops reading an input field, the next input field is considered to begin at the first unread character. The conflicting character, if there is one, is considered unread and is the first character of the next input field or the first character in subsequent read operations on **stdin**.

Table R.8   Type Characters for scanf

Character	Type of Input Expected	Type of Argument
c	When used with **scanf**, specifies single-byte character; when used with **wscanf**, specifies wide character. White-space characters that are ordinarily skipped are read when **c** is specified. To read next non–white-space single-byte character, use **%1s**; to read next non–white-space wide character, use **%1ws**.	Pointer to **char** when used with **scanf**; pointer to **wchar_t** when used with **wscanf**.
C	When used with **scanf**, specifies wide character; when used with **wscanf**, specifies single-byte character. White-space characters that are ordinarily skipped are read when **C** is specified. To read next non–white-space single-byte character, use **%1s**; to read next non–white-space wide character, use **%1ws**.	Pointer to **wchar_t** when used with **scanf**; pointer to **char** when used with **wscanf**.
d	Decimal integer.	Pointer to **int**.
i	Decimal, hexadecimal, or octal integer.	Pointer to **int**.
o	Octal integer.	Pointer to **int**.
u	Unsigned decimal integer.	Pointer to **unsigned int**.
x	Hexadecimal integer.	Pointer to **int**.
e, E, f, g, G	Floating-point value consisting of optional sign (+ or –), series of one or more decimal digits containing decimal point, and optional exponent ("e" or "E") followed by an optionally signed integer value.	Pointer to **float**.
n	No input read from stream or buffer.	Pointer to **int**, into which is stored number of characters successfully read from stream or buffer up to that point in current call to **scanf** or **wscanf**.

Table R.8   Type Characters for scanf (*continued*)

Character	Type of Input Expected	Type of Argument
s	String, up to first white-space character (space, tab or newline). To read strings not delimited by space characters, use set of square brackets ([ ]), as discussed following Table R.7.	When used with **scanf**, signifies single-byte character array; when used with **wscanf**, signifies wide-character array. In either case, character array must be large enough for input field plus terminating null character, which is automatically appended.
S	String, up to first white-space character (space, tab or newline). To read strings not delimited by space characters, use set of square brackets ([ ]), as discussed preceding this table.	When used with **scanf**, signifies wide-character array; when used with **wscanf**, signifies single byte–character array. In either case, character array must be large enough for input field plus terminating null character, which is automatically appended.

The types **c**, **C**, **s**, and **S** are Microsoft extensions and are not ANSI-compatible.

Thus, to read single-byte or wide characters with **scanf** and **wscanf**, use format specifiers as follows.

To Read Character As	Use This Function	With These Format Specifier
single byte	**scanf**	c, **hc**, or **hC**
single byte	**wscanf**	C, **hc**, or **hC**
wide	**wscanf**	c, **lc**, or **lC**
wide	**scanf**	C, **lc**, or **lC**

To scan strings with **scanf** and **wscanf,** use the prefixes **h** and **l** analogously with format type-specifiers **s** and **S**.

See Also   **fscanf, printf, sprintf, sscanf**

Example

```
/* SCANF.C: This program uses the scanf and wscanf functions
 * to read formatted input.
 */

#include <stdio.h>

void main( void )
{
   int   i, result;
   float fp;
   char  c, s[81];
   wchar_t wc, ws[81];

   printf( "\n\nEnter an int, a float, two chars and two strings\n");

   result = scanf( "%d %f %c %C %s %S", &i, &fp, &c, &wc, s, ws );
   printf( "\nThe number of fields input is %d\n", result );
   printf( "The contents are: %d %f %c %C %s %S\n", i, fp, c, wc, s,
           ws);

   wprintf( L"\n\nEnter an int, a float, two chars and two strings\n");

   result = wscanf( L"%d %f %hc %lc %S %ls", &i, &fp, &c, &wc, s, ws );
   wprintf( L"\nThe number of fields input is %d\n", result );
   wprintf( L"The contents are: %d %f %C %c %hs %s\n", i, fp, c, wc, s,
            ws);
}
```

Output

```
Enter an int, a float, two chars and two strings
71
98.6
h
z
Byte characters

The number of fields input is 6
The contents are: 71 98.599998 h z Byte characters

Enter an int, a float, two chars and two strings
36
92.3
y
n
Wide characters

The number of fields input is 6
The contents are: 36 92.300003 y n Wide characters
```

_searchenv, _wsearchenv

void _searchenv(const char *filename, const char *varname, char *pathname);

void _wsearchenv(const wchar_t *filename, const wchar_t *varname, wchar_t *pathname);

_searchenv:	~~ANSI~~	~~UNIX~~	WIN32S
_wsearchenv:	~~ANSI~~	~~UNIX~~	~~WIN32S~~

#include <stdlib.h>   For _searchenv.
#include <wchar.h>   For _wsearchenv use STDLIB.H or WCHAR.H.

Return Value   None

Parameters

filename   Name of file to search for
varname   Environment to search
pathname   Buffer to store complete path

Remarks

The **_searchenv** routine searches for the target file in the specified domain. The *varname* variable can be any environment or user-defined variable that specifies a list of directory paths, such as **PATH**, **LIB**, and **INCLUDE**. **_searchenv** is case sensitive, so *varname* should match the case of the environment variable.

The routine searches first for the file in the current working directory. If it does not find the file, it looks next through the directories specified by the environment variable. If the target file is in one of those directories, the newly created path is copied into *pathname*. You must ensure that there is sufficient space for the constructed path. If the *filename* file is not found, *pathname* contains an empty, null-terminated string.

_wsearchenv is a wide-character version of **_searchenv**; the arguments to **_wsearchenv** are wide-character strings. **_wsearchenv** and **_searchenv** behave identically otherwise.

See Also   **getenv**, **_putenv**

Example

```
/* SEARCHEN.C: This program searches for a file in
 * a directory specified by an environment variable.
 */

#include <stdlib.h>
#include <stdio.h>
```

```
void main( void )
{
   char pathbuffer[_MAX_PATH];
   char searchfile[] = "CL.EXE";
   char envvar[] = "PATH";

   /* Search for file in PATH environment variable: */
   _searchenv( searchfile, envvar, pathbuffer );
   if( *pathbuffer != '\0' )
      printf( "Path for %s: %s\n", searchfile, pathbuffer );
   else
      printf( "%s not found\n", searchfile );
}
```

Output   Path for CL.EXE: C:\MSVC20\BIN\CL.EXE

setbuf

void setbuf(FILE **stream***, char ****buffer***);**

ANSI   UNIX   WIN32S

#include <stdio.h>

Return Value   None

Parameters   *stream*   Pointer to **FILE** structure
                   buffer   User-allocated buffer

Remarks   The **setbuf** function controls buffering for *stream*. The *stream* argument must refer
                   to an open file that has not been read or written. If the *buffer* argument is **NULL**,
                   the stream is unbuffered. If not, the buffer must point to a character array of length
                   BUFSIZ, where **BUFSIZ** is the buffer size as defined in STDIO.H. The user-
                   specified buffer, instead of the default system-allocated buffer for the given stream,
                   is used for I/O buffering. The **stderr** stream is unbuffered by default, but you can
                   use **setbuf** to assign buffers to **stderr**.

                   setbuf has been replaced by **setvbuf**, which is the preferred routine for new code.
                   setbuf is retained for compatibility with existing code.

See Also   **fclose, fflush, fopen, setvbuf**

Example
```
/* SETBUF.C: This program first opens files named DATA1 and
 * DATA2. Then it uses setbuf to give DATA1 a user-assigned
 * buffer and to change DATA2 so that it has no buffer.
 */

#include <stdio.h>
```

```
                void main( void )
                {
                    char buf[BUFSIZ];
                    FILE *stream1, *stream2;

                    if( ((stream1 = fopen( "data1", "a" )) != NULL) &&
                        ((stream2 = fopen( "data2", "w" )) != NULL) )
                    {
                        /* "stream1" uses user-assigned buffer: */
                        setbuf( stream1, buf );
                        printf( "stream1 set to user-defined buffer at: %Fp\n", buf );

                        /* "stream2" is unbuffered              */
                        setbuf( stream2, NULL );
                        printf( "stream2 buffering disabled\n" );
                        _fcloseall();
                    }
                }
```

Output
```
stream1 set to user-defined buffer at: 0012FDA8
stream2 buffering disabled
```

setjmp

int setjmp(jmp_buf *env* **);**

ANSI   UNIX   WIN32S

#include <setjmp.h>

Return Value

setjmp returns 0 after saving the stack environment. If **setjmp** returns as a result of a **longjmp** call, it returns the *value* argument of **longjmp**, or if the *value* argument of **longjmp** is 0, **setjmp** returns 1. There is no error return.

Parameter

env   Variable in which environment is stored

Remarks

The **setjmp** function saves a stack environment, which you can subsequently restore using **longjmp**. When used together, **setjmp** and **longjmp** provide a way to execute a "non-local goto." They are typically used to pass execution control to error-handling or recovery code in a previously called routine without using the normal calling or return conventions.

A call to **setjmp** saves the current stack environment in *env*. A subsequent call to **longjmp** restores the saved environment and returns control to the point just after the corresponding **setjmp** call. All variables (except register variables) accessible to the routine receiving control contain the values they had when **longjmp** was called.

setjmp and **longjmp** do not support C++ object semantics. In C++ programs, use the C++ exception-handling mechanism.

See Also	**longjmp**
Example	See the example for **_fpreset**.

setlocale, _wsetlocale

char *setlocale(int *category***, const char ****locale* **);**

wchar_t *_wsetlocale(int *category***, const wchar_t ****locale* **);**

> setlocale: ANSI   ~~UNIX~~   WIN32S
> **_wsetlocale:**   ~~ANSI~~   ~~UNIX~~   ~~WIN32S~~
>
> **#include <locale.h>**   For **setlocale**.
> **#include <wchar.h>**   For **_wsetlocale** use LOCALE.H or WCHAR.H.

Return Value

If a valid locale and category are given, the function returns a pointer to the string associated with the specified locale and category. If the locale or category is invalid, the function returns a null pointer and the current locale settings of the program are not changed.

For example, the call

```
setlocale( LC_ALL, "English" );
```

sets all categories, returning only the string English_USA.1252. If all categories are not explicitly set by a call to **setlocale**, the function returns a string indicating the current setting of each of the categories, separated by semicolons. If the *locale* argument is a null pointer, **setlocale** returns a pointer to the string associated with the *category* of the program's locale; the program's current locale setting is not changed.

The null pointer is a special directive that tells **setlocale** to query rather than set the international environment. For example, the sequence of calls

```
setlocale( LC_ALL, "English" );        // Set all categories and
                                       // return "English_USA.1252"
setlocale( LC_MONETARY, "French" );    // Set only the LC_MONETARY
                                       // category and return
                                       // "French_France.1252"
setlocale( LC_ALL, NULL );
```

returns

```
LC_COLLATE=English_USA.1252;LC_CTYPE=English_USA.1252;
LC_MONETARY=French_France.1252;LC_NUMERIC=English_USA.1252;
LC_TIME=English_USA.1252
```

which is the string associated with the **LC_ALL** category.

You can use the string pointer returned by **setlocale** in subsequent calls to restore that part of the program's locale information, assuming that your program does not alter the pointer or the string. Later calls to **setlocale** overwrite the string; you can use **_strdup** to save a specific locale string.

Parameters

category   Category affected by locale
locale   Locale name

Remarks

Use the **setlocale** function to set, change, or query some or all of the current program locale information specified by *locale* and *category*. "Locale" refers to the locality (country and language) for which you can customize certain aspects of your program. Some locale-dependent categories include the formatting of dates and the display format for monetary values.

_wsetlocale is a wide-character version of **setlocale**; the *locale* argument and return value of **_wsetlocale** are wide-character strings. **_wsetlocale** and **setlocale** behave identically otherwise.

The *category* argument specifies the parts of a program's locale information that are affected. The macros used for *category* and the parts of the program they affect are as follows:

LC_ALL   All categories, as listed below

LC_COLLATE   The **strcoll, _stricoll, wcscoll, _wcsicoll,** and **strxfrm** functions

LC_CTYPE   The character-handling functions (except **isdigit, isxdigit, mbstowcs,** and **mbtowc,** which are unaffected)

LC_MONETARY   Monetary-formatting information returned by the **localeconv** function

LC_NUMERIC   Decimal-point character for the formatted output routines (such as **printf**), for the data-conversion routines, and for the nonmonetary-formatting information returned by **localeconv**

LC_TIME   The **strftime** and **wcsftime** functions

The *locale* argument is a pointer to a string that specifies the name of the locale. If *locale* points to an empty string, the locale is the implementation-defined native environment. A value of "C" specifies the minimal ANSI conforming environment for C translation. The "C" locale assumes that all **char** data types are 1 byte and that their value is always less than 256. This is the only locale supported in Microsoft Visual C++ version 1.0 and earlier versions of Microsoft C/C++. At program startup, the equivalent of the following statement is executed:

```
setlocale( LC_ALL, "C" );
```

The *locale* argument takes the following form:

```
locale :: "lang[_country[.code_page]]"
          | ".code_page"
          | ""
          | NULL
```

The set of available languages, countries, and code pages includes all those supported by the Win32 NLS API. The set of language and country codes supported by **setlocale** is listed in Appendix A.

If *locale* is a null pointer, **setlocale** queries, rather than sets, the international environment, and returns a pointer to the string associated with the specified *category*. The program's current locale setting is not changed. For example,

```
setlocale( LC_ALL, NULL );
```

returns the string associated with *category*.

The following examples pertain to the **LC_ALL** category. Either of the strings ".OCP" and ".ACP" can be used in place of a code page number to specify use of the system default OEM code page and system-default ANSI code page, respectively.

```
setlocale( LC_ALL, "" );
```
Sets the locale to the default, which is the system-default ANSI code page obtained from the operating system.

```
setlocale( LC_ALL, ".OCP" );
```
Explicitly sets the locale to the current OEM code page obtained from the operating system.

```
setlocale( LC_ALL, ".ACP" );
```
Sets the locale to the ANSI code page obtained from the operating system.

```
setlocale( LC_ALL, "[[lang_ctry]]" );
```
Sets the locale to the language and country indicated, using the default code page obtained from the host operating system.

```
setlocale( LC_ALL, "[[lang_ctry.cp]]" );
```
Sets the locale to the language, country, and code page indicated in the [[*lang_ctry.cp*]] string. You can use various combinations of language, country, and code page. For example:

```
    setlocale( LC_ALL, "French_Canada.1252" );
    setlocale( LC_ALL, "French_Canada.ACP" );    // Set code page
                                                 // to French Canada
                                                 // ANSI default
    setlocale( LC_ALL, "French_Canada.OCP" );    // Set code page
                                                 // to French Canada
                                                 // OEM default
```

```
setlocale( LC_ALL, "[[lang]]" );
```
Sets the locale to the country indicated, using the default country for the language specified, and the system-default ANSI code page for that country as obtained from the host operating system. For example, the following two calls to **setlocale** are functionally equivalent:

```
setlocale( LC_ALL, "English" );

setlocale( LC_ALL, "English_United States.1252" );
```

```
setlocale( LC_ALL, "[[.code_page]]" );
```
Sets the code page to the value indicated, using the default country and language (as defined by the host operating system) for the specified code page.

The category must be either **LC_ALL** or **LC_CTYPE** to effect a change of code page. For example, if the default country and language of the host operating system are "United States" and "English," the following two calls to **setlocale** are functionally equivalent:

```
setlocale( LC_ALL, ".1252" );

setlocale( LC_ALL, "English_United States.1252");
```

See Also   **localeconv, mblen, _mbstrlen, mbstowcs, mbtowc, strcoll** Functions, **strftime, strxfrm, wcstombs, wctomb**

Example
```c
/* LOCALE.C: Sets the current locale to "Germany" using the
 * setlocale function and demonstrates its effect on the strftime
 * function.
 */

#include <stdio.h>
#include <locale.h>
#include <time.h>

void main(void)
{
        time_t ltime;
        struct tm *thetime;
        unsigned char str[100];

        setlocale(LC_ALL, "German");
        time (&ltime);
        thetime = gmtime(&ltime);
```

```
/* %#x is the long date representation, appropriate to
 * the current locale
 */
if (!strftime((char *)str, 100, "%#x",
            (const struct tm *)thetime))
        printf("strftime failed!\n");
else
        printf("In German locale, strftime returns '%s'\n",
            str);

/* Set the locale back to the default environment */
setlocale(LC_ALL, "C");
time (&ltime);
thetime = gmtime(&ltime);

if (!strftime((char *)str, 100, "%#x",
            (const struct tm *)thetime))
        printf("strftime failed!\n");
else
        printf("In 'C' locale, strftime returns '%s'\n",
            str);
}
```

Output

```
In German locale, strftime returns 'Mittwoch, 04. Mai 1994'
In 'C' locale, strftime returns 'Wednesday, May 04, 1994'
```

_setmbcp

int _setmbcp (int *codepage*);

~~ANSI~~ ~~UNIX~~ WIN32S

#include <mbstring.h>

Return Value _setmbcp returns 0 if the code page is set successfully. If an invalid code page value is supplied for *codepage*, the function returns − 1 and the code page setting is unchanged.

Parameter *codepage* New code page setting for locale-independent multibyte routines

Remarks The **_setmbcp** function specifies a new multibyte code page. By default, the run-time system automatically sets the multibyte code page to the system-default ANSI code page. The multibyte code page setting affects all multibyte routines that are not locale-dependent. For a list of the multibyte routines that are dependent on the locale code page rather than the multibyte code page, see "Interpretation of Multibyte-Character Sequences" on page 21.

The multibyte code page also affects multibyte-character processing by the following run-time library routines:

_exec functions	**_mktemp**	**_stat**
_fullpath	**_spawn** functions	**_tempnam**
_makepath	**_splitpath**	**tmpnam**

In addition, all run-time library routines that receive multibyte-character *argv* or *envp* program arguments as parameters (such as the **_exec** and **_spawn** families) process these strings according to the multibyte code page. Hence these routines are also affected by a call to **_setmbcp** that changes the multibyte code page.

The *codepage* argument can be set to any of the following values:

- **_MB_CP_ANSI**   Use ANSI code page obtained from operating system at program startup
- **_MB_CP_OEM**   Use OEM code page obtained from operating system at program startup
- **_MB_CP_SBCS**   Use single-byte code page. When the code page is set to **_MB_CP_SBCS**, a routine such as **_ismbblead** always returns false.
- Any other valid code page value, regardless of whether the value is an ANSI, OEM, or other operating-sytem–supported code page.

See Also   **_getmbcp**

_setmode

int _setmode (int *handle***, int** *mode* **);**

~~ANSI~~   ~~UNIX~~   WIN32S

#include <fcntl.h>
#include <io.h>

Return Value   If successful, **_setmode** returns the previous translation mode. A return value of –1 indicates an error, in which case **errno** is set to either **EBADF**, indicating an invalid file handle, or **EINVAL**, indicating an invalid *mode* argument (neither **_O_TEXT** nor **_O_BINARY**).

Parameters   *handle*   File handle
mode   New translation mode

Remarks

The **_setmode** function sets to *mode* the translation mode of the file given by *handle*. The mode must be one of two manifest constants, **_O_TEXT** or **_O_BINARY**. **_O_TEXT** sets text (translated) mode. Carriage-return–linefeed (CR-LF) combinations are translated into a single linefeed character on input. Linefeed characters are translated into CR-LF combinations on output. **_O_BINARY** sets binary (untranslated) mode, in which these translations are suppressed.

_setmode is typically used to modify the default translation mode of **stdin** and **stdout**, but you can use it on any file. If you apply **_setmode** to the file handle for a stream, call **_setmode** before performing any input or output operations on the stream.

See Also

_creat, **fopen**, **_open**

Example

```
/* SETMODE.C: This program uses _setmode to change
 * stdin from text mode to binary mode.
 */

#include <stdio.h>
#include <fcntl.h>
#include <io.h>

void main( void )
{
    int result;

    /* Set "stdin" to have binary mode: */
    result = _setmode( _fileno( stdin ), _O_BINARY );
    if( result == -1 )
        perror( "Cannot set mode" );
    else
        printf( "'stdin' successfully changed to binary mode\n" );
}
```

Output

```
'stdin' successfully changed to binary mode
```

_set_new_handler

_PNH _set_new_handler(_PNH *pNewHandler* **);**

~~ANSI~~ ~~UNIX~~ WIN32S

#include <new.h>

Return Value

_set_new_handler returns a pointer to the allocated program memory if successful, or 0 if unsuccessful.

Parameter	*pNewHandler* Pointer to a function that you write

Remarks

The C++ **_set_new_handler** function gains control if the **new** operator fails to allocate memory. The run-time system automatically calls **_set_new_handler** when **new** fails. To use **_set_new_handler**, you must write an exception-handling function and then pass it as an argument to **_set_new_handler**. To facilitate declaration of this new handler, the pointer-to-function type, **_PNH**, is defined in NEW.H. **_PNH** is a pointer to a function that returns type **int** and takes an argument of type **size_t**. Use **size_t** to specify the amount of space to be allocated.

_set_new_handler is essentially a garbage-collection scheme. The run-time system retries allocation each time your function returns a nonzero value and fails if your function returns 0.

An occurrence of one of the **_set_new_handler** functions in a program registers the exception-handling function specified in the argument list with the run-time system:

```
#include <new.h>
int handle_program_memory_depletion( size_t )
{
   // Your code
}
void main( void )
{
   _set_new_handler( handle_program_memory_depletion );
   int *pi = new int[BIG_NUMBER];
}
```

You can save the function address that was last passed to the **_set_new_handler** function and reinstate it later:

```
_PNH old_handler = _set_new_handler( my_handler );
   // Code that requires my_handler
   _set_new_handler( old_handler )
   // Code that requires old_handler
```

In a multithreaded environment, handlers are maintained separately for each process and thread. Each new process lacks installed handlers. Each new thread gets a copy of the new handlers of the calling thread. Thus, each process and thread is in charge of its own free-store error handling.

The C++ **_set_new_mode** function sets the new handler mode for **malloc**. The new handler mode indicates whether, on failure, **malloc** is to call the new handler routine as set by **_set_new_handler**. By default, **malloc** does not call the new handler routine on failure to allocate memory. You can override this default behavior so that, when **malloc** fails to allocate memory, **malloc** calls the new handler routine in the same way that the **new** operator does when it fails for the same reason. To override the default, call

```
_set_new_mode(1)
```

early in your program, or link with NEWMODE.OBJ.

For more information on the **new** and **delete** operators, see the *C++ Language Reference*.

See Also   **calloc**, **free**, **realloc**

Example
```
/* HANDLER.CPP: This program uses _set_new_handler to
 * print an error message if the new operator fails. */

#include <stdio.h>
#include <new.h>

/* Allocate memory in chunks of size MemBlock. */
const size_t MemBlock = 1024;

/* Allocate a memory block for the printf function to use in case
 * of memory allocation failure; the printf function uses malloc.
 * The failsafe memory block must be visible globally because the
 * handle_program_memory_depletion function can take one
 * argument only.
 */
char * failsafe = new char[128];

/* Declare a customized function to handle memory-allocation failure.
 * Pass this function as an argument to _set_new_handler.
 */
int handle_program_memory_depletion( size_t );

void main( void )
{
    // Register existence of a new memory handler.
    _set_new_handler( handle_program_memory_depletion );
    size_t *pmemdump = new size_t[MemBlock];
    for( ; pmemdump != 0; pmemdump = new size_t[MemBlock] );
}
int handle_program_memory_depletion( size_t size )
{
    // Release character buffer memory.
    delete failsafe;
    printf( "Allocation failed, " );
    printf( "%u bytes not available.\n", size );
    // Tell new to stop allocation attempts.
    return 0;
}
```

_set_new_mode

int _set_new_mode (int *newhandlermode*);

~~ANSI~~   ~~UNIX~~   WIN32S

#include <new..h>

Return Value	_set_new_mode returns the previous handler mode set for **malloc**. A return value of 1 indicates that, on failure to allocate memory, **malloc** previously called the new handler routine; a return value of 0 indicates that it did not. If the *newhandlermode* argument does not equal 0 or 1, _set_new_mode returns -1.
Parameter	*newhandlermode* New handler mode for **malloc**; valid values are 0 or 1
Remarks	The C++ _set_new_mode function sets the new handler mode for **malloc**. The new handler mode indicates whether, on failure, **malloc** is to call the new handler routine as set by _set_new_handler. By default, **malloc** does not call the new handler routine on failure to allocate memory. You can override this default behavior so that, when **malloc** fails to allocate memory, **malloc** calls the new handler routine in the same way that the **new** operator does when it fails for the same reason. To override the default, call

```
_set_new_mode(1)
```

early in your program, or link with NEWMODE.OBJ.

See Also	**calloc**, **free**, **malloc**, **realloc**, _query_new_handler, _query_new_mode, _set_new_handler

_set_se_translator

typedef void (*_se_translator_function)(unsigned int, struct _EXCEPTION_POINTERS*);

_se_translator_function _set_se_translator(_se_translator_function *se_trans_func*);

~~ANSI~~   ~~UNIX~~   WIN32S

#include <eh.h>
#include <windows.h>

Return Value	_set_se_translator returns a pointer to its argument.
Parameter	*se_trans_func* Pointer to a C structured exception translator function that you write

Remarks   The **_set_se_translator** function provides a way to handle Win32 exceptions (C structured exceptions) as C++ typed exceptions. To allow each C exception to be handled by a C++ **catch** handler, first define a C exception "wrapper" class that can be used, or derived from, in order to attribute a specific class type to a C exception. To use this class, install a custom C exception translator function that is called by the internal exception-handling mechanism each time a C exception is raised. Within your translator function, you can throw any typed exception that can be caught by a matching C++ **catch** handler.

To specify a custom translation function, call **_set_se_translator** with the name of your translation function as its argument. The translator function that you write is called once for each function invocation on the stack that has **try** blocks. There is no default translator function.

The *se_trans_func* function that you write must take an unsigned integer and a pointer to a Win32 **_EXCEPTION_POINTERS** structure as arguments. The arguments are the return values of calls to the Win32 API **GetExceptionCode** and **GetExceptionInformation** functions, respectively.

See Also   **set_terminate, set_unexpected, terminate, unexpected**

set_terminate

typedef void (*terminate_function)();

terminate_function set_terminate(terminate_function *term_func* **);**

ANSI ~~UNIX~~ WIN32S

#include <eh.h>

Return Value   **set_terminate** returns a pointer to its argument.

Parameter   *term_func*   Pointer to a terminate function that you write

Remarks   The **set_terminate** function installs *term_func* as the function called by **terminate**. **set_terminate** is used with C++ exception handling and may be called at any point in your program before the exception is thrown. **terminate** calls **abort** by default. You can change this default by writing your own termination function and calling **set_terminate** with the name of your function as its argument. **terminate** calls the last function given as an argument to **set_terminate**. After performing any desired cleanup tasks, *term_func* should exit the program. If it does not exit (if it returns to its caller), **abort** is called.

The **terminate_function** type is defined in EH.H as a pointer to a user-defined termination function, *term_func*, that returns **void**. Your custom function *term_func* can take no arguments and should not return to its caller. If it does, **abort** is called. An exception may not be thrown from within *term_func*.

See Also   **abort**, **set_unexpected**, **terminate**, **unexpected**

Example   See the example for **terminate**.

set_unexpected

typedef void (*unexpected_function)();

unexpected_function set_unexpected(unexpected_function *unexp_func* **);**

ANSI ~~UNIX~~ WIN32S

#include <eh.h>

Return Value   **set_unexpected** returns a pointer to the previous function given as an argument to **set_unexpected**.

Parameter   *unexp_func*   Pointer to a function that you write to replace the **unexpected** function

Remarks   The **set_unexpected** function installs *unexp_func* as the function called by **unexpected**. **unexpected** is not used in the current C++ exception-handling implementation. The **unexpected_function** type is defined in EH.H as a pointer to a user-defined unexpected function, *unexp_func*, that returns **void**. Your custom *unexp_func* function should not return to its caller.

By default, **unexpected** calls **terminate**. You can change this default behavior by writing your own termination function and calling **set_unexpected** with the name of your function as its argument. **unexpected** calls the last function given as an argument to **set_unexpected**.

Unlike the custom termination function installed by a call to **set_terminate**, an exception can be thrown from within *unexp_func*.

In the current Microsoft implementation of C++ exception handling, **unexpected** calls **terminate** by default and is never called by the exception-handling run-time library. There is no particular advantage to calling **unexpected** rather than **terminate**.

See Also   **abort**, **set_terminate**, **terminate**, **unexpected**

setvbuf

int setvbuf(FILE **stream*, **char** **buffer*, **int** *mode*, **size_t** *size* **);**

ANSI   UNIX   WIN32S

#include <stdio.h>

Return Value   **setvbuf** returns 0 if successful, or a nonzero value if an illegal type or buffer size is specified.

Parameters   *stream*   Pointer to **FILE** structure
buffer   User-allocated buffer
mode   Mode of buffering
size   Buffer size in bytes. Allowable range: $2 < size < 32768$. Internally, the value supplied for *size* is rounded down to the nearest multiple of 2.

Remarks   The **setvbuf** function allows the program to control both buffering and buffer size for *stream*. *stream* must refer to an open file that has not undergone an I/O operation since it was opened. The array pointed to by *buffer* is used as the buffer, unless it is **NULL**, in which case **setvbuf** uses an automatically allocated buffer of length *size*/2 * 2 bytes.

The mode must be **_IOFBF**, **_IOLBF**, or **_IONBF**. If *mode* is **_IOFBF** or **_IOLBF**, then *size* is used as the size of the buffer. If *mode* is **_IONBF**, the stream is unbuffered and *size* and *buffer* are ignored. Values for *mode* and their meanings are:

_IOFBF   Full buffering; that is, *buffer* is used as the buffer and *size* is used as the size of the buffer. If *buffer* is **NULL**, an automatically allocated buffer *size* bytes long is used.

_IOLBF   With MS-DOS, the same as **_IOFBF**.

_IONBF   No buffer is used, regardless of *buffer* or *size*.

See Also   **fclose, fflush, fopen, setbuf**

Example

```c
/* SETVBUF.C: This program opens two streams: stream1
 * and stream2. It then uses setvbuf to give stream1 a
 * user-defined buffer of 1024 bytes and stream2 no buffer.
 */

#include <stdio.h>

void main( void )
{
   char buf[1024];
   FILE *stream1, *stream2;

   if( ((stream1 = fopen( "data1", "a" )) != NULL) &&
       ((stream2 = fopen( "data2", "w" )) != NULL) )
   {
      if( setvbuf( stream1, buf, _IOFBF, sizeof( buf ) ) != 0 )
         printf( "Incorrect type or size of buffer for stream1\n" );
      else
         printf( "'stream1' now has a buffer of 1024 bytes\n" );
      if( setvbuf( stream2, NULL, _IONBF, 0 ) != 0 )
         printf( "Incorrect type or size of buffer for stream2\n" );
      else
         printf( "'stream2' now has no buffer\n" );
      _fcloseall();
   }
}
```

Output

```
'stream1' now has a buffer of 1024 bytes
'stream2' now has no buffer
```

signal

void (*signal(int *sig,* **void(__cdecl ****func* **) (int** *sig* **[[, int** *subcode* **]]))) (int** *sig* **);**

ANSI   UNIX   WIN32S

#include <signal.h>

Return Value

signal returns the previous value of *func* associated with the given signal. For example, if the previous value of *func* was **SIG_IGN**, the return value is also **SIG_IGN**. A return value of **SIG_ERR** indicates an error, in which case **errno** is set to **EINVAL**.

Parameters

sig   Signal value
func   Function to be executed
subcode   Optional subcode to the signal number

Remarks

The **signal** function allows a process to choose one of several ways to handle an interrupt signal from the operating system. The *sig* argument is the interrupt to which **signal** responds; it must be one of the following manifest constants, defined in SIGNAL.H.

sig Value	Description
SIGABRT	Abnormal termination
SIGFPE	Floating-point error
SIGILL	Illegal instruction
SIGINT	CTRL+C signal
SIGSEGV	Illegal storage access
SIGTERM	Termination request

By default, **signal** terminates the calling program with exit code 3, regardless of the value of *sig*.

The *func* argument is an address to a signal handler that you write, or one of the manifest constants **SIG_DFL** or **SIG_IGN**, also defined in SIGNAL.H. If *func* is a function, it is installed as the signal handler for the given signal. The signal handler's prototype requires one formal argument, *sig*, of type **int**. The operating system provides the actual argument through *sig* when an interrupt occurs; the argument is the signal that generated the interrupt. Thus you can use the six manifest constants (listed in the preceding table) inside your signal handler to determine which interrupt occurred and take appropriate action. For example, you can call **signal** twice to assign the same handler to two different signals, then test the *sig* argument inside the handler to take different actions based on the signal received.

If you are testing for floating-point exceptions (**SIGFPE**), *func* points to a function that takes an optional second argument that is one of several manifest constants defined in FLOAT.H of the form **FPE_**xxx. When a **SIGFPE** signal occurs, you can test the value of the second argument to determine the type of floating-point exception and then take appropriate action. This argument and its possible values are Microsoft extensions.

For floating-point exceptions, the value of *func* is not reset upon receiving the signal. To recover from floating-point exceptions, use **setjmp** with **longjmp**. If the function returns, the calling process resumes execution with the floating-point state of the process left undefined.

If the signal handler returns, the calling process resumes execution immediately following the point at which it received the interrupt signal. This is true regardless of the type of signal or operating mode.

Before the specified function is executed, the value of *func* is set to **SIG_DFL**. The next interrupt signal is treated as described for **SIG_DFL**, unless an intervening call to **signal** specifies otherwise. This feature lets you reset signals in the called function.

Because signal-handler routines are usually called asynchronously when an interrupt occurs, your signal-handler function may get control when a run-time operation is incomplete and in an unknown state. The list below summarizes restrictions that determine which functions you can use in your signal-handler routine.

- Do not issue low-level or STDIO.H I/O routines (such as **printf** and **fread**).
- Do not call heap routines or any routine that uses the heap routines (such as **malloc**, **_strdup**, and **_putenv**). See **malloc** for more information.
- Do not use any function that generates a system call (e.g., **_getcwd**, **time**).
- Do not use **longjmp** unless the interrupt is caused by a floating-point exception (i.e., *sig* is **SIGFPE**). In this case, first reinitialize the floating-point package with a call to **_fpreset**.
- Do not use any overlay routines.

A program must contain floating-point code if it is to trap the **SIGFPE** exception with the function. If your program does not have floating-point code and requires the run-time library's signal-handling code, simply declare a volatile double and initialize it to zero:

```
volatile double d = 0.0f;
```

The **SIGILL**, **SIGSEGV**, and **SIGTERM** signals are not generated under Windows NT. They are included for ANSI compatibility. Thus you can set signal handlers for these signals with **signal**, and you can also explicitly generate these signals by calling **raise**.

Signal settings are not preserved in spawned processes created by calls to **_exec** or **_spawn** functions. The signal settings are reset to the default in the new process.

See Also   **abort**, **_exec** Functions, **exit**, **_fpreset**, **_spawn** Functions

sin, sinh

double sin(double *x* **);**

double sinh(double *x* **);**

ANSI   UNIX   WIN32S

#include <math.h>

Return Value

sin returns the sine of *x*. If *x* is greater than or equal to 2^{63}, or less than or equal to -2^{63}, a loss of significance in the result occurs, in which case the function generates a **_TLOSS** error and returns an indefinite (same as a quiet NaN).

sinh returns the hyperbolic sine of *x*. If the result is too large, **sinh** sets **errno** to **ERANGE** and returns ±**HUGE_VAL**. You can modify error handling with **_matherr**.

Parameter

x   Angle in radians

See Also

acos, asin, atan, cos, tan

Example

```
/* SINCOS.C: This program displays the sine, hyperbolic
 * sine, cosine, and hyperbolic cosine of pi / 2.
 */

#include <math.h>
#include <stdio.h>

void main( void )
{
    double pi = 3.1415926535;
    double x, y;

    x = pi / 2;
    y = sin( x );
    printf( "sin( %f ) = %f\n", x, y );
    y = sinh( x );
    printf( "sinh( %f ) = %f\n",x, y );
    y = cos( x );
    printf( "cos( %f ) = %f\n", x, y );
    y = cosh( x );
    printf( "cosh( %f ) = %f\n",x, y );
}
```

Output
```
sin( 1.570796 ) = 1.000000
sinh( 1.570796 ) = 2.301299
cos( 1.570796 ) = 0.000000
cosh( 1.570796 ) = 2.509178
```

_sopen, _wsopen

int _sopen(const char *_filename_, int _oflag_, int _shflag_ [[, int _pmode_]]);

int _wsopen(const wchar_t *_filename_, int _oflag_, int _shflag_ [[, int _pmode_]]);

_sopen: ~~ANSI~~ ~~UNIX~~ WIN32S
_wsopen: ~~ANSI~~ ~~UNIX~~ ~~WIN32S~~

#include <io.h>   For **_sopen**.
#include <wchar.h>   For **_wsopen** use IO.H or WCHAR.H.
#include <fcntl.h>
#include <sys/types.h>
#include <sys/stat.h>
#include <share.h>

Return Value   Each of these functions returns a file handle for the opened file. A return value of −1 indicates an error, in which case **errno** is set to one of the following values:

EACCES   Given path is a directory, or file is read-only, but an open-for-writing operation was attempted.

EEXIST   **_O_CREAT** and **_O_EXCL** flags were specified, but _filename_ already exists.

EINVAL   Invalid _oflag_ or _shflag_ argument.

EMFILE   No more file handles available.

ENOENT   File or path not found.

Parameters   _filename_   Filename
oflag   Type of operations allowed
shflag   Type of sharing allowed
pmode   Permission setting

Remarks

The **_sopen** function opens the file specified by *filename* and prepares the file for shared reading or writing, as defined by *oflag* and *shflag*. **_wsopen** is a wide-character version of **_sopen**; the *filename* argument to **_wsopen** is a wide-character string. **_wsopen** and **_sopen** behave identically otherwise.

The integer expression *oflag* is formed by combining one or more of the following manifest constants, defined in the file FCNTL.H. When two or more constants form the argument *oflag*, they are combined with the bitwise-OR operator (|).

_O_APPEND   Repositions file pointer to end of file before every write operation.

_O_BINARY   Opens file in binary (untranslated) mode. (See **fopen** for a description of binary mode.)

_O_CREAT   Creates and opens new file for writing. Has no effect if file specified by *filename* exists. The *pmode* argument is required when **_O_CREAT** is specified.

_O_CREAT | _O_SHORT_LIVED   Create file as temporary and if possible do not flush to disk. The *pmode* argument is required when **_O_CREAT** is specified.

_O_CREAT | _O_TEMPORARY   Create file as temporary; file is deleted when last file handle is closed. The *pmode* argument is required when **_O_CREAT** is specified.

_O_CREAT | _O_EXCL   Returns error value if file specified by *filename* exists. Applies only when used with **_O_CREAT**.

_O_RANDOM   Specifies primarily random access from disk

_O_RDONLY   Opens file for reading only; cannot be specified with **_O_RDWR** or **_O_WRONLY**.

_O_RDWR   Opens file for both reading and writing; cannot be specified with **_O_RDONLY** or **_O_WRONLY**.

_O_SEQUENTIAL   Specifies primarily sequential access from disk

_O_TEXT   Opens file in text (translated) mode. (For more information, see "Text and Binary Mode File I/O" on page 12 and **fopen**.)

_O_TRUNC   Opens file and truncates it to zero length; the file must have write permission. You cannot specify this flag with **_O_RDONLY**. **_O_TRUNC** used with **_O_CREAT** opens an existing file or creates a new file.

> **Warning**   The **_O_TRUNC** flag destroys the contents of the specified file.

_O_WRONLY   Opens file for writing only; cannot be specified with **_O_RDONLY** or **_O_RDWR**.

To specify the file access mode, you must specify either **_O_RDONLY**, **_O_RDWR**, or **_O_WRONLY**. There is no default value for the access mode.

The argument *shflag* is a constant expression consisting of one of the following manifest constants, defined in SHARE.H.

_SH_DENYRW   Denies read and write access to file

_SH_DENYWR   Denies write access to file

_SH_DENYRD   Denies read access to file

_SH_DENYNO   Permits read and write access

The *pmode* argument is required only when you specify **_O_CREAT**. If the file does not exist, *pmode* specifies the file's permission settings, which are set when the new file is closed the first time. Otherwise *pmode* is ignored. *pmode* is an integer expression that contains one or both of the manifest constants **_S_IWRITE** and **_S_IREAD**, defined in SYS\STAT.H. When both constants are given, they are combined with the bitwise-OR operator. The meaning of *pmode* is as follows:

_S_IWRITE   Writing permitted

_S_IREAD   Reading permitted

_S_IREAD | _S_IWRITE   Reading and writing permitted

If write permission is not given, the file is read-only. With Windows NT, all files are readable; it is not possible to give write-only permission. Thus the modes **_S_IWRITE** and **_S_IREAD | _S_IWRITE** are equivalent.

_sopen applies the current file-permission mask to *pmode* before setting the permissions (see **_umask**).

See Also   **_close**, **_creat**, **fopen**, **_fsopen**, **_open**,

Example   See the example for **_locking**.

_spawn, _wspawn Functions

int _spawnl(int *mode*, const char **cmdname, const char **arg0, const char **arg1, ...
  const char **argn, NULL);

int _wspawnl(int *mode*, const wchar_t **cmdname, const wchar_t **arg0, const wchar_t **arg1, ...
  const wchar_t **argn, NULL);

int _spawnle(int *mode*, const char **cmdname, const char **arg0, const char =*arg1*, ...
  const char **argn, NULL, const char * const **envp);

int _wspawnle(int *mode*, const wchar_t **cmdname, const wchar_t **arg0, const wchar_t **arg1, ...
  const wchar_t **argn, NULL, const wchar_t * const **envp);

int _spawnlp(int *mode*, const char **cmdname, const char **arg0, const char **arg1, ...
  const char **argn, NULL);

int _wspawnlp(int *mode*, const wchar_t **cmdname, const wchar_t **arg0, const wchar_t **arg1, ...
  const wchar_t **argn, NULL);

int _spawnlpe(int *mode*, const char **cmdname, const char **arg0, const char **arg1, ...
  const char **argn, NULL, const char * const **envp);

int _wspawnlpe(int *mode*, const wchar_t **cmdname, const wchar_t **arg0, const wchar_t **arg1, ...
  const wchar_t **argn, NULL, const wchar_t * const **envp);

int _spawnv(int *mode*, const char **cmdname, const char * const **argv);

int _wspawnv(int *mode*, const wchar_t **cmdname, const wchar_t * const **argv);

int _spawnve(int *mode*, const char **cmdname, const char * const **argv, const char
  * const **envp);

int _wspawnve(int *mode*, const wchar_t **cmdname, const wchar_t * const **argv,
  const wchar_t * const **envp);

int _spawnvp(int *mode*, const char **cmdname, const char * const **argv);

int _wspawnvp(int *mode*, const wchar_t **cmdname, const wchar_t * const **argv);

int _spawnvpe(int *mode*, const char **cmdname, const char * const **argv,
  const char * const **envp);

int _wspawnvpe(int *mode*, const wchar_t **cmdname, const wchar_t * const **argv,
  const wchar_t * const **envp);

_spawnl, _spawnle, _spawnlp, _spawnlpe, _spawnlv, _spawnlve, _spawnlp, _spawnlpe: ~~ANSI~~ ~~UNIX~~ WIN32S
_wspawnl, _wspawnle, _wspawnlp, _wspawnlpe, _wspawnlv, _wspawnlve, _wspawnlp, _wspawnlpe: ~~ANSI~~ ~~UNIX~~ ~~WIN32S~~

#include <stdio.h> For _spawn functions.
#include <wchar.h> For **_wspawn** functions use STDIO.H or WCHAR.H.
#include <process.h>

Return Value

The return value from a synchronous **_spawn** or **_wspawn** (**_P_WAIT** specified for *mode*) is the exit status of the new process. The return value from an asynchronous **_spawn** or **_wspawn** (**_P_NOWAIT** or **_P_NOWAITO** specified for *mode*) is the process handle. The exit status is 0 if the process terminated normally. You can set the exit status to a nonzero value if the spawned process specifically calls the **exit** routine with a nonzero argument. If the new process did not explicitly set a positive exit status, a positive exit status indicates an abnormal exit with an abort or an interrupt. A return value of –1 indicates an error (the new process is not started). In this case, **errno** is set to one of the following values:

E2BIG   Argument list exceeds 1024 bytes

EINVAL   *mode* argument is invalid

ENOENT   File or path is not found

ENOEXEC   Specified file is not executable or has invalid executable-file format

ENOMEM   Not enough memory is available to execute new process

Parameters

mode   Execution mode for calling process
cmdname   Path of file to be executed
arg0, ... argn   List of pointers to arguments
argv   Array of pointers to arguments
envp   Array of pointers to environment settings

Remarks

The **_spawn** functions each create and execute a new process. They automatically handle multibyte-character string arguments as appropriate, recognizing multibyte-character sequences according to the multibyte code page currently in use. The **_wspawn** functions are wide-character versions of the **_spawn** functions; they do not handle multibyte-character strings. Otherwise, the **_wspawn** functions behave identically to their **_spawn** counterparts.

Enough memory must be available for loading and executing the new process. The *mode* argument determines the action taken by the calling process before and during **_spawn**. The following values for *mode* are defined in PROCESS.H:

_P_OVERLAY   Overlays calling process with new process, destroying the calling process (same effect as **_exec** calls).

_P_WAIT   Suspends calling process until execution of new process is complete (synchronous **_spawn**).

_P_NOWAIT or **_P_NOWAITO**   Continues to execute calling process concurrently with new process (asynchronous **_spawn**).

_P_DETACH   Continues to execute the calling process; new process is run in the background with no access to the console or keyboard. Calls to **_cwait** against the new process will fail (asynchronous **_spawn**).

The *cmdname* argument specifies the file that is executed as the new process and can specify a full path (from the root), a partial path (from the current working directory), or just a filename. If *cmdname* does not have a filename extension or does not end with a period (**.**), the **_spawn** function first tries the .COM extension, then the .EXE extension, the .BAT extension, and finally the .CMD extension.

If *cmdname* has an extension, only that extension is used. If *cmdname* ends with a period, the **_spawn** call searches for *cmdname* with no extension. The **_spawnlp**, **_spawnlpe**, **_spawnvp**, and **_spawnvpe** functions search for *cmdname* (using the same procedures) in the directories specified by the **PATH** environment variable.

If *cmdname* contains a drive specifier or any slashes (that is, if it is a relative path), the **_spawn** call searches only for the specified file; no path searching is done.

Note To ensure proper overlay initialization and termination, do not use the **setjmp** or **longjmp** function to enter or leave an overlay routine.

Arguments for the Spawned Process

To pass arguments to the new process, give one or more pointers to character strings as arguments in the **_spawn** call. These character strings form the argument list for the spawned process. The combined length of the strings forming the argument list for the new process must not exceed 1024 bytes. The terminating null character ('\0') for each string is not included in the count, but space characters (automatically inserted to separate arguments) are included.

You can pass argument pointers as separate arguments (in **_spawnl**, **_spawnle**, **_spawnlp**, and **_spawnlpe**) or as an array of pointers (in **_spawnv**, **_spawnve**, **_spawnvp**, and **_spawnvpe**). You must pass at least one argument, *arg0* or *argv*[0], to the spawned process. By convention, this argument is the name of the program as you would type it on the command line. A different value does not produce an error.

The **_spawnl**, **_spawnle**, **_spawnlp**, and **_spawnlpe** calls are typically used in cases where the number of arguments is known in advance. The *arg0* argument is usually a pointer to *cmdname*. The arguments *arg1* through *argn* are pointers to the character strings forming the new argument list. Following *argn*, there must be a **NULL** pointer to mark the end of the argument list.

The **_spawnv**, **_spawnve**, **_spawnvp**, and **_spawnvpe** calls are useful when there is a variable number of arguments to the new process. Pointers to the arguments are passed as an array, *argv*. *argv*[1] through *argv*[*n*] are pointers to the character strings forming the new argument list. The argument *argv*[*n* +1] must be a **NULL** pointer to mark the end of the argument list.

Environment of the Spawned Process

Files that are open when a **_spawn** call is made remain open in the new process. In the **_spawnl**, **_spawnlp**, **_spawnv**, and **_spawnvp** calls, the new process inherits the environment of the calling process. You can use the **_spawnle**, **_spawnlpe**, **_spawnve**, and **_spawnvpe** calls to alter the environment for the new process by passing a list of environment settings through the *envp* argument. The argument *envp* is an array of character pointers, each element (except the final element) of which points to a null-terminated string defining an environment variable. Such a string usually has the form *NAME=value* where *NAME* is the name of an environment variable and *value* is the string value to which that variable is set. (Note that *value* is not enclosed in double quotation marks.) The final element of the *envp* array should be **NULL**. When *envp* itself is **NULL**, the spawned process inherits the environment settings of the parent process.

Depending on the setting of the **_fileinfo** global variable, the **_spawn** functions can pass information about open files, including the translation mode, to the new process. The environment information is passed in text form and therefore contains no graphics characters. (For more information, see "**_fileinfo**" on page 42.)

You must explicitly flush (using **fflush** or **_flushall**) or close any stream before calling a **_spawn** function.

New processes created by calls to **_spawn** functions do not preserve signal settings. Instead, the spawned process resets signal settings to the default.

See Also   **abort**, **atexit**, **_exec** Functions, **exit**, **_flushall**, **_getmbcp**, **_onexit**, **_setmbcp**, **system**

_splitpath, _wsplitpath

void _splitpath(const char *_path_, char *_drive_, char *_dir_, char *_fname_, char *_ext_);

void _wsplitpath(const wchar_t *_path_, wchar_t *_drive_, wchar_t *_dir_, wchar_t *_fname_, wchar_t *_ext_);

_splitpath: ~~ANSI~~ ~~UNIX~~   WIN32S
_wsplitpath: ~~ANSI~~ ~~UNIX~~   ~~WIN32S~~

#include <stdlib.h>   For **_splitpath**.
#include <wchar.h>   For **_wsplitpath** use STDLIB.H or WCHAR.H.

Return Value   None

Parameters   _path_   Full path
drive   Optional drive letter, followed by a colon (:)
dir   Optional directory path, including trailing slash. Forward slashes (/), backslashes (\ ), or both may be used.
fname   Base filename (no extension)
ext   Optional filename extension, including leading period (.)

Remarks   The **_splitpath** function breaks a path into its four components. **_splitpath** automatically handles multibyte-character string arguments as appropriate, recognizing multibyte-character sequences according to the multibyte code page currently in use. **_wsplitpath** is a wide-character version of **_splitpath**; the arguments to **_wsplitpath** are wide-character strings. These functions behave identically otherwise.

Each argument is stored in a buffer; the manifest constants **_MAX_DRIVE**, **_MAX_DIR**, **_MAX_FNAME**, and **_MAX_EXT** (defined in STDLIB.H) specify the maximum size necessary for each buffer. The other arguments point to buffers used to store the path elements. After a call to **_splitpath** is executed, these arguments contain empty strings for components not found in _path_. You can pass a **NULL** pointer to **_splitpath** for any component you don't need.

See Also   **_fullpath**, **_getmbcp**, **_makepath**, **_setmbcp**

Example   See the example for **_makepath**.

sprintf, _snprintf, _snwprintf, swprintf

int sprintf(char *buffer*, **const char** *format* [[, *argument*]] ... **);**

int _snprintf(char *buffer*, **size_t** *count*, **const char** *format* [[, *argument*]] ... **);**

int _snwprintf(wchar_t *buffer*, **size_t** *count*, **const wchar_t** *format* [[, *argument*]] ... **);**

int swprintf(wchar_t *buffer*, **const wchar_t** *format* [[, *argument*]] ... **);**

sprintf: ANSI UNIX WIN32S,   **swprintf:** ANSI UNIX ~~WIN32S~~
_snprintf: ~~ANSI~~ ~~UNIX~~ WIN32S,   **_snwprintf:** ~~ANSI~~ ~~UNIX~~ ~~WIN32S~~

#include <stdio.h> For **sprintf** and **_snprintf**.
#include <wchar.h> For **swprintf** and **_snwprintf** use STDIO.H or WCHAR.H.

Return Value

sprintf and **_snprintf** return the number of bytes stored in *buffer*, not counting the terminating null character. For **_snprintf**, if the number of bytes required to store the data exceeds *count*, then *count* bytes of data are stored in *buffer* and a negative value is returned. **swprintf** and **_snwprintf** return the number of wide characters stored in *buffer*, not counting the terminating null wide character. For **_snwprintf**, if the storage required to store the data exceeds *count* wide characters, then *count* wide characters are stored in *buffer* and a negative value is returned.

Parameters

argument   Optional arguments
buffer   Storage location for output
count   Maximum number of characters to store
format   Format-control string

Remarks

The **sprintf** function formats and stores a series of characters and values in *buffer*. Each *argument* (if any) is converted and output according to the corresponding format specification in *format*. The format consists of ordinary characters and has the same form and function as the *format* argument for **printf**. (See **printf** for a description of the format and arguments.) A null character is appended after the last character written. If copying occurs between strings that overlap, the behavior is undefined.

_snprintf differs from **sprintf** in that **_snprintf** writes no more than *count* characters to *buffer*, including a terminating null character, which is always appended unless *count* is zero.

swprintf is a wide-character version of **sprintf**; the pointer arguments to **swprintf** are wide-character strings. The detection of encoding errors in **swprintf** may differ from that in **sprintf**. **swprintf** and **fwprintf** behave identically except that **swprintf** writes output to a string rather than to a destination of type **FILE**.

_snwprintf differs from **swprintf** in that no more than *count* wide characters are written to *buffer*, including a terminating null wide character, which is always appended unless *count* is zero.

See Also   **fprintf**, **printf**, **scanf**, **sscanf**, **vprintf** Functions

Example

```
/* SPRINTF.C: This program uses sprintf to format various
 * data and place them in the string named buffer.
 */

#include <stdio.h>

void main( void )
{
    char  buffer[200], s[] = "computer", c = '1';
    int   i = 35, j;
    float fp = 1.7320534f;

    /* Format and print various data: */
    j  = sprintf( buffer,      "\tString:    %s\n", s );
    j += sprintf( buffer + j, "\tCharacter: %c\n", c );
    j += sprintf( buffer + j, "\tInteger:   %d\n", i );
    j += sprintf( buffer + j, "\tReal:      %f\n", fp );

    printf( "Output:\n%s\ncharacter count = %d\n", buffer, j );
}
```

Output

```
Output:
    String:    computer
    Character: 1
    Integer:   35
    Real:      1.732053

character count = 71
```

sqrt

double sqrt(double *x*);

ANSI   UNIX   WIN32S

#include <math.h>

Return Value   The **sqrt** function returns the square-root of *x*. If *x* is negative, **sqrt** returns an indefinite (same as a quiet NaN). You can modify error handling with **_matherr**.

Parameter   *x*   Nonnegative floating-point value

See Also   **exp**, **log**, **pow**

Example

```
/* SQRT.C: This program calculates a square root. */

#include <math.h>
#include <stdio.h>
#include <stdlib.h>

void main( void )
{
    double question = 45.35, answer;

    answer = sqrt( question );
    if( question < 0 )
        printf( "Error: sqrt returns %.2f\n, answer" );
    else
        printf( "The square root of %.2f is %.2f\n", question, answer );
}
```

Output

```
The square root of 45.35 is 6.73
```

srand

void srand(unsigned int *seed* **);**

ANSI   UNIX   WIN32S

#include <stdlib.h>

Return Value   None

Parameter   *seed*   Seed for random-number generation

Remarks   The **srand** function sets the starting point for generating a series of pseudorandom integers. To reinitialize the generator, use 1 as the *seed* argument. Any other value for *seed* sets the generator to a random starting point. **rand** retrieves the pseudorandom numbers that are generated. Calling **rand** before any call to **srand** generates the same sequence as calling **srand** with *seed* passed as 1.

See Also   **rand**

Example   See the example for **rand**.

sscanf, swscanf

int sscanf(const char **buffer*, **const char** **format* [[, *argument*]] ... **);**

int swscanf(const wchar_t **buffer*, **const wchar_t** **format* [[, *argument*]] ... **);**

sscanf: ANSI UNIX WIN32S
swscanf: ANSI UNIX ~~WIN32S~~

#include <stdio.h>   For **sscanf**.
#include <wchar.h>   For **swscanf** use STDIO.H or WCHAR.H.

Return Value

Each of these functions returns the number of fields successfully converted and assigned; the return value does not include fields that were read but not assigned. A return value of 0 indicates that no fields were assigned. The return value is **EOF** for an error or if the end of the string is reached before the first conversion.

Parameters

buffer   Stored data
format   Format-control string
argument   Optional arguments

Remarks

The **sscanf** function reads data from *buffer* into the location given by each *argument*. Every *argument* must be a pointer to a variable with a type that corresponds to a type specifier in *format*. The *format* argument controls the interpretation of the input fields and has the same form and function as the *format* argument for the **scanf** function; see **scanf** for a complete description of *format*. If copying takes place between strings that overlap, the behavior is undefined.

swscanf is a wide-character version of **sscanf**; the arguments to **swscanf** are wide-character strings. **swscanf** and **sscanf** behave identically otherwise.

See Also

fscanf, scanf, sprintf, _snprintf

Example

```
/* SSCANF.C: This program uses sscanf to read data items
 * from a string named tokenstring, then displays them.
 */

#include <stdio.h>

void main( void )
{
   char   tokenstring[] = "15 12 14...";
   char   s[81];
   char   c;
   int    i;
   float  fp;
```

```
                    /* Input various data from tokenstring: */
                    sscanf( tokenstring, "%s", s );
                    sscanf( tokenstring, "%c", &c );
                    sscanf( tokenstring, "%d", &i );
                    sscanf( tokenstring, "%f", &fp );

                    /* Output the data read */
                    printf( "String    = %s\n", s );
                    printf( "Character = %c\n", c );
                    printf( "Integer:  = %d\n", i );
                    printf( "Real:     = %f\n", fp );
                }
```

Output

```
String    = 15
Character = 1
Integer:  = 15
Real:     = 15.000000
```

_stat, _wstat

int _stat(const char *_path_, struct _stat *_buffer_);

int _wstat(const wchar_t *_path_, struct _stat *_buffer_);

~~ANSI~~ UNIX ~~WIN32S~~

Use **_stat** for compatibility with ANSI naming conventions of non-ANSI functions. Use **stat** and link with OLDNAMES.LIB for UNIX compatibility.

#include <sys/types.h>
#include <sys/stat.h>

Return Value   Each of these functions returns 0 if the file-status information is obtained. A return value of –1 indicates an error, in which case **errno** is set to **ENOENT**, indicating that the filename or path could not be found.

Parameters   _path_   Path of existing file
buffer   Pointer to structure that stores results

Remarks   The **_stat** function obtains information about the file or directory specified by _path_ and stores it in the structure pointed to by _buffer_. **_stat** automatically handles multibyte-character string arguments as appropriate, recognizing multibyte-character sequences according to the multibyte code page currently in use.

_wstat is a wide-character version of **_stat**; the _path_ argument to **_wstat** is a wide-character string. **_wstat** and **_stat** behave identically except that **_wstat** does not handle multibyte-character strings.

The **_stat** structure, defined in SYS\STAT.H, includes the following fields.

gid   Numeric identifier of group that owns file (UNIX-specific)

st_atime   Time of last access of file.

st_ctime   Time of creation of file.

st_dev   Drive number of the disk containing the file (same as **st_rdev**).

st_ino   Number of the information node (the *inode*) for the file (UNIX-specific). On UNIX file systems, the inode describes the file date and time stamps, permissions, and content. When files are soft-linked to one another, they share the same inode. The inode, and therefore **st_ino**, has no meaning in the FAT, HPFS, or NTFS file systems.

st_mode   Bit mask for file-mode information. The **_S_IFDIR** bit is set if *path* specifies a directory; the **_S_IFREG** bit is set if *path* specifies an ordinary file or a device. User read/write bits are set according to the file's permission mode; user execute bits are set according to the filename extension.

st_mtime   Time of last modification of file.

st_nlink   Always 1 on non-NTFS file systems.

st_rdev   Drive number of the disk containing the file (same as **st_dev**).

st_size   Size of the file in bytes.

uid   Numeric identifier of user who owns file (UNIX-specific)

If *path* refers to a device, the size, time, **_dev**, and **_rdev** fields in the **_stat** structure are meaningless. Because STAT.H uses the **_dev_t** type that is defined in TYPES.H, you must include TYPES.H before STAT.H in your code.

See Also   **_access, _fstat, _getmbcp, _setmbcp**

Example
```
/* STAT.C: This program uses the _stat function to
 * report information about the file named STAT.C.
 */

#include <time.h>
#include <sys/types.h>
#include <sys/stat.h>
#include <stdio.h>

void main( void )
{
    struct _stat buf;
    int result;
    char buffer[] = "A line to output";
```

```
                    /* Get data associated with "stat.c": */
                    result = _stat( "stat.c", &buf );

                    /* Check if statistics are valid: */
                    if( result != 0 )
                      perror( "Problem getting information" );
                    else
                    {
                       /* Output some of the statistics: */
                       printf( "File size      : %ld\n", buf.st_size );
                       printf( "Drive          : %c:\n", buf.st_dev + 'A' );
                       printf( "Time modified : %s", ctime( &buf.st_atime ) );
                    }
                  }
```

Output

```
File size     : 745
Drive         : C:
Time modified : Tue May 03 00:00:00 1994
```

_status87, _statusfp

unsigned int _status87(void);

unsigned int _statusfp(void);

~~ANSI~~ ~~UNIX~~ WIN32S

#include <float.h>

Return Value   The bits in the value returned indicate the floating-point status. See the FLOAT.H include file for a complete definition of the bits returned by **_status87**.

Many math library functions modify the 8087/80287 status word, with unpredictable results. Return values from **_clear87** and **_status87** are more reliable if fewer floating-point operations are performed between known states of the floating-point status word.

Remarks   The **_status87** function gets the floating-point status word. The status word is a combination of the 8087/80287/80387 status word and other conditions detected by the 8087/80287/80387 exception handler, such as floating-point stack overflow and underflow. Unmasked exceptions are checked for before returning the contents of the status word. This means that the caller is informed of pending exceptions.

_statusfp is a platform-independent, portable version of **_status87**. It is identical to **_status87** on Intel (x86) platforms and is also supported by the MIPS platform. To ensure that your floating-point code is portable to MIPS, use **_statusfp**. If you are only targeting x86 platforms, use either **_status87** or **_statusfp**.

See Also   **_clear87**, **_control87**

Example

```
/* STATUS87.C: This program creates various floating-point errors and
 * then uses _status87 to display messages indicating these problems.
 * Compile this program with optimizations disabled (/Od). Otherwise,
 * the optimizer removes the code related to the unused floating-
 * point values.
 */

#include <stdio.h>
#include <float.h>

void main( void )
{
   double a = 1e-40, b;
   float  x, y;

   printf( "Status = %.4x - clear\n",_status87() );

   /* Assignment into y is inexact & underflows: */
   y = a;
   printf( "Status = %.4x - inexact, underflow\n", _status87() );

   /* y is denormal: */
   b = y;
   printf( "Status = %.4x - inexact underflow, denormal\n",
           _status87() );

   /* Clear user 8087: */
   _clear87();
}
```

Output

```
Status = 0000 - clear
Status = 0003 - inexact, underflow
Status = 80003 - inexact underflow, denormal
```

strcat, wcscat, _mbscat

char *strcat(char ***string1****, const char *****string2** **);**

wchar_t *wcscat(wchar_t ***string1****, const wchar_t *****string2** **);**

unsigned char *_mbscat(unsigned char ***string1****, const unsigned char *****string2** **);**

strcat: ANSI   UNIX   WIN32S
wcscat, _mbscat: ~~ANSI~~   ~~UNIX~~   ~~WIN32S~~

#include <string.h>   For **strcat**.
#include <wchar.h>   For **wcscat** use STRING.H or WCHAR.H.
#include <mbstring.h>   For **_mbscat** use STRING.H or MBSTRING.H.

Return Value	Each of these functions returns the destination string (*string1*). No return value is reserved to indicate an error.
Parameters	*string1* Null-terminated destination string *string2* Null-terminated source string
Remarks	The **strcat** function appends *string2* to *string1* and terminates the resulting string with a null character. The initial character of *string2* overwrites the terminating null character of *string1*. No overflow checking is performed when strings are copied or appended. The behavior of **strcat** is undefined if the source and destination strings overlap. **wcscat** and **_mbscat** are wide-character and multibyte-character versions of **strcat.** The arguments and return value of **wcscat** are wide-character strings; those of **_mbscat** are multibyte-character strings. These three functions behave identically otherwise.
See Also	**strncat, strncmp, strncpy, _strnicmp, strrchr, strspn**
Example	See the example for **strcpy.**

strchr, wcschr, _mbschr

char *strchr(const char **string***, int** *c* **);**

wchar_t *wcschr(const wchar_t **string***, wint_t** *c* **);**

unsigned char * _mbschr(const unsigned char **string***, unsigned int** *c* **);**

strchr: ANSI   UNIX   WIN32S
wcschr, _mbschr: ~~ANSI~~   ~~UNIX~~   ~~WIN32S~~

#include <string.h>   For **strchr.**
#include <wchar.h>   For **wcschr** use STRING.H or WCHAR.H.
#include <mbstring.h>   For **_mbschr** use STRING.H or MBSTRING.H.

Return Value	Each of these functions returns a pointer to the first occurrence of *c* in *string*, or **NULL** if *c* is not found.
Parameters	*string* Null-terminated source string *c* Character to be located
Remarks	The **strchr** function finds the first occurrence of *c* in *string*, or it returns **NULL** if *c* is not found. The null-terminating character is included in the search. **wcschr** and **_mbschr** are wide-character and multibyte-character versions of **strchr.** The arguments and return value of **wcschr** are wide-character strings; those of **_mbschr** are multibyte-character strings. **_mbschr** recognizes multibyte-character sequences according to the multibyte code page currently in use. These three functions behave identically otherwise.

See Also   **strcspn, strncat, strncmp, strncpy, _strnicmp, strpbrk, strrchr, strstr**

Example

```
/* STRCHR.C: This program illustrates searching for a character
 * with strchr (search forward) or strrchr (search backward). */

#include <string.h>
#include <stdio.h>

int  ch = 'r';

char string[] = "The quick brown dog jumps over the lazy fox";
char fmt1[] =   "         1         2         3         4         5";
char fmt2[] =   "12345678901234567890123456789012345678901234567890";

void main( void )
{
   char *pdest;
   int result;

   printf( "String to be searched: \n\t\t%s\n", string );
   printf( "\t\t%s\n\t\t%s\n\n", fmt1, fmt2 );
   printf( "Search char:\t%c\n", ch );

   /* Search forward. */
   pdest = strchr( string, ch );
   result = pdest - string + 1;
   if( pdest != NULL )
      printf( "Result:\tfirst %c found at position %d\n\n",
              ch, result );
   else
      printf( "Result:\t%c not found\n" );

   /* Search backward. */
   pdest = strrchr( string, ch );
   result = pdest - string + 1;
   if( pdest != NULL )
      printf( "Result:\tlast %c found at position %d\n\n", ch, result );
   else
      printf( "Result:\t%c not found\n" );
}
```

Output

```
String to be searched:
     The quick brown dog jumps over the lazy fox
              1         2         3         4         5
     12345678901234567890123456789012345678901234567890

Search char:   r
Result:   first r found at position 12

Result:   last r found at position 30
```

strcmp, wcscmp, _mbscmp

int **strcmp**(const char *string1*, const char *string2*);

int **wcscmp**(const wchar_t *string1*, const wchar_t *string2*);

int **_mbscmp**(const unsigned char *string1*, const unsigned char *string2*);

strcmp: ANSI UNIX WIN32S

wcscmp, _mbscmp: ~~ANSI~~ ~~UNIX~~ ~~WIN32S~~

#include <string.h>   For **strcmp**.
#include <wchar.h>   For **wcscmp** use STRING.H or WCHAR.H.
#include <mbstring.h>   For **_mbscmp** use STRING.H or MBSTRING.H.

Return Value

The return value for each of these functions indicates the lexicographic relation of *string1* to *string2*.

Value	Relationship of *string1* to *string2*
< 0	*string1* less than *string2*
0	*string1* identical to *string2*
> 0	*string1* greater than *string2*

On an error, **_mbscmp** returns **_NLSCMPERROR**, which is defined in STRING.H and MBSTRING.H.

Parameters

string1, string2   Null-terminated strings to compare

Remarks

The **strcmp** function compares *string1* and *string2* lexicographically and returns a value indicating their relationship. **wcscmp** and **_mbscmp** are wide-character and multibyte-character versions of **strcmp**. The arguments and return value of **wcscmp** are wide-character strings; those of **_mbscmp** are multibyte-character strings. **_mbscmp** recognizes multibyte-character sequences according to the current multibyte code page and returns **_NLSCMPERROR** on an error. For more information, see "Code Pages" on page 20. These three functions behave identically otherwise.

The **strcmp** functions differ from the **strcoll** functions in that **strcmp** comparisons are not affected by locale, whereas the manner of **strcoll** comparisons is determined by the **LC_COLLATE** category of the current locale. For more information on the **LC_COLLATE** category, see **setlocale**.

In the "C" locale, the order of characters in the character set (ASCII character set) is the same as the lexicographic character order. However, in other locales, the order of characters in the character set may differ from the lexicographic order. For example, in certain European locales, the character 'a' (value 0x61) precedes the character 'ä' (value 0xE4) in the character set, but the character 'ä' precedes the character 'a' lexicographically.

In locales for which the character set and the lexicographic character order differ, use **strcoll** rather than **strcmp** for lexicographic comparison of strings according to the **LC_COLLATE** category setting of the current locale. Thus, to perform a lexicographic comparison of the locale in the above example, use **strcoll** rather than **strcmp**. Alternatively, you can use **strxfrm** on the original strings, then use **strcmp** on the resulting strings.

_stricmp, _wcsicmp, and **_mbsicmp** compare strings by first converting them to their lowercase forms.Two strings containing characters located between 'Z' and 'a' in the ASCII table ('[', '\', ']', '^', '_', and '`') compare differently, depending on their case. For example, the two strings "ABCDE" and "ABCD^" compare one way if the comparison is lowercase ("abcde" > "abcd^") and the other way ("ABCDE" < "ABCD^") if the comparison is uppercase.

See Also   memcmp, _memicmp, strcoll Functions, _stricmp, strncmp, _strnicmp, strrchr, strspn, strxfrm

Example

```
/* STRCMP.C */

#include <string.h>
#include <stdio.h>

char string1[] = "The quick brown dog jumps over the lazy fox";
char string2[] = "The QUICK brown dog jumps over the lazy fox";

void main( void )
{
   char tmp[20];
   int result;
   /* Case sensitive */
   printf( "Compare strings:\n\t%s\n\t%s\n\n", string1, string2 );
   result = strcmp( string1, string2 );
   if( result > 0 )
      strcpy( tmp, "greater than" );
   else if( result < 0 )
      strcpy( tmp, "less than" );
   else
      strcpy( tmp, "equal to" );
   printf( "\tstrcmp:   String 1 is %s string 2\n", tmp );
   /* Case insensitive (could use equivalent _stricmp) */
   result = _stricmp( string1, string2 );
   if( result > 0 )
      strcpy( tmp, "greater than" );
   else if( result < 0 )
      strcpy( tmp, "less than" );
   else
      strcpy( tmp, "equal to" );
   printf( "\t_stricmp:  String 1 is %s string 2\n", tmp );
}
```

Output

```
Compare strings:
        The quick brown dog jumps over the lazy fox
        The QUICK brown dog jumps over the lazy fox

        strcmp:    String 1 is greater than string 2
        _stricmp:  String 1 is equal to string 2
```

strcoll Functions

int **strcoll**(const char *string1, const char *string2);

int **wcscoll**(const wchar_t *string1, const wchar_t *string2);

int **_mbscoll**(const unsigned char *string1, const unsigned char *string2);

int **_stricoll**(const char *string1, const char *string2);

int **_wcsicoll**(const wchar_t *string1, const wchar_t *string2);

int **_mbsicoll**(const unsigned char *string1, const unsigned char *string2);

int **_strncoll** (const char *_string1, const char *_string2, size_t count);

int **_wcsncoll** (const wchar_t *_string1, const wchar_t *_string2, size_t count);

int **_mbsncoll**(const unsigned char *string1, const unsigned char *string2, size_t count);

int **_strnicoll**(const char *string1, const char *string2, size_t count);

int **_wcsnicoll**(const wchar_t *string1, const wchar_t *string2 , size_t count);

int **_mbsnicoll**(const unsigned char *string1, const unsigned char *string2, size_t count);

strcoll: ANSI ~~UNIX~~ WIN32S,   **wcscoll:** ANSI ~~UNIX~~ ~~WIN32S~~
_mbscoll, _wcsicoll, _mbsicoll, _wcsncoll, _mbsncoll, _wcsnicoll, _mbsnicoll:
~~ANSI~~ ~~UNIX~~ ~~WIN32S~~
_stricoll, _strncoll, _strnicoll: ~~ANSI~~ ~~UNIX~~ WIN32S

#include <string.h>   For **strcoll, _stricoll, _strncoll,** and **_strnicoll**
#include <wchar.h>   For **wcscoll, _wcsicoll, _wcsncoll,** and **_wcsnicoll** use
STRING.H or WCHAR.H.
#include <mbstring.h>   For **mbscoll, _mbsicoll, _mbsncoll,** and **_mbsnicoll**

Return Value

Each of these functions returns a value indicating the relationship of *string1* to *string2*, as follows:

Value	Relationship of *string1* to *string2*
< 0	*string1* less than *string2*
0	*string1* identical to *string2*
> 0	*string1* greater than *string2*

Each of these functions returns **_NLSCMPERROR** on an error. To use
_NLSCMPERROR, include either STRING.H or MBSTRING.H. The **wcscoll**
functions can fail if *string1* or *string2* contains wide-character codes outside the
domain of the collating sequence. When an error occurs, the **wcscoll** functions may
set **errno** to **EINVAL**. To check for an error on a call to one of these wide-
character functions, set **errno** to 0 and then check **errno** after calling the function.

Parameters

string1, string2   Null-terminated strings to compare
count   Number of characters to compare

Remarks

The single-byte character (SBCS) versions of these functions (**strcoll**, **stricoll**,
_strncoll, and **_strnicoll**) compare *string1* and *string2* according to the
LC_COLLATE category setting of the current locale. These functions differ from
the corresponding **strcmp** functions in that the **strcoll** functions use locale code
page information that provides collating sequences. For string comparisons in
locales in which the character set order and the lexicographic character order differ,
the **strcoll** functions should be used rather than the corresponding **strcmp**
functions. For more information on **LC_COLLATE**, see **setlocale**.

For some code pages and corresponding character sets, the order of characters in
the character set may differ from the lexicographic character order. In the "C"
locale, this is not the case: the order of characters in the ASCII character set is the
same as the lexicographic order of the characters. However, in certain European
code pages, for example, the character 'a' (value 0x61) precedes the character 'ä'
(value 0xE4) in the character set, but the character 'ä' precedes the character 'a'
lexicographically. To perform a lexicographic comparison in such an instance, use
strcoll rather than **strcmp**. Alternatively, you can use **strxfrm** on the original
strings, then use **strcmp** on the resulting strings.

strcoll, **stricoll**, **_strncoll**, and **_strnicoll** automatically handle multibyte-character
strings according to the locale code page currently in use, as do their wide-character
(Unicode) counterparts. The multibyte-character (MBCS) versions of these
functions, however, collate strings on a character basis according to the multibyte
code page currently in use.

Because the **coll** functions collate strings lexicographically for comparison, whereas
the **cmp** functions simply test for string equality, the **coll** functions are much slower
than the corresponding **cmp** versions. Therefore, the **coll** functions should be used
only when there is a difference between the character set order and the
lexicographic character order in the current code page and this difference is of
interest for the comparison.

Additional remarks are summarized in the following table.

strcoll Functions

SBCS	Unicode	MBCS	Description
strcoll	wcscoll	_mbscoll	Collate two strings
_stricoll	_wcsicoll	_mbsicoll	Collate two strings (case insensitive)
_strncoll	_wcsncoll	_mbsncoll	Collate first *count* characters of two strings
_strnicoll	_wcsnicoll	_mbsnicoll	Collate first *count* characters of two strings (case-insensitive)

See Also   localeconv, _mbsnbcoll, setlocale, strcmp, strncmp, _strnicmp, strxfrm

strcpy, wcscpy, _mbscpy

char *strcpy(char *string1, const char *string2);

wchar_t *wcscpy(wchar_t *string1, const wchar_t *string2);

unsigned char *_mbscpy(unsigned char *string1, const unsigned char *string2);

strcpy: ANSI UNIX WIN32S,   wcscpy: ANSI UNIX ~~WIN32S~~
_mbscpy: ~~ANSI~~ UNIX ~~WIN32S~~

#include <string.h>   For strcpy.
#include <wchar.h>   For wcscpy use STRING.H or WCHAR.H.
#include <mbstring.h>   For _mbscpy use STRING.H or MBSTRING.H.

Return Value   Each of these functions returns the destination string. No return value is reserved to indicate an error.

Parameters   *string1*   Destination string
string2   Null-terminated source string

Remarks   The **strcpy** function copies *string2*, including the terminating null character, to the location specified by *string1*. No overflow checking is performed when strings are copied or appended. The behavior of **strcpy** is undefined if the source and destination strings overlap.

wcscpy and **_mbscpy** are wide-character and multibyte-character versions of **strcpy**. The arguments and return value of **wcscpy** are wide-character strings; those of **_mbscpy** are multibyte-character strings. These three functions behave identically otherwise.

See Also   strcat, strcmp, strncat, strncmp, strncpy, _strnicmp, strrchr, strspn

Example

```
/* STRCPY.C: This program uses strcpy
 * and strcat to build a phrase.
 */

#include <string.h>
#include <stdio.h>

void main( void )
{
   char string[80];
   strcpy( string, "Hello world from " );
   strcat( string, "strcpy " );
   strcat( string, "and " );
   strcat( string, "strcat!" );
   printf( "String = %s\n", string );
}
```

Output

```
String = Hello world from strcpy and strcat!
```

strcspn, wcscspn, _mbscspn

size_t strcspn(const char *_string1_, const char *_string2_);

size_t wcscspn(const wchar_t *_string1_, const wchar_t *_string2_);

size_t _mbscspn(const unsigned char *_string1_, const unsigned char *_string2_);

| **strcspn:** ANSI UNIX WIN32S, | **wcscspn:** ANSI UNIX ~~WIN32S~~ |
| **mbscspn:** ~~ANSI~~ UNIX ~~WIN32S~~ | |

#include <string.h>   For **strcspn**.
#include <wchar.h>   For **wcscspn** use STRING.H or WCHAR.H.
#include <mbstring.h>   For **_mbscspn** use STRING.H or MBSTRING.H.

Return Value

Each of these functions returns an integer value specifying the length of the initial segment of _string1_ that consists entirely of characters not in _string2_. If _string1_ begins with a character that is in _string2_, the function returns 0. No return value is reserved to indicate an error.

Parameters

string1   Null-terminated searched string
string2   Null-terminated character set

Remarks

The **strcspn** function returns the index of the first occurrence of a character in _string1_ that belongs to the set of characters in _string2_. Terminating null characters are not included in the search.

wcscspn and **_mbscspn** are wide-character and multibyte-character versions of **strcspn.** The arguments of **wcscspn** are wide-character strings; those of **_mbscspn** are multibyte-character strings. These three functions behave identically otherwise.

See Also

strncat, strncmp, strncpy, _strnicmp, strrchr, strspn

Example

```
/* STRCSPN.C */

#include <string.h>
#include <stdio.h>

void main( void )
{
    char string[] = "xyzabc";
    int  pos;

    pos = strcspn( string, "abc" );
    printf( "First a, b or c in %s is at character %d\n",
            string, pos );
}
```

Output

```
First a, b or c in xyzabc is at character 3
```

_strdate, _wstrdate

char *_strdate(char *datestr**);**

wchar_t *_wstrdate(wchar_t *datestr**);**

> **_strdate:** ~~ANSI~~ ~~UNIX~~ WIN32S
> **_wstrdate:** ~~ANSI~~ ~~UNIX~~ ~~WIN32S~~

> **#include <time.h>**   For **_strdate**.
> **#include <wchar.h>**   For **_wstrdate** use TIME.H or WCHAR.H.

Return Value   Each of these functions returns a pointer to the resulting character string *datestr*.

Parameter   *datestr*   Current date

Remarks   The **_strdate** function copies the date to the buffer pointed to by *datestr,* formatted *mm/dd/yy* where *mm* is two digits representing the month, *dd* is two digits representing the day, and *yy* is the last two digits of the year. For example, the string 12/05/99 represents December 5, 1999. The buffer must be at least 9 bytes long.

_wstrdate is a wide-character version of **_strdate**; the argument and return value of **_wstrdate** are wide-character strings. These functions behave identically otherwise.

See Also   **asctime, ctime, gmtime, localtime, mktime, time, _tzset**

_strdup, _wcsdup, _mbsdup

char * _strdup(const char *string**);**

wchar_t * _wcsdup(const wchar_t *string**);**

unsigned char * _mbsdup(const unsigned char *string**);**

_strdup: ~~ANSI~~ ~~UNIX~~ WIN32S
_wcsdup, _mbsdup: ~~ANSI~~ ~~UNIX~~ ~~WIN32S~~

#include <string.h> For **_strdup**.
#include <wchar.h> For **_wcsdup** use STRING.H or WCHAR.H.
#include <mbstring.h> For **_mbsdup** use STRING.H or MBSTRING.H.

Return Value

Each of these functions returns a pointer to the storage location for the copied string or **NULL** if storage cannot be allocated.

Parameter

string   Null-terminated source string

Remarks

The **_strdup** function calls **malloc** to allocate storage space for a copy of *string* and then copies *string* to the allocated space.

_wcsdup and **_mbsdup** are wide-character and multibyte-character versions of **_strdup**. The arguments and return value of **_wcsdup** are wide-character strings; those of **_mbsdup** are multibyte-character strings. These three functions behave identically otherwise.

Because **_strdup** calls **malloc** to allocate storage space for the copy of *string*, it is good practice always to release this memory by calling the **free** routine on the pointer returned by the call to **_strdup**.

See Also

memset, strcat, strcmp, strncat, strncmp, strncpy, _strnicmp, strrchr, strspn

Example

```
/* STRDUP.C */

#include <string.h>
#include <stdio.h>

void main( void )
{
   char buffer[] = "This is the buffer text";
   char *newstring;
   printf( "Original: %s\n", buffer );
   newstring = _strdup( buffer );
   printf( "Copy:    %s\n", newstring );
   free( newstring );
}
```

Output

```
Original: This is the buffer text
Copy:    This is the buffer text
```

strerror, _strerror

char *strerror(int *errnum* **);**

char *_strerror(const char *string **);**

strerror: ANSI   ~~UNIX~~   WIN32S
_strerror: ~~ANSI~~   ~~UNIX~~   WIN32S

#include <string.h>

Return Value

strerror and **_strerror** return a pointer to the error-message string. Subsequent calls to **strerror** or **_strerror** can overwrite the string.

Parameters

errnum   Error number
string   User-supplied message

Remarks

The **strerror** function maps *errnum* to an error-message string, returning a pointer to the string. Neither **strerror** nor **_strerror** actually prints the message: For that, you need to call an output function such as **fprintf**:

```
if (( _access( "datafile",2 )) == -1 )
    fprintf( stderr, strerror(NULL) );
```

If *string* is passed as **NULL**, **_strerror** returns a pointer to a string containing the system error message for the last library call that produced an error. The error-message string is terminated by the newline character ('\n'). If *string* is not equal to **NULL**, then **_strerror** returns a pointer to a string containing (in order) your string message, a colon, a space, the system error message for the last library call producing an error, and a newline character. Your string message can be, at most, 94 bytes long.

The actual error number for **_strerror** is stored in the variable **errno**. The system error messages are accessed through the variable **_sys_errlist**, which is an array of messages ordered by error number. **_strerror** accesses the appropriate error message by using the **errno** value as an index to the variable **_sys_errlist**. The value of the variable **_sys_nerr** is defined as the maximum number of elements in the **_sys_errlist** array. To produce accurate results, call **_strerror** immediately after a library routine returns with an error. Otherwise, subsequent calls to **strerror** or **_strerror** can overwrite the **errno** value.

_strerror is not part of the ANSI definition but is instead a Microsoft extension to it. Do not use it where portability is desired; for ANSI compatibility, use **strerror** instead.

See Also

clearerr, ferror, perror

Example

See the example for **perror**.

strftime, wcsftime

size_t strftime(char *_string_, size_t _maxsize_, const char *_format_, const struct tm *_timeptr_);

size_t wcsftime(wchar_t *_string_, size_t _maxsize_, const wchar_t *_format_, const struct tm *_timeptr_);

strftime: ANSI   ~~UNIX~~   WIN32S
wcsftime: ANSI   ~~UNIX~~   ~~WIN32S~~

#include <time.h>   For **strftime**.
#include <wchar.h>   For **wcsftime** use TIME.H or WCHAR.H.

Return Value

strftime returns the number of characters placed in _string_ if the total number of resulting characters, including the terminating null, is not more than _maxsize_. **wcsftime** returns the corresponding number of wide characters. Otherwise, the functions return 0, and the contents of the string are indeterminate.

Parameters

string   Output string
maxsize   Maximum length of string
format   Format-control string
timeptr   **tm** data structure

Remarks

The **strftime** and **wcsftime** functions format the **tm** time value in _timeptr_ according to the supplied _format_ argument and store the result in the buffer _string_. At most, _maxsize_ characters are placed in the string. For a description of the fields in the _timeptr_ structure, see **asctime**. **wcsftime** is the wide-character equivalent of **strftime**; its string-pointer argument points to a wide-character string. These functions behave identically otherwise.

The _format_ argument consists of one or more codes; as in **printf**, the formatting codes are preceded by a percent sign (%). Characters that do not begin with % are copied unchanged to _string_. The **LC_TIME** category of the current locale affects the output formatting of **strftime**.(For more information on **LC_TIME**, see **setlocale**.) The formatting codes for **strftime** are listed below:

%a   Abbreviated weekday name

%A   Full weekday name

%b   Abbreviated month name

%B   Full month name

%c   Date and time representation appropriate for locale

%d   Day of month as decimal number (01–31)

%H   Hour in 24-hour format (00–23)

%I   Hour in 12-hour format (01–12)

%j Day of year as decimal number (001–366)

%m Month as decimal number (01–12)

%M Minute as decimal number (00–59)

%p Current locale's A.M./P.M. indicator for 12-hour clock

%S Second as decimal number (00–59)

%U Week of year as decimal number, with Sunday as first day of week (00–51)

%w Weekday as decimal number (0–6; Sunday is 0)

%W Week of year as decimal number, with Monday as first day of week (00–51)

%x Date representation for current locale

%X Time representation for current locale

%y Year without century, as decimal number (00–99)

%Y Year with century, as decimal number

%z, %Z Time-zone name or abbreviation; no characters if time zone is unknown

%% Percent sign

As in the **printf** function, the **#** flag may prefix any formatting code. In that case, the meaning of the format code is changed as follows.

Format Code	Meaning
%#a, %#A, %#b, %#B, %#p, %#X, %#z, %#Z, %#%	# flag is ignored.
%#c	Long date and time representation, appropriate for current locale. For example: "Tuesday, March 16, 1993, 12:41:29".
%#x	Long date representation, appropriate to current locale. For example: "Tuesday, March 16, 1993".
%#d, %#H, %#I, %#j, %#m, %#M, %#S, %#U, %#w, %#W, %#y, %#Y	Remove leading zeros (if any).

See Also   **localeconv, setlocale, strcoll, _stricoll, strxfrm**

Example   See the example for **time**.

_stricmp, _wcsicmp, _mbsicmp

int _stricmp(const char *string1, const char *string2);

int _wcsicmp(const wchar_t *string1, const wchar_t *string2);

int _mbsicmp(const unsigned char *string1, const unsigned char_t *string2);

_stricmp: ~~ANSI~~ ~~UNIX~~ WIN32S
_wcsicmp, _mbsicmp: ~~ANSI~~ ~~UNIX~~ ~~WIN32S~~

#include <string.h>   For _stricmp.
#include <wchar.h>   For _wcsicmp use STRING.H or WCHAR.H.
#include <mbstring.h>   For _mbsicmp use STRING.H or MBSTRING.H.

Return Value   The return value indicates the relation of *string1* to *string2* as follows.

Value	Description
< 0	*string1* less than *string2*
0	*string1* identical to *string2*
> 0	*string1* greater than *string2*

On an error, **_mbsicmp** returns **NLSCMPERROR**, which is defined in STRING.H and MBSTRING.H.

Parameters   *string1, string2*   Null-terminated strings to compare

Remarks   The **_stricmp** function lexicographically compares lowercase versions of *string1* and *string2* and returns a value indicating their relationship. **_stricmp** differs from **_stricoll** in that the **_stricmp** comparison is not affected by locale, whereas the **_stricoll** comparison is according to the **LC_COLLATE** category of the current locale. For more information on the **LC_COLLATE** category, see **setlocale**.

The **_strcmpi** function is equivalent to **_stricmp** and is provided for backward compatibility only.

_wcsicmp and **_mbsicmp** are wide-character and multibyte-character versions of **_stricmp**. The arguments and return value of **_wcsicmp** are wide-character strings; those of **_mbsicmp** are multibyte-character strings. **_mbsicmp** recognizes multibyte-character sequences according to the current multibyte code page and returns **NLSCMPERROR** on an error. (For more information, see "Code Pages" on page 20.) These three functions behave identically otherwise.

_wcsicmp and **wcscmp** behave identically except that **wcscmp** does not convert its arguments to lowercase before comparing them. **_mbsicmp** and **_mbscmp** behave identically except that **_mbscmp** does not convert its arguments to lowercase before comparing them.

See Also   memcmp, _memicmp, strcmp, strcoll Functions, strncmp, _strnicmp, strrchr, _strset, strspn

Example   See the example for strcmp.

strlen, wcslen, _mbslen, _mbstrlen

size_t strlen(const char *string);

size_t wcslen(const wchar_t *string);

size_t _mbslen(const unsigned char *string);

size_t _mbstrlen(const char *string);

> **strlen:**   ANSI   UNIX   WIN32S
> **wcslen:**   ANSI   UNIX   ~~WIN32S~~
> **_mbslen, _mbstrlen:**   ANSI   ~~UNIX~~   ~~WIN32S~~
>
> #include <string.h>   For strlen.
> #include <wchar.h>   For wcslen use STRING.H or WCHAR.H.
> #include <stdlib.h>   For _mbslen and _mbstrlen.

Return Value   Each of these functions returns the number of characters in *string*, excluding the terminal **NULL**. No return value is reserved to indicate an error.

Parameter   *string*   Null-terminated string

Remarks   Each of these functions returns the number of characters in *string*, not including the terminating null character. **wcslen** is a wide-character version of **strlen**; the argument of **wcslen** is a wide-character string. **wcslen** and **strlen** behave identically otherwise.

_mbslen and **_mbstrlen** return the number of multibyte characters in a multibyte-character string. **_mbslen** recognizes multibyte-character sequences according to the multibyte code page currently in use; it does not test for multibyte-character validity. **_mbstrlen** tests for multibyte-character validity and recognizes multibyte-character sequences according to the **LC_CTYPE** category setting of the current locale. For more information about the **LC_CTYPE** category, see **setlocale**.

See Also   strcat, strcmp, strcoll Functions, strcpy, strrchr, _strset, strspn, setlocale

Example

```
/*  STRLEN.C */

#include <string.h>
#include <stdio.h>
#include <conio.h>
#include <dos.h>

void main( void )
{
    char buffer[61] = "How long am I?";
    int  len;
    len = strlen( buffer );
    printf( "'%s' is %d characters long\n", buffer, len );
}
```

Output

```
'How long am I?' is 14 characters long
```

_strlwr, _wcslwr, _mbslwr

char *_strlwr(char *string **);**

wchar_t * _wcslwr(wchar_t *string **);**

unsigned char * _mbslwr (unsigned char *string **);**

_strlwr: ~~ANSI~~   ~~UNIX~~   WIN32S
_wcslwr, _mbslwr: ~~ANSI~~   ~~UNIX~~   ~~WIN32S~~

#include <string.h>   For _strlwr.
#include <wchar.h>   For _wcslwr use STRING.H or WCHAR.H.
#include <mbstring.h>   For _mbslwr use STRING.H or MBSTRING.H.

Return Value

Each of these functions returns a pointer to the converted string. Because the modification is done in place, the pointer returned is the same as the pointer passed as the input argument. No return value is reserved to indicate an error.

Parameter

string   Null-terminated string to convert to lowercase

Remarks

The **_strlwr** function converts any uppercase letters in *string* to lowercase as determined by the **LC_CTYPE** category setting of the current locale. Other characters are not affected. For more information on **LC_CTYPE**, see **setlocale**.

The **_wcslwr** and **_mbslwr** functions are wide-character and multibyte-character versions of **_strlwr**. The argument and return value of **_wcslwr** are wide-character strings; those of **_mbslwr** are multibyte-character strings. These three functions behave identically otherwise.

See Also   **_strupr**

Example

```
/* STRLWR.C: This program uses _strlwr and _strupr to create
 * uppercase and lowercase copies of a mixed-case string.
 */

#include <string.h>
#include <stdio.h>

void main( void )
{
    char string[100] = "The String to End All Strings!";
    char *copy1, *copy2;
    copy1 = _strlwr( _strdup( string ) );
    copy2 = _strupr( _strdup( string ) );
    printf( "Mixed: %s\n", string );
    printf( "Lower: %s\n", copy1 );
    printf( "Upper: %s\n", copy2 );
}
```

Output

```
Mixed: The String to End All Strings!
Lower: the string to end all strings!
Upper: THE STRING TO END ALL STRINGS!
```

strncat, wcsncat, _mbsncat

char *strncat(char **string1***, const char ****string2***, size_t** *count* **);**

wchar_t *wcsncat(wchar_t **string1***, const wchar_t ****string2***, size_t** *count* **);**

unsigned char *_mbsncat(unsigned char **string1***, const unsigned char ****string2***, size_t** *count***);**

strncat: ANSI   UNIX   WIN32S
wcsncat: ANSI   UNIX   ~~WIN32S~~
_mbsncat: ~~ANSI~~   ~~UNIX~~   ~~WIN32S~~

#include <string.h>   For **strncat**.
#include <wchar.h>   For **wcsncat** use STRING.H or WCHAR.H.
#include <mbstring.h>   For **_mbsncat** use STRING.H or MBSTRING.H.

Return Value   Each of these functions returns a pointer to the destination string. No return value is reserved to indicate an error.

Parameters   *string1*   Null-terminated destination string
string2   Null-terminated source string
count   Number of characters to append

Remarks   The **strncat** function appends, at most, the first *count* characters of *string2* to *string1*. The initial character of *string2* overwrites the terminating null character of *string1*. If a null character appears in *string2* before *count* characters are appended, **strncat** appends all characters from *string2*, up to the null character. If *count* is greater than the length of *string2*, the length of *string2* is used in place of *count*. The resulting string is terminated with a null character. If copying takes place between strings that overlap, the behavior is undefined.

wcsncat and **_mbsncat** are wide-character and multibyte-character versions of **strncat**. The string arguments and return value of **wcsncat** are wide-character strings; those of **_mbsncat** are multibyte-character strings. These three functions behave identically otherwise.

See Also   **_mbsnbcat, strcat, strcmp, strcpy, strncmp, strncpy, _strnicmp, strrchr, _strset, strspn**

Example
```
/* STRNCAT.C */

#include <string.h>
#include <stdio.h>

void main( void )
{
   char string[80] = "This is the initial string!";
   char suffix[] = " extra text to add to the string...";
   /* Combine strings with no more than 19 characters of suffix: */
   printf( "Before: %s\n", string );
   strncat( string, suffix, 19 );
   printf( "After:  %s\n", string );
}
```

Output
```
Before: This is the initial string!
After:  This is the initial string! extra text to add
```

strncmp, wcsncmp, _mbsncmp

int strncmp(const char *_string1_, const char *_string2_, size_t _count_);

int wcsncmp(const wchar_t *_string1_, const wchar_t *_string2_, size_t _count_);

int _mbsncmp(const unsigned char *_string1_, const unsigned char _string2_, size_t _count_);

strncmp: ANSI   UNIX   WIN32S
wcsncmp: ANSI   UNIX   ~~WIN32S~~
_mbsncmp: ~~ANSI~~   ~~UNIX~~   WIN32S

#include <string.h>   For **strncmp**.
#include <wchar.h>   For **wcsncmp** use STRING.H or WCHAR.H.
#include <mbstring.h>   For **_mbsncmp** use STRING.H or MBSTRING.H.

Return Value

The return value indicates the relation of the substrings of _string1_ and _string2_ as follows.

Return Value	Description
< 0	_string1_ substring less than _string2_ substring
0	_string1_ substring identical to _string2_ substring
> 0	_string1_ substring greater than _string2_ substring

On an error, **_mbsncmp** returns **_NLSCMPERROR**, which is defined in STRING.H and MBSTRING.H.

Parameters

string1, _string2_   Strings to compare
count   Number of characters to compare

Remarks

The **strncmp** function lexicographically compares, at most, the first _count_ characters in _string1_ and _string2_ and returns a value indicating the relationship between the substrings. **strncmp** is a case-sensitive version of **_strnicmp**. Unlike **strcoll**, **strncmp** is not affected by locale. For more information on the **LC_COLLATE** category, see **setlocale**.

wcsncmp and **_mbsncmp** are wide-character and multibyte-character versions of **strncmp**. The arguments and return value of **wcsncmp** are wide-character strings; those of **_mbsncmp** are multibyte-character strings. **_mbsncmp** recognizes multibyte-character sequences according to the current multibyte code page and returns **_NLSCMPERROR** on an error. (For more information, see "Code Pages" on page 20.) These three functions behave identically otherwise. **wcsncmp** and **_mbsncmp** are case-sensitive versions of **_wcsnicmp** and **_mbsnicmp**.

See Also

_mbsnbcmp, _mbsnbicmp, strcmp, strcoll Functions, _strnicmp, strrchr, _strset, strspn

Example

```
/* STRNCMP.C */
#include <string.h>
#include <stdio.h>

char string1[] = "The quick brown dog jumps over the lazy fox";
char string2[] = "The QUICK brown fox jumps over the lazy dog";

void main( void )
{
   char tmp[20];
   int result;
   printf( "Compare strings:\n\t\t%s\n\t\t%s\n\n", string1, string2 );
   printf( "Function:\tstrncmp (first 10 characters only)\n" );
   result = strncmp( string1, string2 , 10 );
   if( result > 0 )
      strcpy( tmp, "greater than" );
   else if( result < 0 )
      strcpy( tmp, "less than" );
   else
      strcpy( tmp, "equal to" );
   printf( "Result:\t\tString 1 is %s string 2\n\n", tmp );
   printf( "Function:\tstrnicmp _strnicmp (first 10 characters only)\n"
);
   result = _strnicmp( string1, string2, 10 );
   if( result > 0 )
      strcpy( tmp, "greater than" );
   else if( result < 0 )
      strcpy( tmp, "less than" );
   else
      strcpy( tmp, "equal to" );
   printf( "Result:\t\tString 1 is %s string 2\n\n", tmp );
}
```

Output

```
Compare strings:
                The quick brown dog jumps over the lazy fox
                The QUICK brown fox jumps over the lazy dog

Function:    strncmp (first 10 characters only)
Result:      String 1 is greater than string 2

Function:    _strnicmp (first 10 characters only)
Result:      String 1 is equal to string 2
```

strncpy, wcsncpy, _mbsncpy

char *strncpy(char *_string1_**, const char ***_string2_**, size_t** _count_ **);**

wchar_t *wcsncpy(wchar_t *_string1_**, const wchar_t ***_string2_**, size_t** _count_ **);**

unsigned char *_mbsncpy(unsigned char *_string1_**, const unsigned char ***_string2_**, size_t** _count_ **);**

strncpy: ANSI UNIX WIN32S,	**wcsncpy:** ANSI UNIX ~~WIN32S~~
_mbsncpy: ~~ANSI~~ ~~UNIX~~ ~~WIN32S~~	

#include <string.h>   For **strncpy**.
#include <wchar.h>   For **wcsncpy** use STRING.H or WCHAR.H.
#include <mbstring.h>   For **_mbsncpy**.

Return Value

Each of these functions returns _string1_. No return value is reserved to indicate an error.

Parameters

string1   Destination string
string2   Source string
count   Number of characters to be copied

Remarks

The **strncpy** function copies the initial _count_ characters of _string2_ to _string1_ and returns _string1_. If _count_ is less than or equal to the length of _string2_, a null character is not appended automatically to the copied string. If _count_ is greater than the length of _string2_, the destination string is padded with null characters up to length _count_. The behavior of **strncpy** is undefined if the source and destination strings overlap.

wcsncpy and **_mbsncpy** are wide-character and multibyte-character versions of **strncpy**. The arguments and return value of **wcsncpy** and **_mbsncpy** vary accordingly. These three functions behave identically otherwise.

See Also

_mbsnbcpy, strcat, strcmp, strcpy, strncat, strncmp, _strnicmp, strrchr, _strset, strspn

Example

```
/* STRNCPY.C */

#include <string.h>
#include <stdio.h>

void main( void )
{
    char string[100] = "Cats are nice usually";
    printf ( "Before: %s\n", string );
    strncpy( string, "Dogs", 4 );
    strncpy( string + 9, "mean", 4 );
    printf ( "After:  %s\n", string );
}
```

Output

```
Before: Cats are nice usually
After:  Dogs are mean usually
```

_strnicmp, _wcsnicmp, _mbsnicmp

int _strnicmp(const char *string1, const char *string2, size_t count);

int _wcsnicmp(const wchar_t *string1, const wchar_t *string2, size_t count);

int _mbsnicmp(const unsigned char *string1, const unsigned char *string2, size_t count);

_strnicmp: ~~ANSI~~ ~~UNIX~~ WIN32S
_wcsnicmp, _mbsnicmp: ~~ANSI~~ ~~UNIX~~ ~~WIN32S~~

#include <string.h> For **_strnicmp**.
#include <wchar.h> For **_wcsnicmp** use STRING.H or WCHAR.H.
#include <mbstring.h> For **_mbsnicmp** use STRING.H or MBSTRING.H.

Return Value

The return value indicates the relationship between the substrings as follows.

Value	Description
< 0	*string1* substring less than *string2* substring
0	*string1* substring identical to *string2* substring
> 0	*string1* substring greater than *string2* substring

On an error, **_mbsnicmp** returns **_NLSCMPERROR**, which is defined in STRING.H and MBSTRING.H.

Parameters

string1, *string2* Null-terminated strings to compare
count Number of characters to compare

Remarks

The **_strnicmp** function lexicographically compares, at most, the first *count* characters of *string1* and *string2*. The comparison is performed without regard to case; **_strnicmp** is a case-insensitive version of **strncmp**. The comparison ends if a terminating null character is reached in either string before *count* characters are compared. If the strings are equal when a terminating null character is reached in either string before *count* characters are compared, the shorter string is lesser.

Two strings containing characters located between 'Z' and 'a' in the ASCII table ('[', '\', ']', '^', '_', and '`') compare differently, depending on their case. For example, the two strings "ABCDE" and "ABCD^" compare one way if the comparison is lowercase ("abcde" > "abcd^") and the other way ("ABCDE" < "ABCD^") if it is uppercase.

_wcsnicmp and **_mbsnicmp** are wide-character and multibyte-character versions of **_strnicmp**. The arguments and return value of **_wcsnicmp** are wide-character strings; those of **_mbsnicmp** are multibyte-character strings. **_mbsnicmp** recognizes multibyte-character sequences according to the current multibyte code page and returns **_NLSCMPERROR** on an error. (For more information, see "Code Pages" on page 20.) These three functions behave identically otherwise. These functions are not affected by the current locale setting.

See Also   strcat, strcmp, strcpy, strncat, strncmp, strncpy, strrchr, _strset, strspn

Example   See the example for **strncmp**.

_strnset, _wcsnset, _mbsnset

char *_strnset(char *_string_, int _c_, size_t _count_);

wchar_t *_wcsnset(wchar_t *_string_, wchar_t _c_, size_t _count_);

unsigned char *_mbsnset(unsigned char *_string_, unsigned int _c_, size_t _count_);

> _strnset: ~~ANSI~~ ~~UNIX~~ WIN32S
> _wcsnset, _mbsnset: ~~ANSI~~ ~~UNIX~~ ~~WIN32S~~
>
> **#include <string.h>**   For _strnset.
> **#include <wchar.h>**   For **_wcsnset** use STRING.H or WCHAR.H.
> **#include <mbstring.h>**   For **_mbsnset** use STRING.H or MBSTRING.H.

Return Value   Each of these functions returns a pointer to the altered string.

Parameters
string   String to be altered
_c_   Character setting
count   Number of characters to be set

Remarks   The **_strnset** function sets, at most, the first _count_ characters of _string_ to _c_ (converted to **char**). If _count_ is greater than the length of _string_, the length of _string_ is used instead of _count_.

_wcsnset and **_mbsnset** are wide-character and multibyte-character versions of **_strnset**. The string arguments and return value of **_wcsnset** are wide-character strings; those of **_mbsnset** are multibyte-character strings. These three functions behave identically otherwise.

See Also   strcat, strcmp, strcpy, _strset

Example
```
/* STRNSET.C */

#include <string.h>
#include <stdio.h>

void main( void )
{
   char string[15] = "This is a test";
   /* Set not more than 4 characters of string to be *'s */
   printf( "Before: %s\n", string );
   _strnset( string, '*', 4 );
   printf( "After:  %s\n", string );
}
```

Output
```
Before: This is a test
After:  **** is a test
```

strpbrk, wcspbrk, _mbspbrk

char *strpbrk(const char **string1***, const char ****string2***);**

wchar_t *wcspbrk(const wchar_t **string1***, const wchar_t ****string2***);**

unsigned char *_mbspbrk(const unsigned char**string1***, const unsigned char ****string2***);**

> **strpbrk:**   ANSI   UNIX   WIN32S
> **wcspbrk:**   ANSI   UNIX   ~~WIN32S~~
> **_mbspbrk:**   ~~ANSI~~   ~~UNIX~~   WIN32S
>
> **#include <string.h>**   For **strpbrk**.
> **#include <wchar.h>**   For **wcspbrk** use STRING.H or WCHAR.H.
> **#include <mbstring.h>**   For **_mbspbrk** use STRING.H or MBSTRING.H.

Return Value	Each of these functions returns a pointer to the first occurrence of any character from *string2* in *string1*, or a **NULL** pointer if the two string arguments have no characters in common.
Parameters	*string1* Null-terminated, searched string *string2* Null-terminated character set
Remarks	The **strpbrk** function returns a pointer to the first occurrence of a character in *string1* that belongs to the set of characters in *string2*. The search does not include the terminating null character. **wcspbrk** and **_mbspbrk** are wide-character and multibyte-character versions of **strpbrk**. The arguments and return value of **wcspbrk** are wide-character strings; those of **_mbspbrk** are multibyte-character strings. These three functions behave identically otherwise. **_mbspbrk** is similar to **_mbscspn** except that **_mbspbrk** returns a pointer rather than a value of type **size_t**.
See Also	**strcspn, strchr, strrchr**
Example	

```
/* STRPBRK.C */

#include <string.h>
#include <stdio.h>
void main( void )
{
    char string[100] = "The 3 men and 2 boys ate 5 pigs\n";
    char *result;
    /* Return pointer to first 'a' or 'b' in "string" */
    printf( "1: %s\n", string );
    result = strpbrk( string, "0123456789" );
    printf( "2: %s\n", result++ );
    result = strpbrk( result, "0123456789" );
    printf( "3: %s\n", result++ );
    result = strpbrk( result, "0123456789" );
    printf( "4: %s\n", result );
}
```

Output	1: The 3 men and 2 boys ate 5 pigs
	2: 3 men and 2 boys ate 5 pigs
	3: 2 boys ate 5 pigs
	4: 5 pigs

strrchr, wcsrchr, _mbsrchr

char *strrchr(const char **string***, int** *c* **);**

char *wcsrchr(const wchar_t **string***, int** *c* **);**

int _mbsrchr(const unsigned char **string***, unsigned int** *c* **);**

> **strrchr:**   ANSI   UNIX   WIN32S
> **wcsrchr:**   ANSI   UNIX   ~~WIN32S~~
> **_mbsrchr:**   ~~ANSI~~   ~~UNIX~~   ~~WIN32S~~
>
> **#include <string.h>**   For **strrchr**.
> **#include <wchar.h>**   For **wcsrchr** use STRING.H or WCHAR.H.
> **#include <mbstring.h>**   For **_mbsrchr** use STRING.H or MBSTRING.H.

Return Value	Each of these functions returns a pointer to the last occurrence of *c* in *string*, or **NULL** if *c* is not found.
Parameters	*string* Null-terminated string to search *c* Character to be located
Remarks	The **strrchr** function finds the last occurrence of *c* (converted to **char**) in *string*. The search includes the terminating null character.
	wcsrchr and **_mbsrchr** are wide-character and multibyte-character versions of **strrchr**. The arguments and return value of **wcsrchr** are wide-character strings; those of **_mbsrchr** are multibyte-character strings. These three functions behave identically otherwise.
See Also	**strchr, strcspn, _strnicmp, strpbrk, strspn**
Example	See the example for **strchr**.

_strrev, _wcsrev, _mbsrev

char *_strrev(char **string** **);**

wchar_t *_wcsrev(wchar_t **string** **);**

unsigned char *_mbsrev(unsigned char **string** **);**

_strrev: ~~ANSI~~ ~~UNIX~~ WIN32S
_wcsrev, _mbsrev: ~~ANSI~~ ~~UNIX~~ ~~WIN32S~~

#include <string.h>   For _strrev.
#include <wchar.h>   For _wcsrev use STRING.H or WCHAR.H.
#include <mbstring.h>   For_mbsrev use STRING.H or MBSTRING.H.

Return Value   Each of these functions returns a pointer to the altered string. No return value is reserved to indicate an error.

Parameter   *string*   Null-terminated string to reverse

Remarks   The **_strrev** function reverses the order of the characters in *string*. The terminating null character remains in place. **_wcsrev** and **_mbsrev** are wide-character and multibyte-character versions of **_strrev**. The arguments and return value of **_wcsrev** are wide-character strings; those of **_mbsrev** are multibyte-character strings. For **_mbsrev**, the order of bytes in each multibyte character in *string* is not changed. These three functions behave identically otherwise.

See Also   **strcpy, _strset**

Example

```
/* STRREV.C: This program checks an input string to
 * see whether it is a palindrome: that is, whether
 * it reads the same forward and backward. */

#include <string.h>
#include <stdio.h>

void main( void )
{
   char string[100];
   int result;

   printf( "Input a string and I will tell you if it is a ",
           "palindrome: \n" );
   gets( string );

   /* Reverse string and compare (ignore case): */
   result = _stricmp( string, _strrev( _strdup( string ) ) );
   if( result == 0 )
      printf( "The string \"%s\" is a palindrome\n\n", string );
   else
      printf( "The string \"%s\" is not a palindrome\n\n", string );
}
```

Output

```
Input a string and I will tell you if it is a palindrome:
Able was I ere I saw Elba
The string "Able was I ere I saw Elba" is a palindrome
```

_strset, _wcsset, _mbsset

char *_strset(char **string***, int** *c* **);**

wchar_t *_wcsset(wchar_t **string***, wchar_t** *c* **);**

unsigned char *_mbsset(unsigned char **string***, unsigned int** *c* **);**

_strset: ~~ANSI~~ ~~UNIX~~ WIN32S
_wcsset, _mbsset: ~~ANSI~~ ~~UNIX~~ ~~WIN32S~~

#include <string.h>   For _strset.
#include <wchar.h>   For _wcsset use STRING.H or WCHAR.H.
#include <mbstring.h>   For _mbsset use STRING.H or MBSTRING.H.

Return Value   Each of these functions returns a pointer to the altered string. No return value is reserved to indicate an error.

Parameters   *string*   Null-terminated string to be set
c   Character setting

Remarks   The **_strset** function sets all the characters of *string* to *c* (converted to **char**), except the terminating null character. **_wcsset** and **_mbsset** are wide-character and multibyte-character versions of **_strset**. The data types of the arguments and return values vary accordingly. These three functions behave identically otherwise.

See Also   **_mbsnbset, memset, strcat, strcmp, strcpy, _strnset**

Example
```
/* STRSET.C */

#include <string.h>
#include <stdio.h>

void main( void )
{
   char string[] = "Fill the string with something";
   printf( "Before: %s\n", string );
   _strset( string, '*' );
   printf( "After:  %s\n", string );
}
```

Output
```
Before: Fill the string with something
After:  ****************************
```

strspn, _strspnp, wcsspn, _wcsspnp, _mbsspn, _mbsspnp

size_t strspn(const char *string1*, **const char** *string2* **);**

size_t wcsspn(const wchar_t *string1*, **const wchar_t** *string2* **);**

size_t _mbsspn(const unsigned char *string1*, **const unsigned char** *string2* **);**

unsigned char *_mbsspnp(**const unsigned char** *string1*, **const unsigned char** *string2***);**

For the definitions of **_wcsspnp** and **_strspnp**, see TCHAR.H.

> **strspn:**   ANSI   UNIX   WIN32S
> **_strspnp:**   ~~ANSI~~   UNIX   WIN32S
> **wcsspn:**   ANSI   UNIX   ~~WIN32S~~
> **_wcsspnp, _mbsspn, _mbsspnp:**   ~~ANSI~~   ~~UNIX~~   ~~WIN32S~~

> **#include <string.h>**   For **strspn**.
> **#include <tchar.h>**   For **_strspnp** and **_wcsspnp**
> **#include <wchar.h>**   For **wcsspn** use STRING.H or WCHAR.H.
> **#include <mbstring.h>**   For **_mbsspn** and **_mbsspnp** use STRING.H or MBSTRING.H.

Return Value

strspn, **wcsspn**, and **_mbsspn** return an integer value specifying the length of the substring in *string1* that consists entirely of characters in *string2*. For each of these three functions, if *string1* begins with a character not in *string2*, the function returns 0.

The **_mbsspnp** function and **_strspnp** and **_wcsspnp** routines return a pointer to the first character in *string1* that does not belong to the set of characters in *string2*. Each of these three functions returns **NULL** if *string1* consists entirely of characters from *string2*.

For each of these routines, no return value is reserved to indicate an error.

Parameters

string1   Null-terminated string to search
string2   Null-terminated character set

Remarks

The **strspn** function returns the index of the first character in *string1* that does not belong to the set of characters in *string2*. The search does not include terminating null characters.

wcsspn and **_mbsspn** are wide-character and multibyte-character versions of **strspn**. The arguments of **wcsspn** are wide-character strings; those of **_mbsspn** are multibyte-character strings. These three functions behave identically otherwise.

_mbsspnp and **_mbsspn** differ only in that **_mbsspnp** returns a pointer to the multibyte character that is the first character in *string1* that does not belong to the set of characters in *string2*.

The generic-text function **_tcsspnp**, defined in TCHAR.H, maps to **_mbsspnp** if **_MBCS** has been defined, or to **_wcsspnp** if **_UNICODE** has been defined. Otherwise **_tcsspnp** maps to **_strspnp**. **_strspnp** and **_wcsspnp** are single-byte character and wide-character versions of **_mbsspnp**; they behave identically to **_mbsspnp** otherwise. **_strspnp** and **_wcsspnp** are provided only for this mapping and should not be used for any other reason. For more information, see "Using Generic-Text Mappings" on page 23 and Appendix B, "Generic-Text Mappings."

See Also

_mbspnp, strcspn, strncat, strncmp, strncpy, _strnicmp, strrchr

Example

```
/* STRSPN.C: This program uses strspn to determine
 * the length of the segment in the string "cabbage"
 * consisting of a's, b's, and c's. In other words,
 * it finds the first non-abc letter.
 */

#include <string.h>
#include <stdio.h>

void main( void )
{
    char string[] = "cabbage";
    int  result;
    result = strspn( string, "abc" );
    printf( "The portion of '%s' containing only a, b, or c "
            "is %d bytes long\n", string, result );
}
```

Output

```
The portion of 'cabbage' containing only a, b, or c is 5 bytes long
```

strstr, wcsstr, _mbsstr

char *strstr(const char **string1***, const char ****string2***);**

wchar_t *wcsstr(const wchar_t **string1***, const wchar_t ****string2***);**

unsigned char *_mbsstr(const unsigned char **string1***, const unsigned char ****string2***);**

strstr: ANSI ~~UNIX~~ WIN32S
wcsstr: ANSI ~~UNIX~~ ~~WIN32S~~
_mbsstr: ~~ANSI~~ ~~UNIX~~ ~~WIN32S~~

#include <string.h>   For **strstr**.
#include <wchar.h>   For **wcsstr** use STRING.H or WCHAR.H.
#include <mbstring.h>   For **_mbsstr** use STRING.H or MBSTRING.H.

Return Value

Each of these functions returns a pointer to the first occurrence of *string2* in *string1*, or **NULL** if *string2* does not appear in *string1*. If *string2* points to a string of zero length, the function returns *string1*.

Parameters

string1   Null-terminated string to search
string2   Null-terminated string to search for

Remarks

The **strstr** function returns a pointer to the first occurrence of *string2* in *string1*. The search does not include terminating null characters. **wcsstr** and **_mbsstr** are wide-character and multibyte-character versions of **strstr**. The arguments and return value of **wcsstr** are wide-character strings; those of **_mbsstr** are multibyte-character strings. These three functions behave identically otherwise.

See Also

strcspn, strcmp, strpbrk, strrchr, strspn

Example

```
/* STRSTR.C */

#include <string.h>
#include <stdio.h>

char str[] =    "lazy";
char string[] = "The quick brown dog jumps over the lazy fox";
char fmt1[] =   "         1         2         3         4         5";
char fmt2[] =   "12345678901234567890123456789012345678901234567890";
```

```
void main( void )
{
    char *pdest;
    int  result;
    printf( "String to be searched:\n\t%s\n", string );
    printf( "\t%s\n\t%s\n\n", fmt1, fmt2 );
    pdest = strstr( string, str );
    result = pdest - string + 1;
    if( pdest != NULL )
        printf( "%s found at position %d\n\n", str, result );
    else
        printf( "%s not found\n", str );
}
```

Output

```
String to be searched:
    The quick brown dog jumps over the lazy fox
            1         2         3         4         5
    12345678901234567890123456789012345678901234567890

lazy found at position 36
```

_strtime, _wstrtime

char *_strtime(char *_timestr_);

wchar_t *_wstrtime(wchar_t *_timestr_);

_strtime: ~~ANSI~~ ~~UNIX~~ WIN32S
_wstrtime: ~~ANSI~~ ~~UNIX~~ ~~WIN32S~~

#include <time.h>   For _strtime.
#include <wchar.h>   For **_wstrtime** use TIME.H or WCHAR.H.

Return Value   Each of these functions returns a pointer to the resulting character string _timestr_.

Parameter   _timestr_   Time string

Remarks   The **_strtime** function copies the current time into the buffer pointed to by _timestr_. The time is formatted as _hh:mm:ss_ where _hh_ is two digits representing the hour in 24-hour notation, _mm_ is two digits representing the minutes past the hour, and _ss_ is two digits representing seconds. For example, the string 18:23:44 represents 23 minutes and 44 seconds past 6 P.M. The buffer must be at least 9 bytes long.

_wstrtime is a wide-character version of **_strtime**; the argument and return value of **_wstrtime** are wide-character strings. These functions behave identically otherwise.

See Also   **asctime**, **ctime**, **gmtime**, **localtime**, **mktime**, **time**, **_tzset**

Example

```
/* STRTIME.C */

#include <time.h>
#include <stdio.h>

void main( void )
{
    char dbuffer [9];
    char tbuffer [9];
    _strdate( dbuffer );
    printf( "The current date is %s \n", dbuffer );
    _strtime( tbuffer );
    printf( "The current time is %s \n", tbuffer );
}
```

Output

```
The current date is 05/02/94
The current time is 11:32:36
```

strtod, wcstod, strtol, wcstol, strtoul, wcstoul

double strtod(const char **nptr*, **char** **endptr **);**

double wcstod(const wchar_t **nptr*, **wchar_t** **endptr **);**

long strtol(const char **nptr*, **char** **endptr, **int** *base* **);**

long wcstol(const wchar_t **nptr*, **wchar_t** **endptr, **int** *base* **);**

unsigned long strtoul(const char **nptr*, **char** **endptr, **int** *base* **);**

unsigned long wcstoul(const wchar_t **nptr*, **wchar_t** **endptr, **int** *base* **);**

strtod, strtol, strtoul: ANSI   UNIX   WIN32S
wcstod, **wcstol**, **wcstoul:**   ANSI   UNIX   ~~WIN32S~~

#include <stdlib.h>   For **strtod**, **strtol**, and **strtoul**.
#include <wchar.h>   For **wcstod**, **wcstol**, and **wcstoul** use STDLIB.H or
WCHAR.H.

Return Value

strtod returns the value of the floating-point number, except when the representation would cause an overflow, in which case the function returns +/–**HUGE_VAL**. The sign of **HUGE_VAL** matches the sign of the value that cannot be represented. **strtod** returns 0 if no conversion can be performed or an underflow occurs.

strtol returns the value represented in the string *nptr*, except when the representation would cause an overflow, in which case it returns **LONG_MAX** or **LONG_MIN**. **strtoul** returns the converted value, if any, or **ULONG_MAX** on overflow. Each of these functions returns 0 if no conversion can be performed.

wcstod, **wcstol**, and **wcstoul** return values analogously to **strtod**, **strtol**, and **strtoul,** respectively.

For all six functions in this group, **errno** is set to **ERANGE** if overflow or underflow occurs.

Parameters

nptr   Null-terminated string to convert
endptr   Pointer to character that stops scan
base   Number base to use

Remarks

The **strtod**, **strtol**, and **strtoul** functions convert *nptr* to a double-precision value, a long-integer value, or an unsigned long-integer value, respectively.

The input string *nptr* is a sequence of characters that can be interpreted as a numerical value of the specified type. Each function stops reading the string *nptr* at the first character it cannot recognize as part of a number. This may be the terminating null character. For **strtol** or **strtoul**, this terminating character can also be the first numeric character greater than or equal to *base*.

For all six functions in the **strtod** group, the current locale's **LC_NUMERIC** category setting determines recognition of the radix character in *nptr;* for more information, see **setlocale.**If *endptr* is not **NULL**, a pointer to the character that stopped the scan is stored at the location pointed to by *endptr*. If no conversion can be performed (no valid digits were found or an invalid base was specified), the value of *nptr* is stored at the location pointed to by *endptr*.

strtod expects *nptr* to point to a string of the following form:

[[*whitespace*]] [[*sign*]] [*digits*] [[*.digits*]] [[{**d** | **D** | **e** | **E**}[[*sign*]]*digits*]]

A *whitespace* may consist of space or tab characters, which are ignored; *sign* is either plus (+) or minus (–); and *digits* are one or more decimal digits. If no digits appear before the radix character, at least one must appear after the radix character. The decimal digits can be followed by an exponent, which consists of an introductory letter (**d**, **D**, **e**, or **E**) and an optionally signed integer. If neither an exponent part nor a radix character appears, a radix character is assumed to follow the last digit in the string. The first character that does not fit this form stops the scan.

The **strtol** and **strtoul** functions expect *nptr* to point to a string of the following form:

[[*whitespace*]] [[{+ | –}]] [[**0** [[{ **x** | **X** }]]]] [[*digits*]]

If *base* is between 2 and 36, then it is used as the base of the number. If *base* is 0, the initial characters of the string pointed to by *nptr* are used to determine the base. If the first character is 0 and the second character is not 'x' or 'X', the string is interpreted as an octal integer; otherwise, it is interpreted as a decimal number. If the first character is '0' and the second character is 'x' or 'X', the string is interpreted as a hexadecimal integer. If the first character is '1' through '9', the string is interpreted as a decimal integer. The letters 'a' through 'z' (or 'A' through 'Z') are assigned the values 10 through 35; only letters whose assigned values are less than *base* are permitted. **strtoul** allows a plus (+) or minus (–) sign prefix; a leading minus sign indicates that the return value is negated.

wcstod, **wcstol**, and **wcstoul** are wide-character versions of **strtod**, **strtol**, and **strtoul,** respectively; the *nptr* argument to each of these wide-character functions is a wide-character string. Otherwise, each of these wide-character functions behaves identically to its single-byte–character counterpart.

See Also   **atof, localeconv, setlocale**

Example
```
/* STRTOD.C: This program uses strtod to convert a
 * string to a double-precision value; strtol to
 * convert a string to long integer values; and strtoul
 * to convert a string to unsigned long-integer values.
 */
```

```
#include <stdlib.h>
#include <stdio.h>

void main( void )
{
    char    *string, *stopstring;
    double x;
    long    l;
    int     base;
    unsigned long ul;
    string = "3.1415926This stopped it";
    x = strtod( string, &stopstring );
    printf( "string = %s\n", string );
    printf("    strtod = %f\n", x );
    printf("    Stopped scan at: %s\n\n", stopstring );
    string = "-10110134932This stopped it";
    l = strtol( string, &stopstring, 10 );
    printf( "string = %s", string );
    printf("    strtol = %ld", l );
    printf("    Stopped scan at: %s", stopstring );
    string = "10110134932";
    printf( "string = %s\n", string );
    /* Convert string using base 2, 4, and 8: */
    for( base = 2; base <= 8; base *= 2 )
    {
        /* Convert the string: */
        ul = strtoul( string, &stopstring, base );
        printf( "    strtol = %ld (base %d)\n", ul, base );
        printf( "    Stopped scan at: %s\n", stopstring );
    }
}
```

Output

```
string = 3.1415926This stopped it
    strtod = 3.141593
    Stopped scan at: This stopped it

string = -10110134932This stopped it    strtol = -2147483647    Stopped
scan at: This stopped itstring = 10110134932
    strtol = 45 (base 2)
    Stopped scan at: 34932
    strtol = 4423 (base 4)
    Stopped scan at: 4932
    strtol = 2134108 (base 8)
    Stopped scan at: 932
```

strtok, wcstok, _mbstok

char *strtok(char **string1***, const char ****string2***);**

wchar_t *wcstok(wchar_t **string1***, const wchar_t ****string2***);**

unsigned char *_mbstok*(unsigned char**string1***, const unsigned char ****string2***);**

strtok: ANSI   UNIX   WIN32S
wcstok: ANSI   UNIX   ~~WIN32S~~
_mbstok: ~~ANSI~~   ~~UNIX~~   ~~WIN32S~~

#include <string.h>   For **strtok**.
#include <wchar.h>   For **wcstok** use STRING.H or WCHAR.H.
#include <mbstring.h>   For**_mbstok** use STRING.H or MBSTRING.H.

Return Value

The first time one of these functions is called, it returns a pointer to the first token in *string1*. In each subsequent call to the function on the same token string, the function returns a pointer to the next token in the string. The function returns **NULL** when there are no more tokens. All tokens are null-terminated.

Parameters

string1   String containing token(s)
string2   Set of delimiter characters

Remarks

The **strtok** function finds the next token in *string1*. The set of characters in *string2* specifies possible delimiters of the token to be found in *string1* on the current call. **wcstok** and **_mbstok** are wide-character and multibyte-character versions of **strtok**. The arguments and return value of **wcstok** are wide-character strings; those of **_mbstok** are multibyte-character strings. These three functions behave identically otherwise.

On the first call to **strtok**, the function skips leading delimiters and returns a pointer to the first token in *string1*, terminating the token with a null character. More tokens can be broken out of the remainder of *string1* by a series of calls to **strtok**. Each call to **strtok** modifies *string1* by inserting a null character after the token returned by that call. To read the next token from *string1*, call **strtok** with a **NULL** value for the *string1* argument. The **NULL** *string1* argument causes **strtok** to search for the next token in the modified *string1*. The *string2* argument can take any value from one call to the next so that the set of delimiters may vary.

See Also

strcspn, strspn, setlocale

Example

```
/* STRTOK.C: In this program, a loop uses strtok
 * to print all the tokens (separated by commas
 * or blanks) in the string named "string".
 */

#include <string.h>
#include <stdio.h>
```

```
char string[] = "A string\tof ,,tokens\nand some  more tokens";
char seps[]   = " ,\t\n";
char *token;
void main( void )
{
   printf( "%s\n\nTokens:\n", string );
   /* Establish string and get the first token: */
   token = strtok( string, seps );
   while( token != NULL )
   {
      /* While there are tokens in "string" */
      printf( " %s\n", token );
      /* Get next token: */
      token = strtok( NULL, seps );
   }
}
```

Output

```
A string    of ,,tokens
and some   more tokens

Tokens:
 A
 string
 of
 tokens
 and
 some
 more
 tokens
```

_strupr, _wcsupr, _mbsupr

char *_strupr(char *_string_ **);**

wchar_t * _wcsupr(wchar_t *_string_ **);**

unsigned char * _mbsupr (unsigned char *_string_ **);**

_strupr: ~~ANSI~~ ~~UNIX~~ WIN32S
_wcsupr, _mbsupr: ~~ANSI~~ ~~UNIX~~ ~~WIN32S~~

#include <string.h>   For _strupr.
#include <wchar.h>   For _wcsupr use STRING.H or WCHAR.H.
#include <mbstring.h>   For _mbsupr use STRING.H or MBSTRING.H.

Return Value   These functions return a pointer to the altered string. Because the modification is done in place, the pointer returned is the same as the pointer passed as the input argument. No return value is reserved to indicate an error.

Parameter   _string_   String to capitalize

Remarks

The **_strupr** function converts, in place, each lowercase letter in *string* to uppercase. The conversion is determined by the **LC_CTYPE** category setting of the current locale. Other characters are not affected. For more information on **LC_CTYPE**, see **setlocale**.

_wcsupr and **_mbsupr** are wide-character and multibyte-character versions of **_strupr**. The argument and return value of **_wcsupr** are wide-character strings; those of **_mbsupr** are multibyte-character strings. These three functions behave identically otherwise.

See Also   **_strlwr**

Example   See the example for **_strlwr**.

strxfrm, wcsxfrm

size_t strxfrm(char * *string1* **, const char *** *string2* **, size_t** *count* **);**

size_t wcsxfrm(wchar_t * *string1* **, const wchar_t *** *string2* **, size_t** *count* **);**

strxfrm: ANSI   ~~UNIX~~   WIN32S
wcsxfrm: ~~ANSI~~   ~~UNIX~~   ~~WIN32S~~

#include <string.h>   For **strxfrm**.
#include <wchar.h>   For **wcsxfrm** include STRING.H or WCHAR.H.

Return Value

Each of these functions returns the length of the transformed string, not counting the terminating null character. If the return value is greater than or equal to *count*, the content of *string1* is unpredictable. On an error, each of the functions sets **errno** and returns **(size_t)** –1.

Parameters

string1   Destination string
string2   Source string
count   Maximum number of characters to place in *string1*

Remarks

The **strxfrm** function transforms the string pointed to by *string2* into a new collated form that is stored in *string1*. No more than *count* characters, including the null character, are transformed and placed into the resulting string. The transformation is made using the current locale's **LC_COLLATE** category setting. For more information on **LC_COLLATE**, see **setlocale**.

After the transformation, a call to **strcmp** with the two transformed strings yields results identical to those of a call to **strcoll** applied to the original two strings. As with **strcoll** and **stricoll**, **strxfrm** automatically handles multibyte-character strings as appropriate.

wcsxfrm is a wide-character version of **strxfrm**; the string arguments of **wcsxfrm** are wide-character pointers. For **wcsxfrm**, after the string transformation, a call to **wcscmp** with the two transformed strings yields results identical to those of a call to **wcscoll** applied to the original two strings. **wcsxfrm** and **strxfrm** behave identically otherwise.

In the "C" locale, the order of the characters in the character set (ASCII character set) is the same as the lexicographic order of the characters. However, in other locales, the order of characters in the character set may differ from the lexicographic character order. For example, in certain European locales, the character 'a' (value 0x61) precedes the character 'ä' (value 0xE4) in the character set, but the character 'ä' precedes the character 'a' lexicographically.

In locales for which the character set and the lexicographic character order differ, use **strxfrm** on the original strings and then **strcmp** on the resulting strings to produce a lexicographic string comparison according to the current locale's **LC_COLLATE** category setting. Thus, to compare two strings lexicographically in the above locale, use **strxfrm** on the original strings, then **strcmp** on the resulting strings. Alternatively, you can use **strcoll** rather than **strcmp** on the original strings.

The value of the following expression is the size of the array needed to hold the **strxfrm** transformation of the source string:

```
1 + strxfrm( NULL, string, 0 )
```

In the "C" locale only, **strxfrm** is equivalent to the following:

```
strncpy( _string1, _string2, _count );
return( strlen( _string1 ) );
```

See Also   **localeconv, setlocale, strcmp, strncmp, strcoll** Functions

_swab

void _swab(char *_src_, char *_dest_, int _n_);

~~ANSI~~ UNIX WIN32S

#include <stdlib.h>

Return Value   None

Parameters   _src_   Data to be copied and swapped
dest   Storage location for swapped data
_n_   Number of bytes to be copied and swapped

Remarks

The **_swab** function copies *n* bytes from *src*, swaps each pair of adjacent bytes, and stores the result at *dest*. The integer *n* should be an even number to allow for swapping. **_swab** is typically used to prepare binary data for transfer to a machine that uses a different byte order.

Use **_swab** for compatibility with ANSI naming conventions of non-ANSI functions. Use **swab** and link with OLDNAMES.LIB for UNIX compatibility.

Example

```
/* SWAB.C illustrates:
 *        _swab
 */

#include <stdlib.h>
#include <stdio.h>

char from[] = "BADCFEHGJILKNMPORQTSVUXWZY";
char to[] =   "..........................";

void main()
{
    printf( "Before:\t%s\n\t%s\n\n", from, to );
    _swab( from, to, sizeof( from ) );
    printf( "After:\t%s\n\t%s\n\n", from, to );
}
```

Output

```
Before:   BADCFEHGJILKNMPORQTSVUXWZY
          ..........................

After:    BADCFEHGJILKNMPORQTSVUXWZY
          ABCDEFGHIJKLMNOPQRSTUVWXYZ
```

system, _wsystem

int system(const char *command **);**

int _wsystem(const wchar_t *command **);**

ANSI   UNIX   ~~WIN32S~~

#include <process.h>
#include <stdlib.h>   For **system** use STDLIB.H (for ANSI compatibility) or PROCESS.H.
#include <wchar.h>   For **_wsystem** use PROCESS.H, STDLIB.H, or WCHAR.H.

Return Value

If *command* is **NULL** and the command interpreter is found, the function returns a nonzero value. If the command interpreter is not found, it returns 0 and sets **errno** to **ENOENT**. If *command* is not **NULL**, **system** returns the value that is returned by the command interpreter. It returns the value 0 only if the command interpreter returns the value 0. A return value of −1 indicates an error, and **errno** is set to one of the following values:

E2BIG   Argument list (which is system-dependent) is too big.

ENOENT   Command interpreter cannot be found.

ENOEXEC   Command-interpreter file has invalid format and is not executable.

ENOMEM   Not enough memory is available to execute command; or available memory has been corrupted; or invalid block exists, indicating that process making call was not allocated properly.

Parameter

command   Command to be executed

Remarks

The **system** function passes *command* to the command interpreter, which executes the string as an operating-system command. **system** refers to the **COMSPEC** and **PATH** environment variables that locate the command-interpreter file (the file named CMD.EXE in Windows NT). If *command* points to an empty string, the function simply checks to see whether the command interpreter exists.

You must explicitly flush (using **fflush** or **_flushall**) or close any stream before calling **system**.

_wsystem is a wide-character version of **_system**; the *command* argument to **_wsystem** is a wide-character string. These functions behave identically otherwise.

See Also

_exec Functions, **exit**, **_flushall**, **_spawn** Functions

Example

```
/* SYSTEM.C: This program uses
 * system to TYPE its source file.
 */

#include <process.h>

void main( void )
{
    system( "type system.c" );
}
```

Output

```
/* SYSTEM.C: This program uses
 * system to TYPE its source file.
 */
#include <process.h>
void main( void )
{
    system( "type system.c" );
}
```

tan, tanh

double tan(double *x* **);**

double tanh(double *x* **);**

ANSI   UNIX   WIN32S

#include <math.h>

Return Value   **tan** returns the tangent of *x*. If *x* is greater than or equal to 2^{63}, or less than or equal to -2^{63}, a loss of significance in the result occurs, in which case the function generates a **_TLOSS** error and returns an indefinite (same as a quiet NaN). You can modify error handling with **_matherr**.

tanh returns the hyperbolic tangent of *x*. There is no error return.

Parameter   *x*   Angle in radians

See Also   **acos, asin, atan, cos, sin**

Example
```
/* TAN.C:  This program displays the tangent of pi / 4
 * and the hyperbolic tangent of the result.
 */

#include <math.h>
#include <stdio.h>

void main( void )
{
    double pi = 3.1415926535;
    double x, y;

    x = tan( pi / 4 );
    y = tanh( x );
    printf( "tan( %f ) = %f\n", x, y );
    printf( "tanh( %f ) = %f\n", y, x );
}
```

Output
```
tan( 1.000000 ) = 0.761594
tanh( 0.761594 ) = 1.000000
```

_tell

long _tell(int *handle* **);**

~~ANSI~~ ~~UNIX~~ WIN32S

#include <io.h>

Return Value   A return value of – 1L indicates an error, and **errno** is set to **EBADF** to indicate an invalid file-handle argument. On devices incapable of seeking, the return value is undefined.

Parameter   *handle*   Handle referring to open file

Remarks   The **_tell** function gets the current position of the file pointer (if any) associated with the *handle* argument. The position is expressed as the number of bytes from the beginning of the file.

See Also   **ftell, _lseek**

Example
```
/* TELL.C:  This program uses _tell to tell the
 * file pointer position after a file read.
 */

#include <io.h>
#include <stdio.h>
#include <fcntl.h>

void main( void )
{
   int  fh;
   char buffer[500];

   if( (fh = _open( "tell.c", _O_RDONLY )) != -1 )
   {
      if( _read( fh, buffer, 500 ) > 0 )
         printf( "Current file position is: %d\n", _tell( fh ) );
      _close( fh );
   }
}
```

Output   `Current file position is: 418`

_tempnam, _wtempnam, tmpnam, _wtmpnam

char *_tempnam(char **dir***, char ****prefix***);**

wchar_t *_wtempnam(wchar_t **dir***, wchar_t ****prefix***);**

char *tmpnam(char **string***);**

wchar_t *_wtmpnam(wchar_t **string***);**

> **_tempnam:** ~~ANSI~~ UNIX WIN32S
> **_wtempnam, _wtmpnam:** ~~ANSI~~ UNIX ~~WIN32S~~
> **tmpnam:** ANSI UNIX WIN32S

Use **_tempnam** for compatibility with ANSI naming conventions of non-ANSI functions. Use **tempnam** and link with OLDNAMES.LIB for UNIX compatibility.

#include <stdio.h>   For **_tempnam** and **tmpnam**.
#include <wchar.h>   For **_wtempnam** and **_wtmpnam** use STDIO.H or WCHAR.H.

Return Value

Each of these functions returns a pointer to the name generated, unless it is impossible to create this name or the name is not unique. If the name cannot be created or if a file with that name already exists, **tmpnam** and **_tempnam** return **NULL**. **_tempnam** and **_wtempnam** also return **NULL** if the file search fails.

Parameters

prefix   Filename prefix
dir   Target directory to be used if TMP not defined
string   Pointer to temporary name

Remarks

The **tmpnam** function generates a temporary filename that can be used to open a temporary file without overwriting an existing file.

This name is stored in *string*. If *string* is **NULL**, then **tmpnam** leaves the result in an internal static buffer. Thus any subsequent calls destroy this value. If *string* is not **NULL**, it is assumed to point to an array of at least **L_tmpnam** bytes (the value of **L_tmpnam** is defined in STDIO.H). The function generates unique filenames for up to **TMP_MAX** calls.

The character string that **tmpnam** creates consists of the path prefix, defined by the entry **P_tmpdir** in the file STDIO.H, followed by a sequence consisting of the digit characters '0' through '9'; the numerical value of this string is in the range 1–65,535. Changing the definitions of **L_tmpnam** or **P_tmpdir** in STDIO.H does not change the operation of **tmpnam**.

_tempnam creates a temporary filename for use in another directory. This filename is different from that of any existing file. The *prefix* argument is the prefix to the filename. **_tempnam** uses **malloc** to allocate space for the filename; the program is responsible for freeing this space when it is no longer needed. **_tempnam** looks for the file with the given name in the following directories, listed in order of precedence.

Directory Used	Conditions
Directory specified by **TMP**	**TMP** environment variable is set, and directory specified by **TMP** exists.
dir argument to **_tempnam**	**TMP** environment variable is not set, or directory specified by **TMP** does not exist.
P_tmpdir in STDIO.H	*dir* argument is **NULL**, or *dir* is name of nonexistent directory.
Current working directory	**P_tmpdir** does not exist.

_tempnam and **tmpnam** automatically handle multibyte-character string arguments as appropriate, recognizing multibyte-character sequences according to the OEM code page obtained from the operating system. **_wtempnam** is a wide-character version of **_tempnam**; the arguments and return value of **_wtempnam** are wide-character strings. **_wtempnam** and **_tempnam** behave identically except that **_wtempnam** does not handle multibyte-character strings. **_wtmpnam** is a wide-character version of **tmpnam**; the argument and return value of **_wtmpnam** are wide-character strings. **_wtmpnam** and **tmpnam** behave identically except that **_wtmpnam** does not handle multibyte-character strings.

See Also   **_getmbcp, malloc, _setmbcp, tmpfile**

Example

```
/* TEMPNAM.C: This program uses tmpnam to create a unique
 * filename in the current working directory, then uses
 * _tempnam to create a unique filename with a prefix of stq.
 */

#include <stdio.h>

void main( void )
{
    char *name1, *name2;

    /* Create a temporary filename for the current working directory: */
    if( ( name1 = tmpnam( NULL ) ) != NULL )
        printf( "%s is safe to use as a temporary file.\n", name1 );
    else
        printf( "Cannot create a unique filename\n" );
```

```
    /* Create a temporary filename in temporary directory with the
     * prefix "stq". The actual destination directory may vary
     * depending on the state of the TMP environment variable and
     * the global variable P_tmpdir.
     */
    if( ( name2 = _tempnam( "c:\\tmp", "stq" ) ) != NULL )
        printf( "%s is safe to use as a temporary file.\n", name2 );
    else
        printf( "Cannot create a unique filename\n" );
}
```

Output

```
\s12. is safe to use as a temporary file.
C:\temp\stq2 is safe to use as a temporary file.
```

terminate

void terminate(void);

ANSI ~~UNIX~~ WIN32S

#include <eh.h>

Return Value   None

Remarks   The **terminate** function is used with C++ exception handling and is called in the following cases:

- A matching catch handler cannot be found for a thrown C++ exception.
- An exception is thrown by a destructor function during stack unwind.
- The stack is corrupted after throwing an exception.

terminate calls **abort** by default. You can change this default by writing your own termination function and calling **set_terminate** with the name of your function as its argument. **terminate** calls the last function given as an argument to **set_terminate**.

See Also   **abort, _set_se_translator, set_terminate, set_unexpected, unexpected**

Example

```
/* TERMINAT.CPP:    */
#include <eh.h>
#include <process.h>
#include <iostream.h>

void term_func();
void main()
{

    int i = 10, j = 0, result;
    set_terminate( term_func );
    try
    {
        if( j == 0 )
            throw "Divide by zero!";
        else
            result = i/j;

    }
    catch( int )
    {
        cout << "Caught some integer exception.\n";
    }
    cout << "This should never print.\n";

}
void term_func()
{
    cout << "term_func() was called by terminate().\n";

    // ... cleanup tasks performed here

    // If this function does not exit, abort is called.

    exit(-1);
}
```

Output   term_func() was called by terminate().

time

time_t time(time_t * *timer* **);**

ANSI   UNIX   WIN32S

#include <time.h>

Return Value   **time** returns the time in elapsed seconds. There is no error return.

Parameter   *timer*   Storage location for time

Remarks   The **time** function returns the number of seconds elapsed since midnight (00:00:00),
January 1, 1970, universal coordinated time, according to the system clock. The
return value is stored in the location given by *timer*. This parameter may be **NULL**,
in which case the return value is not stored.

See Also   **asctime, _ftime, gmtime, localtime, _utime**

Example

```
/* TIMES.C illustrates various time and date functions including:
 *      time            _ftime          ctime       asctime
 *      localtime       gmtime          mktime      _tzset
 *      _strtime        _strdate        strftime
 *
 * Also the global variable:
 *      _tzname
 */

#include <time.h>
#include <stdio.h>
#include <sys/types.h>
#include <sys/timeb.h>
#include <string.h>

void main()
{
    char tmpbuf[128], ampm[] = "AM";
    time_t ltime;
    struct _timeb tstruct;
    struct tm *today, *gmt, xmas = { 0, 0, 12, 25, 11, 93 };

    /* Set time zone from TZ environment variable. If TZ is not set,
     * operating system default is used, otherwise PST8PDT is used
     * (Pacific standard time, daylight savings).
     */
    _tzset();

    /* Display operating system-style date and time. */
    _strtime( tmpbuf );
    printf( "OS time:\t\t\t%s\n", tmpbuf );
    _strdate( tmpbuf );
    printf( "OS date:\t\t\t%s\n", tmpbuf );
```

```
    /* Get UNIX-style time and display as number and string. */
    time( &ltime );
    printf( "Time in seconds since UCT 1/1/70:\t%ld\n", ltime );
    printf( "UNIX time and date:\t\t\t%s", ctime( &ltime ) );

    /* Display UCT. */
    gmt = gmtime( &ltime );
    printf( "Universal coordinated time:\t\t%s", asctime( gmt ) );

    /* Convert to time structure and adjust for PM if necessary. */
    today = localtime( &ltime );
    if( today->tm_hour > 12 )
    {
strcpy( ampm, "PM" );
today->tm_hour -= 12;
    }
    if( today->tm_hour == 0 )   /* Adjust if midnight hour. */
today->tm_hour = 12;

    /* Note how pointer addition is used to skip the first 11
     * characters and printf is used to trim off terminating
     * characters.
     */
    printf( "12-hour time:\t\t\t\t%.8s %s\n",
        asctime( today ) + 11, ampm );

    /* Print additional time information. */
    _ftime( &tstruct );
    printf( "Plus milliseconds:\t\t\t%u\n", tstruct.millitm );
    printf( "Zone difference in seconds from UCT:\t%u\n",
            tstruct.timezone );
    printf( "Time zone name:\t\t\t\t%s\n", _tzname[0] );
    printf( "Daylight savings:\t\t\t%s\n",
            tstruct.dstflag ? "YES" : "NO" );

    /* Make time for noon on Christmas, 1993. */
    if( mktime( &xmas ) != (time_t)-1 )
printf( "Christmas\t\t\t\t%s\n", asctime( &xmas ) );

    /* Use time structure to build a customized time string. */
    today = localtime( &ltime );

    /* Use strftime to build a customized time string. */
    strftime( tmpbuf, 128,
        "Today is %A, day %d of %B in the year %Y.\n", today );
    printf( tmpbuf );
}
```

Output

```
OS time:                15:39:57
OS date:                03/26/93
Time in seconds since UCT 1/1/70:   733189197
UNIX time and date:          Fri Mar 26 15:39:57 1993
Universal coordinated time:      Fri Mar 26 23:39:57 1993
12-hour time:           03:39:57 PM
Plus milliseconds:          160
Zone difference in seconds from UCT:   480
Time zone name:             PST
Daylight savings:           NO
Christmas           Sat Dec 25 12:00:00 1993

Today is Friday, day 26 of March in the year 1993.
```

tmpfile

FILE *tmpfile(void);

ANSI   UNIX   WIN32S

#include <stdio.h>

Return Value

If successful, **tmpfile** returns a stream pointer. Otherwise, it returns a **NULL** pointer.

Remarks

The **tmpfile** function creates a temporary file and returns a pointer to that stream. If the file cannot be opened, **tmpfile** returns a **NULL** pointer. This temporary file is automatically deleted when the file is closed, when the program terminates normally, or when **_rmtmp** is called, assuming that the current working directory does not change. The temporary file is opened in **w+b** (binary read/write) mode.

See Also

_rmtmp, _tempnam

Example

```
/* TMPFILE.C: This program uses tmpfile to create a
 * temporary file, then deletes this file with _rmtmp.
 */

#include <stdio.h>
```

```
                    void main( void )
                    {
                       FILE *stream;
                       char tempstring[] = "String to be written";
                       int  i;

                       /* Create temporary files. */
                       for( i = 1; i <= 3; i++ )
                       {
                          if( (stream = tmpfile()) == NULL )
                             perror( "Could not open new temporary file\n" );
                          else
                             printf( "Temporary file %d was created\n", i );
                       }

                       /* Remove temporary files. */
                       printf( "%d temporary files deleted\n", _rmtmp() );
                    }
```

Output

```
Temporary file 1 was created
Temporary file 2 was created
Temporary file 3 was created
3 temporary files deleted
```

__ toascii, tolower, _tolower, towlower, toupper, _toupper, towupper

int __toascii(int *c*);

int tolower(int *c*);

int _tolower(int *c*);

int towlower(wint_t *c*);

int toupper(int *c*);

int _toupper(int *c*);

int towupper(wint_t *c*);

__ **toascii**, **_tolower**, **_toupper**: ~~ANSI~~ UNIX   WIN32S
tolower, **toupper**, **towlower**, **towupper**: ANSI   UNIX   WIN32S

Use __ **toascii** for compatibility with ANSI naming conventions of non-ANSI functions. Use **toascii** and link with OLDNAMES.LIB for UNIX compatibility.

#include <ctype.h>   For single-byte character **to** functions (__ **toascii**, **tolower**, **_tolower**, **toupper**, and **_toupper**).
#include <wchar.h>   For **tow** functions use CTYPE.H or WCHAR.H.

Return Value

Each of the **to** routines converts a copy of *c*, if possible, and returns the result. For all **to** routines, there is no return value reserved to indicate an error.

Parameter

c   Character to convert

Remarks

Each of the **to** functions and its associated macro, if any, converts a single character, as described in the following table.

Function	Macro	Description
__ **toascii**	__ **toascii**	Converts *c* to ASCII character
tolower	**tolower**	Converts *c* to lowercase if appropriate
_tolower	**_tolower**	Converts *c* to lowercase
towlower	None	Converts *c* to corresponding wide-character lowercase letter
toupper	**toupper**	Converts *c* to uppercase if appropriate
_toupper	**_toupper**	Converts *c* to uppercase
towupper	None	Converts c to corresponding wide-character uppercase letter

To use the function versions of the **to** routines that are also defined as macros, either remove the macro definitions with **#undef** directives or do not include CTYPE.H. If you use the /Za compiler option, the compiler uses the function version of **toupper** or **tolower**. Declarations of the **tolower** and **toupper** functions are in STDLIB.H.

The __ **toascii** routine sets all but the low-order 7 bits of *c* to 0, so that the converted value represents a character in the ASCII character set. If *c* already represents an ASCII character, *c* is unchanged.

The **tolower** and **toupper** routines:

- Are dependent on the **LC_CTYPE** category of the current locale (**tolower** calls **isupper** and **toupper** calls **islower**).

- Convert c if c represents a convertible letter of the appropriate case in the current locale and the opposite case exists for that locale. Otherwise, c is unchanged.

The **_tolower** and **_toupper** routines:

- Are locale-independent, much faster versions of **tolower** and **toupper.**

- Can be used only when **isascii**(c) and either **isupper**(c) or **islower**(c), respectively, are true.

- Have undefined results if c is not an ASCII letter of the appropriate case for converting.

The **towlower** and **towupper** functions return a converted copy of c if and only if both of the following conditions are true. Otherwise, c is unchanged.

- c is a wide character of the appropriate case (that is, for which **iswupper** or **iswlower,** respectively, is true).

- There is a corresponding wide character of the target case (that is, for which **iswlower** or **iswupper,** respectively, is true).

See Also

is Functions

Example

```
/* TOUPPER.C: This program uses toupper and tolower to
 * analyze all characters between 0x0 and 0x7F. It also
 * applies _toupper and _tolower to any code in this
 * range for which these functions make sense.
 */

#include <conio.h>
#include <ctype.h>
#include <string.h>

char msg[] = "Some of THESE letters are Capitals\r\n";
char *p;
```

```
void main( void )
{
   _cputs( msg );

   /* Reverse case of message. */
   for( p = msg; p < msg + strlen( msg ); p++ )
   {
      if( islower( *p ) )
         _putch( _toupper( *p ) );
      else if( isupper( *p ) )
         _putch( _tolower( *p ) );
      else
         _putch( *p );
   }
}
```

Output

```
Some of THESE letters are Capitals
sOME OF these LETTERS ARE cAPITALS
```

_tzset

void _tzset(void);

~~ANSI~~ UNIX   WIN32S

Use **_tzset** for compatibility with ANSI naming conventions of non-ANSI functions. Use **tzset** and link with OLDNAMES.LIB for UNIX compatibility.

#include <time.h>

Return Value   None

Remarks

The **_tzset** function uses the current setting of the environment variable **TZ** to assign values to three global variables: **_daylight**, **_timezone**, and **_tzname**. These variables are used by the **_ftime** and **localtime** functions to make corrections from universal coordinated time (UCT) to local time, and by the **time** function to compute UCT from system time. Use the following syntax to set the **TZ** environment variable:

set TZ=*tzn*[[+ | –]]*hh*[[:*mm*[[:*ss*]]]][[*dzn*]]

tzn   Three-letter time-zone name, such as PST. You must specify the correct offset from UCT.

hh   Difference in hours between UCT and local time. Optionally signed.

mm   Minutes. Separated from *hh* by a colon (**:**).

ss   Seconds. Separated from *mm* by a colon (**:**).

dzn   Three-letter daylight-saving-time zone such as PDT. If daylight saving time is never in effect in the locality, set **TZ** without a value for *dzn*.

For example, to set the **TZ** environment variable to correspond to the current time zone in Germany, you can use one of the following statements:

```
set TZ=GST1GDT
set TZ=GST+1GDT
```

These strings use GST to indicate German standard time, assume that Germany is one hour ahead of UCT, and assume that daylight savings time is in effect.

If the **TZ** value is not set, **_tzset** attempts to use the time zone information specified by the operating system. In Windows NT, this information is specified in the Control Panel's Date/Time application. If **_tzset** cannot obtain this information, it uses PST8PDT by default, which signifies the Pacific time zone.

Based on the **TZ** environment variable value, the following values are assigned to the global variables **_daylight**, **_timezone**, and **_tzname** when **_tzset** is called:

Global Variable	Description	Default Value
_daylight	Nonzero value if a daylight-saving-time zone is specified in **TZ** setting; otherwise, 0	1
_timezone	Difference in seconds between UCT and local time.	28000 (28000 seconds equals 8 hours)
_tzname[0]	String value of time-zone name from **TZ** environmental variable; empty if **TZ** has not been set	PST
_tzname[1]	String value of daylight-saving-time zone; empty if daylight-saving-time zone is omitted from **TZ** environmental variable	PDT

The default values shown in the preceding table for **_daylight** and the **_tzname** array correspond to "PST8PDT." If the DST zone is omitted from the **TZ** environmental variable, the value of **_daylight** is 0 and the **_ftime**, **gmtime**, and **localtime** functions return 0 for their DST flags. For more information, see "**_daylight**, **_timezone**, and **_tzname**" on page 38.

See Also   asctime, _ftime, gmtime, localtime, time, _utime

Example

```
/* TZSET.C: This program first sets up the time zone by
 * placing the variable named TZ=EST5 in the environment
 * table. It then uses _tzset to set the global variables
 * named _daylight, _timezone, and _tzname.
 */

#include <time.h>
#include <stdlib.h>
#include <stdio.h>

void main( void )
{
    if( _putenv( "TZ=EST5EDT" ) == -1 )
    {
        printf( "Unable to set TZ\n" );
        exit( 1 );
    }
    else
    {
        _tzset();
        printf( "_daylight = %d\n", _daylight );
        printf( "_timezone = %ld\n", _timezone );
        printf( "_tzname[0] = %s\n", _tzname[0] );
    }
    exit( 0 );
}
```

Output

```
_daylight = 1
_timezone = 18000
_tzname[0] = EST
```

_ultoa, _ultow

char *_ultoa(unsigned long *value*, **char ****string*, **int** *radix* **);**

wchar_t *_ultow (unsigned long *value*, **wchar_t ****string*, **int** *radix* **);**

_ultoa: ~~ANSI~~ ~~UNIX~~ WIN32S
_ultow: ~~ANSI~~ UNIX ~~WIN32S~~

#include <stdlib.h>   For **_ultoa**.
#include <wchar.h>   For **_ultow** use STDLIB.H or WCHAR.H.

Return Value   Each of these functions returns a pointer to *string*. There is no error return.

Parameters   *value*   Number to be converted
string   String result
radix   Base of *value*

Remarks   The **_ultoa** function converts *value* to a null-terminated character string and stores the result (up to 33 bytes) in *string*. No overflow checking is performed. *radix* specifies the base of *value*; *radix* must be in the range 2–36. **_ultow** is a wide-character version of **_ultoa**.

See Also   **_itoa, _ltoa**

Example   See the example for **_itoa**.

_umask

int _umask(int *pmode* **);**

~~ANSI~~ UNIX WIN32S

Use **_umask** for compatibility with ANSI naming conventions of non-ANSI functions. Use **umask** and link with OLDNAMES.LIB for UNIX compatibility.

#include <sys/types.h>
#include <sys/stat.h>
#include <io.h>

Return Value   **_umask** returns the previous value of *pmode*. There is no error return.

Parameter   *pmode*   Default permission setting

Remarks   The **_umask** function sets the file-permission mask of the current process to the mode specified by *pmode*. The file-permission mask modifies the permission setting of new files created by **_creat**, **_open**, or **_sopen**. If a bit in the mask is 1, the corresponding bit in the file's requested permission value is set to 0 (disallowed). If a bit in the mask is 0, the corresponding bit is left unchanged. The permission setting for a new file is not set until the file is closed for the first time.

The argument *pmode* is a constant expression containing one or both of the manifest constants **_S_IREAD** and **_S_IWRITE**, defined in SYS.H. When both constants are given, they are joined with the bitwise-OR operator (|). If the *pmode* argument is **_S_IREAD**, reading is not allowed (the file is write-only). If the *pmode* argument is **_S_IWRITE**, writing is not allowed (the file is read-only). For example, if the write bit is set in the mask, any new files will be read-only. Note that with MS-DOS and Windows NT, all files are readable; it is not possible to give write-only permission. Therefore, setting the read bit with **_umask** has no effect on the file's modes.

See Also   **_chmod, _creat, _mkdir, _open**

Example
```c
/* UMASK.C: This program uses _umask to set
 * the file-permission mask so that all future
 * files will be created as read-only files.
 * It also displays the old mask.
 */

#include <sys/stat.h>
#include <sys/types.h>
#include <io.h>
#include <stdio.h>

void main( void )
{
    int oldmask;

    /* Create read-only files: */
    oldmask = _umask( _S_IWRITE );
    printf( "Oldmask = 0x%.4x\n", oldmask );
}
```

Output   `Oldmask = 0x0000`

unexpected

void unexpected(void);

ANSI ~~UNIX~~ WIN32S

#include <eh.h>

Return Value   None

Remarks   The **unexpected** routine is not used with the current implemenation of C++ exception handling. **unexpected** calls **terminate** by default. You can change this default behavior by writing a custom termination function and calling **set_unexpected** with the name of your function as its argument. **unexpected** calls the last function given as an argument to **set_unexpected**.

See Also   abort, _set_se_translator, set_terminate, set_unexpected, terminate

ungetc, ungetwc

int ungetc(int *c*, **FILE** **stream*);

wint_t ungetwc(wint_t *c*, **FILE** **stream*);

> **ungetc:**   ANSI   UNIX   WIN32S
> **ungetwc:**   ANSI   UNIX   ~~WIN32S~~
>
> **#include <stdio.h>**   For **ungetc**.
> **#include<wchar.h>**   For **ungetwc** use STDIO.H or WCHAR.H.

Return Value   If successful, each of these functions returns the character argument *c*. If *c* cannot be pushed back or if no character has been read, the input stream is unchanged and **ungetc** returns **EOF**; **ungetwc** returns **WEOF**.

Parameters   *c*   Character to be pushed
stream   Pointer to **FILE** structure

Remarks   The **ungetc** function pushes the character *c* back onto *stream* and clears the end-of-file indicator. The stream must be open for reading. A subsequent read operation on *stream* starts with *c*. An attempt to push **EOF** onto the stream using **ungetc** is ignored.

Characters placed on the stream by **ungetc** may be erased if **fflush**, **fseek**, **fsetpos**, or **rewind** is called before the character is read from the stream. The file-position indicator will have the value it had before the characters were pushed back. The external storage corresponding to the stream is unchanged. On a successful **ungetc** call against a text stream, the file-position indicator is unspecified until all the pushed-back characters are read or discarded. On each successful **ungetc** call against a binary stream, the file-position indicator is decremented; if its value was 0 before a call, the value is undefined after the call.

Results are unpredictable if **ungetc** is called twice without a read or file-positioning operation between the two calls. After a call to **fscanf**, a call to **ungetc** may fail unless another read operation (such as **getc**) has been performed. This is because **fscanf** itself calls **ungetc**.

ungetwc is a wide-character version of **ungetc**. However, on each successful **ungetwc** call against a text or binary stream, the value of the file-position indicator is unspecified until all pushed-back characters are read or discarded.

See Also   **getc, putc**

Example

```
/* UNGETC.C: This program first converts a character
 * representation of an unsigned integer to an integer. If
 * the program encounters a character that is not a digit,
 * the program uses ungetc to replace it in the  stream.
 */

#include <stdio.h>
#include <ctype.h>

void main( void )
{
   int ch;
   int result = 0;

   printf( "Enter an integer: " );

   /* Read in and convert number: */
   while( ((ch = getchar()) != EOF) && isdigit( ch ) )
      result = result * 10 + ch - '0';     /* Use digit. */
   if( ch != EOF )
      ungetc( ch, stdin );                  /* Put nondigit back. */
   printf( "Number = %d\nNext character in stream = '%c'",
            result, getchar() );
}
```

Output

```
Enter an integer: 521a
Number = 521
Next character in stream = 'a'
```

_ungetch

int _ungetch(int *c* **);**

~~ANSI~~   ~~UNIX~~   WIN32S

#include <conio.h>

Return Value   _ungetch returns the character *c* if it is successful. A return value of **EOF** indicates an error.

Parameter   *c*   Character to be pushed

Remarks   The **_ungetch** function pushes the character *c* back to the console, causing *c* to be the next character read by **_getch** or **_getche**. **_ungetch** fails if it is called more than once before the next read. The *c* argument may not be **EOF**.

See Also   **_cscanf, _getch**

Example

```
/* UNGETCH.C: In this program, a white-space delimited
 * token is read from the keyboard. When the program
 * encounters a delimiter, it uses _ungetch to replace
 * the character in the keyboard buffer.
 */

#include <conio.h>
#include <ctype.h>
#include <stdio.h>

void main( void )
{
   char buffer[100];
   int count = 0;
   int ch;
   ch = _getche();
   while( isspace( ch ) )         /* Skip preceding white space. */
      ch = _getche();
   while( count < 99 )            /* Gather token. */
   {
      if( isspace( ch ) )         /* End of token. */
         break;
      buffer[count++] = (char)ch;
      ch = _getche();
   }
   _ungetch( ch );               /* Put back delimiter. */
   buffer[count] = '\0';         /* Null terminate the token. */
   printf( "\ntoken = %s\n", buffer );
}
```

Output

```
White
token = White
```

_unlink, _wunlink

int **_unlink**(const char *filename*);

int **_wunlink**(const wchar_t *filename*);

_unlink: ~~ANSI~~   UNIX   WIN32S
_wunlink: ~~ANSI~~   UNIX   ~~WIN32S~~

Use **_unlink** for compatibility with ANSI naming conventions of non-ANSI functions. Use **unlink** and link with OLDNAMES.LIB for UNIX compatibility.

#include <io.h>
#include <stdio.h>   For **_unlink**.
#include <wchar.h>   For **_wunlink** use STDIO.H or WCHAR.H.

Return Value

Each of these functions returns 0 if successful. Otherwise, the function returns –1 and sets **errno** to **EACCES**, which means the path specifies a read-only file, or to **ENOENT**, which means the file or path is not found or the path specified a directory.

Parameter

filename   Name of file to remove

Remarks

The **_unlink** function deletes the file specified by *filename*. **_wunlink** is a wide-character version of **_unlink**; the *filename* argument to **_wunlink** is a wide-character string. These functions behave identically otherwise.

See Also

_close, remove

Example

```
/* UNLINK.C: This program uses _unlink to delete UNLINK.OBJ. */

#include <stdio.h>

void main( void )
{
    if( _unlink( "unlink.obj" ) == -1 )
        perror( "Could not delete 'UNLINK.OBJ'" );
    else
        printf( "Deleted 'UNLINK.OBJ'\n" );
}
```

Output

```
Deleted 'UNLINK.OBJ'
```

_utime, _wutime

int _utime(char **filename***, struct _utimbuf ****times***);**

int _wutime(wchar_t **filename***, struct _utimbuf ****times***);**

> **_utime:** ~~ANSI~~ UNIX WIN32S
> **_wutime:** ~~ANSI~~ UNIX ~~WIN32S~~
>
> Use **_utime** for compatibility with ANSI naming conventions of non-ANSI functions. Use **utime** and link with OLDNAMES.LIB for UNIX compatibility.
>
> **#include <sys/types.h>**
> **#include <sys/utime.h>**   For **_utime**.
> **#include <wchar.h>**   For **_wutime** use UTIME.H or WCHAR.H.

Return Value

Each of these functions returns 0 if the file-modification time was changed. A return value of –1 indicates an error, in which case **errno** is set to one of the following values:

EACCES   Path specifies directory or read-only file

EINVAL   Invalid *times* argument

EMFILE   Too many open files (the file must be opened to change its modification time)

ENOENT   Path or filename not found

Parameters

filename   Path or filename
times   Pointer to stored time values

Remarks

The **_utime** function sets the modification time for the file specified by *filename*. The process must have write access to the file in order to change the time. Under Windows NT, you can change the access time and the modication time in the **_utimbuf** structure. If *times* is a **NULL** pointer, the modification time is set to the current time. Otherwise, *times* must point to a structure of type **_utimbuf**, defined in SYS\UTIME.H.

The **_utimbuf** structure stores file access and modification times used by **_utime** to change file-modification dates. The structure has the following fields, which are both of type **time_t**:

actime   Time of file access

modtime   Time of file modification

_utime is identical to **_futime** except that the *filename* argument of **_utime** is a filename or a path to a file, rather than a handle to an open file.

_wutime is a wide-character version of **_utime**; the *filename* argument to **_wutime** is a wide-character string. These functions behave identically otherwise.

See Also   **asctime, ctime, _fstat, _ftime, _futime, gmtime, localtime, _stat, time**

Example

```
/* UTIME.C: This program uses _utime to set the
 * file-modification time to the current time.
 */

#include <stdio.h>
#include <stdlib.h>
#include <sys/types.h>
#include <sys/utime.h>

void main( void )
{
   /* Show file time before and after. */
   system( "dir utime.c" );
   if( _utime( "utime.c", NULL ) == -1 )
      perror( "_utime failed\n" );
   else
      printf( "File time modified\n" );
   system( "dir utime.c" );
}
```

Output

```
 Volume in drive C is CDRIVE
 Volume Serial Number is 0E17-1702

 Directory of C:\code

05/02/94  10:00p                      451 utime.c
               1 File(s)              451 bytes
                              83,320,832 bytes free
 Volume in drive C is CDRIVE
 Volume Serial Number is 0E17-1702

 Directory of C:\code

05/02/94  10:00p                      451 utime.c
               1 File(s)              451 bytes
                              83,320,832 bytes free
File time modified
```

va_arg, va_end, va_start

type **va_arg(va_list** *arg_ptr***,** *type* **);**

void va_end(va_list *arg_ptr* **);**

void va_start(va_list *arg_ptr* **);**   (UNIX version)

void va_start(va_list *arg_ptr***,** *prev_param* **);**   (ANSI version)

ANSI   UNIX   WIN32S

#include <stdarg.h>   Required for ANSI compatibility.
#include <varargs.h>   Required for UNIX V compatibility.
#include <stdio.h>

Return Value   **va_arg** returns the current argument; **va_start** and **va_end** do not return values.

Parameters   *type*   Type of argument to be retrieved
arg_ptr   Pointer to list of arguments
prev_param   Parameter preceding first optional argument (ANSI only)

Remarks   The **va_arg**, **va_end**, and **va_start** macros provide a portable way to access the arguments to a function when the function takes a variable number of arguments. Two versions of the macros are available: The macros defined in STDARG.H conform to the ANSI C standard, and the macros defined in VARARGS.H are compatible with the UNIX System V definition. The macros are:

va_alist   Name of parameter to called function (UNIX version only)

va_arg   Macro to retrieve current argument

va_dcl   Declaration of **va_alist** (UNIX version only)

va_end   Macro to reset *arg_ptr*

va_list   **typedef** for pointer to list of arguments

va_start   Macro to set *arg_ptr* to beginning of list of optional arguments (UNIX version only)

Both versions of the macros assume that the function takes a fixed number of required arguments, followed by a variable number of optional arguments. The required arguments are declared as ordinary parameters to the function and can be accessed through the parameter names. The optional arguments are accessed through the macros in STDARG.H or VARARGS.H, which set a pointer to the first optional argument in the argument list, retrieve arguments from the list, and reset the pointer when argument processing is completed.

The ANSI C standard macros, defined in STDARG.H, are used as follows:

- All required arguments to the function are declared as parameters in the usual way. **va_dcl** is not used with the STDARG.H macros.

- **va_start** sets *arg_ptr* to the first optional argument in the list of arguments passed to the function. The argument *arg_ptr* must have **va_list** type. The argument *prev_param* is the name of the required parameter immediately preceding the first optional argument in the argument list. If *prev_param* is declared with the register storage class, the macro's behavior is undefined. **va_start** must be used before **va_arg** is used for the first time.

- **va_arg** retrieves a value of *type* from the location given by *arg_ptr* and increments *arg_ptr* to point to the next argument in the list, using the size of *type* to determine where the next argument starts. **va_arg** can be used any number of times within the function to retrieve arguments from the list.

- After all arguments have been retrieved, **va_end** resets the pointer to **NULL**.

The UNIX System V macros, defined in VARARGS.H, operate somewhat differently:

- Any required arguments to the function can be declared as parameters in the usual way.

- The last (or only) parameter to the function represents the list of optional arguments. This parameter must be named **va_alist** (not to be confused with **va_list**, which is defined as the type of **va_alist**).

- **va_dcl** appears after the function definition and before the opening left brace of the function. This macro is defined as a complete declaration of the **va_alist** parameter, including the terminating semicolon; therefore, no semicolon should follow **va_dcl**.

- Within the function, **va_start** sets *arg_ptr* to the beginning of the list of optional arguments passed to the function. **va_start** must be used before **va_arg** is used for the first time. The argument *arg_ptr* must have **va_list** type.

- **va_arg** retrieves a value of *type* from the location given by *arg_ptr* and increments *arg_ptr* to point to the next argument in the list, using the size of *type* to determine where the next argument starts. **va_arg** can be used any number of times within the function to retrieve the arguments from the list.

- After all arguments have been retrieved, **va_end** resets the pointer to **NULL**.

See Also   **vfprintf**

Example

```
/* VA.C: The program below illustrates passing a variable
 * number of arguments using the following macros:
 *      va_start                va_arg              va_end
 *      va_list                 va_dcl (UNIX only)
 */
```

```c
#include <stdio.h>
#define ANSI              /* Comment out for UNIX version     */
#ifdef ANSI               /* ANSI compatible version          */
#include <stdarg.h>
int average( int first, ... );
#else                     /* UNIX compatible version          */
#include <varargs.h>
int average( va_list );
#endif

void main( void )
{
   /* Call with 3 integers (-1 is used as terminator). */
   printf( "Average is: %d\n", average( 2, 3, 4, -1 ) );

   /* Call with 4 integers. */
   printf( "Average is: %d\n", average( 5, 7, 9, 11, -1 ) );

   /* Call with just -1 terminator. */
   printf( "Average is: %d\n", average( -1 ) );
}

/* Returns the average of a variable list of integers. */
#ifdef ANSI               /* ANSI compatible version     */
int average( int first, ... )
{
   int count = 0, sum = 0, i = first;
   va_list marker;

   va_start( marker, first );       /* Initialize variable arguments. */
   while( i != -1 )
   {
      sum += i;
      count++;
      i = va_arg( marker, int);
   }
   va_end( marker );                /* Reset variable arguments.     */
   return( sum ? (sum / count) : 0 );
}

#else       /* UNIX compatible version must use old-style definition.
*/
int average( va_alist )
va_dcl
{
   int i, count, sum;
   va_list marker;
```

```
                va_start( marker );              /* Initialize variable arguments. */
                for( sum = count = 0; (i = va_arg( marker, int)) != -1; count++ )
                    sum += i;
                va_end( marker );                /* Reset variable arguments.      */
                return( sum ? (sum / count) : 0 );
            }
            #endif
```

Output

```
Average is: 3
Average is: 8
Average is: 0
```

vprintf, vwprintf, vfprintf, vfwprintf, vsprintf, vswprintf, _vsnprintf, _vsnwprintf

int vfprintf(FILE **stream,* **const char** **format,* **va_list** *argptr* **);**

int vfwprintf(FILE **stream,* **const wchar_t** **format,* **va_list** *argptr***);**

int vprintf(const char **format,* **va_list** *argptr* **);**

int vwprintf(const wchar_t **format,* **va_list** *argptr* **);**

int vsprintf(char **buffer,* **const char** **format,* **va_list** *argptr* **);**

int vswprintf(wchar_t **buffer,* **size_t** *count,* **const wchar_t** **format,* **va_list** *argptr* **);**

int _vsnprintf(char **buffer,* **size_t** *count,* **const char** **format,* **va_list** *argptr* **);**

int _vsnwprintf(wchar_t **buffer,* **size_t** *count,* **const wchar_t** **format,* **va_list** *argptr* **);**

vprintf, vfprintf, vsprintf: ANSI   UNIX   WIN32S
vwprintf, vfwprintf, vswprintf: ANSI   UNIX   ~~WIN32S~~
_vsnprintf: ~~ANSI~~   ~~UNIX~~   WIN32S
_vsnwprintf: ~~ANSI~~   ~~UNIX~~   ~~WIN32S~~

#include <stdio.h>   For single-byte–character **vprintf** functions.
#include <varargs.h>   Required for UNIX System V compatibility.
#include <stdarg.h>   Required for ANSI compatibility.
#include <wchar.h>   For **vwprintf, vfwprintf, vswprintf,** and **_vsnwprintf,** use STDIO.H or WCHAR.H.

Return Value   The return value for these functions is the number of characters written, not including the terminating null character, or a negative value if an output error occurs. For **vswprintf**, a negative value is also returned if *count* or more wide characters are requested to be written. For **_vsnprintf**, if the number of bytes to write exceeds *buffer*, then *count* bytes are written and –1 is returned.

Parameters

stream   Pointer to **FILE** structure
format   Format specification
argptr   Pointer to list of arguments
buffer   Storage location for output
count   Maximum number of bytes to write

Remarks

The **vprintf** functions are similar to their counterpart functions as listed in the following table. However, each **vprintf** function accepts a pointer to an argument list, whereas each of the counterpart functions accepts an argument list.

These functions format data for output to destinations as follows.

Function	Counterpart Function	Output Destination
vfprintf	**fprintf**	*stream*
vfwprintf	**fwprintf**	*stream*
vprintf	**printf**	**stdout**
vwprintf	**wprintf**	**stdout**
vsprintf	**sprintf**	memory pointed to by *buffer*
vswprintf	**swprintf**	memory pointed to by *buffer*
_vsnprintf	**_snprintf**	memory pointed to by *buffer*
_vsnwprintf	**_snwprintf**	memory pointed to by *buffer*

The *argptr* argument has type **va_list**, which is defined in VARARGS.H and STDARG.H. The *argptr* variable must be initialized by **va_start,** and may be reinitialized by subsequent **va_arg** calls; *argptr* then points to the beginning of a list of arguments that are converted and transmitted for output according to the corresponding specifications in the *format* argument. *format* has the same form and function as the *format* argument for **printf**. None of these functions invokes **va_end.** For a more complete description of each **vprintf** function, see the description of its counterpart function as listed in the preceding table.

_vsnprintf differs from **vsprintf** in that it writes no more than *count* bytes to *buffer*.

vfwprintf, **_vsnwprintf**, **vswprintf**, and **vwprintf** are wide-character versions of **vfprintf**, **_vsnprintf**, **vsprintf,** and **vprintf**, respectively; in each of these wide-character functions, *buffer* and *format* are wide-character strings. Otherwise, each wide-character function behaves identically to its SBCS counterpart function.

For **vsprintf**, **vswprintf**, **_vsnprintf** and **_vsnwprintf**, if copying occurs between strings that overlap, the behavior is undefined.

See Also

fprintf, **printf**, **sprintf**, **va_arg**

wcstombs

size_t wcstombs(char *_mbstr_, const wchar_t *_wcstr_, size_t _count_);

ANSI   ~~UNIX~~   WIN32S

#include <stdlib.h>

Return Value

If **wcstombs** successfully converts the multibyte string, it returns the number of bytes written into the multibyte output string, excluding the terminating **NULL** (if any). If the *mbstr* argument is **NULL**, **wcstombs** returns the required size of the destination string. If **wcstombs** encounters a wide character it cannot be convert to a multibyte character, it returns –1 cast to type **size_t**.

Parameters

mbstr   The address of a sequence of multibyte characters

wcstr   The address of a sequence of wide characters

count   The maximum number of bytes that can be stored in the multibyte output string

Remarks

The **wcstombs** function converts the wide-character string pointed to by *wcstr* to the corresponding multibyte characters and stores the results in the *mbstr* array. The *count* parameter indicates the maximum number of bytes that can be stored in the multibyte output string (that is, the size of *mbstr*). In general, it is not known how many bytes will be required when converting a wide-character string. Some wide characters will require only one byte in the output string; others require two. If there are two bytes in the multibyte output string for every wide character in the input string (including the wide character **NULL**), the result is guaranteed to fit.

If **wcstombs** encounters the wide-character null character (L'\0') either before or when *count* occurs, it converts it to an 8-bit 0 and stops. Thus, the multibyte character string at *mbstr* is null-terminated only if **wcstombs** encounters a wide-character null character during conversion. If the sequences pointed to by *wcstr* and *mbstr* overlap, the behavior of **wcstombs** is undefined.

If the *mbstr* argument is **NULL**, **wcstombs** returns the required size of the destination string.

See Also

mblen, mbstowcs, mbtowc, wctomb

Example

```
/* WCTOMB.CPP illustrates the behavior of the wctomb function */

#include <stdio.h>
#include <stdlib.h>

void main( void )
{
    int i;
    wchar_t wc = L'a';
    char *pmbnull = NULL;
    char *pmb = (char *)malloc( sizeof( char ) );

    printf( "Convert a wide character:\n" );
    i = wctomb( pmb, wc );
    printf( "\tCharacters converted: %u\n", i );
    printf( "\tMultibyte character: %.1s\n\n", pmb );

    printf( "Attempt to convert when target is NULL:\n" );
    i = wctomb( pmbnull, wc );
    printf( "\tCharacters converted: %u\n", i );
    printf( "\tMultibyte character: %.1s\n", pmbnull );
}
```

Output

```
Convert wide-character string:
    Characters converted: 1
    Multibyte character: H
```

wctomb

int wctomb(char *_mbchar_, wchar_t _wchar_);

ANSI   ~~UNIX~~   WIN32S

#include <stdlib.h>

Return Value

If **wctomb** converts the wide character to a multibyte character, it returns the number of bytes (which is never greater than **MB_CUR_MAX**) in the wide character. If _wchar_ is the wide-character null character (L'\0'), **wctomb** returns 1. If the conversion is not possible in the current locale, **wctomb** returns −1.

Parameters

mbchar   The address of a multibyte character
wchar   A wide character

Remarks

The **wctomb** function converts its _wchar_ argument to the corresponding multibyte character and stores the result at _mbchar_. You can call the function from any point in any program.

See Also

mblen, mbstowcs, mbtowc, wcstombs

Example

```
/* WCTOMB.CPP illustrates the behavior of the wctomb function */

#include <stdio.h>
#include <stdlib.h>

void main( void )
{
   int i;
   wchar_t wc = L'a';
   char *pmbnull = NULL;
   char *pmb = (char *)malloc( sizeof( char ) );

   printf( "Convert a wide character:\n" );
   i = wctomb( pmb, wc );
   printf( "\tCharacters converted: %u\n", i );
   printf( "\tMultibyte character: %.1s\n\n", pmb );

   printf( "Attempt to convert when target is NULL:\n" );
   i = wctomb( pmbnull, wc );
   printf( "\tCharacters converted: %u\n", i );
   printf( "\tMultibyte character: %.1s\n", pmbnull );
}
```

Output

```
Convert a wide character:
   Characters converted: 1
   Multibyte character: a

Attempt to convert when target is NULL:
   Characters converted: 0
   Multibyte character: (
```

_write

int _write(int *handle*, **const void** **buffer*, **unsigned int** *count* **);**

~~ANSI~~   UNIX   WIN32S

Use **_write** for compatibility with ANSI naming conventions of non-ANSI functions. Use **write** and link with OLDNAMES.LIB for UNIX compatibility.

#include <io.h>

Return Value

If successful, **_write** returns the number of bytes actually written. If the actual space remaining on the disk is less than the size of the buffer the function is trying to write to the disk, **_write** fails and does not flush any of the buffer's contents to the disk. A return value of –1 indicates an error. In this case, **errno** is set to one of two values: **EBADF**, which means the file handle is invalid or the file is not opened for writing, or **ENOSPC**, which means there is not enough space left on the device for the operation.

If the file is opened in text mode, each linefeed character is replaced with a carriage-return–linefeed pair in the output. The replacement does not affect the return value.

Parameters

handle   Handle of file into which data is written
buffer   Data to be written
count   Number of bytes

Remarks

The **_write** function writes *count* bytes from *buffer* into the file associated with *handle*. The write operation begins at the current position of the file pointer (if any) associated with the given file. If the file is open for appending, the operation begins at the current end of the file. After the write operation, the file pointer is increased by the number of bytes actually written.

When writing to files opened in text mode, **_write** treats a CTRL+Z character as the logical end-of-file. When writing to a device, **_write** treats a CTRL+Z character in the buffer as an output terminator.

See Also

fwrite, **_open**, **_read**

Example

```
/* WRITE.C: This program opens a file for output
 * and uses _write to write some bytes to the file. */

#include <io.h>
#include <stdio.h>
#include <stdlib.h>
#include <fcntl.h>
#include <sys/types.h>
#include <sys/stat.h>

char buffer[] = "This is a test of '_write' function";

void main( void )
{
   int fh;
   unsigned byteswritten;

   if( (fh = _open( "write.o", _O_RDWR | _O_CREAT,
                              _S_IREAD | _S_IWRITE )) != -1 )
   {
      if(( byteswritten = _write( fh, buffer, sizeof( buffer ))) == -1 )
         perror( "Write failed" );
      else
         printf( "Wrote %u bytes to file\n", byteswritten );

      _close( fh );
   }
}
```

Output

```
Wrote 36 bytes to file
```

_wtoi, _wtol

int _wtoi(const wchar_t *__string__);

long _wtol(const wchar_t *__string__);

~~ANSI~~   UNIX   ~~WIN32S~~

#include <stdlib.h>
#include <wchar.h>   Use STDLIB.H or WCHAR.H.

Return Value

Each function returns the **int** or **long** value produced by interpreting the input characters as a number. If the input cannot be converted to a value of the appropriate type, **_wtoi** returns 0 and **_wtol** returns 0L. The return value is undefined in case of overflow.

Parameter

string   String to be converted

Remarks

The **_wtoi** function converts a wide-character string to an integer value. **_wtol** converts a wide-character string to a long integer value. The input string is a sequence of characters that can be interpreted as a numerical value of the specified type. The output value is affected by the setting of the **LC_NUMERIC** category of the current locale. (For more information on the **LC_NUMERIC** category, see **setlocale.**The function stops reading the input string at the first character that it cannot recognize as part of a number. This character may be the null character (L'\0') terminating the string.

The *string* argument for these functions has the form

[[*whitespace*]] [[*sign*]]*digits*

A *whitespace* consists of space and/or tab characters, which are ignored. *sign* is either plus (+) or minus (−). *digits* is one or more decimal digits. **_wtoi** and **_wtol** do not recognize decimal points or exponents.

See Also

atoi, _ecvt, _fcvt, _gcvt

Example

See the example for **atoi.**

A P P E N D I X   A

Language and Country Strings

The *locale* argument to the **setlocale** function can be composed of any combination of three separate string options: language, country, and code page. The *locale* argument takes the following form:

```
locale  "lang[_country[.code_page]]"
        | ".code_page"
        | ""
        | NULL
```

This appendix lists the language and country strings available to **setlocale**. All country and language codes currently supported by the Win32 NLS API are supported by **setlocale**.

Language Strings

The following language strings are recognized by **setlocale**. Any language not supported by the operating system is not accepted by **setlocale**. The three-letter language-string codes are NT-specific.

Primary Language	Sublanguage	Language String
Chinese	Chinese	"chinese"
Chinese	Chinese (simplified)	"chinese-simplified" or "chs"
Chinese	Chinese (traditional)	"chinese-traditional" or "cht"
Czech	Czech	"csy" or "czech"
Danish	Danish	"dan"or "danish"
Dutch	Dutch (Belgian)	"belgian", "dutch-belgian", or "nlb"
Dutch	Dutch (default)	"dutch" or "nld"
English	English (Australian)	"australian", "ena", or "english-aus"
English	English (Canadian)	"canadian", "enc", or "english-can"
English	English (default)	"english"

Primary Language	Sublanguage	Language String
English	English (New Zealand)	"english-nz" or "enz"
English	English (UK)	"eng", "english-uk", or "uk"
English	English (USA)	"american", "american english", "american-english", "english-american", "english-us", "english-usa", "enu", "us", or "usa"
Finnish	Finnish	"fin" or "finnish"
French	French (Belgian)	"frb" or "french-belgian"
French	French (Canadian)	"frc" or "french-canadian"
French	French (default)	"fra"or "french"
French	French (Swiss)	"french-swiss" or "frs"
German	German (Austrian)	"dea" or "german-austrian"
German	German (default)	"deu" or "german"
German	German (Swiss)	"des", "german-swiss", or "swiss"
Greek	Greek	"ell" or "greek"
Hungarian	Hungarian	"hun" or "hungarian"
Icelandic	Icelandic	"icelandic" or "isl"
Italian	Italian (default)	"ita" or "italian"
Italian	Italian (Swiss)	"italian-swiss" or "its"
Japanese	Japanese	"japanese" or "jpn"
Korean	Korean	"kor" or "korean"
Norwegian	Norwegian (Bokmal)	"nor" or "norwegian-bokmal"
Norwegian	Norwegian (default)	"norwegian"
Norwegian	Norwegian (Nynorsk)	"non" or "norwegian-nynorsk"
Polish	Polish	"plk" or "polish"
Portuguese	Portuguese (Brazilian)	"portuguese-brazilian" or "ptb"
Portuguese	Portuguese (default)	"portuguese" or "ptg"
Russian	Russian (default)	"rus" or "russian"
Slovak	Slovak	"sky" or "slovak"
Spanish	Spanish (default)	"esp" or "spanish"
Spanish	Spanish (Mexican)	"esm" or "spanish-mexican"
Spanish	Spanish (Modern)	"esn" or "spanish-modern"
Swedish	Swedish	"sve" or "swedish"
Turkish	Turkish	"trk" or "turkish"

Country Strings

The following is a list of country strings recognized by **setlocale**. Strings for countries that are not supported by the operating system are not accepted by **setlocale**. Three-letter country-name codes are from ISO/IEC (International Organization for Standardization, International Electrotechnical Commission) specification 3166.

Country	Country String
Australia	"aus" or "australia"
Austria	"austria" or "aut"
Belgium	"bel" or "belgium"
Brazil	"bra" or "brazil"
Canada	"can" or "canada"
Czech Republic	"cze" or "czech"
Denmark	"denmark" or "dnk"
Finland	"fin" or "finland"
France	"fra" or "france"
Germany	"deu" or "germany"
Greece	"grc" or "greece"
Hong Kong	"hkg", "hong kong", or "hong-kong"
Hungary	"hun" or "hungary"
Iceland	"iceland" or "isl"
Ireland	"ireland" or "irl"
Italy	"ita" or "italy"
Japan	"japan" or "jpn"
Mexico	"mex" or "mexico"
Netherlands	"nld", "holland", or "netherlands"
New Zealand	"new zealand", "new-zealand", "nz", or "nzl"
Norway	"nor" or "norway"
People's Republic of China	"china", "chn", "pr china", or "pr-china"
Poland	"pol" or "poland"
Portugal	"prt" or "portugal"
Russia	"rus" or "russia"

Country	Country String
Singapore	"sgp" or "singapore"
Slovak Repubic	"svk" or "slovak"
South Korea	"kor", "korea", "south korea", or "south-korea"
Spain	"esp" or "spain"
Sweden	"swe" or "sweden"
Switzerland	"che" or "switzerland"
Taiwan	"taiwan" or "twn"
Turkey	"tur" or "turkey"
United Kingdom	"britain", "england", "gbr", "great britain", "uk", "united kingdom", or "united-kingdom"
United States of America	"america", "united states", "united-states", "us", or "usa"

A P P E N D I X   B

Generic-Text Mappings

To simplify writing code for international markets, many generic-text mappings are defined in TCHAR.H. These mappings are for data types, variables, and other objects, and depend on whether the constant **_UNICODE** or **_MBCS** has been defined in your program. For more information, see "Using Generic-Text Mappings" on page 23. Generic-text mappings are Microsoft extensions that are not ANSI-compatible.

Generic-Text Data Type Mappings

Generic-Text Data Type Name	SBCS (_UNICODE, _MBCS Not Defined)	_MBCS Defined	_UNICODE Defined
_TCHAR	char	char	wchar_t
_TINT	int	int	wint_t
_TSCHAR	signed char	signed char	wchar_t
_TUCHAR	unsigned char	unsigned char	wchar_t
_TXCHAR	char	unsigned char	wchar_t
_T or **_TEXT**	No effect (removed by preprocessor)	No effect (removed by preprocessor)	L (converts following character or string to its Unicode counterpart)

The following generic-text constant, global variable, and standard-type mappings are defined in TCHAR.H.

Generic-Text Constant, Global Variable, and Standard Type Mappings

Generic-Text– Object Name	SBCS (_UNICODE, _MBCS Not Defined)	_MBCS Defined	_UNICODE Defined
_TEOF	EOF	EOF	WEOF
_tenviron	_environ	_environ	_wenviron
_tfinddata_t	_finddata_t	_finddata_t	_wfinddata_t

The following generic-text routine mappings are also defined in TCHAR.H. **_tccpy** and **_tclen** map to functions in the MBCS model; they are mapped to macros or inline functions in the SBCS and Unicode models for completeness.

Generic-Text Routine and Other Mappings

Generic-Text Routine Name	SBCS (_UNICODE, _MBCS Not Defined)	_MBCS Defined	_UNICODE Defined
_fgettc	fgetc	fgetc	fgetwc
_fgettchar	fgetchar	fgetchar	_fgetwchar
_fgetts	fgets	fgets	fgetws
_fputtc	fputc	fputc	fputwc
_fputtchar	fputchar	fputchar	_fputwchar
_fputts	fputs	fputs	fputws
_ftprintf	fprintf	fprintf	fwprintf
_ftscanf	fscanf	fscanf	fwscanf
_gettc	getc	getc	getwc
_gettchar	getchar	getchar	getwchar
_getts	gets	gets	getws
_istalnum	isalnum	_ismbcalnum	iswalnum
_istalpha	isalpha	_ismbcalpha	iswalpha
_istascii	__isascii	__isascii	iswascii
_istcntrl	iscntrl	iscntrl	iswcntrl
_istdigit	isdigit	_ismbcdigit	iswdigit
_istgraph	isgraph	_ismbcgraph	iswgraph
_istlead	Always returns false	_ismbblead	Always returns false
_istleadbyte	Always returns false	isleadbyte	Always returns false
_istlegal	Always returns true	_ismbclegal	Always returns true
_istlower	islower	_ismbclower	iswlower
_istprint	isprint	_ismbcprint	iswprint
_istpunct	ispunct	_ismbcpunct	iswpunct
_istspace	isspace	_ismbcspace	iswspace
_istupper	isupper	_ismbcupper	iswupper
_istxdigit	isxdigit	isxdigit	iswxdigit
_itot	_itoa	_itoa	_itow
_ltot	_ltoa	_ltoa	_ltow

Generic-Text Routine and Other Mappings (*continued*)

Generic-Text Routine Name	SBCS (_UNICODE, _MBCS Not Defined)	_MBCS Defined	_UNICODE Defined
_puttc	putc	putc	putwc
_puttchar	putchar	putchar	putwchar
_putts	puts	puts	putws
_tmain	main	main	wmain
_sntprintf	_snprintf	_snprintf	_snwprintf
_stprintf	sprintf	sprintf	swprintf
_stscanf	sscanf	sscanf	swscanf
_taccess	_access	_access	_waccess
_tasctime	asctime	asctime	_wasctime
_tccpy	Maps to macro or inline function	_mbccpy	Maps to macro or inline function
_tchdir	_chdir	_chdir	_wchdir
_tclen	Maps to macro or inline function	_mbclen	Maps to macro or inline function
_tchmod	_chmod	_chmod	_wchmod
_tcreat	_creat	_creat	_wcreat
_tcscat	strcat	_mbscat	wcscat
_tcschr	strchr	_mbschr	wcschr
_tcsclen	strlen	_mbslen	wcslen
_tcscmp	strcmp	_mbscmp	wcscmp
_tcscoll	strcoll	strcoll	wcscoll
_tcscpy	strcpy	_mbscpy	wcscpy
_tcscspn	strcspn	_mbscspn	wcscspn
_tcsdec	_strdec	_mbsdec	_wcsdec
_tcsdup	_strdup	_mbsdup	_wcsdup
_tcsftime	strftime	strftime	wcsftime
_tcsicmp	_stricmp	_mbsicmp	_wcsicmp
_tcsicoll	_stricoll	_stricoll	_wcsicoll
_tcsinc	_strinc	_mbsinc	_wcsinc
_tcslen	strlen	_mbslen	wcslen
_tcslwr	_strlwr	_mbslwr	_wcslwr
_tcsnbcnt	_strncnt	_mbsnbcnt	_wcnscnt
_tcsncat	strncat	_mbsnbcat	wcsncat
_tcsnccat	strncat	_mbsncat	wcsncat

Generic-Text Routine and Other Mappings (*continued*)

Generic-Text Routine Name	SBCS (_UNICODE, _MBCS Not Defined)	_MBCS Defined	_UNICODE Defined
_tcsncmp	strncmp	_mbsnbcmp	wcsncmp
_tcsnccmp	strncmp	_mbsncmp	wcsncmp
_tcsnccnt	_strncnt	_mbsnccnt	_wcsncnt
_tcsnccpy	strncpy	_mbsncpy	wcsncpy
_tcsncicmp	_strnicmp	_mbsnicmp	_wcsnicmp
_tcsncpy	strncpy	_mbsnbcpy	wcsncpy
_tcsncset	_strnset	_mbsnset	_wcsnset
_tcsnextc	_strnextc	_mbsnextc	_wcsnextc
_tcsnicmp	_strnicmp	_mbsnicmp	_wcsnicmp
_tcsnicoll	_strnicoll	_strnicoll	_wcsnicoll
_tcsninc	_strninc	_mbsninc	_wcsninc
_tcsnccnt	_strncnt	_mbsnccnt	_wcsncnt
_tcsnset	_strnset	_mbsnbset	_wcsnset
_tcspbrk	strpbrk	_mbspbrk	wcspbrk
_tcsspnp	_strspnp	_mbsspnp	_wcsspnp
_tcsrchr	strrchr	_mbsrchr	wcsrchr
_tcsrev	_strrev	_mbsrev	_wcsrev
_tcsset	_strset	_mbsset	_wcsset
_tcsspn	strspn	_mbsspn	wcsspn
_tcsstr	strstr	_mbsstr	wcsstr
_tcstod	strtod	strtod	wcstod
_tcstok	strtok	_mbstok	wcstok
_tcstol	strtol	strtol	wcstol
_tcstoul	strtoul	strtoul	wcstoul
_tcsupr	_strupr	_mbsupr	_wcsupr
_tcsxfrm	strxfrm	strxfrm	wcsxfrm
_tctime	ctime	ctime	_wctime
_texecl	_execl	_execl	_wexecl
_texecle	_execle	_execle	_wexecle
_texeclp	_execlp	_execlp	_wexeclp
_texeclpe	_execlpe	_execlpe	_wexeclpe
_texecv	_execv	_execv	_wexecv
_texecve	_execve	_execve	_wexecve

Generic-Text Routine and Other Mappings (*continued*)

Generic-Text Routine Name	SBCS (_UNICODE, _MBCS Not Defined)	_MBCS Defined	_UNICODE Defined
_texecvp	_execvp	_execvp	_wexecvp
_texecvpe	_execvpe	_execvpe	_wexecvpe
_tfdopen	_fdopen	_fdopen	_wfdopen
_tfindfirst	_findfirst	_findfirst	_wfindfirst
_tfindnext	_findnext	_findnext	_wfindnext
_tfopen	fopen	fopen	_wfopen
_tfreopen	freopen	freopen	_wfreopen
_tfsopen	_fsopen	_fsopen	_wfsopen
_tfullpath	_fullpath	_fullpath	_wfullpath
_tgetcwd	_getcwd	_getcwd	_wgetcwd
_tgetenv	getenv	getenv	_wgetenv
_tmain	main	main	wmain
_tmakepath	_makepath	_makepath	_wmakepath
_tmkdir	_mkdir	_mkdir	_wmkdir
_tmktemp	_mktemp	_mktemp	_wmktemp
_tperror	perror	perror	_wperror
_topen	_open	_open	_wopen
_totlower	tolower	_mbctolower	towlower
_totupper	toupper	_mbctoupper	towupper
_tpopen	_popen	_popen	_wpopen
_tprintf	printf	printf	wprintf
_tremove	remove	remove	_wremove
_trename	rename	rename	_wrename
_trmdir	_rmdir	_rmdir	_wrmdir
_tsearchenv	_searchenv	_searchenv	_wsearchenv
_tscanf	scanf	scanf	wscanf
_tsetlocale	setlocale	setlocale	_wsetlocale
_tsopen	_sopen	_sopen	_wsopen
_tspawnl	_spawnl	_spawnl	_wspawnl
_tspawnle	_spawnle	_spawnle	_wspawnle
_tspawnlp	_spawnlp	_spawnlp	_wspawnlp
_tspawnlpe	_spawnlpe	_spawnlpe	_wspawnlpe
_tspawnv	_spawnv	_spawnv	_wspawnv

Generic-Text Routine and Other Mappings (*continued*)

Generic-Text Routine Name	SBCS (_UNICODE, _MBCS Not Defined)	_MBCS Defined	_UNICODE Defined
_tspawnve	_spawnve	_spawnve	_wspawnve
_tspawnvp	_spawnvp	_spawnvp	_tspawnvp
_tspawnvpe	_spawnvpe	_spawnvpe	_tspawnvpe
_tsplitpath	_splitpath	_splitpath	_wsplitpath
_tstat	_stat	_stat	_wstat
_tstrdate	_strdate	_strdate	_wstrdate
_tstrtime	_strtime	_strtime	_wstrtime
_tsystem	system	system	_wsystem
_ttempnam	_tempnam	_tempnam	_wtempnam
_ttmpnam	tmpnam	tmpnam	_wtmpnam
_ttoi	atoi	atoi	_wtoi
_ttol	atol	atol	_wtol
_tutime	_utime	_utime	_wutime
_tWinMain	WinMain	WinMain	wWinMain
_ultot	_ultoa	_ultoa	_ultow
_ungettc	ungetc	ungetc	ungetwc
_vftprintf	vfprintf	vfprintf	vfwprintf
_vsntprintf	_vsnprintf	_vsnprintf	_vsnwprintf
_vstprintf	vsprintf	vsprintf	vswprintf
_vtprintf	vprintf	vprintf	vwprintf

Index

N

NaN
  definition of 201
  output from printf function 283
New processes, loading and executing, _exec, _wexec functions 104
New processes *See* Spawned processes 334
NEWMODE.OBJ, linking with, for malloc failures 323
_nextafter function 263
Numbers
  converting doubles to strings, _ecvt function 100
  pseudorandom, generating, rand function 294

O

_off_t standard type 44
offsetof macro 263
_onexit function 263
_onexit_t standard type 44
_open function 265
_open_osfhandle function 268
Opening files
  fopen, _wfopen functions 134
  for file sharing, _sopen, _wsopen functions 331
  _open, _wopen functions 265
Operating systems
  specifying versions 43
  variable mode 43
_osver variable 43
_outp function 269
_outpd function 269
_outpw function 269

P

Parent process defined 31
Paths
  breaking into components, _splitpath, _wsplitpath functions 338
  creating, _makepath, _wmakepath functions 222
  getting current directory
    _getcwd, _wgetcwd functions 170
    _getdcwd, _wgetdcwd functions 172
_pclose function 270
perror function 270
_pgmptr variable 43
PID *See* _getpid function
_pipe function 272
Pipes
  closing streams, _pclose function 270
  creating for reading, writing, _pipe function 272
_PNH standard type 44
_popen function 275

Ports, I/O routines 17
pow function 277
Powers, calculating, pow function 277
Preprocessor directives for generic-text mappings 23
printf function
  flag directives (list) 281
  output, indefinite (quiet NaN) 283
  precision specification 282
  size, distance specification 284
  type characters (list) 280
  use 278
  width specification 282
Printf function family, floating-point support for 9
Printing
  characters, values to output streams, printf, wprintf 278
  error messages
    perror, _wperror functions 270
    strerror, _strerror functions 356
  to console, _cprintf function 86
Process control routines (list) 30–32
Process identification number, getting, _getpid function 177
Processes
  identification, _getpid function 177
  new, loading and executing, _exec, _wexec functions 104
  terminating calling, exit, _exit functions 109
Processing at exit, atexit function 56
Programs
  aborting, abort routines 54
  executing, sending signal to, raise function 294
  identifying program logic errors, assert macro
  saving current state, setjmp function 313
ptrdiff_t standard type 44
putc, putwc, putchar, putwchar functions 286
_putch function 287
_putenv function 288
puts, putws functions 289
Putting strings to the console, _cputs function 87
_putw function 290

Q

qsort function 292
_query_new_handler function 291
_query_new_mode function 292
Quick-sort algorithm, qsort function 292
Quiet NaN, output from printf function 283
Quotients, computing, ldiv function 205

R

raise function 294
rand function 294
Random number generation, rand function 294
Random starting point, setting, srand function 341

Y

Contributors to *Run-Time Library Reference*

Richard Carlson, Index Editor
David Donovan, Production
Richard Edwards, Writer
Marilyn Johnstone, Writer
Seth Manheim, Writer
Mark Olson, Art Director
Aldon Schwimmer, Writer
Jeff Thomas, Editor

iostream Class Library Reference

Microsoft® Visual C++™

Development System for Windows™ and Windows NT™
Version 2.0

Microsoft Corporation

Contents

Figure

Introduction

Microsoft Visual C++™ contains the C++ iostream class library, which supports object-oriented input and output. This library follows the syntax that the authors of the C++ language originally established and thus represents a de facto standard for C++ input and output.

About This Book

Chapter 1, "iostream Programming," provides information you need to get started using iostream classes. After reading this material, you will begin to understand how to write programs that process formatted text character streams and binary disk files and how to customize the library in limited ways. The chapter includes advanced information on how to derive iostream classes and create custom multiparameter "manipulators." These topics will get you started on extending the library and doing specialized formatting. You will also learn about the relationship between the iostream classes and their subsidiary buffer classes. You can then apply some of the iostream library design principles to your own class libraries.

Chapter 2, "Alphabetic Microsoft iostream Class Library Reference," begins with a detailed class hierarchy diagram. The iostream class library reference follows, arranged by classes in alphabetic order. Each class description includes a summary of each member, arranged by category, followed by alphabetical listings of member functions (public and protected), overloaded operators, data members, and manipulators.

Public and protected class members are documented only when they are normally used in application programs or derived classes. See the class header files for a complete listing of class members.

Note For information on Microsoft product support, see Microsoft Support Services in *Introducing Visual C++*.

Document Conventions

This book uses the following document conventions:

Example	Description
STDIO.H	Uppercase letters indicate filenames, segment names, registers, and terms used at the operating-system command level.
char, _alloca, __cdecl	Bold type indicates C and C++ keywords, operators, language-specific characters, and library routines. Within discussions of syntax, bold type indicates that the text must be entered exactly as shown.
	Many constants, functions, and keywords begin with either a single or double underscore. These are required as part of the name. For example, the compiler recognizes the **__cplusplus** manifest constant only when the leading double underscore is included.
	It may be difficult at first glance to distinguish a single underscore from a double underscore because the two run together on the screen. Therefore, the width of the character(s) is your guide. The sample term **alloca**, in the left column above, has one leading underscore, while the term **cdecl** has two.
expression	Words in italics indicate placeholders for information you must supply, such as a filename. Italic type is also used occasionally for emphasis in the text.
[*option*]	Items inside square brackets are optional.
**#pragma pack {1	2}**	Braces and a vertical bar indicate a choice among two or more items. You must choose one of these items unless square brackets ([ ]) surround the braces.
`#include <io.h>`	This font is used for examples, user input, program output, and error messages in text.
CL [*option...*] *file...*	Three dots (an ellipsis) following an item indicate that more items having the same form may appear.

`while()`
`{`
`   .`
`   .`
`   .`
`}`
	A column or row of three dots tells you that part of an example program has been intentionally omitted.

CTRL+ENTER	Small capital letters are used to indicate the names of keys on the keyboard. When you see a plus sign (+) between two key names, you should hold down the first key while pressing the second.
	The carriage-return key, sometimes marked as a bent arrow on the keyboard, is called ENTER.
"argument"	Quotation marks enclose a new term the first time it is defined in text.
"C string"	Some C constructs, such as strings, require quotation marks.
Dynamic-Link Library (DLL)	The first time an acronym is used, it is usually spelled out.
Microsoft Specific →	Some features documented in this book have special usage constraints, such as Microsoft specific information— features defined by Microsoft C implementation that are implementation dependent or undefined in the ANSI standard. A heading identifying the nature of the exception, followed by an arrow, marks the beginning of these exception features.
END Microsoft Specific	**END** followed by the exception heading marks the end of text about a feature which has a usage constraint.

C H A P T E R   1

iostream Programming

This chapter begins with a general description of the iostream classes and then describes output streams, input streams, and input/output streams. The end of the chapter provides information about advanced iostream programming.

What Is a Stream?

Like C, C++ does not have built-in input/output capability. All C++ compilers, however, come bundled with a systematic, object-oriented I/O package, known as the iostream classes. The "stream" is the central concept of the iostream classes. You can think of a stream object as a "smart file" that acts as a source and destination for bytes. A stream's characteristics are determined by its class and by customized insertion and extraction operators.

Through device drivers, the disk operating system deals with the keyboard, screen, printer, and communication ports as extended files. The iostream classes interact with these extended files. Built-in classes support reading from and writing to memory with syntax identical to that for disk I/O, which makes it easy to derive stream classes.

Input/Output Alternatives

This product provides several options for I/O programming:

- C run-time library direct, unbuffered I/O
- ANSI C run-time library stream I/O
- Console and port direct I/O
- The Microsoft Foundation Class Library
- The Microsoft iostream Class Library

The iostream classes are useful for buffered, formatted text I/O. They are also useful for unbuffered or binary I/O if you need a C++ programming interface and decide not to use the Microsoft Foundation classes. The iostream classes are an object-oriented I/O alternative to the C run-time functions.

You can use iostream classes with the Microsoft® Windows™ operating system. String and file streams work without restrictions, but the character-mode stream objects **cin**, **cout**, **cerr**, and **clog** are inconsistent with the Windows graphical user interface. You can also derive custom stream classes that interact directly with the Windows environment. If you link with the QuickWin library, however, the **cin**, **cout**, **cerr**, and **clog** objects are assigned to special windows because they are connected to the predefined files **stdin**, **stdout**, and **stderr**.

You cannot use iostream classes in tiny-model programs because tiny-model programs cannot contain static objects such as **cin** and **cout**.

The iostream Class Hierarchy

The class hierarchy diagram at the beginning of Chapter 2 shows some relationships between iostream classes. There are additional "member" relationships between the **ios** and **streambuf** families. Use the diagram to locate base classes that provide inherited member functions for derived classes.

Output Streams

An output stream object is a destination for bytes. The three most important output stream classes are **ostream**, **ofstream**, and **ostrstream**.

The **ostream** class, through the derived class **ostream_withassign**, supports the predefined stream objects:

- **cout**   standard output
- **cerr**   standard error with limited buffering
- **clog**   similar to **cerr** but with full buffering

Objects are rarely constructed from **ostream** or **ostream_withassign**; predefined objects are generally used. In some cases, you can reassign predefined objects after program startup. The **ostream** class, which can be configured for buffered or unbuffered operation, is best suited to sequential text-mode output. All functionality of the base class, **ios**, is included in **ostream**. If you construct an object of class **ostream**, you must specify a **streambuf** object to the constructor.

The **ofstream** class supports disk file output. If you need an output-only disk, construct an object of class **ofstream**. You can specify whether **ofstream** objects accept binary or text-mode data before or after opening the file. Many formatting options and member functions apply to **ofstream** objects, and all functionality of the base classes **ios** and **ostream** is included.

If you specify a filename in the constructor, that file is automatically opened when the object is constructed. Otherwise, you can use the **open** member function after invoking the default constructor, or you can construct an **ofstream** object based on an open file that is identified by a file descriptor.

Like the run-time function **sprintf**, the **ostrstream** class supports output to in-memory strings. To create a string in memory using I/O stream formatting, construct an object of class **ostrstream**. Because **ostrstream** objects are write-only, your program must access the resulting string through a pointer to **char**.

Constructing Output Stream Objects

If you use only the predefined **cout**, **cerr**, or **clog** objects, you don't need to construct an output stream. You must use constructors for:

- File streams
- String streams

Output File Stream Constructors

You can construct an output file stream in one of three ways:

- Use the default constructor, then call the **open** member function.

```
ofstream myFile; // Static or on the stack
myFile.open( "filename", iosmode );

ofstream* pmyFile = new ofstream; // On the heap
pmyFile->open( "filename", iosmode );
```

- Specify a filename and mode flags in the constructor call.

```
ofstream myFile( "filename", iosmode );
```

- Specify an integer file descriptor for a file already open for output. You can specify unbuffered output or a pointer to your own buffer.

```
int fd = _open( "filename", dosmode );
ofstream myFile1( fd );  // Buffered mode (default)
ofstream myFile2( fd, NULL, 0 );  // Unbuffered mode ofstream
myFile3( fd, pch, buflen);  // User-supplied buffer
```

Output String Stream Constructors

To construct an output string stream, you can use one of two **ostrstream** constructors. One dynamically allocates its own storage, and the other requires the address and size of a preallocated buffer.

- The dynamic constructor is used like this:

```
char* sp;
ostrstream myString;
myString << "this is a test" << ends;
sp = myString.str();   // Get a pointer to the string
```

The **ends** "manipulator" adds the necessary terminating null character to the string.

- The constructor that requires the preallocated buffer is used like this:

```
char s[32];
ostrstream myString( s, sizeof( s ) );
myString << "this is a test" << ends; // Text stored in s
```

Using Insertion Operators and Controlling Format

This section shows how to control format and how to create insertion operators for your own classes. The insertion (<<) operator, which is preprogrammed for all standard C++ data types, sends bytes to an output stream object. Insertion operators work with predefined "manipulators," which are elements that change the default format of integer arguments.

Output Width

To align output, you specify the output width for each item by placing the **setw** manipulator in the stream or by calling the **width** member function. This example right aligns the values in a column at least 10 characters wide:

```
#include <iostream.h>

void main()
{
   double values[] = { 1.23, 35.36, 653.7, 4358.24 };
   for( int i = 0; i < 4; i++ )
   {
      cout.width(10);
      cout << values[i] << '\n';
   }
}
```

The output looks like this:

```
    1.23
   35.36
   653.7
 4358.24
```

Leading blanks are added to any value fewer than 10 characters wide.

To pad a field, use the **fill** member function, which sets the value of the padding character for fields that have a specified width. The default is a blank. To pad the column of numbers with asterisks, modify the previous **for** loop as follows:

```
for( int i = 0; i < 4; i++ )
{
    cout.width( 10 );
    cout.fill( '*' );
    cout << values[i] << endl
}
```

The **endl** manipulator replaces the newline character ('\n'). The output looks like this:

```
******1.23
*****35.36
****653.7
***4358.24
```

To specify widths for data elements in the same line, use the **setw** manipulator:

```
#include <iostream.h>
#include <iomanip.h>

void main()
{
    double values[] = { 1.23, 35.36, 653.7, 4358.24 };
    char *names[] = { "Zoot", "Jimmy", "Al", "Stan" };
    for( int i = 0; i < 4; i++ )
        cout << setw( 6 )  << names[i]
             << setw( 10 ) << values[i] << endl;
}
```

The **width** member function is declared in IOSTREAM.H. If you use **setw** or any other manipulator *with arguments*, you must include IOMANIP.H. In the output, strings are printed in a field of width 6 and integers in a field of width 10:

```
Zoot        1.23
Jimmy      35.36
   Al      653.7
 Stan    4358.24
```

Neither **setw** nor **width** truncates values. If formatted output exceeds the width, the entire value prints, subject to the stream's precision setting. Both **setw** and **width** affect the following field only. Field width reverts to its default behavior (the necessary width) after one field has been printed. However, the other stream format options remain in effect until changed.

Alignment

Output streams default to right-aligned text. To left align the names in the previous example and right align the numbers, replace the **for** loop as follows:

```
for ( int i = 0; i < 4; i++ )
   cout << setiosflags( ios::left )
        << setw( 6 ) << names[i]
        << resetiosflags( ios::left )
        << setw( 10 ) << values[i] << endl;
```

The output looks like this:

```
Zoot        1.23
Jimmy      35.36
Al        653.7
Stan     4358.24
```

The left-align flag is set by using the **setiosflags** manipulator with the **ios::left** enumerator. This enumerator is defined in the **ios** class, so its reference must include the **ios::** prefix. The **resetiosflags** manipulator turns off the left-align flag. Unlike **width** and **setw**, the effect of **setiosflags** and **resetiosflags** is permanent.

Precision

The default value for floating-point precision is six. For example, the number 3466.9768 prints as 3466.98. To change the way this value prints, use the **setprecision** manipulator. The manipulator has two flags, **ios::fixed** and **ios::scientific**. If **ios::fixed** is set, the number prints as 3466.976800. If **ios::scientific** is set, it prints as 3.4669773+003.

To display the floating-point numbers in the previous "Alignment" section with one significant digit, replace the **for** loop as follows:

```
for ( int i = 0; i < 4; i++ )
   cout << setiosflags( ios::left )
        << setw( 6 )
        << names[i]
        << resetiosflags( ios::left )
        << setw( 10 )
        << setprecision( 1 )
        << values[i]
        << endl;
```

The program prints this list:

```
Zoot        1
Jimmy     4e+001
Al        7e+002
Stan      4e+003
```

To eliminate scientific notation, insert this statement before the **for** loop:

```
cout << setiosflags( ios::fixed );
```

With fixed notation, the program prints with one digit after the decimal point.

```
Zoot        1.2
Jimmy      35.4
Al        653.7
Stan     4358.2
```

If you change the **ios::fixed** flag to **ios::scientific**, the program prints this:

```
Zoot    1.2e+000
Jimmy   3.5e+001
Al      6.5e+002
Stan    4.4e+003
```

Again, the program prints one digit after the decimal point. If *either* **ios::fixed** or **ios::scientific** is set, the precision value determines the number of digits after the decimal point. If neither flag is set, the precision value determines the total number of significant digits. The **resetiosflags** manipulator clears these flags.

Radix

The **dec**, **oct**, and **hex** manipulators set the default radix for input and output. For example, if you insert the **hex** manipulator into the output stream, the object correctly translates the internal data representation of integers into a hexadecimal output format. The numbers are displayed with digits a through f in lowercase if the **ios::uppercase** flag is clear (the default); otherwise, they are displayed in uppercase. The default radix is **dec** (decimal).

Output File Stream Member Functions

Output stream member functions have three types: those that are equivalent to manipulators, those that perform unformatted write operations, and those that otherwise modify the stream state and have no equivalent manipulator or insertion operator. For sequential, formatted output, you might use only insertion operators and manipulators. For random-access binary disk output, you use other member functions, with or without insertion operators.

The open Function

To use an output file stream (**ofstream**), you must associate that stream with a specific disk file in the constructor or the **open** function. If you use the **open** function, you can reuse the same stream object with a series of files. In either case, the arguments describing the file are the same.

When you open the file associated with an output stream, you generally specify an **open_mode** flag. You can combine these flags, which are defined as enumerators in the **ios** class, with the bitwise OR (|) operator.

Flag	Function
ios::app	Opens an output file for appending.
ios::ate	Opens an existing file (either input or output) and seeks the end.
ios::in	Opens an input file. Use **ios::in** as an **open_mode** for an **ofstream** file to prevent truncating an existing file.
ios::out	Opens an output file. When you use **ios::out** for an **ofstream** object without **ios::app**, **ios::ate**, or **ios::in**, **ios::trunc** is implied.
ios::nocreate	Opens a file only if it already exists; otherwise the operation fails.
ios::noreplace	Opens a file only if it does not exist; otherwise the operation fails.
ios::trunc	Opens a file and deletes the old file (if it already exists).
ios::binary	Opens a file in binary mode (default is text mode).

Three common output stream situations involve mode options:

- Creating a file. If the file already exists, the old version is deleted.

```
ostream ofile( "FILENAME" );  // Default is ios::out
ofstream ofile( "FILENAME", ios::out ); // Equivalent to above
```

- Appending records to an existing file or creating one if it does not exist.

```
ofstream ofile( "FILENAME", ios::app );
```

■ Opening two files, one at a time, on the same stream.

```
ofstream ofile();
ofile.open( "FILE1", ios::in );
// Do some output
ofile.close(); // FILE1 closed
ofile.open( "FILE2", ios::in );
// Do some more output
ofile.close(); // FILE2 closed
// When ofile goes out of scope it is destroyed.
```

The put Function

The **put** function writes one character to the output stream. The following two statements are the same by default, but the second is affected by the stream's format arguments:

```
cout.put( 'A' ); // Exactly one character written
cout << 'A'; // Format arguments 'width' and 'fill' apply
```

The write Function

The **write** function writes a block of memory to an output file stream. The length argument specifies the number of bytes written. This example creates an output file stream and writes the binary value of the Date structure to it:

```
#include <fstream.h>

struct Date
{
    int mo, da, yr;
};

void main()
{
    Date dt = { 6, 10, 92 };
    ofstream tfile( "date.dat" , ios::binary );
    tfile.write( (char *) &dt, sizeof dt );
}
```

The **write** function does not stop when it reaches a null character, so the complete class structure is written. The function takes two arguments: a **char** pointer and a count of characters to write. Note the required cast to **char*** before the address of the structure object.

The seekp and tellp Functions

An output file stream keeps an internal pointer that points to the position where data is to be written next. The **seekp** member function sets this pointer and thus provides random-access disk file output. The **tellp** member function returns the file position.

For examples that use the input stream equivalants to **seekp** and **tellp**, see "The seekg and **tellg** Functions" on page 19.

The close Function

The **close** member function closes the disk file associated with an output file stream. The file must be closed to complete all disk output. If necessary, the **ofstream** destructor closes the file for you, but you can use the **close** function if you need to open another file for the same stream object.

The output stream destructor automatically closes a stream's file only if the constructor or the **open** member function opened the file. If you pass the constructor a file descriptor for an already-open file or use the **attach** member function, you must close the file explicitly.

Error Processing Functions

Use these member functions to test for errors while writing to a stream:

Function	Return value
bad	Returns **TRUE** if there is an unrecoverable error.
fail	Returns **TRUE** if there is an unrecoverable error or an "expected" condition, such as a conversion error, or if the file is not found. Processing can often resume after a call to **clear** with a zero argument.
good	Returns **TRUE** if there is no error condition (unrecoverable or otherwise) and the end-of-file flag is not set.
eof	Returns **TRUE** on the end-of-file condition.
clear	Sets the internal error state. If called with the default arguments, it clears all error bits.
rdstate	Returns the current error state. For a complete description of error bits, see the *Class Library Reference*.

The **!** operator is overloaded to perform the same function as the **fail** function. Thus the expression

```
if( !cout)...
```

is equivalent to

```
if( cout.fail() )...
```

The **void*()** operator is overloaded to be the opposite of the **!** operator; thus the expression

```
if( cout)...
```

is equal to

```
if( !cout.fail() )...
```

The **void*()** operator is not equivalent to **good** because it doesn't test for the end of file.

The Effects of Buffering

The following example shows the effects of buffering. You might expect the program to print please wait, wait 5 seconds, and then proceed. It won't necessarily work this way, however, because the output is buffered.

```
#include <iostream.h>
#include <time.h>

void main()
{
    time_t tm = time( NULL ) + 5;
    cout << "Please wait...";
    while ( time( NULL ) < tm )
        ;
    cout << "\nAll done" << endl;
}
```

To make the program work logically, the **cout** object must empty itself when the message is to appear. To flush an **ostream** object, send it the **flush** manipulator:

```
cout << "Please wait..." << flush;
```

This step flushes the buffer, ensuring the message prints before the wait. You can also use the **endl** manipulator, which flushes the buffer and outputs a carriage return–linefeed, or you can use the **cin** object. This object (with the **cerr** or **clog** objects) is usually tied to the **cout** object. Thus, any use of **cin** (or of the **cerr** or **clog** objects) flushes the **cout** object.

Binary Output Files

Streams were originally designed for text, so the default output mode is text. In text mode, the newline character (hexadecimal 10) expands to a carriage return–linefeed (16-bit only). The expansion can cause problems, as shown here:

```
#include <fstream.h>
int iarray[2] = { 99, 10 };
void main()
{
    ofstream os( "test.dat" );
    os.write( (char *) iarray, sizeof( iarray ) );
}
```

You might expect this program to output the byte sequence { 99, 0, 10, 0 }; instead, it outputs { 99, 0, 13, 10, 0 }, which causes problems for a program expecting binary input. If you need true binary output, in which characters are written untranslated, you have several choices:

- Construct a stream as usual, then use the **setmode** member function, which changes the mode after the file is opened:

```
ofstream ofs ( "test.dat" );
ofs.setmode( filebuf::binary );
ofs.write( char*iarray, 4 ); // Exactly 4 bytes written
```

- Specify binary output by using the **ofstream** constuctor mode argument:

```
#include <fstream.h>
#include <fcntl.h>
#include <io.h>
int iarray[2] = { 99, 10 };
void main()
{
    ofstream os( "test.dat", ios::binary );
    ofs.write( iarray, 4 ); // Exactly 4 bytes written
}
```

- Use the **binary** manipulator instead of the **setmode** member function:

```
ofs << binary;
```

  Use the **text** manipulator to switch the stream to text translation mode.

- Open the file using the run-time **_open** function with a binary mode flag:

```
filedesc fd = _open( "test.dat",
                _O_BINARY | _O_CREAT | _O_WRONLY );
ofstream ofs( fd );
ofs.write( ( char* ) iarray, 4 ); // Exactly 4 bytes written
```

Overloading the << Operator for Your Own Classes

Output streams use the insertion (<<) operator for standard types. You can also overload the << operator for your own classes.

The **write** function example showed the use of a `Date` structure. A date is an ideal candidate for a C++ class in which the data members (month, day, and year) are hidden from view. An output stream is the logical destination for displaying such a structure. This code displays a date using the **cout** object:

```
Date dt( 1, 2, 92 );
cout << dt;
```

To get **cout** to accept a Date object after the insertion operator, overload the insertion operator to recognize an **ostream** object on the left and a Date on the right. The overloaded << operator function must then be declared as a friend of class Date so it can access the private data within a Date object.

```
#include <iostream.h>

class Date
{
    int mo, da, yr;
public:
    Date( int m, int d, int y )
    {
        mo = m; da = d; yr = y;
    }
    friend ostream& operator<< ( ostream& os, Date& dt );
};

ostream& operator<< ( ostream& os, Date& dt )
{
    os << dt.mo << '/' << dt.da << '/' << dt.yr;
    return os;
}

void main()
{
    Date dt( 5, 6, 92 );
    cout << dt;
}
```

When you run this program, it prints the date:

```
5/6/92
```

The overloaded operator returns a reference to the original **ostream** object, which means you can combine insertions:

```
cout << "The date is" << dt << flush;
```

Writing Your Own Manipulators Without Arguments

Writing manipulators that don't use arguments requires neither class derivation nor use of complex macros. Suppose your printer requires the pair <ESC>[to enter bold mode. You can insert this pair directly into the stream:

```
cout << "regular " << '\033' << '[' << "boldface" << endl;
```

Or you can define the bold manipulator, which inserts the characters:

```
ostream& bold( ostream& os ) {
    return os << '\033' << '[';
}
cout << "regular " << bold << "boldface" << endl;
```

The globally defined bold function takes an **ostream** reference argument and returns the **ostream** reference. It is not a member function or a friend because it doesn't need access to any private class elements. The bold function connects to the stream because the stream's **<<** operator is overloaded to accept that type of function, using a declaration that looks something like this:

```
ostream& ostream::operator<< ( ostream& (*_f)( ostream& ) ); {
    (*_f)( *this );
    return *this;
}
```

You can use this feature to extend other overloaded operators. In this case, it is incidental that bold inserts characters into the stream. The function is called when it is inserted into the stream, not necessarily when the adjacent characters are printed. Thus, printing could be delayed because of the stream's buffering.

Input Streams

An input stream object is a source of bytes. The three most important input stream classes are **istream**, **ifstream**, and **istrstream**.

The **istream** class is best used for sequential text-mode input. You can configure objects of class **istream** for buffered or unbuffered operation. All functionality of the base class, **ios**, is included in **istream**. You will rarely construct objects from class **istream**. Instead, you will generally use the predefined **cin** object, which is actually an object of class **istream_withassign**. In some cases, you can assign **cin** to other stream objects after program startup.

The **ifstream** class supports disk file input. If you need an input-only disk file, construct an object of class **ifstream**. You can specify binary or text-mode data. If you specify a filename in the constructor, the file is automatically opened when the object is constructed. Otherwise, you can use the **open** function after invoking the default constructor. Many formatting options and member functions apply to **ifstream** objects. All functionality of the base classes **ios** and **istream** is included in **ifstream**.

Like the library function **sscanf**, the **istrstream** class supports input from in-memory strings. To extract data from a character array that has a null terminator, allocate and initialize the string, then construct an object of class **istrstream**.

Constructing Input Stream Objects

If you use only the **cin** object, you don't need to construct an input stream. You must construct an input stream if you use:

- File stream
- String stream

Input File Stream Constructors

There are three ways to create an input file stream:

- Use the **void**-argument constructor, then call the **open** member function:

```
ifstream myFile; // On the stack
myFile.open( "filename", iosmode );

ifstream* pmyFile = new ifstream; // On the heap
pmyFile->open( "filename", iosmode );
```

- Specify a filename and mode flags in the constructor invocation, thereby opening the file during the construction process:

```
ifstream myFile( "filename", iosmode );
```

- Specify an integer file descriptor for a file already open for input. In this case you can specify unbuffered input or a pointer to your own buffer:

```
int fd = _open( "filename", dosmode );
ifstream myFile1( fd );  // Buffered mode (default)
ifstream myFile2( fd, NULL, 0 );  // Unbuffered mode
ifstream myFile3( fd, pch, buflen );  // User-supplied buffer
```

Input String Stream Constructors

Input string stream constructors require the address of preallocated, preinitialized storage:

```
char s[] = "123.45";
double amt;
istrstream myString( s );
myString >> amt; // Amt should contain 123.45
```

Using Extraction Operators

The extraction operator (>>), which is preprogrammed for all standard C++ data types, is the easiest way to get bytes from an input stream object.

Formatted text input extraction operators depend on white space to separate incoming data values. This is inconvenient when a text field contains multiple words or when commas separate numbers. In such a case, one alternative is to use the unformatted input member function **getline** to read a block of text with white space included, then parse the block with special functions. Another method is to derive an input stream class with a member function such as `GetNextToken`, which can call **istream** members to extract and format character data.

Testing for Extraction Errors

Output error processing functions, discussed in "Error Processing Functions" on page 10, apply to input streams. Testing for errors during extraction is important. Consider this statement:

```
cin >> n;
```

If n is a signed integer, a value greater than 32,767 (the maximum allowed value, or MAX_INT) sets the stream's **fail** bit, and the **cin** object becomes unusable. All subsequent extractions result in an immediate return with no value stored.

Input Stream Manipulators

Many manipulators, such as **setprecision**, are defined for the **ios** class and thus apply to input streams. Few manipulators, however, actually affect input stream objects. Of those that do, the most important are the radix manipulators, **dec**, **oct**, and **hex**, which determine the conversion base used with numbers from the input stream.

On extraction, the **hex** manipulator enables processing of various input formats. For example, c, C, 0xc, 0xC, 0Xc, and 0XC are all interpreted as the decimal integer 12. Any character other than 0 through 9, A through F, a through f, x, and X terminates the numeric conversion. Thus the sequence `"124n5"` is converted to the number 124 with the **ios::fail** bit set.

Input Stream Member Functions

Input stream member functions are used for disk input.

The open Function

If you are using an input file stream (**ifstream**), you must associate that stream with a specific disk file. You can do this in the constructor, or you can use the **open** function. In either case, the arguments are the same.

You generally specify an **open_mode** flag when you open the file associated with an input stream (the default mode is **ios::in**). For a list of the **open_mode** flags, see "The open Function" on page 8. The flags can be combined with the bitwise OR (|) operator.

To read a file, first use the **fail** member function to determine whether it exists:

```
istream ifile( "FILENAME", ios::nocreate );
if ( ifile.fail() )
// The file does not exist ...
```

The get Function

The unformatted **get** member function works like the **>>** operator with two exceptions. First, the **get** function includes white-space characters, whereas the extractor excludes white space when the **ios::skipws** flag is set (the default). Second, the **get** function is less likely to cause a tied output stream (**cout**, for example) to be flushed.

A variation of the **get** function specifies a buffer address and the maximum number of characters to read. This is useful for limiting the number of characters sent to a specific variable, as this example shows:

```
#include <iostream.h>

void main()
{
   char line[25];
   cout << " Type a line terminated by carriage return\n>";
   cin.get( line, 25 );
   cout << ' ' << line;
}
```

In this example, you can type up to 24 characters and a terminating character. Any remaining characters can be extracted later.

The getline Function

The **getline** member function is similar to the **get** function. Both functions allow a third argument that specifies the terminating character for input. The default value is the newline character. Both functions reserve one character for the required terminating character. However, **get** leaves the terminating character in the stream and **getline** removes the terminating character.

The following example specifies a terminating character for the input stream:

```
#include <iostream.h>

void main()
{
   char line[100];
   cout << " Type a line terminated by 't'" << endl;
   cin.getline( line, 100, 't' );
   cout << line;
}
```

The read Function

The **read** member function reads bytes from a file to a specified area of memory. The length argument determines the number of bytes read. If you do not include that argument, reading stops when the physical end of file is reached or, in the case of a text-mode file, when an embedded **EOF** character is read.

This example reads a binary record from a payroll file into a structure:

```
#include <fstream.h>
#include <fcntl.h>
#include <io.h>

void main()
{
    struct
    {
        double salary;
        char name[23];
    } employee;

    ifstream is( "payroll", ios::binary | ios::nocreate );
    if( is ) {  // ios::operator void*()
        is.read( (char *) &employee, sizeof( employee ) );
        cout << employee.name << ' ' << employee.salary << endl;
    }
    else {
        cout << "ERROR: Cannot open file 'payroll'." << endl;
    }
}
```

The program assumes that the data records are formatted exactly as specified by the structure with no terminating carriage-return or linefeed characters.

The seekg and tellg Functions

Input file streams keep an internal pointer to the position in the file where data is to be read next. You set this pointer with the **seekg** function, as shown here:

```
#include <fstream.h>

void main()
{
    char ch;
```

```
        ifstream tfile( "payroll", ios::binary | ios::nocreate );
        if( tfile ) {
           tfile.seekg( 8 );       // Seek 8 bytes in (past salary)
           while ( tfile.good() ) { // EOF or failure stops the reading
              tfile.get( ch );
              if( !ch ) break; // quit on null
              cout << ch;
           }
        }
        else {
           cout << "ERROR: Cannot open file 'payroll'." << endl;
        }
     }
```

To use **seekg** to implement record-oriented data management systems, multiply the fixed-length record size by the record number to obtain the byte position relative to the end of the file, then use the **get** object to read the record.

The **tellg** member function returns the current file position for reading. This value is of type **streampos**, a **typedef** defined in IOSTREAM.H. The following example reads a file and displays messages showing the positions of spaces.

```
#include <fstream.h>

void main()
{
   char ch;
ifstream tfile( "payroll", ios::binary | ios::nocreate );
   if( tfile ) {
       while ( tfile.good() ) {
           streampos here = tfile.tellg();
           tfile.get( ch );
           if ( ch == ' ' )
               cout << "\nPosition " << here << " is a space";
       }
   }
   else {
      cout << "ERROR: Cannot open file 'payroll'." << endl;
   }
}
```

The close Function

The **close** member function closes the disk file associated with an input file stream and frees the operating system file handle. The **ifstream** destructor closes the file for you (unless you called the **attach** function or passed your own file descriptor to the constructor), but you can use the **close** function if you need to open another file for the same stream object.

Overloading the >> Operator for Your Own Classes

Input streams use the extraction (>>) operator for the standard types. You can write similar extraction operators for your own types; your success depends on using white space precisely.

Here is an example of an extraction operator for the Date class presented earlier:

```
istream& operator>> ( istream& is, Date& dt )
{
    is >> dt.mo >> dt.da >> dt.yr;
    return is;
}
```

Input/Output Streams

An **iostream** object is a source and/or a destination for bytes. The two most important I/O stream classes, both derived from **iostream**, are **fstream** and **strstream**. These classes inherit the functionality of the **istream** and **ostream** classes described previously.

The **fstream** class supports disk file input and output. If you need to read from and write to a particular disk file in the same program, construct an **fstream** object. An **fstream** object is a single stream with two logical substreams, one for input and one for output. Although the underlying buffer contains separately designated positions for reading and writing, those positions are tied together.

The **strstream** class supports input and output of in-memory strings.

Custom Manipulators with Arguments

This section describes how to create output stream manipulators with one or more arguments, and how to use manipulators for non-output streams.

Output Stream Manipulators with One Argument (int or long)

The iostream class library provides a set of macros for creating parameterized manipulators. Manipulators with a single **int** or **long** argument are a special case. To create an output stream manipulator that accepts a single **int** or **long** argument (like **setw**), you must use the **OMANIP** macro, which is defined in IOMANIP.H. This example defines a fillblank manipulator that inserts a specified number of blanks into the stream:

```
#include <iostream.h>
#include <iomanip.h>

ostream& fb( ostream& os, int l )
{
   for( int i=0; i < l; i++ )
        os << ' ';
   return os;
}

OMANIP(int) fillblank( int l )
{
   return OMANIP(int) ( fb, l );
}

void main()
{
    cout << "10 blanks follow" << fillblank( 10 ) << ".\n";
}
```

The IOMANIP.H header file contains a macro that expands **OMANIP(int)** into a class, **__OMANIP_int**, which includes a constructor and an overloaded **ostream** insertion operator for an object of the class. In the previous example, the fillblank function calls the **__OMANIP_int** constructor to return an object of class **__OMANIP_int**. Thus, fillblank can be used with an **ostream** insertion operator. The constructor calls the fb function.

The **OMANIP** macro represents an advanced use of C++. It will be superseded once C++ accommodates parameterized types. In the meantime, it is easier to adapt the previous code than to analyze the syntax. The expression **OMANIP(long)** expands to another built-in class, **__OMANIP_long**, which accommodates functions with a long integer argument.

Other One-Argument Output Stream Manipulators

To create manipulators that take arguments other than **int** and **long**, you must use the **IOMANIPdeclare** macro, which declares the classes for your new type, as well as the **OMANIP** macro.

The following example uses a class money, which is a **long** type. The setpic manipulator attaches a formatting "picture" string to the class that can be used by the overloaded stream insertion operator of the class money. The picture string is stored as a static variable in the money class rather than as data member of a stream class, so you do not have to derive a new output stream class.

```
#include <iostream.h>
#include <iomanip.h>
#include <string.h>

typedef char* charp;
IOMANIPdeclare( charp );

class money {
private:
    long value;
    static char *szCurrentPic;
public:
    money( long val ) { value = val; }
    friend ostream& operator << ( ostream& os, money m ) {
        // A more complete function would merge the picture
        // with the value rather than simply appending it
        os << m.value << '[' << money::szCurrentPic << ']';
        return os;
    }
    friend ostream& setpic( ostream& os, char* szPic ) {
        money::szCurrentPic = new char[strlen( szPic ) + 1];
        strcpy( money::szCurrentPic, szPic );
        return os;
    }
};
char *money::szCurrentPic;  // Static pointer to picture

OMANIP(charp) setpic(charp c)
{
    return OMANIP(charp) (setpic, c);
}

void main()
{
    money amt = 35235.22;
    cout << setiosflags( ios::fixed );
    cout << setpic( "###,###,###.##" ) << "amount = " << amt << endl;
}
```

Output Stream Manipulators with More Than One Argument

The following example shows how to write a manipulator, fill, to insert a specific number of a particular character. The manipulator, which takes two arguments, is similar to setpic in the previous example. The difference is that the character pointer type declaration is replaced by a structure declaration.

```
#include <iostream.h>
#include <iomanip.h>

struct fillpair {
        char ch;
        int  cch;
};

IOMANIPdeclare( fillpair );

ostream& fp( ostream& os, fillpair pair )
{
    for ( int c = 0; c < pair.cch; c++ ) {
        os << pair.ch;
    }
    return os;
}

OMANIP(fillpair) fill( char ch, int cch )
{
    fillpair pair;

    pair.cch = cch;
    pair.ch  = ch;
    return OMANIP (fillpair)( fp, pair );
}

void main()
{
    cout << "10 dots coming" << fill( '.', 10 ) << "done" << endl;
}
```

This example can be rewritten so that the manipulator definition is in a separate program file. In this case, the header file must contain these declarations:

```
struct fillpair {
        char ch;
        int  cch;
};
IOMANIPdeclare( fillpair );
ostream& fp( ostream& o, fillpair pair );
OMANIP(fillpair) fill( char ch, int cch );
```

Custom Manipulators for Input and Input/Output Streams

The **OMANIP** macro works with **ostream** and its derived classes. The **SMANIP**, **IMANIP**, and **IOMANIP** macros work with the classes **ios**, **istream**, and **iostream**, respectively.

Using Manipulators with Derived Stream Classes

Suppose you define a manipulator, xstream, that works with the **ostream** class. The manipulator will work with all classes derived from **ostream**. Further suppose you need manipulators that work only with xstream. In this case, you must add an overloaded insertion operator that is not a member of **ostream**:

```
xstream& operator<< ( xstream& xs, xstream& (*_f)( xstream& ) ) {
    (*_f)( xs );
    return xs;
}
```

The manipulator code looks like this:

```
xstream& bold( xstream& xs ) {
    return xs << '\033' << '[';
}
```

If the manipulator needs to access xstream protected data member functions, you can declare the bold function as a friend of the xstream class.

Deriving Your Own Stream Classes

Like any C++ class, a stream class can be derived to add new member functions, data members, or manipulators. If you need an input file stream that tokenizes its input data, for example, you can derive from the **ifstream** class. This derived class can include a member function that returns the next token by calling its base class's public member functions or extractors. You may need new data members to hold the stream object's state between operations, but you probably won't need to use the base class's protected member functions or data members.

For the straightforward stream class derivation, you need only write the necessary constructors and the new member functions.

The streambuf Class

Unless you plan to make major changes to the iostream library, you do not need to work much with the **streambuf** class, which does most of the work for the other stream classes. In most cases, you will create a modified output stream by deriving only a new **streambuf** class and connecting it to the **ostream** class.

Why Derive a Custom streambuf Class?

Existing output streams communicate to the file system and to in-memory strings. You can create streams that address a memory-mapped video screen, a window as defined by Microsoft Windows, a new physical device, and so on. A simpler method is to alter the byte stream as it goes to a file system device.

A streambuf Derivation Example

The following example modifies the **cout** object to print in two-column landscape (horizontal) mode on a printer that uses the PCL control language (for example, Hewlett-Packard LaserJet printer). As the test driver program shows, all member functions and manipulators that work with the original **cout** object work with the special version. The application programming interface is the same.

The example is divided into three source files:

- HSTREAM.H—the LaserJet class declaration that must be included in the implementation file and application file

- HSTREAM.CPP—the LaserJet class implementation that must be linked with the application

- EXIOS204.CPP—the test driver program that sends output to a LaserJet printer

HSTREAM.H contains only the class declaration for hstreambuf, which is derived from the **filebuf** class and overrides the appropriate **filebuf** virtual functions.

```
// hstream.h - HP LaserJet output stream header
#include <fstream.h> // Accesses filebuf class
#include <string.h>
#include <stdio.h> // for sprintf

class hstreambuf : public filebuf
{
public:
    hstreambuf( int filed );
    virtual int sync();
    virtual int overflow( int ch );
    ~hstreambuf();
private:
    int column, line, page;
    char* buffer;
    void convert( long cnt );
    void newline( char*& pd, int& jj );
    void heading( char*& pd, int& jj );
    void pstring( char* ph, char*& pd, int& jj );
};
```

```
ostream& und( ostream& os );
ostream& reg( ostream& os );
```

HSTREAM.CPP contains the `hstreambuf` class implementation.

```
// hstream.cpp  - HP LaserJet output stream
#include "hstream.h"

const int REG  = 0x01;   // Regular font code
const int UND  = 0x02;   // Underline font code
const int CR   = 0x0d;   // Carriage return character
const int NL   = 0x0a;   // Newline character
const int FF   = 0x0c;   // Formfeed character
const int TAB  = 0x09;   // Tab character
const int LPP  = 57;     // Lines per page
const int TABW = 5;      // Tab width

// Prolog defines printer initialization (font, orientation, etc.
char prolog[] =
{ 0x1B, 0x45,                          // Reset printer
  0x1B, 0x28, 0x31, 0x30, 0x55,          // IBM PC char set
  0x1B, 0x26, 0x6C, 0x31, 0x4F,          // Landscape
  0x1B, 0x26, 0x6C, 0x38, 0x44,        // 8 lines per inch
  0x1B, 0x26, 0x6B, 0x32, 0x53};       // Lineprinter font

// Epilog prints the final page and terminates the output
char epilog[] = { 0x0C, 0x1B, 0x45 };   // Formfeed, reset

char uon[] = { 0x1B, 0x26, 0x64, 0x44, 0 }; // Underline on
char uoff[] = { 0x1B, 0x26, 0x64, 0x40, 0 };// Underline off

hstreambuf::hstreambuf( int filed ) : filebuf( filed )
{
    column = line = page = 0;
    int size = sizeof( prolog );
    setp( prolog, prolog + size );
    pbump( size );   // Puts the prolog in the put area
    filebuf::sync(); // Sends the prolog to the output file
    buffer = new char[1024]; // Allocates destination buffer
}
```

```
hstreambuf::~hstreambuf()
{
    sync(); // Makes sure the current buffer is empty
    delete buffer; // Frees the memory
    int size = sizeof( epilog );
    setp( epilog, epilog + size );
    pbump( size );   // Puts the epilog in the put area
    filebuf::sync(); // Sends the epilog to the output file
}
virtual int hstreambuf::sync()
{
    long count = out_waiting();
    if ( count ) {
        convert( count );
    }
    return filebuf::sync();
}


virtual int hstreambuf::overflow( int ch )
{
    long count = out_waiting();
    if ( count ) {
        convert( count );
    }
    return filebuf::overflow( ch );
}
// The following code is specific to the HP LaserJet printer

// Converts a buffer to HP, then writes it
void hstreambuf::convert( long cnt )
{
    char *bufs, *bufd; // Source, destination pointers
    int j = 0;

    bufs = pbase();
    bufd = buffer;
    if( page == 0 ) {
        newline( bufd, j );
    }
    for( int i = 0; i < cnt; i++ ) {
        char c = *( bufs++ );  // Gets character from source buffer
        if( c >= ' ' ) {        // Character is printable
            * ( bufd++ ) = c;
            j++;
            column++;
        }
```

```
        else if( c == NL ) {           // Moves down one line
                *( bufd++ ) = c;       // Passes character through
                j++;
                line++;
                newline( bufd, j ); // Checks for page break, etc.
        }
        else if( c == FF ) {     // Ejects paper on formfeed
            line = line - line % LPP + LPP;
            newline( bufd, j ); // Checks for page break, etc.
        }
        else if( c == TAB ) {    // Expands tabs
            do {
                *( bufd++ ) = ' ';
                j++;
                column++;
            } while ( column % TABW );
        }
        else if( c == UND ) { // Responds to und manipulator
            pstring( uon, bufd, j );
        }
        else if( c == REG ) { // Responds to reg manipulator
            pstring( uoff, bufd, j );
        }
    }
    setp( buffer, buffer + 1024 ); // Sets new put area
    pbump( j ); // Tells number of characters in the dest buffer
}

// simple manipulators - apply to all ostream classes
ostream& und( ostream& os ) // Turns on underscore mode
{
    os << (char) UND; return os;
}

ostream& reg( ostream& os ) // Turns off underscore mode
{
    os << (char) REG; return os;
}
```

```
void hstreambuf::newline( char*& pd, int& jj ) {
// Called for each newline character
    column = 0;
    if ( ( line % ( LPP*2 ) ) == 0 ) { // Even page
        page++;
        pstring( "\033&a+0L", pd, jj );  // Set left margin to zero
        heading( pd, jj );               // Print heading
        pstring( "\033*p0x77Y", pd, jj );// Cursor to (0,77) dots
    }
    if ( ( ( line % LPP ) == 0 ) && ( line % ( LPP*2 ) ) != 0 ) {
    //  Odd page; prepare to move to right column
        page++;
        pstring( "\033*p0x77Y", pd, jj ); // Cursor to (0,77) dots
        pstring( "\033&a+88L", pd, jj );  // Left margin to col 88
    }
}


void hstreambuf::heading( char*& pd, int& jj ) // Prints heading
{
    char hdg[20];
    int i;

    if( page > 1 ) {
        *( pd++ ) = FF;
        jj++;
    }
    pstring( "\033*p0x0Y", pd, jj ); // Top of page
    pstring( uon, pd, jj );          // Underline on
    sprintf( hdg, "Page %-3d", page );
    pstring( hdg, pd, jj );
    for( i=0; i < 80; i++ ) {        // Pads with blanks
        *( pd++ ) = ' ';
        jj++;
    }
    sprintf( hdg, "Page %-3d", page+1 ) ;
    pstring( hdg, pd, jj );
    for( i=0; i < 80; i++ ) {        // Pads with blanks
        *( pd++ ) = ' ';
        jj++;
    }
    pstring( uoff, pd, jj ); // Underline off
}
```

```
// Outputs a string to the buffer
void hstreambuf::pstring( char* ph, char*& pd, int& jj )
{
    int len = strlen( ph );
    strncpy( pd, ph, len );
    pd += len;
    jj += len;
}
```

EXIOS204.CPP reads text lines from the **cin** object and writes them to the modified **cout** object.

```
// exios204.cpp
// hstream Driver program copies cin to cout until end of file
#include "hstream.h"

hstreambuf hsb( 1 ); // 1=stdout

void main()
{
    char line[200];
    cout = &hsb; // Associates the HP LaserJet streambuf to cout
    while( 1 ) {
        cin.getline( line, 200 );
        if( !cin.good() ) break;
        cout << line << endl;
    }
}
```

Here are the main points in the preceding code:

- The new class `hstreambuf` is derived from **filebuf**, which is the buffer class for disk file I/O. The **filebuf** class writes to disk in response to commands from its associated **ostream** class. The `hstreambuf` constructor takes an argument that corresponds to the operating system file number, in this case 1, for **stdout**. This constructor is invoked by this line:

  ```
  hstreambuf hsb( 1 );
  ```

- The **ostream_withassign** assignment operator associates the `hstreambuf` object with the **cout** object:

  ```
  ostream& operator =( streambuf* sbp );
  ```

  This statement in EXIOS204.CPP executes the assignment:

  ```
  cout = &hsb;
  ```

- The `hstreambuf` constructor prints the prolog that sets up the laser printer, then allocates a temporary print buffer.

- The destructor outputs the epilog text and frees the print buffer when the object goes out of scope, which happens after the exit from **main**.

- The **streambuf** virtual **overflow** and **sync** functions do the low-level output. The hstreambuf class overrides these functions to gain control of the byte stream. The functions call the private convert member function.

- The convert function processes the characters in the hstreambuf buffer and stores them in the object's temporary buffer. The **filebuf** functions process the temporary buffer.

- The details of convert relate more to the PCL language than to the iostream library. Private data members keep track of column, line, and page numbers.

- The und and reg manipulators control the underscore print attribute by inserting codes 0x02 and 0x03 into the stream. The convert function later translates these codes into printer-specific sequences.

- The program can be extended easily to embellish the heading, add more formatting features, and so forth.

- In a more general program, the hstreambuf class could be derived from the **streambuf** class rather than the **filebuf** class. The **filebuf** derivation shown gets the most leverage from existing iostream library code, but it makes assumptions about the implementation of **filebuf**, particularly the **overflow** and **sync** functions. Thus you cannot necessarily expect this example to work with other derived **streambuf** classes or with **filebuf** classes provided by other software publishers.

C H A P T E R   2

Alphabetic Microsoft iostream Class Library Reference

iostream Class Hierarchy Diagram

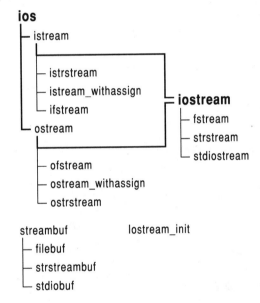

iostream Class List

Abstract Stream Base Class

ios   Stream base class.

Input Stream Classes

istream   General-purpose input stream class and base class
                            for other input streams.

ifstream   Input file stream class.

istream_withassign   Input stream class for **cin**.

istrstream   Input string stream class.

Output Stream Classes

ostream   General-purpose output stream class and base class
                            for other output streams.

ofstream   Output file stream class.

ostream_withassign   Output stream class for **cout**, **cerr**, and **clog**.

ostrstream   Output string stream class.

Input/Output Stream Classes

iostream   General-purpose input/output stream class and base
                            class for other input/output streams.

fstream   Input/output file stream class.

strstream   Input/output string stream class.

stdiostream   Input/output class for standard I/O files.

Stream Buffer Classes

streambuf   Abstract stream buffer base class.

filebuf   Stream buffer class for disk files.

strstreambuf   Stream buffer class for strings.

stdiobuf   Stream buffer class for standard I/O files.

Predefined Stream Initializer Class

Iostream_init   Predefined stream initializer class.

class filebuf : public streambuf

#include <fstream.h>

The **filebuf** class is a derived class of **streambuf** that is specialized for buffered disk file I/O. The buffering is managed entirely within the Microsoft iostream Class Library. **filebuf** member functions call the run-time low-level I/O routines (the functions declared in IO.H) such as **_sopen**, **_read**, and **_write**.

The file stream classes, **ofstream**, **ifstream**, and **fstream**, use **filebuf** member functions to fetch and store characters. Some of these member functions are virtual functions of the **streambuf** class.

The reserve area, put area, and get area are introduced in the **streambuf** class description. The put area and the get area are always the same for **filebuf** objects. Also, the get pointer and put pointers are tied; when one moves, so does the other.

Construction/Destruction — Public Members

filebuf
> Constructs a **filebuf** object.

~filebuf
> Destroys a **filebuf** object.

Operations — Public Members

open
> Opens a file and attaches it to the **filebuf** object.

close
> Flushes any waiting output and closes the attached file.

setmode
> Sets the file's mode to binary or text.

attach
> Attaches the **filebuf** object to an open file.

Status/Information — Public Members

fd
> Returns the stream's file descriptor.

is_open
> Tests whether the file is open.

See Also   **ifstream, ofstream, streambuf, strstreambuf, stdiobuf**

Member Functions

filebuf::attach

filebuf* attach(filedesc *fd* **);**

Attaches this **filebuf** object to the open file specified by *fd*.

Return Value

The function returns **NULL** when the stream is already attached to a file; otherwise it returns the address of the **filebuf** object.

Parameter

fd

A file descriptor as returned by a call to the run-time function **_open** or **_sopen**. **filedesc** is a **typedef** equivalent to **int**.

---

filebuf::close

filebuf* close();

Flushes any waiting output, closes the file, and disconnects the file from the **filebuf** object.

Return Value

If an error occurs, the function returns **NULL** and leaves the **filebuf** object in a closed state. If there is no error, the function returns the address of the **filebuf** object and clears its error state.

See Also

filebuf::open

---

filebuf::fd

filedesc fd() const;

Returns the file descriptor associated with the **filebuf** object; **filedesc** is a **typedef** equivalent to **int**.

Return Value

The value is supplied by the underlying file system. The function returns **EOF** if the object is not attached to a file.

See Also

filebuf::attach

filebuf::filebuf

filebuf();

filebuf(filedesc *fd* **);**

filebuf(filedesc *fd,* **char*** *pr,* **int** *nLength* **);**

Parameters

fd
> A file descriptor as returned by a call to the run-time function **_sopen**. **filedesc** is a **typedef** equivalent to **int**.

pr
> Pointer to a previously allocated reserve area of length *nLength*.

nLength
> The length (in bytes) of the reserve area.

Remarks

The three filebuf constructors are described as follows:

filebuf()
> Constructs a **filebuf** object without attaching it to a file.

filebuf(filedesc)
> Constructs a **filebuf** object and attaches it to an open file.

filebuf(filedesc, char*, int)
> Constructs a **filebuf** object, attaches it to an open file, and initializes it to use a specified reserve area.

filebuf::~filebuf

~filebuf();

Remarks

Closes the attached file only if that file was opened by the **open** member function.

filebuf::is_open

int is_open() const;

Return Value

Returns a nonzero value if this **filebuf** object is attached to an open disk file identified by a file descriptor; otherwise 0.

See Also

filebuf::open

filebuf::open

filebuf* open(const char* *szName*, **int** *nMode*, **int** *nProt* = **filebuf::openprot**);

Opens a disk file and attaches it with this **filebuf** object.

Return Value If the file is already open, or if there is an error while opening the file, the function returns **NULL**; otherwise it returns the **filebuf** address.

Parameters *szName*
 The name of the file to be opened during construction.

nMode
 An integer containing mode bits defined as **ios** enumerators that can be combined with the OR (|) operator. See the **ofstream** constructor for a list of the enumerators.

nProt
 The file protection specification; defaults to the static integer **filebuf::openprot**, which is equivalent to the operating system default (**filebuf::sh_compat** for MS-DOS). The possible values of *nProt* are:

- **filebuf::sh_compat**   Compatibility share mode (MS-DOS only).
- **filebuf::sh_none**   Exclusive mode—no sharing.
- **filebuf::sh_read**   Read sharing allowed.
- **filebuf::sh_write**   Write sharing allowed.

 You can combine the **filebuf::sh_read** and **filebuf::sh_write** modes with the logical OR (||) operator.

See Also **filebuf::is_open, filebuf::close, filebuf::~filebuf**

---

filebuf::setmode

int setmode(int *nMode* = **filebuf::text**);

Parameter *nMode*
 An integer that must be one of the static **filebuf** constants. The *nMode* parameter must have one of the following values:

- **filebuf::text**   Text mode (newline characters translated to and from carriage return-linefeed pairs under MS-DOS).
- **filebuf::binary**   Binary mode (no translation).

Return Value   The previous mode if there is no error; otherwise 0.

Remarks   Sets the binary/text mode of the stream's **filebuf** object.

See Also   **ios binary** manipulator, **ios text** manipulator

class fstream : public iostream

#include <fstream.h>

The **fstream** class is an **iostream** derivative specialized for combined disk file input and output. Its constructors automatically create and attach a **filebuf** buffer object.

See **filebuf** class for information on the get and put areas and their associated pointers. Although the **filebuf** object's get and put pointers are theoretically independent, the get area and the put area are not active at the same time. When the stream's mode changes from input to output, the get area is emptied and the put area is reinitialized. When the mode changes from output to input, the put area is flushed and the get area is reinitialized. Thus, either the get pointer or the put pointer is null at all times.

Construction/Destruction—Public Members

fstream
> Constructs an **fstream** object.

~fstream
> Destroys an **fstream** object.

Operations—Public Members

open
> Opens a file and attaches it to the **filebuf** object and thus to the stream.

close
> Flushes any waiting output and closes the stream's file.

setbuf
> Attaches the specified reserve area to the stream's **filebuf** object.

setmode
> Sets the stream's mode to binary or text.

attach
> Attaches the stream (through the **filebuf** object) to an open file.

Status/Information—Public Members

rdbuf
> Gets the stream's **filebuf** object.

fd
> Returns the file descriptor associated with the stream.

is_open
> Tests whether the stream's file is open.

See Also   **ifstream, ofstream, strstream, stdiostream, filebuf**

Member Functions

fstream::attach

void attach(filedesc *fd* **);**

Attaches this stream to the open file specified by *fd*.

Parameter
fd
A file descriptor as returned by a call to the run-time function **_open** or **_sopen**; **filedesc** is a **typedef** equivalent to **int**.

Remarks
The function fails when the stream is already attached to a file. In that case, the function sets **ios::failbit** in the stream's error state.

See Also
filebuf::attach, **fstream::fd**

---

fstream::close

void close();

Remarks
Calls the **close** member function for the associated **filebuf** object. This function, in turn, flushes any waiting output, closes the file, and disconnects the file from the **filebuf** object. The **filebuf** object is not destroyed.

The stream's error state is cleared unless the call to **filebuf::close** fails.

See Also
filebuf::close, **fstream::open**, **fstream::is_open**

---

fstream::fd

filedesc fd() const;

Remarks
Returns the file descriptor associated with the stream. **filedesc** is a **typedef** equivalent to **int**. Its value is supplied by the underlying file system.

See Also
filebuf::fd, **fstream::attach**

fstream::fstream

fstream();

fstream(const char* *szName*, int *nMode*, int *nProt* = filebuf::openprot);

fstream(filedesc *fd*);

fstream(filedesc *fd*, char* *pch*, int *nLength*);

Parameters

szName

The name of the file to be opened during construction.

nMode

An integer that contains mode bits defined as **ios** enumerators that can be combined with the bitwise OR (|) operator. The *nMode* parameter must have one of the following values:

- **ios::app**   The function performs a seek to the end of file. When new bytes are written to the file, they are always appended to the end, even if the position is moved with the **ostream::seekp** function.

- **ios::ate**   The function performs a seek to the end of file. When the first new byte is written to the file, it is appended to the end, but when subsequent bytes are written, they are written to the current position.

- **ios::in**   The file is opened for input. The original file (if it exists) will not be truncated.

- **ios::out**   The file is opened for output.

- **ios::trunc**   If the file already exists, its contents are discarded. This mode is implied if **ios::out** is specified, and **ios::ate**, **ios::app**, and **ios:in** are not specified.

- **ios::nocreate**   If the file does not already exist, the function fails.

- **ios::noreplace**   If the file already exists, the function fails.

- **ios::binary**   Opens the file in binary mode (the default is text mode).

Note that there is no **ios::in** or **ios::out** default mode for **fstream** objects. You must specify both modes if your **fstream** object must both read and write files.

nProt

The file protection specification; defaults to the static integer **filebuf::openprot**, which is equivalent to the operating system default, **filebuf::sh_compat**, under MS-DOS. The possible *nProt* values are as follows:

- **filebuf::sh_compat**   Compatibility share mode (MS-DOS only).
- **filebuf::sh_none**   Exclusive mode—no sharing.
- **filebuf::sh_read**   Read sharing allowed.
- **filebuf::sh_write**   Write sharing allowed.

The **filebuf::sh_read** and **filebuf::sh_write** modes can be combined with the logical OR (‖) operator.

fd

A file descriptor as returned by a call to the run-time function **_open** or **_sopen**. **filedesc** is a **typedef** equivalent to **int**.

pch

Pointer to a previously allocated reserve area of length *nLength*. A **NULL** value (or *nLength* = 0) indicates that the stream will be unbuffered.

nLength

The length (in bytes) of the reserve area (0 = unbuffered).

Remarks

The four **fstream** constructors are:

- **fstream( )**   Constructs an **fstream** object without opening a file.
- **fstream(const char*, int, int)**   Contructs an **fstream** object, opening the specified file.
- **fstream(filedesc)**   Constructs an **fstream** object that is attached to an open file.
- **fstream(filedesc, char*, int)**   Constructs an **fstream** object that is associated with a **filebuf** object. The **filebuf** object is attached to an open file and to a specified reserve area.

All **fstream** constructors construct a **filebuf** object. The first three use an internally allocated reserve area, but the fourth uses a user-allocated area. The user-allocated area is not automatically released during destruction.

fstream::~fstream

~fstream();

Remarks

Flushes the buffer, then destroys an **fstream** object, along with its associated **filebuf** object. The file is closed only if it was opened by the constructor or by the **open** member function.

The **filebuf** destructor releases the reserve buffer only if it was internally allocated.

fstream::is_open

int is_open() const;

Return Value   Returns a nonzero value if this stream is attached to an open disk file identified by a file descriptor; otherwise 0.

See Also   **filebuf::is_open, fstream::open, fstream::close**

---

fstream::open

void open(const char* *szName***, int** *nMode***, int** *nProt* **= filebuf::openprot);**

Opens a disk file and attaches it to the stream's **filebuf** object.

Parameters   *szName*
     The name of the file to be opened during construction.

    nMode
     An integer containing mode bits defined as **ios** enumerators that can be combined with the OR (|) operator. See the **fstream** constructor for a list of the enumerators. There is no default; a valid mode must be specified.

    nProt
     The file protection specification; defaults to the static integer **filebuf::openprot**. See the **fstream** constructor for a list of the other allowed values.

Remarks   If the **filebuf** object is already attached to an open file, or if a **filebuf** call fails, the **ios::failbit** is set. If the file is not found, then the **ios::failbit** is set only if the **ios::nocreate** mode was used.

See Also   **filebuf::open, fstream::fstream, fstream::close, fstream::is_open**

---

fstream::rdbuf

filebuf* rdbuf() const;

Remarks   Returns a pointer to the **filebuf** buffer object that is associated with this stream. (This is not the character buffer; the **filebuf** object contains a pointer to the character area.)

fstream::setbuf

streambuf* setbuf(char* *pch*, **int** *nLength* **);**

Attaches the specified reserve area to the stream's **filebuf** object.

Return Value

If the file is open and a buffer has already been allocated, the function returns **NULL**; otherwise it returns a pointer to the **filebuf** cast as a **streambuf**. The reserve area will not be released by the destructor.

Parameters

pch
A pointer to a previously allocated reserve area of length *nLength*. A **NULL** value indicates an unbuffered stream.

nLength
The length (in bytes) of the reserve area. A length of 0 indicates an unbuffered stream.

fstream::setmode

int setmode(int *nMode* = **filebuf::text);**

Sets the binary/text mode of the stream's **filebuf** object. It can be called only after the file is opened.

Return Value

The previous mode; −1 if the parameter is invalid, the file is not open, or the mode cannot be changed.

Parameter

nMode
An integer that must be one of the following static **filebuf** constants:

- **filebuf::text**   Text mode (newline characters translated to and from carriage-return–linefeed pairs).

- **filebuf::binary**   Binary mode (no translation).

See Also

ios binary manipulator, **ios text** manipulator

class ifstream : public istream

#include <fstream.h>

The **ifstream** class is an **istream** derivative specialized for disk file input. Its constructors automatically create and attach a **filebuf** buffer object.

The **filebuf** class documentation describes the get and put areas and their associated pointers. Only the get area and the get pointer are active for the **ifstream** class.

Construction/Destruction — Public Members

ifstream

Constructs an **ifstream** object.

~ifstream

Destroys an **ifstream** object.

Operations — Public Members

open

Opens a file and attaches it to the **filebuf** object and thus to the stream.

close

Closes the stream's file.

setbuf

Associates the specified reserve area to the stream's **filebuf** object.

setmode

Sets the stream's mode to binary or text.

attach

Attaches the stream (through the **filebuf** object) to an open file.

Status/Information — Public Members

rdbuf

Gets the stream's **filebuf** object.

fd

Returns the file descriptor associated with the stream.

is_open

Tests whether the stream's file is open.

See Also   **filebuf, streambuf, ofstream, fstream**

Member Functions

ifstream::attach

void attach(filedesc *fd* **);**

Attaches this stream to the open file specified by *fd*.

Parameter   *fd*

A file descriptor as returned by a call to the run-time function **_open** or **_sopen**; **filedesc** is a **typedef** equivalent to **int**.

Remarks   The function fails when the stream is already attached to a file. In that case, the function sets **ios::failbit** in the stream's error state.

See Also   **filebuf::attach, ifstream::fd**

ifstream::close

void close();

Remarks   Calls the **close** member function for the associated **filebuf** object. This function, in turn, closes the file and disconnects the file from the **filebuf** object. The **filebuf** object is not destroyed.

The stream's error state is cleared unless the call to **filebuf::close** fails.

See Also   **filebuf::close, ifstream::open, ifstream::is_open**

ifstream::fd

filedesc fd() const;

Return Value   Returns the file descriptor associated with the stream; **filedesc** is a **typedef** equivalent to **int**. Its value is supplied by the underlying file system.

See Also   **filebuf::fd, ifstream::attach**

ifstream::ifstream

ifstream();

ifstream(const char* *szName*, **int** *nMode* = **ios::in, int** *nProt* =
filebuf::openprot);

ifstream(filedesc *fd* **);**

ifstream(filedesc *fd*, **char*** *pch*, **int** *nLength* **);**

szName
The name of the file to be opened during construction.

nMode
An integer that contains mode bits defined as **ios** enumerators that can be
combined with the bitwise OR (|) operator. The *nMode* parameter must have
one of the following values:

- **ios::in**   The file is opened for input (default).

- **ios::nocreate**   If the file does not already exist, the function fails.

- **ios::binary**   Opens the file in binary mode (the default is text mode).

Note that the **ios::nocreate** flag is necessary if you intend to test for the file's
existence (the usual case).

nProt
The file protection specification; defaults to the static integer **filebuf::openprot**
that is equivalent to **filebuf::sh_compat**. The possible *nProt* values are:

- **filebuf::sh_compat**   Compatibility share mode.

- **filebuf::sh_none**   Exclusive mode—no sharing.

- **filebuf::sh_read**   Read sharing allowed.

- **filebuf::sh_write**   Write sharing allowed.

To combine the **filebuf::sh_read** and **filebuf::sh_write** modes, use the logical
OR (||) operator.

fd
A file descriptor as returned by a call to the run-time function **_open** or **_sopen**;
filedesc is a **typedef** equivalent to **int**.

pch
Pointer to a previously allocated reserve area of length *nLength*. A **NULL** value
(or *nLength* = 0) indicates that the stream will be unbuffered.

nLength
The length (in bytes) of the reserve area (0 = unbuffered).

Remarks   The four **ifstream** constructors are:

- **ifstream()**   Constructs an **ifstream** object without opening a file.
- **ifstream(const char*, int, int)**   Contructs an **ifstream** object, opening the specified file.
- **ifstream(filedesc)**   Constructs an **ifstream** object that is attached to an open file.
- **ifstream(filedesc, char*, int)**   Constructs an **ifstream** object that is associated with a **filebuf** object. The **filebuf** object is attached to an open file and to a specified reserve area.

All **ifstream** constructors construct a **filebuf** object. The first three use an internally allocated reserve area, but the fourth uses a user-allocated area.

ifstream::~ifstream

~ifstream();

Remarks   Destroys an **ifstream** object along with its associated **filebuf** object. The file is closed only if it was opened by the constructor or by the **open** member function.

The **filebuf** destructor releases the reserve buffer only if it was internally allocated.

ifstream::is_open

int is_open() const;

Return Value   Returns a nonzero value if this stream is attached to an open disk file identified by a file descriptor; otherwise 0.

See Also   **filebuf::is_open, ifstream::open, ifstream::close**

ifstream::open

void open(const char* *szName***, int** *nMode* **= ios::in, int** *nProt* **= filebuf::openprot);**

Parameters

szName
> The name of the file to be opened during construction.

nMode
> An integer containing bits defined as **ios** enumerators that can be combined with the OR (|) operator. See the **ifstream** constructor for a list of the enumerators. The **ios::in** mode is implied.

nProt
> The file protection specification; defaults to the static integer **filebuf::openprot**. See the **ifstream** constructor for a list of the other allowed values.

Remarks

Opens a disk file and attaches it to the stream's **filebuf** object. If the **filebuf** object is already attached to an open file, or if a **filebuf** call fails, the **ios::failbit** is set. If the file is not found, then the **ios::failbit** is set only if the **ios::nocreate** mode was used.

See Also

filebuf::open, ifstream::ifstream, ifstream::close, ifstream::is_open

---

ifstream::rdbuf

filebuf* rdbuf() const;

Return Value

Returns a pointer to the **filebuf** buffer object that is associated with this stream. (This is not the character buffer; the **filebuf** object contains a pointer to the character area.)

---

ifstream::setbuf

streambuf* setbuf(char* *pch***, int** *nLength* **);**

Attaches the specified reserve area to the stream's **filebuf** object.

Return Value

If the file is open and a buffer has already been allocated, the function returns **NULL**; otherwise it returns a pointer to the **filebuf**, which is cast as a **streambuf**. The reserve area will not be released by the destructor.

Parameters

pch
> A pointer to a previously allocated reserve area of length *nLength*. A **NULL** value indicates an unbuffered stream.

nLength
> The length (in bytes) of the reserve area. A length of 0 indicates an unbuffered stream.

ifstream::setmode

int setmode(int *nMode* **= filebuf::text);**

Return Value
> The previous mode; –1 if the parameter is invalid, the file is not open, or the mode cannnot be changed.

Parameter

nMode
> An integer that must be one of the following static **filebuf** constants:
>
> - **filebuf::text**   Text mode (newline characters translated to and from carriage return–linefeed pairs).
> - **filebuf::binary**   Binary mode (no translation).

Remarks
> This function sets the binary/text mode of the stream's **filebuf** object. It may be called only after the file is opened.

See Also
> **ios binary** manipulator, **ios text** manipulator

class ios

#include <iostream.h>

As the iostream class heirarchy diagram (on page 33) shows, **ios** is the base class for all the input/output stream classes. While **ios** is not technically an abstract base class, you will not usually construct **ios** objects, nor will you derive classes directly from **ios**. Instead, you will use the derived classes **istream** and **ostream** or other derived classes.

Even though you will not use **ios** directly, you will be using many of the inherited member functions and data members described here. Remember that these inherited member function descriptions are not duplicated for derived classes.

Data Members (static)—Public Members

basefield

Mask for obtaining the conversion base flags (**dec**, **oct**, or **hex**).

adjustfield

Mask for obtaining the field padding flags (**left**, **right**, or **internal**).

floatfield

Mask for obtaining the numeric format (**scientific** or **fixed**).

Construction/Destruction—Public Members

ios

Constructor for use in derived classes.

~ios

Virtual destructor.

Flag and Format Access Functions—Public Members

flags

Sets or reads the stream's format flags.

setf

Manipulates the stream's format flags.

unsetf

Clears the stream's format flags.

fill

Sets or reads the stream's fill character.

precision

Sets or reads the stream's floating-point format display precision.

width

Sets or reads the stream's output field width.

Status-Testing Functions—Public Members

good
Indicates good stream status.

bad
Indicates a serious I/O error.

eof
Indicates end of file.

fail
Indicates a serious I/O error or a possibly recoverable I/O formatting error.

rdstate
Returns the stream's error flags.

clear
Sets or clears the stream's error flags.

User-Defined Format Flags—Public Members

bitalloc
Provides a mask for an unused format bit in the stream's private flags variable (static function).

xalloc
Provides an index to an unused word in an array reserved for special-purpose stream state variables (static function).

iword
Converts the index provided by **xalloc** to a reference (valid only until the next **xalloc**).

pword
Converts the index provided by **xalloc** to a pointer (valid only until the next **xalloc**).

Other Functions—Public Members

delbuf
Controls the connection of **streambuf** deletion with **ios** destruction.

rdbuf
Gets the stream's **streambuf** object.

sync_with_stdio
Synchronizes the predefined objects **cin**, **cout**, **cerr**, and **clog** with the standard I/O system.

tie
Ties a specified **ostream** to this stream.

Operators — Public Members

operator void*()

Converts a stream to a pointer that can be used only for error checking.

operator !()

Returns a nonzero value if a stream I/O error occurs.

ios Manipulators

dec

Causes the interpretation of subsequent fields in decimal format (the default mode).

hex

Causes the interpretation of subsequent fields in hexadecimal format.

oct

Causes the interpretation of subsequent fields in octal format.

binary

Sets the stream's mode to binary (stream must have an associated **filebuf** buffer).

text

Sets the stream's mode to text, the default mode (stream must have an associated **filebuf** buffer).

Parameterized Manipulators

(#include <iomanip.h> required)

setiosflags

Sets the stream's format flags.

resetiosflags

Resets the stream's format flags.

setfill

Sets the stream's fill character.

setprecision

Sets the stream's floating-point display precision.

setw

Sets the stream's field width (for the next field only).

See Also   **istream, ostream**

Member Functions

ios::bad

int bad() const;

Return Value   Returns a nonzero value to indicate a serious I/O error. This is the same as setting the **badbit** error state. Do not continue I/O operations on the stream in this situation.

See Also   **ios::good, ios::fail, ios::rdstate**

ios::bitalloc

static long bitalloc();

Remarks   Provides a mask for an unused format bit in the stream's private flags variable (static function). The **ios** class currently defines 15 format flag bits accessible through **flags** and other member functions. These bits reside in a 32-bit private **ios** data member and are accessed through enumerators such as **ios::left** and **ios::hex**.

The **bitalloc** member function provides a mask for a previously unused bit in the data member. Once you obtain the mask, you can use it to set or test the corresponding custom flag bit in conjunction with the **ios** member functions and manipulators listed under "See Also."

See Also   **ios::flags, ios::setf, ios::unsetf, ios setiosflags** manipulator, **ios resetiosflags** manipulator

ios::clear

void clear(int *nState* = 0);

Parameter   *nState*
     If 0, all error bits are cleared; otherwise bits are set according to the following masks (**ios** enumerators) that can be combined using the bitwise OR (|) operator. The *nState* parameter must have one of the following values:

- **ios::goodbit**   No error condition (no bits set).
- **ios::eofbit**   End of file reached.
- **ios::failbit**   A possibly recoverable formatting or conversion error.
- **ios::badbit**   A severe I/O error.

Remarks   Sets or clears the error-state flags. The **rdstate** function can be used to read the current error state.

See Also   ios::rdstate, ios::good, ios::bad, ios::eof

ios::delbuf

void delbuf(int *nDelFlag* **);**

int delbuf() const;

Parameter   *nDelFlag*
A nonzero value indicates that **~ios** should delete the stream's attached **streambuf** object. A 0 value prevents deletion.

Remarks   The first overloaded **delbuf** function assigns a value to the stream's buffer-deletion flag. The second function returns the current value of the flag.

This function is public only because it is accessed by the **Iostream_init** class. Treat it as protected.

See Also   ios::rdbuf, ios::~ios

ios::eof

int eof() const;

Return Value   Returns a nonzero value if end of file has been reached. This is the same as setting the **eofbit** error flag.

ios::fail

int fail() const;

Return Value   Returns a nonzero value if any I/O error (not end of file) has occurred. This condition corresponds to either the **badbit** or **failbit** error flag being set. If a call to **bad** returns 0, you can assume that the error condition is nonfatal and that you can probably continue processing after you clear the flags.

See Also   **ios::bad**, **ios::clear**

---

ios::fill

char fill(char *cFill*);

char fill() const;

Return Value   The first overloaded function sets the stream's internal fill character variable to *cFill* and returns the previous value. The default fill character is a space.

The second **fill** function returns the stream's fill character.

Parameter   *cFill*
    The new fill character to be used as padding between fields.

See Also   **ios setfill** manipulator

---

ios::flags

long flags(long *lFlags*);

long flags() const;

Return Value   The first overloaded **flags** function sets the stream's internal flags variable to *lFlags* and returns the previous value.

The second function returns the stream's current flags.

Parameter   *lFlags*
    The new format flag values for the stream. The values are specified by the following bit masks (**ios** enumerators) that can be combined using the bitwise OR (|) operator. The *lFlags* parameter must have one of the following values:

- **ios::skipws**   Skip white space on input.
- **ios::left**   Left-align values; pad on the right with the fill character.
- **ios::right**   Right-align values; pad on the left with the fill character (default alignment).
- **ios::internal**   Add fill characters after any leading sign or base indication, but before the value.
- **ios::dec**   Format numeric values as base 10 (decimal) (default radix).
- **ios::oct**   Format numeric values as base 8 (octal).
- **ios::hex**   Format numeric values as base 16 (hexadecimal).
- **ios::showbase**   Display numeric constants in a format that can be read by the C++ compiler.
- **ios::showpoint**   Show decimal point and trailing zeros for floating-point values.
- **ios::uppercase**   Display uppercase A through F for hexadecimal values and E for scientific values.
- **ios::showpos**   Show plus signs (+) for positive values.
- **ios::scientific**   Display floating-point numbers in scientific format.
- **ios::fixed**   Display floating-point numbers in fixed format.
- **ios::unitbuf**   Cause **ostream::osfx** to flush the stream after each insertion. By default, **cerr** is unit buffered.
- **ios::stdio**   Cause **ostream::osfx** to flush stdout and stderr after each insertion.

See Also   **ios::setf, ios::unsetf, ios setiosflags** manipulator, **ios resetiosflags** manipulator, **ios::adjustfield, ios::basefield, ios::floatfield**

---

ios::good

int good() const;

Return Value   Returns a nonzero value if all error bits are clear. Note that the **good** member function is not simply the inverse of the **bad** function.

See Also   **ios::bad, ios::fail, ios::rdstate**

ios::init

Protected →
void init(streambuf* *psb* **);**
END Protected

Parameter   *psb*
                   A pointer to an existing streambuf object.

Remarks   Associates an object of a **streambuf**-derived class with this stream and, if
                   necessary, deletes a dynamically created stream buffer object that was previously
                   associated. The **init** function is useful in derived classes with the protected default
                   istream, **ostream**, and **iostream** constructors. Thus, an **ios**-derived class
                   constructor can construct and attach its own predetermined stream buffer object.

See Also   **istream::istream, ostream::ostream, iostream::iostream**

ios::ios

ios(streambuf* *psb* **);**

Parameter   *psb*
                   A pointer to an existing streambuf object.

Remarks   Constructor for **ios**. You will seldom need to invoke this constructor except in
                   derived classes. Generally, you will be deriving classes not from **ios** but from
                   istream, **ostream**, and **iostream**.

ios::~ios

virtual ~ios();

Remarks   Virtual destructor for **ios**.

ios::iword

long& iword(int *nIndex* **) const;**

Parameters   *nIndex*
                   An index to a table of words that are associated with the **ios** object.

Remarks   The **xalloc** member function provides the index to the table of special-purpose words. The **pword** function converts that index to a reference to a 32-bit word.

See Also   **ios::xalloc, ios::pword**

---

ios::precision

int precision(int *np*);

int precision() const;

Return Value   The first overloaded **precision** function sets the stream's internal floating-point precision variable to *np* and returns the previous value. The default precision is six digits. If the display format is scientific or fixed, the precision indicates the number of digits after the decimal point. If the format is automatic (neither floating point nor fixed), the precision indicates the total number of significant digits.

The second function returns the stream's current precision value.

Parameter   *np*
                     An integer that indicates the number of significant digits or significant decimal digits to be used for floating-point display.

See Also   **ios setprecision** manipulator

---

ios::pword

void*& pword(int *nIndex*) const;

Parameter   *nIndex*
                     An index to a table of words that are associated with the **ios** object.

Remarks   The **xalloc** member function provides the index to the table of special-purpose words. The **pword** function converts that index to a reference to a pointer to a 32-bit word.

See Also   **ios::xalloc, ios::iword**

ios::rdbuf

streambuf* rdbuf() const;

Return Value   Returns a pointer to the **streambuf** object that is associated with this stream. The **rdbuf** function is useful when you need to call **streambuf** member functions.

ios::rdstate

int rdstate() const;

Return Value   Returns the current error state as specified by the following masks (**ios** enumerators):

- **ios::goodbit**   No error condition.
- **ios::eofbit**   End of file reached.
- **ios::failbit**   A possibly recoverable formatting or conversion error.
- **ios::badbit**   A severe I/O error or unknown state.

The returned value can be tested against a mask with the AND (**&**) operator.

See Also   **ios::clear**

ios::setf

long setf(long *lFlags* **);**

long setf(long *lFlags***, long** *lMask* **);**

Return Value   The first overloaded **setf** function turns on only those format bits that are specified by 1s in *lFlags*. It returns a **long** that contains the previous value of all the flags.

The second function alters those format bits specified by 1s in *lMask*. The new values of those format bits are determined by the corresponding bits in *lFlags*. It returns a **long** that contains the previous value of all the flags.

Parameters

lFlags

Format flag bit values. See the **flags** member function for a list of format flags. To combine these flags, use the bitwise OR (I) operator.

lMask

Format flag bit mask.

See Also   **ios::flags**, **ios::unsetf**, **ios setiosflags** manipulator

ios::sync_with_stdio

static void sync_with_stdio();

Remarks

Synchronizes the C++ streams with the standard I/O system. The first time this function is called, it resets the predefined streams (**cin**, **cout**, **cerr**, **clog**) to use a **stdiobuf** object rather than a **filebuf** object. After that, you can mix I/O using these streams with I/O using **stdin**, **stdout**, and **stderr**. Expect some performance decrease because there is buffering both in the stream class and in the standard I/O file system.

After the call to **sync_with_stdio**, the **ios::stdio** bit is set for all affected predefined stream objects, and **cout** is set to unit buffered mode.

ios::tie

ostream* tie(ostream* *pos* **);**

ostream* tie() const;

Return Value

The first overloaded **tie** function ties this stream to the specified **ostream** and returns the value of the previous tie pointer or **NULL** if this stream was not previously tied. A stream tie enables automatic flushing of the **ostream** when more characters are needed, or there are characters to be consumed.

By default, **cin** is initially tied to **cout** so that attempts to get more characters from standard input may result in flushing standard output. In addition, **cerr** and **clog** are tied to **cout** by default.

The second function returns the value of the previous tie pointer or **NULL** if this stream was not previously tied.

Parameter

pos

A pointer to an **ostream** object.

ios::unsetf

long unsetf(long *lFlags* **);**

Return Value Clears the format flags specified by 1s in *lFlags*. It returns a **long** that contains the previous value of all the flags.

Parameter *lFlags*
Format flag bit values. See the **flags** member function for a list of format flags.

See Also **ios::flags, ios::setf, ios resetiosflags** manipulator

---

ios::width

int width(int *nw* **);**

int width() const;

Return Value The first overloaded **width** function sets the stream's internal field width variable to *nw*. When the width is 0 (the default), inserters insert only the number of characters necessary to represent the inserted value. When the width is not 0, the inserters pad the field with the stream's fill character, up to *nw*. If the unpadded representation of the field is larger than *nw*, the field is not truncated. Thus, *nw* is a minimum field width.

The internal width value is reset to 0 after each insertion or extraction.

The second overloaded **width** function returns the current value of the stream's width variable.

Parameter *nw*
The minimum field width in characters.

See Also **ios setw** manipulator

---

ios::xalloc

static int xalloc();

Return Value Provides extra **ios** object state variables without the need for class derivation. It does so by returning an index to an unused 32-bit word in an internal array. This index can subsequently be converted into a reference or pointer by using the **iword** or **pword** member functions.

Any call to **xalloc** invalidates values returned by previous calls to **iword** and **pword**.

See Also   **ios::iword, ios::pword**

Operators

ios::operator void* ()

operator void* () const;

An operator that converts a stream to a pointer that can be compared to 0

Return Value   The conversion returns 0 if either **failbit** or **badbit** is set in the stream's error state.See **rdstate** for a description of the error state masks. A nonzero pointer is not meant to be dereferenced.

See Also   **ios::good, ios::fail**

ios::operator ! ()

int operator !() const;

Return Value   Returns a nonzero value if either **failbit** or **badbit** is set in the stream's error state. See **rdstate** for a description of the error state masks.

See Also   **ios::good, ios::fail**

ios::adjustfield

static const long adjustfield;

Remarks   A mask for obtaining the padding flag bits (**left, right,** or **internal**).

See Also	**ios::flags**
Example	```

```
extern ostream os;
if( ( os.flags() & ios::adjustfield ) == ios::left ) .....
```

ios::basefield

static const long basefield;

Remarks	A mask for obtaining the current radix flag bits (**dec**, **oct**, or **hex**).
See Also	**ios::flags**
Example	

```
extern ostream os;
if( ( os.flags() & ios::basefield ) == ios::hex ) .....
```

ios::floatfield

static const long floatfield;

Remarks	A mask for obtaining floating-point format flag bits (**scientific** or **fixed**).
See Also	**ios::flags**
Example	

```
extern ostream os;
if( ( os.flags() & ios::floatfield ) == ios::scientific ) .....
```

Manipulators

ios& binary

binary

Remarks	Sets the stream's mode to binary. The default mode is text.
	The stream must have an associated **filebuf** buffer.
See Also	**ios text** manipulator, **ofstream::setmode**, **ifstream::setmode**, **filebuf::setmode**

ios& dec

dec

Remarks   Sets the format conversion base to 10 (decimal).

See Also   **ios hex** manipulator, **ios oct** manipulator

ios& hex

hex

Remarks   Sets the format conversion base to 16 (hexadecimal).

See Also   **ios dec** manipulator, **ios oct** manipulator

ios& oct

oct

Remarks   Sets the format conversion base to 8 (octal).

See Also   **ios dec** manipulator, **ios hex** manipulator

resetiosflags

SMANIP(long) resetiosflags(long *lFlags*);

#include <iomanip.h>

Parameter   *lFlags*
        Format flag bit values. See the **flags** member function for a list of format flags.
        To combine these flags, use the OR (I) operator.

Remarks   This parameterized manipulator clears only the specified format flags. This setting
remains in effect until you change it.

setfill

SMANIP(int) setfill(int *nFill*);

#include <iomanip.h>

Parameter

nFill
    The new fill character to be used as padding between fields.

Remarks

This parameterized manipulator sets the stream's fill character. The default is a space. This setting remains in effect until the next change.

---

setiosflags

SMANIP(long) setiosflags(long *lFlags*);

#include <iomanip.h>

Parameter

lFlags
    Format flag bit values. See the **flags** member function for a list of format flags. To combine these flags, use the OR (|) operator.

Remarks

This parameterized manipulator sets only the specified format flags. This setting remains in effect until the next change.

---

setprecision

SMANIP(int) setprecision(int *np*);

#include <iomanip.h>

Parameter

np
    An integer that indicates the number of significant digits or significant decimal digits to be used for floating-point display.

Remarks

This parameterized manipulator sets the stream's internal floating-point precision variable to *np*. The default precision is six digits. If the display format is scientific or fixed, then the precision indicates the number of digits after the decimal point. If the format is automatic (neither floating point nor fixed), then the precision indicates the total number of significant digits. This setting remains in effect until the next change.

setw

SMANIP(int) setw(int *nw* **);**

#include <iomanip.h>

Parameter

nw
> The field width in characters.

Remarks

This parameterized manipulator sets the stream's internal field width parameter. See the **width** member function for more information. This setting remains in effect only for the next insertion.

---

ios& text

text

Sets the stream's mode to text (the default mode).

Remarks

The stream must have an associated **filebuf** buffer.

See Also

ios binary manipulator, **ofstream::setmode**, **ifstream::setmode**, **filebuf::setmode**

class iostream : public istream, public ostream

#include <iostream.h>

The **iostream** class provides the basic capability for sequential and random-access I/O. It inherits functionality from the **istream** and **ostream** classes.

The **iostream** class works in conjunction with classes derived from **streambuf** (for example, **filebuf**). In fact, most of the **iostream** "personality" comes from its attached **streambuf** class. You can use **iostream** objects for sequential disk I/O if you first construct an appropriate **filebuf** object. More often, you will use objects of classes **fstream** and **strstream**.

Derivation

For derivation suggestions, see the **istream** and **ostream** classes.

Public Members

iostream

Constructs an **iostream** object that is attached to an existing **streambuf** object.

~iostream

Destroys an **iostream** object.

Protected Members

iostream

Acts as a **void**-argument **iostream** constructor.

See Also

istream, ostream, fstream, strstream, stdiostream

Member Functions

iostream::iostream

Public →
iostream(streambuf* *psb* **);**
END Public

Protected →
iostream( );
END Protected

Parameter   *psb*
> A pointer to an existing **streambuf** object (or an object of a derived class).

Remarks   Constructs an object of type **iostream**.

See Also   **ios::init**

---

iostream::~iostream

virtual ~iostream();

Remarks   Virtual destructor for the **iostream** class.

class Iostream_init

#include <iostream.h>

The **Iostream_init** class is a static class that initializes the predefined stream objects **cin**, **cout**, **cerr**, and **clog**. A single object of this class is constructed "invisibly" in response to any reference to the predefined objects. The class is documented for completeness only. You will not normally construct objects of this class.

Public Members

Iostream_init
> A constructor that initializes **cin**, **cout**, **cerr**, and **clog**.

~Iostream_init
> The destructor for the **Iostream_init** class.

Member Functions

Iostream_init::Iostream_init

Iostream_init();

Remarks   **Iostream_init** constructor that initializes **cin**, **cout**, **cerr**, and **clog**. For internal use only.

Iostream_init::~Iostream_init

~Iostream_init();

Remarks   **Iostream_init** destructor. For internal use only.

class istream : virtual public ios

#include <iostream.h>

The **istream** class provides the basic capability for sequential and random-access input. An **istream** object has a **streambuf**-derived object attached, and the two classes work together; the **istream** class does the formatting, and the **streambuf** class does the low-level buffered input.

You can use **istream** objects for sequential disk input if you first construct an appropriate **filebuf** object. More often, you will use the predefined stream object **cin** (which is actually an object of class **istream_withassign**), or you will use objects of classes **ifstream** (disk file streams) and **istrstream** (string streams).

Derivation

It is not always necessary to derive from **istream** to add functionality to a stream; consider deriving from **streambuf** instead, as illustrated in "Deriving Your Own Stream Classes" on page 24. The **ifstream** and **istrstream** classes are examples of **istream**-derived classes that construct member objects of predetermined derived **streambuf** classes. You can add manipulators without deriving a new class.

If you add new extraction operators for a derived **istream** class, then the rules of C++ dictate that you must reimplement all the base class extraction operators. See the "Derivation" section of class **ostream** for an efficient reimplementation technique.

Construction/Destruction—Public Members

istream

Constructs an **istream** object attached to an existing object of a **streambuf**-derived class.

~istream

Destroys an **istream** object.

Prefix/Suffix Functions—Public Members

ipfx

Check for error conditions prior to extraction operations (input prefix function).

isfx

Called after extraction operations (input suffix function).

Input Functions—Public Members

get

Extracts characters from the stream up to, but not including, delimiters.

getline

Extracts characters from the stream (extracts and discards delimiters).

read
> Extracts data from the stream.

ignore
> Extracts and discards characters.

peek
> Returns a character without extracting it from the stream.

gcount
> Counts the characters extracted in the last unformatted operation.

eatwhite
> Extracts leading white space.

Other Functions — Public Members

putback
> Puts characters back to the stream.

sync
> Synchronizes the stream buffer with the external source of characters.

seekg
> Changes the stream's get pointer.

tellg
> Gets the value of the stream's get pointer.

Operators — Public Members

operator >>
> Extraction operator for various types.

Protected Members

istream
> Constructs an **istream** object.

Manipulators

ws
> Extracts leading white space.

See Also   **streambuf, ifstream, istrstream, istream_withassign**

Member Functions

istream::eatwhite

void eatwhite();

Remarks   Extracts white space from the stream by advancing the get pointer past spaces and tabs.

See Also   **istream ws** manipulator

istream::gcount

int gcount() const;

Remarks   Returns the number of characters extracted by the last unformatted input function. Formatted extraction operators may call unformatted input functions and thus reset this number.

See Also   **istream::get, istream::getline, istream::ignore, istream::read**

istream::get

int get();&

istream& get(char* *pch*, **int** *nCount*, **char** *delim* = '\n');

istream& get(unsigned char* *puch*, **int** *nCount*, **char** *delim* = '\n');

istream& get(signed char* *psch*, **int** *nCount*, **char** *delim* = '\n');& **istream& get(char&** *rch*);

istream& get(unsigned char& *ruch*);

istream& get(signed char& *rsch*);& **istream& get(streambuf&** *rsb*, **char** *delim* = '\n');

Parameters	*pch, puch, psch*
	A pointer to a character array.
	nCount
	The maximum number of characters to store, including the terminating **NULL**.
	delim
	The delimiter character (defaults to newline).
	rch, ruch, rsch
	A reference to a character.
	rsb
	A reference to an object of a **streambuf**-derived class.

Remarks   These functions extract data from an input stream as follows:

Variation	Description
get();	Extracts a single character from the stream and returns it.
get(char*, int, char);	Extracts characters from the stream until either *delim* is found, the limit *nCount* is reached, or the end of file is reached. The characters are stored in the array followed by a null terminator.
get(char&);	Extracts a single character from the stream and stores it as specified by the reference argument.
get(streambuf&, char);	Gets characters from the stream and stores them in a **streambuf** object until the delimiter is found or the end of the file is reached. The **ios::failbit** flag is set if the **streambuf** output operation fails.

In all cases, the delimiter is neither extracted from the stream nor returned by the function. The **getline** function, in contrast, extracts but does not store the delimiter.

See Also   **istream::getline**, **istream::read**, **istream::ignore**, **istream::gcount**

---

istream::getline

istream& getline(char* *pch*, **int** *nCount*, **char** *delim* = '\n');

istream& getline(unsigned char* *puch*, **int** *nCount*, **char** *delim* = '\n');

istream& getline(signed char* *psch*, **int** *nCount*, **char** *delim* = '\n');

Parameters *pch, puch, psch*
A pointer to a character array.

nCount
The maximum number of characters to store, including the terminating **NULL**.

delim
The delimiter character (defaults to newline).

Remarks Extracts characters from the stream until either the delimiter *delim* is found, the limit *nCount*–1 is reached, or end of file is reached. The characters are stored in the specified array followed by a null terminator. If the delimiter is found, it is extracted but not stored.

The **get** function, in contrast, neither extracts nor stores the delimiter.

See Also **istream::get**, **istream::read**

istream::ignore

istream& ignore(int *nCount* **= 1, int** *delim* **= EOF);**

Parameters *nCount*
The maximum number of characters to extract.

delim
The delimiter character (defaults to **EOF**).

Remarks Extracts and discards up to *nCount* characters. Extraction stops if the delimiter *delim* is extracted or the end of file is reached. If *delim* = **EOF** (the default), then only the end of file condition causes termination. The delimiter character is extracted.

istream::ipfx

int ipfx(int *need* **= 0);**

Return Value A nonzero return value if the operation was successful; 0 if the stream's error state is nonzero, in which case the function does nothing.

Parameter *need*
Zero if called from formatted input functions; otherwise the minimum number of characters needed.

Remarks	This input prefix function is called by input functions prior to extracting data from the stream. Formatted input functions call **ipfx(0)**, while unformatted input functions usually call **ipfx(1)**.

Any **ios** object tied to this stream is flushed if *need* = 0 or if there are fewer than *need* characters in the input buffer. Also, **ipfx** extracts leading white space if **ios::skipws** is set.

See Also   **istream::isfx**

---

istream::isfx

void isfx();

Remarks   This input suffix function is called at the end of every extraction operation.

---

istream::istream

Public →
istream(streambuf* *psb*);
END Public

Protected →
istream( );
END Protected

Parameter   *psb*
    A pointer to an existing object of a **streambuf**-derived class.

Remarks   Constructs an object of type **istream**.

See Also   **ios::init**

---

istream::~istream

virtual ~istream();

Remarks   Virtual destructor for the **istream** class.

istream::peek

int peek();

Return Value   Returns the next character without extracting it from the stream. Returns **EOF** if the stream is at end of file or if the **ipfx** function indicates an error.

---

istream::putback

istream& putback(char *ch* **);**

Parameter   *ch*
                  The character to put back; must be the character previously extracted.

Remarks   Puts a character back into the input stream. The **putback** function may fail and set the error state. If *ch* does not match the character that was previously extracted, the result is undefined.

---

istream::read

istream& read(char* *pch*, **int** *nCount* **);**

istream& read(unsigned char* *puch*, **int** *nCount* **);**

istream& read(signed char* *psch*, **int** *nCount* **);**

Parameters   *pch, puch, psch*
                  A pointer to a character array.

                  nCount
                  The maximum number of characters to read.

Remarks   Extracts bytes from the stream until the limit *nCount* is reached or until the end of file is reached. The **read** function is useful for binary stream input.

See Also   **istream::get, istream::getline, istream::gcount, istream::ignore**

istream::seekg

istream& seekg(streampos *pos* **);**

istream& seekg(streamoff *off*, **ios::seek_dir** *dir* **);**

Parameters

pos
    The new position value; **streampos** is a **typedef** equivalent to **long**.

off
    The new offset value; **streamoff** is a **typedef** equivalent to **long**.

dir
    The seek direction. Must be one of the following enumerators:

- **ios::beg**   Seek from the beginning of the stream.
- **ios::cur**   Seek from the current position in the stream.
- **ios::end**   Seek from the end of the stream.

Remarks

Changes the get pointer for the stream. Not all derived classes of **istream** need support positioning; it is most often used with file-based streams.

See Also

istream::tellg, ostream::seekp, ostream::tellp

istream::sync

int sync();

Synchronizes the stream's internal buffer with the external source of characters.

Return Value

EOF to indicate errors.

Remarks

Synchronizes the stream's internal buffer with the external source of characters. This function calls the virtual **streambuf::sync** function so you can customize its implementation by deriving a new class from **streambuf**.

See Also

streambuf::sync

istream::tellg

streampos tellg();

Gets the value for the stream's **get** pointer.

Return Value   A **streampos** type, corresponding to a **long**.

See Also   **istream::seekg, ostream::tellp, ostream::seekp**

Operators

istream::operator >>

istream& operator >>(char* *psz* **);**

istream& operator >>(unsigned char* *pusz* **);**

istream& operator >>(signed char* *pssz* **);**

istream& operator >>(char& *rch* **);**

istream& operator >>(unsigned char& *ruch* **);**

istream& operator >>(signed char& *rsch* **);**

istream& operator >>(short& *s* **);**

istream& operator >>(unsigned short& *us* **);**

istream& operator >>(int& *n* **);**

istream& operator >>(unsigned int& *un* **);**

istream& operator >>(long& *l* **);**

istream& operator >>(unsigned long& *ul* **);**

istream& operator >>(float& *f* **);**

istream& operator >>(double& *d* **);**

istream& operator >>(long double& *ld* **);** (16-bit only)

istream& operator >>(streambuf* *psb* **);**

istream& operator >>(istream& (**fcn***)(istream&));**

istream& operator >>(ios& (**fcn***)(ios&));**

Remarks   These overloaded operators extract their argument from the stream. With the last
two variations, you can use manipulators that are defined for both **istream** and **ios**.

Manipulators

istream& ws

ws

Remarks Extracts leading white space from the stream by calling the **eatwhite** function.

See Also **istream::eatwhite**

class istream_withassign : public istream

#include <iostream.h>

The **istream_withassign** class is a variant of **istream** that allows object assignment. The predefined object **cin** is an object of this class and thus may be reassigned at run time to a different **istream** object. For example, a program that normally expects input from **stdin** could be temporarily directed to accept its input from a disk file.

Predefined Objects

The **cin** object is a predefined object of class **ostream_withassign**. It is connected to **stdin** (standard input, file descriptor 0).

The objects **cin**, **cerr**, and **clog** are tied to **cout** so that use of any of these may cause **cout** to be flushed.

Construction/Destruction — Public Members
istream_withassign
　　Constructs an **istream_withassign** object.

~istream_withassign
　　Destroys an **istream_withassign** object.

Operators—Public Members
operator =
　　Indicates an assignment operator.

See Also　　**ostream_withassign**

Member Functions

istream_withassign::istream_withassign

istream_wit

hassign(streambuf* *psb* **);**

istream_withassign();

Parameter　　*psb*
　　A pointer to an existing object of a **streambuf**-derived class.

Remarks   The first constructor creates a ready-to-use object of type **istream_withassign**, complete with attached **streambuf** object.

The second constructor creates an object but does not initialize it. You must subsequently use the second variation of the **istream_withassign** assignment operator to attach the **streambuf** object, or use the first variation to initialize this object to match the specified **istream** object.

See Also   **istream_withassign::operator =**

istream_withassign::~istream_withassign

~**istream_withassign**();

Remarks   Destructor for the **istream_withassign** class.

Operators

istream_withassign::operator =

istream& operator =(const istream& *ris* **);**

istream& operator =(streambuf* *psb* **);**

Remarks   The first overloaded assignment operator assigns the specified **istream** object to this **istream_withassign** object.

The second operator attaches a **streambuf** object to an existing **istream_withassign** object, and it initializes the state of the **istream_withassign** object. This operator is often used in conjunction with the **void**-argument constructor.

See Also   **istream_withassign::istream_withassign, cin**

Example

```
char buffer[100];
class xistream; // A special-purpose class derived from istream
extern xistream xin; // An xistream object constructed elsewhere

cin = xin; // cin is reassigned to xin
cin >> buffer; // xin used instead of cin
```

Example

```
char buffer[100];
extern filedesc fd; // A file descriptor for an open file
filebuf fb( fd ); // Construct a filebuf attached to fd

cin = &fb;      // fb associated with cin
cin >> buffer; // cin now gets its intput from the fb file
```

class istrstream : public istream

#include <strstrea.h>

The **istrstream** class supports input streams that have character arrays as a source. You must allocate a character array before constructing an **istrstream** object. You can use **istream** operators and functions on this character data. A get pointer, working in the attached **strstreambuf** class, advances as you extract fields from the stream's array. Use **istream::seekg** to go backwards. If the get pointer reaches the end of the string (and sets the **ios::eof** flag), you must call **clear** before **seekg**.

Construction/Destruction — Public Members

istrstream
> Constructs an **istrstream** object.

~istrstream
> Destroys an **istrstream** object.

Other Functions — Public Members

rdbuf
> Returns a pointer to the stream's associated **strstreambuf** object.

str
> Returns a character array pointer to the string stream's contents.

See Also   **strstreambuf, streambuf, strstream, ostrstream**

Member Functions

istrstream::istrstream

istrstream(char* *psz* **);**

istrstream(char* *pch*, **int** *nLength* **);**

Parameters   *psz*
> A null-terminated character array (string).

pch
> A character array that is not necessarily null terminated.

nLength
> Size (in characters) of *pch*. If 0, then *pch* is assumed to point to a null-terminated array; if less than 0, then the array length is assumed to be unlimited.

Remarks   The first constructor uses the specified *psz* buffer to make an **istrstream** object with length corresponding to the string length.

The second constructor makes an **istrstream** object out of the first *nLength* characters of the *pch* buffer.

Both constructors automatically construct a **strstreambuf** object that manages the specified character buffer.

istrstream::~istrstream

~istrstream();

Remarks   Destroys an **istrstream** object and its associated **strstreambuf** object. The character buffer is not released because it was allocated by the user prior to **istrstream** construction.

istrstream::rdbuf

strstreambuf* rdbuf() const;

Return Value   Returns a pointer to the **strstreambuf** buffer object that is associated with this stream. Note that this is not the character buffer itself; the **strstreambuf** object contains a pointer to the character area.

See Also   **istrstream::str**

istrstream::str

char* str();

Return Value   Returns a pointer to the string stream's character array. This pointer corresponds to the array used to construct the **istrstream** object.

See Also   **istrstream::istrstream**

class ofstream : public ostream

#include <fstream.h>

The **ofstream** class is an **ostream** derivative specialized for disk file output. All of its constructors automatically create and associate a **filebuf** buffer object.

The **filebuf** class documentation describes the get and put areas and their associated pointers. Only the put area and the put pointer are active for the **ofstream** class.

Construction/Destruction — Public Members

ofstream
Constructs an **ofstream** object.

~ofstream
Destroys an **ofstream** object.

Operations — Public Members

open
Opens a file and attaches it to the **filebuf** object and thus to the stream.

close
Flushes any waiting output and closes the stream's file.

setbuf
Associates the specified reserve area to the stream's **filebuf** object.

setmode
Sets the stream's mode to binary or text.

attach
Attaches the stream (through the **filebuf** object) to an open file.

Status/Information — Public Members

rdbuf
Gets the stream's **filebuf** object.

fd
Returns the file descriptor associated with the stream.

is_open
Tests whether the stream's file is open.

See Also   **filebuf, streambuf, ifstream, fstream**

Member Functions

ofstream::attach

void attach(filedesc *fd* **);**

Parameter   *fd*

A file descriptor as returned by a call to the run-time function **_open** or **_sopen**; **filedesc** is a **typedef** equivalent to **int**.

Remarks   Attaches this stream to the open file specified by *fd*. The function fails when the stream is already attached to a file. In that case, the function sets **ios::failbit** in the stream's error state.

See Also   **filebuf::attach**, **ofstream::fd**

ofstream::close

void close();

Remarks   Calls the **close** member function for the associated **filebuf** object. This function, in turn, flushes any waiting output, closes the file, and disconnects the file from the **filebuf** object. The **filebuf** object is not destroyed.

The stream's error state is cleared unless the call to **filebuf::close** fails.

See Also   **filebuf::close**, **ofstream::open**, **ofstream::is_open**

ofstream::fd

filedesc fd() const;

Return Value   Returns the file descriptor associated with the stream. **filedesc** is a **typedef** equivalent to **int**. Its value is supplied by the underlying file system.

See Also   **filebuf::fd**, **ofstream::attach**

ofstream::is_open

int is_open() const;

Return Value   Returns a nonzero value if this stream is attached to an open disk file identified by a file descriptor; otherwise 0.

See Also   **filebuf::is_open**, **ofstream::open**, **ofstream::close**

---

ofstream::ofstream

ofstream();

ofstream(const char* *szName*, **int** *nMode* = **ios::out, int** *nProt* = **filebuf::openprot);**

ofstream(filedesc *fd* **);**

ofstream(filedesc *fd*, **char*** *pch*, **int** *nLength* **);**

Parameters   *szName*
The name of the file to be opened during construction.

nMode
An integer that contains mode bits defined as **ios** enumerators that can be combined with the bitwise OR (|) operator. The *nMode* parameter must have one of the following values:

- **ios::app**   The function performs a seek to the end of file. When new bytes are written to the file, they are always appended to the end, even if the position is moved with the **ostream::seekp** function.

- **ios::ate**   The function performs a seek to the end of file. When the first new byte is written to the file, it is appended to the end, but when subsequent bytes are written, they are written to the current position.

- **ios::in**   If this mode is specified, then the original file (if it exists) will not be truncated.

- **ios::out**   The file is opened for output (implied for all **ofstream** objects).

- **ios::trunc**   If the file already exists, its contents are discarded. This mode is implied if **ios::out** is specified and **ios::ate**, **ios::app**, and **ios:in** are not specified.

- **ios::nocreate**   If the file does not already exist, the function fails.

- **ios::noreplace**   If the file already exists, the function fails.

- **ios::binary**   Opens the file in binary mode (the default is text mode).

nProt

The file protection specification; defaults to the static integer **filebuf::openprot** that is equivalent to **filebuf::sh_compat**. The possible *nProt* values are:

- **filebuf::sh_compat**   Compatibility share mode.
- **filebuf::sh_none**   Exclusive mode; no sharing.
- **filebuf::sh_read**   Read sharing allowed.
- **filebuf::sh_write**   Write sharing allowed.

To combine the **filebuf::sh_read** and **filebuf::sh_write** modes, use the logical OR (‖) operator.

fd

A file descriptor as returned by a call to the run-time function **_open** or **_sopen**; **filedesc** is a **typedef** equivalent to **int**.

pch

Pointer to a previously allocated reserve area of length *nLength*. A **NULL** value (or *nLength* = 0) indicates that the stream will be unbuffered.

nLength

The length (in bytes) of the reserve area (0 = unbuffered).

Remarks

The four **ofstream** constructors are:

Constructor	Description
ofstream()	Constructs an **ofstream** object without opening a file.
ofstream(const char*, int, int)	Contructs an **ofstream** object, opening the specified file.
ofstream(filedesc)	Constructs an **ofstream** object that is attached to an open file.
ofstream(filedesc, char*, int)	Constructs an **ofstream** object that is associated with a **filebuf** object. The **filebuf** object is attached to an open file and to a specified reserve area.

All **ofstream** constructors construct a **filebuf** object. The first three use an internally allocated reserve area, but the fourth uses a user-allocated area. The user-allocated area is not automatically released during destruction.

ofstream::~ofstream

~ofstream();

Remarks

Flushes the buffer, then destroys an **ofstream** object along with its associated **filebuf** object. The file is closed only if was opened by the constructor or by the **open** member function.

The **filebuf** destructor releases the reserve buffer only if it was internally allocated.

ofstream::open

void **open**(const char* *szName*, int *nMode* = **ios::out**, int *nProt* = **filebuf::openprot**);

Parameters

szName
    The name of the file to be opened during construction.

nMode
    An integer containing mode bits defined as **ios** enumerators that can be combined with the OR (|) operator. See the **ofstream** constructor for a list of the enumerators. The **ios::out** mode is implied.

nProt
    The file protection specification; defaults to the static integer **filebuf::openprot**. See the **ofstream** constructor for a list of the other allowed values.

Remarks

Opens a disk file and attaches it to the stream's **filebuf** object. If the **filebuf** object is already attached to an open file, or if a **filebuf** call fails, the **ios::failbit** is set. If the file is not found, the **ios::failbit** is set only if the **ios::nocreate** mode was used.

See Also

filebuf::open, **ofstream::ofstream**, **ofstream::close**, **ofstream::is_open**

ofstream::rdbuf

filebuf* rdbuf() const;

Return Value

Returns a pointer to the **filebuf** buffer object that is associated with this stream. (Note that this is not the character buffer; the **filebuf** object contains a pointer to the character area.)

Example

```
extern ofstream ofs;
int fd = ofs.rdbuf()->fd(); // Get the file descriptor for ofs
```

ofstream::setbuf

streambuf* setbuf(char* *pch*, **int** *nLength* **);**

Attaches the specified reserve area to the stream's **filebuf** object.

Return Value

If the file is open and a buffer has already been allocated, the function returns **NULL**; otherwise it returns a pointer to the **filebuf** cast as a **streambuf**. The reserve area will not be released by the destructor.

Parameters

pch

A pointer to a previously allocated reserve area of length *nLength*. A **NULL** value indicates an unbuffered stream.

nLength

The length (in bytes) of the reserve area. A length of 0 indicates an unbuffered stream.

ofstream::setmode

int setmode(int *nMode* **= filebuf::text);**

Return Value

The previous mode; –1 if the parameter is invalid, the file is not open, or the mode cannnot be changed.

Parameter

nMode

An integer that must be one of the following static **filebuf** constants:

- **filebuf::text**   Text mode (newline characters translated to and from carriage return–linefeed pairs).
- **filebuf::binary**   Binary mode (no translation).

Remarks

This function sets the binary/text mode of the stream's **filebuf** object. It may be called only after the file is opened.

See Also

ios binary manipulator, **ios text** manipulator

class ostream : virtual public ios

#include <iostream.h>

The **ostream** class provides the basic capability for sequential and random-access output. An **ostream** object has a **streambuf**-derived object attached, and the two classes work together; the **ostream** class does the formatting, and the **streambuf** class does the low-level buffered output.

You can use **ostream** objects for sequential disk output if you first construct an appropriate **filebuf** object. (The **filebuf** class is derived from **streambuf**.) More often, you will use the predefined stream objects **cout**, **cerr**, and **clog** (actually objects of class **ostream_withassign**), or you will use objects of classes **ofstream** (disk file streams) and **ostrstream** (string streams).

All of the **ostream** member functions write unformatted data; formatted output is handled by the insertion operators.

Derivation

It is not always necessary to derive from **ostream** to add functionality to a stream; consider deriving from **streambuf** instead, as illustrated in "Deriving Your Own Stream Classes" on page 24. The **ofstream** and **ostrstream** classes are examples of **ostream**-derived classes that construct member objects of predetermined derived **streambuf** classes. You can add manipulators without deriving a new class.

If you add new insertion operators for a derived **ostream** class, then the rules of C++ dictate that you must reimplement all the base class insertion operators. If, however, you reimplement the operators through inline equivalence, no extra code will be generated.

Construction/Destruction — Public Members

ostream
> Constructs an **ostream** object that is attached to an existing **streambuf** object.

~ostream
> Destroys an **ostream** object.

Prefix/Suffix Functions — Public Members

opfx
> Output prefix function, called prior to insertion operations to check for error conditions, and so forth.

osfx
> Output suffix function, called after insertion operations; flushes the stream's buffer if it is unit buffered.

Unformatted Output — Public Members

put

Inserts a single byte into the stream.

write

Inserts a series of bytes into the stream.

Other Functions — Public Members

flush

Flushes the buffer associated with this stream.

seekp

Changes the stream's put pointer.

tellp

Gets the value of the stream's put pointer.

Operators — Public Members

operator <<

Insertion operator for various types.

Manipulators

endl

Inserts a newline sequence and flushes the buffer.

ends

Inserts a null character to terminate a string.

flush

Flushes the stream's buffer.

Example

```
class xstream : public ostream
{
public:
    // Constructors, etc.
    // ........
    inline xstream& operator << ( char ch ) // insertion for char
    {
        return (xstream&)ostream::operator << ( ch );
    }
    // ........
    // Insertions for other types
};
```

See Also   **streambuf, ofstream, ostrstream, cout, cerr, clog**

Member Functions

ostream::flush

ostream& flush();

Remarks   Flushes the buffer associated with this stream. The **flush** function calls the **sync** function of the associated **streambuf**.

See Also   **ostream flush** manipulator, **streambuf::sync**

ostream::opfx

int opfx();

Return Value   If the **ostream** object's error state is not 0, **opfx** returns 0 immediately; otherwise it returns a nonzero value.

Remarks   This output prefix function is called before every insertion operation. If another **ostream** object is tied to this stream, the **opfx** function flushes that stream.

ostream::osfx

void osfx();

Remarks   This output suffix function is called after every insertion operation. It flushes the **ostream** object if **ios::unitbuf** is set, or **stdout** and **stderr** if **ios::stdio** is set.

ostream::ostream

Public →
ostream(streambuf* *psb* **);**
End Public

Protected →
ostream( );
END Protected

Parameter	*psb*
	A pointer to an existing object of a **streambuf**-derived class.
Remarks	Constructs an object of type **ostream**.
See Also	**ios::init**

ostream::~ostream

virtual ~ostream();

Remarks   Destroys an **ostream** object. The output buffer is flushed as appropriate. The attached **streambuf** object is destroyed only if it was allocated internally within the **ostream** constructor.

ostream::put

ostream& put(char *ch* **);**

Parameter   *ch*
The character to insert.

Remarks   This function inserts a single character into the output stream.

ostream::seekp

ostream& seekp(streampos *pos* **);**

ostream& seekp(streamoff *off*, **ios::seek_dir** *dir* **);**

Parameters   *pos*
The new position value; **streampos** is a **typedef** equivalent to **long**.

off
The new offset value; **streamoff** is a **typedef** equivalent to **long**.

dir
The seek direction specified by the enumerated type **ios::seek_dir**, with values including:

- **ios::beg**   Seek from the beginning of the stream.

- **ios::cur**   Seek from the current position in the stream.
- **ios::end**   Seek from the end of the stream.

Remarks   Changes the position value for the stream. Not all derived classes of **ostream** need support positioning. For file streams, the position is the byte offset from the beginning of the file; for string streams, it is the byte offset from the beginning of the string.

See Also   **ostream::tellp**, **istream::seekg**, **istream::tellg**

ostream::tellp

streampos tellp();

Return Value   A **streampos** type that corresponds to a **long**.

Remarks   Gets the position value for the stream. Not all derived classes of **ostream** need support positioning. For file streams, the position is the byte offset from the beginning of the file; for string streams, it is the byte offset from the beginning of the string. Gets the value for the stream's put pointer.

See Also   **ostream::seekp**, **istream::tellg**, **istream::seekg**

ostream::write

ostream& write(const char* *pch*, **int** *nCount* **);**

ostream& write(const unsigned char* *puch*, **int** *nCount* **);**

ostream& write(const signed char* *psch*, **int** *nCount* **);**

Parameters   *pch, puch, psch*
A pointer to a character array.

nCount
The number of characters to be written.

Remarks   Inserts a specified number of bytes from a buffer into the stream. If the underlying file was opened in text mode, additional carriage return characters may be inserted. The **write** function is useful for binary stream output.

Operators

ostream::operator <<

ostream& operator <<(char *ch* **);**

ostream& operator <<(unsigned char *uch* **);**

ostream& operator <<(signed char *sch* **);**

ostream& operator <<(const char* *psz* **);**

ostream& operator <<(const unsigned char* *pusz* **);**

ostream& operator <<(const signed char* *pssz* **);**

ostream& operator <<(short *s* **);**

ostream& operator <<(unsigned short *us* **);**

ostream& operator <<(int *n* **);**

ostream& operator <<(unsigned int *un* **);**

ostream& operator <<(long *l* **);**

ostream& operator <<(unsigned long *ul* **);**

ostream& operator <<(float *f* **);**

ostream& operator <<(double *d* **);**

ostream& operator <<(long double *ld* **);** (16-bit only)

ostream& operator <<(const void* *pv* **);**

ostream& operator <<(streambuf* *psb* **);**

ostream& operator <<(ostream& (*fcn***)(ostream&));**

ostream& operator <<(ios& (*fcn***)(ios&));**

Remarks   These overloaded operators insert their argument into the stream. With the last two
variations, you can use manipulators that are defined for both **ostream** and **ios**.

Manipulators

ostream& endl

endl

Remarks   This manipulator, when inserted into an output stream, inserts a newline character and then flushes the buffer.

ostream& ends

ends

Remarks   This manipulator, when inserted into an output stream, inserts a null-terminator character. It is particularly useful for **ostrstream** objects.

ostream& flush

flush

Remarks   This manipulator, when inserted into an output stream, flushes the output buffer by calling the **streambuf::sync** member function.

See Also   **ostream::flush, streambuf::sync**

class ostream_withassign : public ostream

#include <iostream.h>

The **ostream_withassign** class is a variant of **ostream** that allows object assignment. The predefined objects **cout**, **cerr**, and **clog** are objects of this class and thus may be reassigned at run time to a different **ostream** object. For example, a program that normally sends output to **stdout** could be temporarily directed to send its output to a disk file.

Predefined Objects

The three predefined objects of class **ostream_withassign** are connected as follows:

cout   Standard output (file descriptor 1).

cerr   Unit buffered standard error (file descriptor 2).

clog   Fully buffered standard error (file descriptor 2).

Unit buffering, as used by **cerr**, means that characters are flushed after each insertion operation. The objects **cin**, **cerr**, and **clog** are tied to **cout** so that use of any of these will cause **cout** to be flushed.

Construction/Destruction — Public Members

ostream_withassign
    Constructs an **ostream_withassign** object.

~ostream_withassign
    Destroys an **ostream_withassign** object.

Operators — Public Members

operator =
    Assignment operator.

See Also   **istream_withassign**

Member Functions

ostream_withassign::ostream_withassign

ostream_withassign(streambuf * *psb* **);**

ostream_withassign();

Parameter *psb*
A pointer to an existing object of a **streambuf**-derived class.

Remarks The first constructor makes a ready-to-use object of type **ostream_withassign**,
with an attached **streambuf** object.

The second constructor makes an object but does not initialize it. You must
subsequently use the **streambuf** assignment operator to attach the **streambuf**
object, or use the **ostream** assignment operator to initialize this object to match the
specified object.

See Also **ostream_withassign::operator =**

ostream_withassign::~ostream_withassign

~ostream_withassign();

Remarks Destructor for the **ostream_withassign** class.

Operators

ostream_withassign::operator =

ostream& operator =(const ostream&_os);

ostream& operator =(streambuf*_sp_ **);**

Remarks   The first overloaded assignment operator assigns the specified **ostream** object to this **ostream_withassign** object.

The second operator attaches a **streambuf** object to an existing **ostream_withassign** object, and initializes the state of the **ostream_withassign** object. This operator is often used in conjunction with the **void**-argument constructor.

See Also   **ostream_withassign::ostream_withassign, cout**

Example

```
filebuf fb( "test.dat" ); // Filebuf object attached to "test.dat"
cout = &fb;          // fb associated with cout
cout << "testing"; // Message goes to "test.dat" instead of stdout
```

class ostrstream : public ostream

#include <strstrea.h>

The **ostrstream** class supports output streams that have character arrays as a destination. You can allocate a character array prior to construction, or the constructor can internally allocate an expandable array. You can then use all the **ostream** operators and functions to fill the array.

Be aware that there is a put pointer working behind the scenes in the attached **strstreambuf** class. This pointer advances as you insert fields into the stream's array. The only way you can make it go backwards is to use the **ostream::seekp** function. If the put pointer reaches the end of user-allocated memory (and sets the **ios::eof** flag), you must call **clear** before **seekp**.

Construction/Destruction — Public Members

ostrstream
Constructs an **ostrstream** object.

~ostrstream
Destroys an **ostrstream** object.

Other Functions — Public Members

pcount
Returns the number of bytes that have been stored in the stream's buffer.

rdbuf
Returns a pointer to the stream's associated **strstreambuf** object.

str
Returns a character array pointer to the string stream's contents and freezes the array.

See Also   **strstreambuf, streambuf, strstream, istrstream**

Member Functions

ostrstream::ostrstream

ostrstream();

ostrstream(char* *pch*, **int** *nLength*, **int** *nMode* = **ios::out);**

Parameters

pch
A character array that is large enough to accommodate future output stream activity.

nLength
The size (in characters) of *pch*. If 0, then *pch* is assumed to point to a null-terminated array and **strlen(** *pch* **)** is used as the length; if less than 0, the array is assumed to have infinite length.

nMode
The stream-creation mode, which must be one of the following enumerators as defined in class **ios**:

- **ios::out**   Default; storing begins at *pch*.

- **ios::ate**   The *pch* parameter is assumed to be a null-terminated array; storing begins at the **NULL** character.

- **ios::app**   Same as **ios::ate**.

Remarks

The first constructor makes an **ostrstream** object that uses an internal, dynamic buffer.

The second constructor makes an **ostrstream** object out of the first *nLength* characters of the *pch* buffer. The stream will not accept characters once the length reaches *nLength*.

ostrstream::~ostrstream

~ostrstream();

Remarks

Destroys an **ostrstream** object and its associated **strstreambuf** object, thus releasing all internally allocated memory. If you used the **void**-argument constructor, the internally allocated character buffer is released; otherwise, you must release it.

An internally allocated character buffer will not be released if it was previously frozen by an **str** or **strstreambuf::freeze** function call.

See Also   **ostrstream::str**, **strstreambuf::freeze**

---

ostrstream::pcount

int pcount() const;

Return Value   Returns the number of bytes stored in the buffer. This information is especially useful when you have stored binary data in the object.

---

ostrstream::rdbuf

strstreambuf* rdbuf() const;

Return Value   Returns a pointer to the **strstreambuf** buffer object that is associated with this stream. This is not the character buffer; the **strstreambuf** object contains a pointer to the character area.

See Also   **ostrstream::str**

---

ostrstream::str

char* str();

Return Value   Returns a pointer to the internal character array. If the stream was built with the **void**-argument constructor, **str** freezes the array. You must not send characters to a frozen stream, and you are responsible for deleting the array. You can, however, subsequently unfreeze the array by calling **rdbuf->freeze(0)**.

If the stream was built with the constructor that specified the buffer, the pointer contains the same address as the array used to construct the **ostrstream** object.

See Also   **ostrstream::ostrstream**, **ostrstream::rdbuf**, **strstreambuf::freeze**

class stdiobuf : public streambuf

#include <stdiostr.h>

The run-time library supports three conceptual sets of I/O functions: iostreams (C++ only), standard I/O (the functions declared in STDIO.H), and low-level I/O (the functions declared in IO.H). The **stdiobuf** class is a derived class of **streambuf** that is specialized for buffering to and from the standard I/O system.

Because the standard I/O system does its own internal buffering, the extra buffering level provided by **stdiobuf** may reduce overall input/output efficiency. The **stdiobuf** class is useful when you need to mix iostream I/O with standard I/O (**printf** and so forth).

You can avoid use of the **stdiobuf** class if you use the **filebuf** class. You must also use the stream class's **ios::flags** member function to set the **ios::stdio** format flag value.

Construction/Destruction — Public Members
stdiobuf
> Constructs a **stdiobuf** object from a **FILE** pointer.

~stdiobuf
> Destroys a **stdiobuf** object.

Other Functions — Public Members
stdiofile
> Gets the file that is attached to the **stdiofile** object.

See Also   **stdiostream, filebuf, strstreambuf, ios::flags**

Member Functions

stdiobuf::stdiobuf

stdiobuf(FILE* *fp*);

Parameter   *fp*
> A standard I/O file pointer (can be obtained through an **fopen** or **_fsopen** call).

Remarks   Objects of class **stdiobuf** are constructed from open standard I/O files, including **stdin**, **stdout**, and **stderr**. The object is unbuffered by default.

stdiobuf::~stdiobuf

~stdiobuf();

Remarks   Destroys a **stdiobuf** object and, in the process, flushes the put area. The destructor does not close the attached file.

stdiobuf::stdiofile

FILE* stdiofile();

Remarks   Returns the standard I/O file pointer associated with a **stdiobuf** object.

class stdiostream : public iostream

#include <stdiostr.h>

The **stdiostream** class makes I/O calls (through the **stdiobuf** class) to the standard I/O system, which does its own internal buffering. Calls to the functions declared in STDIO.H, such as **printf**, can be mixed with **stdiostream** I/O calls.

This class is included for compatibility with earlier stream libraries. You can avoid use of the **stdiostream** class if you use the **ostream** or **istream** class with an associated **filebuf** class. You must also use the stream class's **ios::flags** member function to set the **ios::stdio** format flag value.

The use of the **stdiobuf** class may reduce efficiency because it imposes an extra level of buffering. Do not use this feature unless you need to mix iostream library calls with standard I/O calls for the same file.

Construction/Destruction — Public Members

stdiostream

Constructs a **stdiostream** object that is associated with a standard I/O **FILE** pointer.

~stdiostream

Destroys a **stdiostream** object (virtual).

Other Functions — Public Members

rdbuf

Gets the stream's **stdiobuf** object.

See Also   **stdiobuf, ios::flags**

Member Functions

stdiostream::rdbuf

stdiobuf* rdbuf() const;

Return Value   Returns a pointer to the **stdiobuf** buffer object that is associated with this stream. The **rdbuf** function is useful when you need to call **stdiobuf** member functions.

stdiostream::stdiostream

stdiostream(FILE* *fp* **);**

Parameter

fp

A standard I/O file pointer (can be obtained through an **fopen** or **_fsopen** call). Could be **stdin**, **stdout**, or **stderr**.

Remarks

Objects of class **stdiostream** are constructed from open standard I/O files. An unbuffered **stdiobuf** object is automatically associated, but the standard I/O system provides its own buffering.

Example

```
stdiostream myStream( stdout );
```

stdiostream::~stdiostream

~stdiostream();

Remarks

This destructor destroys the **stdiobuf** object associated with this stream; however, the attached file is not closed.

class streambuf

#include <iostream.h>

All the iostream classes in the **ios** hierarchy depend on an attached **streambuf** class for the actual I/O processing. This class is an abstract class, but the iostream class library contains the following derived buffer classes for use with streams:

- **filebuf**   Buffered disk file I/O.
- **strstreambuf**   Stream data held entirely within an in-memory byte array.
- **stdiobuf**   Disk I/O with buffering done by the underlying standard I/O system.

All **streambuf** objects, when configured for buffered processing, maintain a fixed memory buffer, called a reserve area, that can be dynamically partitioned into a get area for input, and a put area for output. These areas may or may not overlap. With the protected member functions, you can access and manipulate a get pointer for character retrieval and a put pointer for character storage. The exact behavior of the buffers and pointers depends on the implementation of the derived class.

The capabilities of the iostream classes can be extended significantly through the derivation of new **streambuf** classes. The **ios** class tree supplies the programming interface and all formatting features, but the **streambuf** class does the real work. The **ios** classes call the **streambuf** public members, including a set of virtual functions.

The **streambuf** class provides a default implementation of certain virtual member functions. The "Default Implementation" section for each such function suggests function behavior for the derived class.

Character Input Functions — Public Members

in_avail

Returns the number of characters in the get area.

sgetc

Returns the character at the get pointer, but does not move the pointer.

snextc

Advances the get pointer, then returns the next character.

sbumpc

Returns the current character, and then advances the get pointer.

stossc

Moves the get pointer forward one position, but does not return a character.

sputbackc
Attempts to move the get pointer back one position.

sgetn
Gets a sequence of characters from the **streambuf** object's buffer.

Character Output Functions—Public Members

out_waiting
Returns the number of characters in the put area.

sputc
Stores a character in the put area and advances the put pointer.

sputn
Stores a sequence of characters in the **streambuf** object's buffer and advances the put pointer.

Construction/Destruction—Public Members

~streambuf
Virtual destructor.

Diagnostic Functions—Public Members

dbp
Prints buffer statistics and pointer values.

Virtual Functions—Public Members

sync
Empties the get area and the put area.

setbuf
Attempts to attach a reserve area to the **streambuf** object.

seekoff
Seeks to a specified offset.

seekpos
Seeks to a specified position.

overflow
Empties the put area.

underflow
Fills the get area if necessary.

pbackfail
Augments the **sputbackc** function.

Construction/Destruction—Protected Members

streambuf
Constructors for use in derived classes.

Other Protected Member Functions — Protected Members

base

Returns a pointer to the start of the reserve area.

ebuf

Returns a pointer to the end of the reserve area.

blen

Returns the size of the reserve area.

pbase

Returns a pointer to the start of the put area.

pptr

Returns the put pointer.

epptr

Returns a pointer to the end of the put area.

eback

Returns the lower bound of the get area.

gptr

Returns the get pointer.

egptr

Returns a pointer to the end of the get area.

setp

Sets all the put area pointers.

setg

Sets all the get area pointers.

pbump

Increments the put pointer.

gbump

Increments the get pointer.

setb

Sets up the reserve area.

unbuffered

Tests or sets the **streambuf** buffer state variable.

allocate

Allocates a buffer, if needed, by calling **doalloc**.

doallocate

Allocates a reserve area (virtual function).

Member Functions

streambuf::allocate

Protected →
int allocate();
END Protected

Return Value   Calls the virtual function **doallocate** to set up a reserve area. If a reserve area already exists or if the **streambuf** object is unbuffered, **allocate** returns 0. If the space allocation fails, **allocate** returns **EOF**.

See Also   **streambuf::doallocate, streambuf::unbuffered**

streambuf::base

Protected →
char* base( ) const;
END Protected

Return Value   Returns a pointer to the first byte of the reserve area. The reserve area consists of space between the pointers returned by **base** and **ebuf**.

See Also   **streambuf::ebuf, streambuf::setb, streambuf::blen**

streambuf::blen

Protected →
int blen() const;
END Protected

Return Value   Returns the size, in bytes, of the reserve area.

See Also   **streambuf::base, streambuf::ebuf, streambuf::setb**

streambuf::dbp

void dbp( );

Remarks

Writes ASCII debugging information directly on **stdout**. Treat this function as part of the protected interface.

Some sample output follows:

```
STREAMBUF DEBUG INFO: this = 00E7:09DC
 base()=00E7:0A0C, ebuf()=00E7:0C0C,  blen()=512
eback()=0000:0000, gptr()=0000:0000, egptr()=0000:0000
pbase()=00E7:0A0C, pptr()=00E7:0A22, epptr()=00E7:0C0C
```

streambuf::doallocate

Protected →
virtual int doallocate( );
END Protected

Return Value

Called by **allocate** when space is needed. The **doallocate** function must allocate a reserve area, then call **setb** to attach the reserve area to the **streambuf** object. If the reserve area allocation fails, **doallocate** returns **EOF**.

Remarks

By default, this function attempts to allocate a reserve area using operator **new**.

See Also

streambuf::allocate, streambuf::setb

streambuf::eback

Protected →
char* eback( ) const;
END Protected

Return Value

Returns the lower bound of the get area. Space between the **eback** and **gptr** pointers is available for putting a character back into the stream.

See Also

streambuf::sputbackc, streambuf::gptr

streambuf::ebuf

Protected →
char* ebuf( ) const;
END Protected

Return Value   Returns a pointer to the byte after the last byte of the reserve area. The reserve area consists of space between the pointers returned by **base** and **ebuf**.

See Also   **streambuf::base, streambuf::setb, streambuf::blen**

---

streambuf::egptr

Protected →
char* egptr( ) const;
END Protected

Return Value   Returns a pointer to the byte after the last byte of the get area.

See Also   **streambuf::setg, streambuf::eback, streambuf::gptr**

---

streambuf::epptr

Protected →
char* epptr( ) const;
END Protected

Return Value   Returns a pointer to the byte after the last byte of the put area.

See Also   **streambuf::setp, streambuf::pbase, streambuf::pptr**

streambuf::gbump

Protected →
void gbump(int *nCount* **);**
END Protected

Parameter   *Count*
              The number of bytes to increment the get pointer. May be positive or negative.

Remarks   Increments the get pointer. No bounds checks are made on the result.

See Also   **streambuf::pbump**

---

streambuf::gptr

Protected →
char* gptr( ) const;
END Protected

Return Value   Returns a pointer to the next character to be fetched from the **streambuf** buffer.
              This pointer is known as the get pointer.

See Also   **streambuf::setg, streambuf::eback, streambuf::egptr**

---

streambuf::in_avail

int in_avail( ) const;

Return Value   Returns the number of characters in the get area that are available for fetching.
              These characters are between the **gptr** and **egptr** pointers and may be fetched with
              a guarantee of no errors.

---

streambuf::out_waiting

int out_waiting( ) const;

Return Value   Returns the number of characters in the put area that have not been sent to the final
              output destination. These characters are between the **pbase** and **pptr** pointers.

streambuf::overflow

virtual int overflow(int *nCh* **= EOF) = 0;**

Return Value   **EOF** to indicate an error.

Parameter   *nCh*
        EOF or the character to output.

Remarks   The virtual **overflow** function, together with the **sync** and **underflow** functions, defines the characteristics of the **streambuf**-derived class. Each derived class might implement **overflow** differently, but the interface with the calling stream class is the same.

The **overflow** function is most frequently called by public **streambuf** functions like **sputc** and **sputn** when the put area is full, but other classes, including the stream classes, can call **overflow** anytime.

The function "consumes" the characters in the put area between the **pbase** and **pptr** pointers and then reinitializes the put area. The **overflow** function must also consume *nCh* (if *nCh* is not **EOF**), or it might choose to put that character in the new put area so that it will be consumed on the next call.

The definition of "consume" varies among derived classes. For example, the **filebuf** class writes its characters to a file, while the **strsteambuf** class keeps them in its buffer and (if the buffer is designated as dynamic) expands the buffer in response to a call to **overflow**. This expansion is achieved by freeing the old buffer and replacing it with a new, larger one. The pointers are adjusted as necessary.

Default Implementation   No default implementation. Derived classes must define this function.

See Also   **streambuf::pbase, streambuf::pptr, streambuf::setp, streambuf::sync, streambuf::underflow**

---

streambuf::pbackfail

virtual int pbackfail(int *nCh* **);**

Return Value   The *nCh* parameter if successful; otherwise **EOF**.

Parameter   *nCh*
        The character used in a previous **sputbackc** call.

Remarks	This function is called by **sputbackc** if it fails, usually because the **eback** pointer equals the **gptr** pointer. The **pbackfail** function should deal with the situation, if possible, by such means as repositioning the external file pointer.
Default implementation	Returns EOF.
See Also	**streambuf::sputbackc**

streambuf::pbase

Protected →
char* pbase( ) const;
END Protected

Return Value	Returns a pointer to the start of the put area. Characters between the **pbase** pointer and the **pptr** pointer have been stored in the buffer but not flushed to the final output destination.
See Also	**streambuf::pptr, streambuf::setp, streambuf::out_waiting**

streambuf::pbump

Protected →
void pbump(int *nCount*);
END Protected

Parameter	*nCount* The number of bytes to increment the put pointer. May be positive or negative.
Remarks	Increments the put pointer. No bounds checks are made on the result.
See Also	**streambuf::gbump, streambuf::setp**

streambuf::pptr

Protected →
char* pptr( ) const;
END Protected

Return Value	Returns a pointer to the first byte of the put area. This pointer is known as the put pointer and is the destination for the next character(s) sent to the **streambuf** object.
See Also	**streambuf::epptr**, **streambuf::pbase**, **streambuf::setp**

streambuf::sbumpc

int sbumpc( );

Return Value	Returns the current character, then advances the get pointer. Returns **EOF** if the get pointer is currently at the end of the sequence (equal to the **egptr** pointer).
See Also	**streambuf::epptr**, **streambuf::gbump**

streambuf::seekoff

virtual streampos seekoff(streamoff *off*, **ios::seek_dir** *dir*, **int** *nMode* = **ios::in | ios::out);**

Return Value	The new position value. This is the byte offset from the start of the file (or string). If both **ios::in** and **ios::out** are specified, the function returns the output position. If the derived class does not support positioning, the function returns **EOF**.
Parameters	*off* The new offset value; **streamoff** is a **typedef** equivalent to **long**. *dir* One of the following seek directions specified by the enumerated type **seek_dir**: • **ios::beg** Seek from the beginning of the stream. • **ios::cur** Seek from the current position in the stream. • **ios::end** Seek from the end of the stream. *nMode* An integer that contains a bitwise OR (	) combination of the enumerators **ios::in** and **ios::out**.
Remarks	Changes the position for the **streambuf** object. Not all derived classes of **streambuf** need to support positioning; however, the **filebuf**, **strstreambuf**, and **stdiobuf** classes do support positioning. Classes derived from **streambuf** often support independent input and output position values. The *nMode* parameter determines which value(s) is set.

Default Implementation	Returns EOF.
See Also	**streambuf::seekpos**

streambuf::seekpos

virtual streampos seekpos(streampos *pos*, **int** *nMode* = **ios::in | ios::out**);

Return Value

The new position value. If both **ios::in** and **ios::out** are specified, the function returns the output position. If the derived class does not support positioning, the function returns **EOF**.

Parameters

pos
> The new position value; **streampos** is a **typedef** equivalent to **long**.

nMode
> An integer that contains mode bits defined as **ios** enumerators that can be combined with the OR (|) operator. See **ofstream::ofstream** for a listing of the enumerators.

Remarks

Changes the position, relative to the beginning of the stream, for the **streambuf** object. Not all derived classes of **streambuf** need to support positioning; however, the **filebuf**, **strstreambuf**, and **stdiobuf** classes do support positioning.

Classes derived from **streambuf** often support independent input and output position values. The *nMode* parameter determines which value(s) is set.

Default Implementation

Calls **seekoff((streamoff)** *pos*, **ios::beg**, *nMode*). Thus, to define seeking in a derived class, it is usually necessary to redefine only **seekoff**.

See Also

streambuf::seekoff

streambuf::setb

Protected →
void setb(char* *pb*, **char*** *peb*, **int** *nDelete* = **0**);
END Protected

Parameters   *pb*
> The new value for the base pointer.

peb
> The new value for the **ebuf** pointer.

nDelete
> Flag that controls automatic deletion. If *nDelete* is not 0, the reserve area will be deleted when: (1) the base pointer is changed by another **setb** call, or (2) the **streambuf** destructor is called.

Remarks   Sets the values of the reserve area pointers. If both *pb* and *peb* are **NULL**, there is no reserve area. If *pb* is not **NULL** and *peb* is **NULL**, the reserve area has a length of 0.

See Also   **streambuf::base, streambuf::ebuf**

---

streambuf::setbuf

virtual streambuf* setbuf(char* *pr,* **int** *nLength* **);**

Return Value   A **streambuf** pointer if the buffer is accepted; otherwise **NULL**.

Parameters   *pr*
> A pointer to a previously allocated reserve area of length *nLength*. A **NULL** value indicates an unbuffered stream.

nLength
> The length (in bytes) of the reserve area. A length of 0 indicates an unbuffered stream.

Remarks   Attaches the specified reserve area to the **streambuf** object. Derived classes may or may not use this area.

Default Implementation   Accepts the request if there is not a reserved area already.

streambuf::setg

Protected →
void setg(char* *peb*, **char*** *pg*, **char*** *peg*);
END Protected

Parameters
    peb
        The new value for the **eback** pointer.

    pg
        The new value for the **gptr** pointer.

    peg
        The new value for the **egptr** pointer.

Remarks
    Sets the values for the get area pointers.

See Also
    streambuf::eback, streambuf::gptr, streambuf::egptr

streambuf::setp

Protected →
void setp(char* *pp*, **char*** *pep*);
END Protected

Parameters
    pp
        The new value for the **pbase** and **pptr** pointers.

    pep
        The new value for the **epptr** pointer.

Remarks
    Sets the values for the put area pointers.

See Also
    streambuf::pptr, streambuf::pbase, streambuf::epptr

streambuf::sgetc

int sgetc( );

Remarks
    Returns the character at the get pointer. The **sgetc** function does not move the get pointer. Returns **EOF** if there is no character available.

See Also
    streambuf::sbumpc, streambuf::sgetn, streambuf::snextc, streambuf::stossc

streambuf::sgetn

int sgetn(char* *pch*, int *nCount*);

Return Value   The number of characters fetched.

Parameters   *pch*
> A pointer to a buffer that will receive characters from the **streambuf** object.

nCount
> The number of characters to get.

Remarks   Gets the *nCount* characters that follow the get pointer and stores them in the area starting at *pch*. When fewer than *nCount* characters remain in the **streambuf** object, **sgetn** fetches whatever characters remain. The function repositions the get pointer to follow the fetched characters.

See Also   **streambuf::sbumpc, streambuf::sgetc, streambuf::snextc, streambuf::stossc**

---

streambuf::snextc

int snextc( );

Return Value   First tests the get pointer, then returns **EOF** if it is already at the end of the get area. Otherwise, it moves the get pointer forward one character and returns the character that follows the new position. It returns **EOF** if the pointer has been moved to the end of the get area.

See Also   **streambuf::sbumpc, streambuf::sgetc, streambuf::sgetn, streambuf::stossc**

---

streambuf::sputbackc

int sputbackc(char *ch*);

Return Value   **EOF** on failure.

Parameter   *ch*
> The character to be put back to the **streambuf** object.

Remarks   Moves the get pointer back one character. The *ch* character must match the character just before the get pointer.

See Also   **streambuf::sbumpc, streambuf::pbackfail**

streambuf::sputc

int sputc(int *nCh* **);**

Return Value   The number of characters successfully stored; **EOF** on error.

Parameter   *nCh*
        The character to store in the **streambuf** object.

Remarks   Stores a character in the put area and advances the put pointer.

This public function is available to code outside the class, including the classes derived from **ios**. A derived **streambuf** class can gain access to its buffer directly by using protected member functions.

See Also   **streambuf::sputn**

---

streambuf::sputn

int sputn(const char* *pch***, int** *nCount* **);**

Return Value   The number of characters stored. This number is usually *nCount* but could be less if an error occurs.

Parameters   *pch*
        A pointer to a buffer that contains data to be copied to the **streambuf** object.
        nCount
        The number of characters in the buffer.

Remarks   Copies *nCount* characters from *pch* to the **streambuf** buffer following the put pointer. The function repositions the put pointer to follow the stored characters.

See Also   **streambuf::sputc**

---

streambuf::stossc

void stossc( );

Remarks   Moves the get pointer forward one character. If the pointer is already at the end of the get area, the function has no effect.

See Also   **streambuf::sbumpc, streambuf::sgetn, streambuf::snextc, streambuf::sgetc**

streambuf::streambuf

Protected →
streambuf( );

streambuf(char* *pr*, int *nLength*);
END Protected

Parameters

pr
A pointer to a previously allocated reserve area of length *nLength*. A **NULL** value indicates an unbuffered stream.

nLength
The length (in bytes) of the reserve area. A length of 0 indicates an unbuffered stream.

Remarks

The first constructor makes an uninitialized **streambuf** object. This object is not suitable for use until a **setbuf** call is made. A derived class constructor usually calls **setbuf** or uses the second constructor.

The second constructor initializes the **streambuf** object with the specified reserve area or marks it as unbuffered.

See Also

streambuf::setbuf

---

streambuf::~streambuf

Public →
virtual ~streambuf( );
END Public

Remarks

The **streambuf** destructor flushes the buffer if the stream is being used for output.

---

streambuf::sync

virtual int sync( );

Return Value

EOF if an error occurs.

Remarks

The virtual **sync** function, with the **overflow** and **underflow** functions, defines the characteristics of the **streambuf**-derived class. Each derived class might implement **sync** differently, but the interface with the calling stream class is the same.

The **sync** function flushes the put area. It also empties the get area and, in the process, sends any unprocessed characters back to the source, if necessary.

Default Implementation   Returns 0 if the get area is empty and there are no more characters to output; otherwise, it returns **EOF**.

See Also   **streambuf::overflow**

streambuf::unbuffered

Protected →
void unbuffered(int *nState* **);**

int unbuffered() const;
END Protected

Parameter   *nState*
        The value of the buffering state variable; 0 = buffered, nonzero = unbuffered.

Remarks   The first overloaded **unbuffered** function sets the value of the **streambuf** object's buffering state. This variable's primary purpose is to control whether the **allocate** function automatically allocates a reserve area.

The second function returns the current buffering state variable.

See Also   **streambuf::allocate**, **streambuf::doallocate**

streambuf::underflow

mfvirtual int underflow() = 0;

Remarks   The virtual **underflow** function, with the **sync** and **overflow** functions, defines the characteristics of the **streambuf**-derived class. Each derived class might implement **underflow** differently, but the interface with the calling stream class is the same.

The **underflow** function is most frequently called by public **streambuf** functions like **sgetc** and **sgetn** when the get area is empty, but other classes, including the stream classes, can call **underflow** anytime.

The **underflow** function supplies the get area with characters from the input source. If the get area contains characters, **underflow** returns the first character. If the get area is empty, it fills the get area and returns the next character (which it leaves in the get area). If there are no more characters available, then **underflow** returns **EOF** and leaves the get area empty.

In the **strstreambuf** class, **underflow** adjusts the **egptr** pointer to access storage that was dynamically allocated by a call to **overflow**.

Default Implementation

No default implementation. Derived classes must define this function.

class strstream : public iostream

#include <strstrea.h>

The **strstream** class supports I/O streams that have character arrays as a source and destination. You can allocate a character array prior to construction, or the constructor can internally allocate a dynamic array. You can then use all the input and output stream operators and functions to fill the array.

Be aware that a put pointer and a get pointer are working independently behind the scenes in the attached **strstreambuf** class. The put pointer advances as you insert fields into the stream's array, and the get pointer advances as you extract fields. The **ostream::seekp** function moves the put pointer, and the **istream::seekg** function moves the get pointer. If either pointer reaches the end of the string (and sets the **ios::eof** flag), you must call **clear** before seeking.

Construction/Destruction — Public Members

strstream
Constructs a **strstream** object.

~strstream
Destroys a **strstream** object.

Other Functions — Public Members

pcount
Returns the number of bytes that have been stored in the stream's buffer.

rdbuf
Returns a pointer to the stream's associated **strstreambuf** object.

str
Returns a pointer to the string stream's character buffer and freezes it.

See Also   **strstreambuf, streambuf, istrstream, ostrstream**

Member Functions

strstream::pcount

int pcount() const;

Return Value
Returns the number of bytes stored in the buffer. This information is especially useful when you have stored binary data in the object.

strstream::rdbuf

strstreambuf* rdbuf() const;

Return Value
Returns a pointer to the **strstreambuf** buffer object that is associated with this stream. This is not the character buffer; the **strstreambuf** object contains a pointer to the character area.

See Also
strstream::str

strstream::str

char* str();

Return Value
Returns a pointer to the internal character array. If the stream was built with the **void**-argument constructor, then **str** freezes the array. You must not send characters to a frozen stream, and you are responsible for deleting the array. You can unfreeze the the stream by calling **rdbuf->freeze(0)**.

If the stream was built with the constructor that specified the buffer, the pointer contains the same address as the array used to construct the **ostrstream** object.

See Also
strstreambuf::freeze, strstream::rdbuf

strstream::strstream

strstream();

strstream(char* *pch*, **int** *nLength*, **int** *nMode* **);**

Parameters

pch

A character array that is large enough to accommodate future output stream activity.

nLength

The size (in characters) of *pch*. If 0, *pch* is assumed to point to a null-terminated array; if less than 0, the array is assumed to have infinite length.

nMode

The stream creation mode, which must be one of the following enumerators as defined in class **ios**:

- **ios::in**   Retrieval begins at the beginning of the array.

- **ios::out**   By default, storing begins at *pch*.

- **ios::ate**   The *pch* parameter is assumed to be a null-terminated array; storing begins at the **NULL** character.

- **ios::app**   Same as **ios::ate**.

The use of the **ios::in** and **ios::out** flags is optional for this class; both input and output are implied.

Remarks

The first constructor makes an **strstream** object that uses an internal, dynamic buffer that is initially empty.

The second constructor makes an **strstream** object out of the first *nLength* characters of the *psc* buffer. The stream will not accept characters once the length reaches *nLength*.

---

strstream::~strstream

~strstream();

Remarks

Destroys a **strstream** object and its associated **strstreambuf** object, thus releasing all internally allocated memory. If you used the **void**-argument constructor, the internally allocated character buffer is released; otherwise, you must release it.

An internally allocated character buffer will not be released if it was previously frozen by calling **rdbuf->freeze(0)**.

See Also

strstream::rdbuf

class strstreambuf : public streambuf

#include <strstrea.h>

The **strstreambuf** class is a derived class of **streambuf** that manages an in-memory character array.

The file stream classes, **ostrstream**, **istrstream**, and **strstream**, use **strstreambuf** member functions to fetch and store characters. Some of these member functions are virtual functions defined for the **streambuf** class.

The reserve area, put area, and get area were introduced in the **streambuf** class description. For **strsteambuf** objects, the put area is the same as the get area, but the **get** pointer and the **put** pointer move independently.

Construction/Destruction — Public Members

strstreambuf
> Constructs a **strstreambuf** object.

~strstreambuf
> Destroys a strstreambuf object.

Other Functions — Public Members

freeze
> Freezes a stream.

str
> Returns a pointer to the string.

See Also
istrstream, ostrstream, filebuf, stdiobuf

Member Functions

strstreambuf::freeze

void freeze(int n = 1);

Parameter
> n
> > A 0 value permits automatic deletion of the current array and its automatic growth (if it is dynamic); a nonzero value prevents deletion.

Remarks	If a **strstreambuf** object has a dynamic array, memory is usually deleted on destruction and size adjustment. The **freeze** function provides a way to prevent that automatic deletion. Once an array is frozen, no further input or output is permitted. The results of such operations are undefined.

The **freeze** function can also unfreeze a frozen buffer.

See Also   strstreambuf::str

strstreambuf::str

char* str();

Return Value   Returns a pointer to the object's internal character array. If the **strstreambuf** object was constructed with a user-supplied buffer, that buffer address is returned. If the object has a dynamic array, **str** freezes the array. You must not send characters to a frozen **strstreambuf** object, and you are responsible for deleting the array. If a dynamic array is empty, then **str** returns **NULL**.

Use the **freeze** function with a 0 parameter to unfreeze a **strstreambuf** object.

See Also   strstreambuf::freeze

strstreambuf::strstreambuf

strstreambuf();

strstreambuf(int *nBytes* **);**

strstreambuf(char* *pch*, **int** *n*, **char*** *pstart* = **0** **);**

strstreambuf(unsigned char* *puch*, **int** *n*, **unsigned char*** *pustart* = **0** **);**

strstreambuf(signed char* *psch*, **int** *n*, **signed char*** *psstart* = **0** **);**

strstreambuf(void* (**falloc***)(long), void (****ffree***)(void*));**

Parameters   *nBytes*
     The initial length of a dynamic stream buffer.

pch, puch, psch
     A pointer to a character buffer that will be attached to the object. The **get** pointer is initialized to this value.

n
> One of the following integer parameters:
>
> - positive   *n* bytes, starting at *pch*, is used as a fixed-length stream buffer.
> - 0   The *pch* parameter points to the start of a null-terminated string that constitutes the stream buffer (terminator excluded).
> - negative   The *pch* parameter points to a stream buffer that continues indefinitely.

pstart, pustart, psstart
> The initial value of the **put** pointer.

falloc
> A memory-allocation function with the prototype **void** * **falloc(long)**. The default is **new**.

ffree
> A function that frees allocated memory with the prototype **void ffree(void** * **)**. The default is **delete**.

Remarks

The four **streambuf** constructors are described as follows:

Constructor	Description
strstreambuf()	Constructs an empty **strstreambuf** object with dynamic buffering. The buffer is allocated internally by the class and grows as needed, unless it is frozen.
strstreambuf(int)	Constructs an empty **strstreambuf** object with a dynamic buffer *n* bytes long to start with. The buffer is allocated internally by the class and grows as needed, unless it is frozen.
strstreambuf(char*, **int, char*** **)**	Constructs a **strstreambuf** object from already-allocated memory as specified by the arguments. There are constructor variations for both unsigned and signed character arrays.
strstreambuf(void*(*), **void(*))**	Constructs an empty **strstreambuf** object with dynamic buffering. The *falloc* function is called for allocation. The **long** parameter specifies the buffer length and the function returns the buffer address. If the *falloc* pointer is **NULL**, operator **new** is used. The *ffree* function frees memory allocated by *falloc*. If the *ffree* pointer is **NULL**, the operator **delete** is used.

strstreambuf::~strstreambuf

~strstreambuf();

Remarks

Destroys a **strstreambuf** object and releases internally allocated dynamic memory unless the object is frozen. The destructor does not release user-allocated memory.

Index

O

W

Width
    internal field variable, setting, ios::width 63
    streams, setting internal field parameter, setw 68
width member function, ios class 63
write member function
    ofstream class 9
    ostream class 97

X

xalloc member function, ios class 63